All the Things We Were

Also by Louise Tanner

MISS BANNISTER'S GIRLS
HERE TODAY

A Scrapbook of the People, Politics, and
Popular Culture in the Tragicomic Years
Between the Crash and Pearl Harbor

All the Things We Were

by Louise Tanner

Doubleday & Company, Inc.
Garden City, New York
1968

The drawing from *The Shadow* used at the beginning of Chapter 4: copyright © 1936 by Street & Smith Publications, Inc.; copyright © renewed 1964 by The Conde Nast Publications, Inc. Reproduced by permission.

Grateful acknowledgment is made to the following for the use of copyrighted material:

A. S. BARNES & COMPANY, INC.
Excerpts from *The Tumult and the Shouting*, by Grantland Rice. Reprinted by permission.

CHAPPELL & CO., INC.
Lines from "A Little Skipper from Heaven Above," by Cole Porter. Copyright © 1936 by Chappell & Co., Inc. Copyright renewed. "But in the Morning No!" by Cole Porter. Copyright © 1939 by Chappell & Co., Inc. Copyright renewed. Reprinted by permission.

COMMANDER PUBLICATIONS AND LEO FEIST, INC.
Lines from "I'm an Old Cowhand," by Johnny Mercer. Copyright 1936 by Leo Feist, Inc. United States copyright renewal 1964 by Johnny Mercer. Reprinted by permission.

GENERAL MILLS, INC.
Lines from a Wheaties commercial, "Raise the Flag for Hudson High, Boys!" Copyright © 1936 General Mills, Inc. Reprinted by permission.

PEPSICO
Lines from a Pepsi-Cola jingle. Copyright © 1940 by the Pepsi-Cola Company. Reprinted by permission.

THE RICHMOND ORGANIZATION
Lines from "Rock Island Line." New words and new music arrangement by Huddie Ledbetter. Edited with new additional material by Alan Lomax. © Copyright 1959 Folkways Music Publishers, Inc., New York, N.Y. Reprinted by permission.

IRVING SETTEL
Excerpts from *A Pictorial History of Radio*, by Irving Settel. Reprinted by permission.

M. WITMARK & SONS
Lines from "Shuffle Off to Buffalo," by Al Dubin and Harry Warren. Copyright 1932 by M. Witmark & Sons. Reprinted by permission.

LEO FEIST, INC.
Special lyrics to "Smile for Me," by Phil Baxter for Fitch Shampoo commercial. Copyright 1932 (renewed) by Leo Feist, Inc., New York, N.Y. Reprinted by permission.

For my son Mike and his friends, who burst in with title suggestions while switching my radio to the "WMCA Good Guys" and "Murray the K." You didn't come up with a title, but you gave me an ending.

Coming Attractions

Illustrations follow page 170

PHOTO CREDITS

UPI—Nos. 1, 2, 3, 6, 8, 12, 14, 15
Brown Brothers—No. 16
Museum of Modern Art—No. 7
Standard Brands, Inc.—No. 4
The Wonderful Era of the Great Dance Bands by Leo
    Walker, published by Howell-North—No. 13

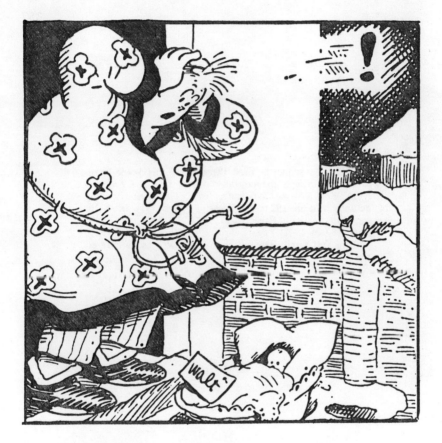

The Skeezix sequence used throughout this book is reproduced through the courtesy of the *Chicago Tribune-
New York News* Syndicate, Inc. The first drawing
actually ran in 1921; the second (Page xxi) in 1926;
Page 19 in 1934; Page 37 in 1937; Page 139 in 1939;
Page 187 in 1942; Page 241 in 1944; Page 291 in 1949;
and the full family portrait shows our hero as he entered
the 1960s.

Introduction

The winters of one's childhood are always colder. But nostalgia warms.

Nostalgia is very In now. The roaring twenties inspired musical productions like *The Boy Friend* and a revival of those prolapsed womb dresses which belonged to the ugliest era in fashion history. The Thirties have succeeded the Twenties in our memories, just as they once did in fact. A museum runs a Camp Retrospective with tapes of Bing Crosby singing "My Little Buckaroo," reruns of Ruby Keeler kissing Dick Powell in *Gold Diggers of 1933*. There are showcases full of Big Little Books of *Flash Gordon* and *Tailspin Tommy*.

Anyone who remembers the landscape of the Thirties with even vague accuracy might question the view of a more prosperous generation which sees the entire period as Campy. Not long ago an exhibition of 1930s' protest pictures was reviewed in the newspapers as an amusing bit of pop. It is hard to look at the pictures without suppressing a smile. All the villains of the isolationist morality play were there . . . the World War I veterans in helmets and puttees . . . the mutilated legionnaire . . . the bloated war profiteer . . . even an occasional sinister priest. Evil strikebreakers roughed up pickets. A man slept underneath a newspaper on a park bench while a few feet away a chauffeur heedlessly walked a Pekingese. (You just know that the chauffeur was bonded to some Fifth Avenue matron and not rented by the hour, as he would be years later, a status symbol from Carey Cadillac.) The smile you can't quite suppress is the product of the well-known and sudden shock of recognition. The men in puttees recall the day when you heard about somebody's father who suffered from "shell shock." Perhaps a mutilated man in a legionnaire's cap sold you a poppy in the street. After the smile, the child of the Thirties would involuntarily say, "But dammit—" The man on the park bench was once all too real. The strikebreakers, no matter what the propaganda value, were an illustration of the real story—rarely stressed to stockholders—of Henry Ford's relationship with the CIO. In November 1937, when people were still rioting in protest against inadequate relief checks, a Siamese cat named Prince Rahula made the trip from Bar Harbor to Panama City as the sole occupant of an A-deck stateroom and bath.

It is the latter sort of tidbit which obscures the view from the peak we now occupy in our various Dariens. Nostalgia today is a national pastime and a big business. In the Thirties war was hell. In the Sixties the crusade to make the world safe for democracy breeds its own form of hilarity. Snoopy, canine hero of the comic strip *Peanuts,* dreams of Sopwith Camels and bursts out occasionally with choruses of "It's a Long Way to Tipperary." A collection of comic books, bought for $100 by an enterprising Los Angeles man, has already fetched him $25,000. His most expensive edition, of course, was Detective Comics #27 (1939) which first introduced the public to Batman and Robin. Aerospace engineers devoured *Buck Rogers.* Playgoers flocked to see *Superman* on Broadway in 1966. Disc jockeys reminisce about Oliver Warbucks and Punjab.* A British designer turns out Little Orphan Annie dresses. "Trivia" at one time seemed destined to be "the Game" of the 1960s. It involved the swapping of unrelated nostalgic tidbits. Name all of Our Gang. Who played Fu-Manchu? Whose money was Groucho Marx (alias Hugo Quackenbush, alias Wolf J. Flywheel) usually after in the movies?

It could be the gangster of the Thirties who exemplifies nostalgic upgrading most handily. He has been elevated to a position of respectability in our minds, so that we almost regret his passing. The proprietress of a chic men's store recently restaged Al Capone's

* Full name: Punjab-Ohile

funeral in an old Mafia hangout in the east Bronx, not long ago. The cortege was composed of those beautiful 1932 cars. *Esquire* recalled the "dear dead days" when crime paid (how hard they labored to convince us that it didn't in endless movie shorts of gangland greats going up that last mile in a salvo of gunfire). The new gangsters, according to *Esquire,* are punks. The gangsters of the Thirties had style . . . Underworld Image . . . the crook look. Take elegant Larry Fay, "the milk racket czar in white hat and cigarette," Vincent Coll and mob, who stare from *Esquire's* pages with facial expressions that seem to say, "We ain't talkin', Copper."

The gangsters of the Thirties, like movie stars, always seemed a little larger than life. J. Edgar Hoover's G-Men waged all-out war on Pretty Boy Floyd, Baby Face Nelson, Alvin (Creepy) Karpis, Big Frenchy de Mange, Legs Diamond, Dutch Schultz, Two Gun Crowley, Owney Madden, Machine Gun Kelly, and of course Public Enemy Number One—John Dillinger. Bonnie and Clyde are big in the movies and debate rages in the New York *Times* as to whether they are real American folk heroes. Time has mellowed our memories of the Thirties. When Al Capone was finally nabbed for income tax evasion, when Dillinger was cornered at last in 1934 outside that movie theater, none of us realized how lucky we had been to have them around.

Yet, the winters of one's childhood are always colder and they were never worse than in those desolate days just after the great crash. In those early years of the Depression, if he were lucky, a child would ride about in the rumble seat of a square Model A Ford. The blood is thicker when you are eight years old. A chilling breeze that froze the inside of the nostrils was the norm in a "flivver" that shook and protested at thirty miles an hour against the bumps and unexpected cave-ins of a rural road. But there was consolation in the fact that things weren't much cozier inside in the heaterless front seat occupied by the old folks.

Everyone looked half frozen along the roadside of that bleak Depression landscape which was leading so many intellectuals to say yes to the question of "Why not Communism?" Granville Hicks, one who gave an affirmative answer for a time, recalls shabby men standing idle on corners in Troy, New York. Between Troy and

Albany the train whirled past Hoovervilles beside the railroad tracks—shacks thrown together from packing boxes and hunks of corrugated iron. In Bennington, Vermont, there were people who had flocked home from the cities. (While the Depression did not permanently halt the population flow toward the towns, there were many—ill-equipped to wrest a living from the soil—who tried to make a go of it in some improvised shelter on an edge of Pa and Ma's already bankrupt farm.) Skinny young Vermonters gazed at the road from a rural slum.

In Harlan County, Kentucky—one of the areas worst hit by the Depression—coal miners lived on dandelions and blackberries and children were so hungry that they gnawed at their own hands. Protests against farm foreclosure were so bitter that in various parts of the country the National Guard was being called out. In Bucks County, Pennsylvania, a farmer's union—with the aid of Communist agitators—had managed to save a lot of people's land. (The term exurbia was unknown—as was the type of gentleman farmer who later resided there and found that it was hard to make ends meet on $60,000 a year.) In an Indiana "Shedtown" a couple lived with an indoor chicken brooder, an oil lamp, a wooden tray and a box—raising chickens "fer eatin' and not fer sale."

Things were no better in the towns. In Muncie, Indiana, there were scabrous buildings with the lath exposed; budgets allowed nothing for food, let alone maintenance. Around the edges of town might be a hobo camp. If there were docks, people haunted them to find spoiled vegetables, a bone with a bit of meat on it for a stew. In the homeland of opportunity people lived in sewer pipes and fifty men fought over a garbage pail. Commuters stood on suburban railroad station platforms making bright normal pleasantries, as if they were setting off for the day's work. But the office was mythical and the day's work was their futile search for work.

It is easy to go through the time between the Crash and Pearl Harbor cafeteria style, selecting only the most appetizing items. At the drop of a hat, a friend will sing you the Jack Armstrong song, and we will all agree that nobody today writes music like Cole Porter. To listen to us, one gets the impression that Depression America was a kind of slightly dented Utopia. There never was a comedian as funny as Fred Allen, a song as catchy as "Don't Be

That Way," as played by Benny Goodman. Happiness was Carole Lombard wading through a high-pile white rug, Duke Ellington playing "Sophisticated Lady" at a white piano. But there was so much in that Depression landscape to look back on in horror. When we walk down Memory Lane, we seldom revisit the average bleak American street of 1931.

How much do we really remember about the Thirties, now that remembering them has become big business?

The tabloid Thirties are little help. Looking through bound copies of *The Daily News* is to realize that then as now, the man on the street did not care to reflect unduly on his plight. To be sure, the newspapers showed the hunger marches. But they much preferred to focus their flashes on episodes like the Lindbergh kidnaping, or the Bruno Richard Hauptmann trial (forerunner, perhaps, of the "trial" Lee Harvey Oswald has had posthumously), or Judge Crater. The papers' contribution to history tends to give us vice-girl Vivian Gordon strangled in Van Cortlandt Park—and of Vivian's daughter, Benita, then in high school, who wrote in her diary: "2:15 P.M. I'm tired . . . I am turning on the gas."

Crime continued to be creative and colorful. Ivar Kreuger, the Match King, was an international scoundrel and 1932 suicide. Winnie Ruth Judd stepped into the baggage room of the Southern Pacific Railway in Los Angeles in 1932 to claim a valise, a locker, and a trunk—which, as it turned out, contained the butchered bodies of two women. Wiley Post, the famed one-eyed airman, was killed in 1935, and Amelia Earhart disappeared in 1937. There was Howard Hughes, then as now, and in those days Mr. Hughes was a promoter of airplanes and starlets—the starlets usually went further—and there was Douglas "Wrong Way" Corrigan, who took off in a light plane for Los Angeles and landed in Dublin, a "mistake" which endeared him to the Irish and to the lovers of goof-offs on both sides of the water. Yet these crimes or comedies were editorial distractions in this most political of decades. The primary concern of one and all was to find a remedy for a sick economy, one which would get the ailing patient through the day. Perhaps distraction was part of the cure. But in looking back, no one should be so distracted now that they fail to remember—or sense—the icy quiet of idleness . . . the men who really did stand in line in the morning to get apples to sell or who stood in other lines for a flop, watery coffee, and mush. There were those who stood in line in that bitter day in 1930 to find out what was left of the old nest egg. The Bank of the United States, formidable title, had gone broke. Men rushed police guards. Women screamed as they held up their passbooks trying to salvage their life savings from "the bank that couldn't fail."

Nostalgia warms now, but keeping warm was the big problem then. The poor became infinitely resourceful at making a tin shack "tight for the winter," putting cardboard in their shoes to plug up a leaking sole, gathering scrapwood to keep the furnace going, spending a dime to go to a movie for two blissful double features worth of fetid warm air.

With the inauguration of Franklin D. Roosevelt, hopes sprang up again on those desolate street corners. The massive wave of bank failures in 1932 led to a bank holiday in 1933. A wild carnival air seized the country at times; people were unsure of reality, on the brink of hysteria. But there were methods that kept people firmly on the ground. With the banks closed, scrip was issued in Akron, Ohio. The bottle with a refund due became legal tender in places like Hartford.

The brain trusts began to assemble in Washington and with them came the endless catalog of alphabetical agencies—CCC for Civilian Conservation Corps, AAA for Agricultural Adjustment Administration, NRA for National Recovery Administration, PWA for Public Works Administration, TVA for Tennessee Valley Authority—all set up during the breathless period known as the First Hundred Days. There was the NYA or National Youth Administration to keep young people in college. On May 6, 1935, the Works Progress Administration, or WPA, was established to provide work for the jobless. It was a source of jokes for everyone. In the same year the Social Security Act was passed over the heads of a group of dissenters who, it is interesting to recall, included the AF of L, the National Association of Manufacturers, and the Communist Party.

"Relief." The NRA. The Model A. Fox Movietone showed us moving pictures of the ranters Huey Long, Father Coughlin, Gerald L. K. Smith, Dr. Francis Townsend, who peddled their economic and social panaceas to alarmingly large crowds.

Noisy events bracket the Thirties. Like the Crash, Pearl Harbor knocked the underpinnings out from under every basic American assumption. The campus pacifist suddenly acquired a new direction. Instead of worrying about getting rid of the wheat surplus, we soon stood in line for cigarettes, butter, and sugar. Instead of looking forward to endless dreary years of unemployment, a college man tended to step right in to a job (mostly uniformed, to be sure). Forgotten were the truths that a child of the Thirties learned at Mother's knee. We had learned that war is hell, Europeans a bunch of cynical opportunists, our frontiers were in our own back yard. We had to be on guard against all appeals to youthful idealism lest we become embroiled like our fathers in the folly of a foreign war.

Today the patriotic duties of the young, so we tell them, include underwriting the aspirations of nations unformed in 1939. They should take courses in Bantu so as not to insult their beneficiaries by misspelling names. They must live with thoughts that would have set up riots on Peace Day in 1936—the thought, for instance, that no sacrifice is too great to beat the Russians to the moon. We urge them to accept with resignation ever-mounting taxes to pay for napalm bombs to be dropped on Asiatic rice paddies.

The Thirties were the years which changed the very structure of the American personality. The psychological gap between rich and poor would never again be as great as it was in 1930. Our faith in science and technology would never again be as childlike as it was in that interregnum between the self-starter and the second-stage rocket—when nobody considered that the scientists who brought us nylons were capable of turning out a world-ending bomb. We would never again be such proud provincials as we were in that decade when the world shrank before our eyes, when the woes of Europe came into our movie houses and radios along with Lew Lehr and Myrt and Marge.

All things considered, why does it seem so difficult to remember those years in detail? Alistair Cooke wrote a moving introduction to his story of the Alger Hiss trial. Among other things, he explained that a respectable figure like Alger Hiss, in the climate of the Thirties, might easily have seen no conflict between his loyalties to America and his loyalty to the Communist Party. As far as the general public was concerned, Cooke's book, written only a decade after the New Deal, might have described conditions in the Holy Roman Empire.

Nostalgia for the Thirties may be most prevalent among those least affected by the Depression. The poor, who spent those years reversing shirt collars, splitting sheets up the middle, and sewing them together, relining their winter coats, or standing in line for a government check, are now either dead or no longer so poor. But in any case, when they think back, memory mercifully fails them. Others—those who could afford such things then—remember now that barbers, laundresses, and music teachers came to the house. There were several mails a day and no nonsense about zip codes. Hospitals were quiet, and most of them uncrowded. Secretaries worked on Saturdays and knew how to spell. Doctors made house calls; cab drivers made change. In fact with cabbies then, the mere sight of a ten-dollar bill would have them into a drugstore and back with ten singles before you could say "knife"; they followed well-dressed pedestrians down the street, watching eagerly for signs of fatigue. If the gap between rich and poor has narrowed, it has done so with some falling off in the service trades. Many of those who lament the current downfall of standards are simply annoyed because it is no longer possible to get a girl to live in and work twelve hours a day for six dollars a week.

Of course there is a slightly different group, who remember rent parties and assorted hardships and the spirit of sharing in the Village. These are the rebellious children of upper-class or upper-middle-class parents who, during the Thirties, wrote home to their horrified families that they were sharing living quarters with some hirsute lady comrade who looked like the madam of a fancy house in Minsk. For some, their early struggles were genuine enough. Sometimes the job at the necktie counter at Macy's failed. But in the background there was often a parent against whom one was rebelling—Daddy in Peoria, Mother in Dallas—playing a waiting game. The prodigal would be welcomed back home if he wearied of putting the milk out on the window sill, buying co-op soap, and brushing his teeth with salt. Mary McCarthy took care of a lot of this in *The Group*.

It may be that one significant difference is that it has been a long time now since anyone has spoken of "progress" quite that simply or painted a "futuristic" oil. Today it is tomorrow which terrifies us. We may escape into a romanticized world of Ovaltine shakers, '32 Hupmobiles, and Dixie Cup pictures of the stars. But those of us who do are either too young to have really known that peculiar period, or too successful and glazed to remember it accurately. This is not true of everyone. One suspects that the Thirties are often the source of hidden trauma that the analysis dredges up from the unconscious. One housewife can never quite kick the childhood habit of saving things—worn-out underwear, a lampshade with a rip that can be turned to the wall, worthless bank books. The vice president of a large company, in a setting of rare books and modern art, seems temperamentally and spiritually unfit to talk revolution. Yet he still lapses on occasion into the idiom of class struggle, a habit he acquired in the early Thirties when he shared an apartment with two Communists and shelled peas as they discussed Bukharin. Children of an age which still used the word thrift are shocked by nylons that run after one wearing. A successful editor remarks that he's always pleasantly surprised to be working, and always delighted when his car starts on the first try.

At what moment in the past did the gun moll become a historical figure? Whatever became of Rochelle Hudson or Dr. Alexis Carrel's mechanical heart? When did nose and throat specialists stop using argyrol packs? (And what indeed ever happened to nose and throat specialists?) Whatever happened to the movie heroine who understudied the star and got her big chance to tap dance on some Busby Berkeley pyramid of drums? When did the Black Hand become the Cosa Nostra and when did people stop saying "Comes the Revolution"?

Go up to the attic. Can you find the Roscoe Turner pilot's wings, the scale model of Sir Malcolm Campbell's Bluebird, the Lou Gehrig baseball, the autographed picture of Mel Ott, the bumper plate urging "Repeal." We are like amnesiacs searching for our identity. Somewhere in all that junk there must be a clue. Everybody knows by now who Lamont Cranston is. But who in hell am I?

Chapter 1

The Lean Years in Funnyland

"I'm sure this is the way the last Eskimo told us to come, Corky," said the little boy with the wild cowlick, as he lay in bed dreaming of Christmas in 1929. Skeezix, hero of the comic strip *Gasoline Alley,* was embarking on a fantasy voyage to the North Pole. As he explored the delights of Santa's workshop, a younger boy, Corky, dozed in an adjoining crib. A few months before, General Motors, which stood at 72¾ at the peak of the Bull Market, had fallen to 36. Radio Corporation Common which was 101 at the peak, fell to a poet-panic 26, U.S. Steel from 261¾ to 150. If the knowledge had caused a mass defenestration of Wall Street tycoons, Skeezix and Corky didn't realize it. This innocent pair had little more on their minds than Donder and Blitzen and the flashlight they were going to buy for Uncle Walt Wallet.

The middle-class homes of Funnyland were deaf to the rumblings of a changing world. The doings of the comic characters make a fascinating contrast with what was going on in the rest of the paper. The events which were to change our lives obtruded in only the most marginal manner upon a Shangri-la of grammatical error, dropped final g's, and delayed physical development—Little Orphan Annie had run around prepubescent since November 2, 1924. Skeezix and Corky—unique in that they were subject to the normal growing process—were also unusual in other respects. They were always doing what we were. Through their eyes we can see a whole era unfold.

In this way they differed from other comic strip heroes whose weekly adventures were eagerly awaited by legions of young readers. Dick Tracy, Mutt and Jeff, Terry and the Pirates, Smilin' Jack, Skippy, Blondie, the Katzenjammer Kids, Popeye, Moon Mullins, Mr. and Mrs., the Timid Soul, Winnie Winkle the Bread-Winner, Tillie the Toiler, Reg'lar Fellers, Harold Teen, Flash Gordon, and Superman had made their appearance by the late Thirties. So did Prince Valiant—drawn by Hal Foster, "The Rembrandt of King Features." Prince Valiant's Arthurian background branded him in the eyes of his youthful followers as bordering dangerously on the educational.

The comic book belonged to the war years, the comic strip to the Depression. When Kayo Mullins slept in a bureau drawer, hundreds of boys bedded down in similar surroundings. Everyone identified with these Sunday visitors. The comics had many by-products. King Features was big business. There were the Lucky Bucks which could be cut out of the paper when one was through it. Lucky Bucks were funny money which featured a picture of Jiggs or Happy Hooligan instead of Washington or Benjamin Franklin. Movie serials were made from Flash Gordon and Dick Tracy. There were the Big Little Books, chunky volumes depicting some comic strip hero in a context unrelated to the current adventure. Skeezix's Big Little Book alter ego was a year younger than his comic strip personality. The Big Little Book Skeezix was in shorts after Sunday Skeezix had graduated to knickers. In many schoolyards pornographers peddled their wares in Big Little Book form. Here one could find one's Sunday favorites engaged in observing a Black Sabbath.

The early Thirties had many features which were spillovers from the Twenties—along with dance marathons and Prohibition gin. Little Orphan Annie was timeless. Winnie Winkle the Bread-Winner had originally been a flapper. Gasoline Alley and Harold Teen burst onto the scene in 1919. Harold Teen, whose hair was slicked down in two smooth sections, divided by a "part" in the middle of his head, a fashion originally inspired by Rudolph Valentino, remained throughout the Depression as a sort of out-of-phase sheik. His friends who gathered at the Sugar Bowl—Lilacs, the wayward elf Shadow Smart, his arch enemy Poison Pembroke, and his sometime rival Beezie ("J. Beelzebub") Binks—dressed in modified Oxford Bag pants and coonskin coats. They spoke an idiom ("yowsah," "fan mah brow," "hot pups," "hello growin' pains," "yeggs," "fems") which in spirit if not in letter belonged to the age of jazz and gin.

What were you up to, Harold Teen—on the night of December 23, 1929? As Skeezix dreamed of Eskimos and reindeer, Christmas was uppermost in Harold's thoughts too. As neighborhood theaters showed Joe E. Brown and Marilyn Miller in *Sally,* as women were "making their mark in Talkicland," as the U.S. acted to "de-hootch the Yuletide," Harold was praying to Santa Claus: "Dear Santa, I'm rather ashamed to ask you for a new bear coat for Christmas. You have so many other needy cases. Still, I'm not thinking of myself, dear Santa Claus. It would mean so much to her to have me well dressed."

"Her" was, of course, Lillums Lovewell. She had worn galoshes and a cloche hat during the Twenties. She could still melt Harold by lapsing into baby talk—"You are a great big mans, Harold." She was his "lil lambie," his "lollypopsie," his "radiator," his "moulton mama." In his love-stricken condition, he hummed endlessly "Life is jes' a bowl of cherries."

Skeezix's origins dated back to the day of coonskin, and cranks—the kind once used to start cars. Back in 1921 Uncle Walt Wallet was a member of a group of automobile buffs who spent their lives supine under the chassis of a flivver. The automobile in 1921 was in its infancy. A plot cooked up by Uncle Walt and Uncle Avery to set their car on fire to collect the insurance died a-borning because "There's so much water in the gasoline we've been getting lately, it would put the fire out."

Skeezix was deposited on Uncle Walt's doorstep on February 14, 1921. For a week the neighbors were amused by the spectacle of a bachelor trying to cope with a new little life. On February 16, Uncle Walt had yet to grasp the fact that Skeezix was a boy. A day earlier he complained that his doorstep bundle should have come with feeding instructions, like an alligator from Florida.

Uncle Walt later married Auntie Blossom. Skeezix's adoption, had the usual fallopian repercussions. The union was later blessed by Corky, and a girl named Judy.

Throughout the Thirties some of those jalopies Uncle Walt and Uncle Avery had tinkered with transported Skeezix and Harold to dates, to the soda fountain, to the beach. As they maddened motorists with their stately pace of 20 mph, their used cars were a menace not only to pedestrians but they were frightening the pants off Chrysler, GM, and Ford, who hadn't yet begun to build in obsolescence.

Harold Teen was frozen permanently in adolescence. Skeezix, whose prepubescent period roughly paralleled that of Jackie Cooper, was a kiddie-strip hero. Barring such famous boy adventurers of Funnyland as Terry of *Terry and the Pirates* and Dick Tracy's redheaded idolator Junior, who participated in a violent world, most kiddie-strip heroes inhabited a Booth Tarkington landscape, curiously at odds with the real world. Prerequisites for a kiddie strip were a small town and a gang which convened in a clubhouse.

Where were Jimmie Dugan of *Reg'lar Fellers* and Winnie Winkle's little brother Perry during the lean winter of 1931 and 1932? Jimmie and the Duffy boys were pitching Lou Gehrig baseballs around at the Reg'lar Fellers Club. Perry was playing with his friends from the Rinkydink Club.

Perry wore a velvet suit topped by a red coat with a matching wide-brimmed red sailor hat. Neither this sissy garb nor the fact that he had a girl's haircut ever evoked the slightest comment from his peers. Jimmie Dugan of *Reg'lar Fellers* wore a jacket, necktie, and knickers to play catch. Rain or shine, summer or winter, Jimmie and the Duffys, Skippy Skinner and Perry Winkle wore hats, a formality which in the bareheaded space age the Hat Institute has tried in vain to revive.

Jimmie Dugan had idiosyncracies in mannerisms and dress left over from the high-button-shoes era. They went well with the New York *Herald Tribune*'s nostalgic Webster cartoons: "They Don't Speak Our Language," "Life's Darkest Moment," "The Timid Soul," "The Thrill That Comes Once in a Lifetime." Webster's characters crawled under the flaps of circus tents. Some of them even *wore* high button shoes.

In the winter the small towns of Funnyland were blanketed with clean white snow. Only occasionally did the Tarkington Funnyland feel the impact of hard times, as in the delightful Webster Bridge cartoon showing four bums in a hobo jungle discussing the Vanderbilt Club convention.

The boy in the kiddie strip often had an older sister who was one of Funnyland's career girls. Perry Winkle's sister Winnie was permanently employed despite falling sales curves. Any ups and downs she experienced concerned the heart rather than the pocketbook. Winnie often picked a lemon in the garden of love. Once she posed as an heiress to attract Count Raymond Beleares de la Chartreuse, only to discover that his credentials were as suspect as her own. In the dénouement of sportsmanship, she said, "Some count! But what a hairdresser." Tillie the Toiler often went off in pursuit of such exotic creatures as "Nick Keever, the all-star performer from Haywire University," but she always came back *faute de mieux* to her waist-high boy friend, faithful old Mac.

Blondie started out in the steno pool with a half-pint suitor called Hiho Hennepin, until Dagwood Bumstead won her away and lured her into the world of diapers and two o'clock feedings. Realism did occasionally obtrude into a *Blondie* strip. Someone once expressed a desire to buy a car and salesmen materialized from behind fences and ashcans, brandishing order blanks.

For the most part the home and office situation of Funnyland contained little to offend the "rugged individualism" of Herbert Hoover. There were jobs for anyone who wanted to work, even ten-year-old go-getters like Smitty, who had been working since 1922. He was still in short pants and still serving a boss who had never heard of the NRA, of its head General Hugh Johnson, or of those subversive laws governing the employment of children.

Meanwhile, how were things in the real world?

In 1931 W. K. Vanderbilt, sitting in a dining room off the coast of Spain on his 264-foot yacht *Alva,* read the latest report from Wall Street. The Vanderbilt family's stock, which had once stood at 250, was plummeting to its rock-bottom depth of $10 a share. "Central has hit 25," he recorded in his diary, "it is time to go home."

By 1931 the Little Bull Market which had given brief promise of better things to come had played itself out. By the end of 1932

General Motors, Radio Corporation Common, and U.S. Steel had tumbled respectively from 36 to 7⅝; from 26 to 2½, and from 150 to 21¼. Business as a whole was running at a loss of over $5,000,000,000.

The financial structure of the country was tottering. Scandal would touch Charles Mitchell of the National City Bank. The Senate Banking Committee would dare to question the practices of the august House of Morgan. For some, it was even advisable to skip town. Samuel Insull, Midwest Utilities mogul, found it expedient to go halfway round the world to avoid embarrassing questions. A process server slapped a notice on the door of New York's absentee Mayor Jimmy Walker for an unpaid bill his wife had run up in palmier days. Quipped the *News:* "Mrs. Walker's a Walker With Shoes at Forty Bucks." Soon the Mayor's ordeal before the Seabury Committee would blow the lid off Tammany's little tin box. By 1933 a survey showed some seventy thousand householders had lost their homes—with an estimated thousand homes a day falling into the mortgage holder's hands.

Those Tarkington-like comic strip streets gave no clue of the workers in Soviet uniforms who paraded bearing signs, "American Workers Refuse to Starve." The 1932 Bonus March on Washington was turned back by the United States Army after the Veterans had set up shop on Anacostia Flats. The Bonus Army Bank stood ready to do a land-office business in case Congress passed the Bonus Bill. When Congress didn't comply, someone with a wry sense of humor put up a sign saying, "This Bank Just Failed."

A New York *Daily News* reporter in 1931 visited Unemployed City, a collection of shacks and dugouts in a vacant lot—typical of what were known as "Hoovervilles" all over the country. He was invited by the inhabitants to forage for the ingredients of a stew, which was cooked in a communal pot with no-questions-asked origins.

And what about the snow that was a feature of Funnyland's old-fashioned winters? Sandwiched among the trunk murders and "heart balm" suits in 1933 was the news that a blizzard which killed sixteen people in the Midwest and stopped trains for five days in Missoula, Montana, brought serendipity to nineteen thousand New York unemployed. They were taken on at fifty cents an hour to augment the Sanitation Department's regular force. The children of Funnyland, sledding over the white hills, were unaware that a blizzard could have sociological implications.

As for the true-life Tillie the Toilers of the early Thirties, one group was put to work on a project in 1933, after a long interlude of being out of work. More than two-thirds broke down and wept as they discovered they had almost forgotten how to type and take dictation. The New York tabloids, whose readers liked their sociology with a dash of spice, read with a thrill of horror of the fate of many real-life Winnies, Tillies, and Blondies: "Vice Ring Preys on Jobless Girl." None of Tillie's or Winnie's bogus counts or college smoothies ever tried to lure them into a bordello.

Like the jalopy, another unwanted legacy from the Twenties was Prohibition. On January 16, 1920, the Eighteenth Amendment to the Constitution went into effect, outlawing liquor. The Volstead Act was passed shortly thereafter to reinforce it. Not since the Civil War had an issue so divided the country. The Grays and the Blues had nothing on the Wets and the Drys. But from the outset it seemed evident that Prohibition wasn't working out. The tiny band of Prohibition agents had been unable to patrol the interminable coastline to head off smugglers or to supervise the purity of "near beer" or to curtail home brewing experiments with bathtub gin. Throughout the Twenties rum ships had operated outside the twelve-mile limit, and people had sipped illicit cocktails in the curtained anonymity of the speakeasy. Kingpin of those gangsters, who used to fill people with lead and now fill us with nostalgia, was Scarface Al Capone. Like most of the crew, he got his start in bootlegging.

In 1931 a square-jawed newcomer turned up in Funnyland. Dick Tracy's first case involved a murder in a speakeasy. Hasty exits were facilitated by mysterious secret panels. The place enjoyed the protection of a crooked lawyer named Habeas. The proprietress, Texie, whirled unexpectedly through a panel to confront Tracy with a gun. Texie's prototype, the immortal Texas Guinan, in the early Thirties became an anachronism. The author of the Prohibition Law announced in 1932 that, given another chance, he would vote against it. Franklin D. Roosevelt campaigning against Herbert Hoover announced, "I too want Repeal." A 1931 cartoon showed

Columbia at a party on the arm of a ramrodlike figure named Prohibition. She was ogling a more fun-loving swain. "I think I'll give this bimbo the gate," she said to Repeal, "you look good to me."

By December 1933 the country was legally wet again. Repeal's first gift to Columbia was 3.2 beer. There was a landmark Christmas in 1934. No longer were the festivities marred, as they had been in the past, by such headlines as "Christmas Hootch Kills Seven," and "One Drink Costs Man Eyesight."

In 1934, stores were throwing down the gauntlet to gift givers with holiday liquor events. Santa's bag of goodies included imported champagne at $3.69 a bottle. Holiday baskets ($7.99 complete) included 1 bottle of Derbyshire gin, 1 quart of Founder Rye whiskey, 1 bottle imported Ben Nevis Scotch whiskey. The Derbyshire gin by itself came to 93¢ a fifth. For the first time in a long time you could use the bathtub for bathing, with the NRA eagle smiling his blessing.

After 1933 the bootleggers had to rechannel their energies. Kidnapings were big after Repeal. Some speakeasies became posh restaurants or nightclubs—as did Sherman Billingsley's Stork Club and Jack and Charlie's 21. The war with gangland went on unabated with the focus shifting somewhat west and south. Texas badman Clyde Barrow and his cigar-smoking sweetheart Bonnie Parker were killed in a gun duel near Acadia, Louisiana. J. Edgar Hoover's G-Men gunned down John Dillinger, Public Enemy Number One, outside a Chicago movie theater in 1934. Public Enemy Number Two—Owney Madden—prepared to rid himself of his first wife Dorothy, so that he could wed Miss Agnes Denby of Hot Springs, Arkansas. Unlike Dillinger, Madden had a long lifeline. It was healthier perhaps to be runner up. Dick Tracy and Junior turned from the speakeasy to trap malefactors with more generalized interests. There was Larceny Lu and a mad scientist named Dr. Hump. With the passing of Prohibition the evildoer of the Thirties could shift his center of operation from the still to the chemistry lab.

A legacy which dated back not to Tarkington but to the days of Uncle Remus and Artemus Ward was the Depression's attitude toward minorities. Skeezix's maid could say without fear of protest from the NAACP, "I doesn't have to be independent on nobody for what I wants done," or "You tote these cakes ova to Miss Sniff's for the church suppa just as if you' Auntie Blossom was here!" A Negro manservant in *Harold Teen* hands around a tray of drinks with the words "Yah ah come, Massa. Yassuh! Yassuh!"

Amusing malapropisms were standard speech for Negroes, but the Negro was not the only one abused. When Reg'lar Feller Pinhead Duffy took violin lessons, his brother Puddinhead remarked, "Mom took the cotton out of her ears yestiddy for the foist time." When Jimmie Dugan acquired his Lou Gehrig baseball he threw what he described as "incoives," "outcoives," "downcoives," and "upcoives." Nobody wrote in protest that every unlettered Reg'lar Feller had an Irish name. The comic effect of Captain Katzenjammer's *echt Deutsch* speech patterns were akin to Jimmie and Puddinhead's "deses" and "doses."

The bottom might drop out of everything but Funnyland followed its formulae. Webster's Caspar Milquetoast would tremble in his shoes when the office boy asked for his autograph because once, long ago, someone told him it was unwise to sign anything. Hans und Fritz Katzenjammer concocted weekly deviltry to plague Mama, der Captain und der Inspector. The formula—one prank, one spanking per Sunday. Jiggs would be dragged off dressed in soup and fish, while lusting for poker and corned beef. Bunky of *Parlor, Bedroom and Sink* was ambulatory though always in baby clothes. Like Toots and Casper's son Buttercup, Bunky might be rated today as an under-achiever. He challenged his tormentor Fagan with the monotonous observation, "Youse is a viper." Buttercup's vocabulary was even more meager, consisting of the single word "goo."

Most durable survivor of the ancien régime was Little Orphan Annie's beloved Daddy Warbucks. As his very name implied, he was a walking testimonial to the economics of Adam Smith. His ups and downs, separations and reconciliations with Annie were dizzying. The formula hasn't changed much to this day. The year 1931 might find him in a flophouse. By 1932 he was comfortably installed in a mansion with a Cockney butler who was given to such remarks as, "Madam is a bit hindisposed." He was opposed by bad people—like Homer Jackal—who tended to question his sanity. Shallow people—his wife of 1932, for instance, named Trixie —also schemed to get their mitts on his millions. One could tell right away that Trixie had the wrong values because she disliked a) Orphan Annie, and b) the country, being driven to squawks and ee-yows by the very sight of a cow.

There were other rough diamonds, who even in the flophouse period recognized Warbucks' quality, sensing that beneath that bum's shrubbery there lurked a "man of distinction."

"Yessir," one such sterling fellow remarked, "I've always admired that bird Warbucks more'n any other guy in the world. Never saw him personally (He was, of course, looking at him.) but his pictures tell the story. He's a scrapper. None of yer pussyfootin' sick snobs. Robbin' widows an' orphans. He took his away from guys that could give him a battle." It was the ethic of Carnegie and Rockefeller. Warbucks' reputation for decency stemmed from the fact that he never groined anyone who couldn't groin him back.

Yet if Adam Smith was out of fashion, one had only to turn to the advertising pages to see why.

"Avoid that Christmas fatigue, gedunk," said a 1931 Harold Teen cartoon, pinpointing one of Funnyland's great Depression pastimes: hunting up cut-rate gifts for the loved ones. It was the thought that counted with Harold when he gave Lillums a simple bunch of wildflowers or when Reg'lar Feller Jimmie Dugan gave his father a ten-cent bottle of metal polish to shine his gold tooth.

The newspaper ads at Christmastime throughout the Thirties mirrored the disastrous deflation that had hit every item in Santa's workshop. A "velocipede" in 1932, regularly $7.95, was marked down to $4.95 on easy terms of 25¢ a week. Shoes for Kayo Mullins could be had for 77¢, cotton pajamas for 69¢, a shirt and tie combination came to 50¢, a leatherette jacket to $1.95. Boys' three-piece knicker sets of the type sported by Jimmie Dugan cost $3.88. For a dollar more a boy could have a hat, a *vest,* and "two pairs of full-cut knickers." The Depression practice of marking down Christmas merchandise was in direct opposition to current Yuletide custom. Cutting the price of an object around December 1st represented the retailer's last hope of ever getting rid of it.

The shirt and necktie combination represented a form of merchandising that went with a buyer's market. Everything from rhinestone clips to grip developers were given away to followers of radio serials. Customers were lured into the Bijou with offers of free dishes. For every young couple who did over the living room with the aid of Raleigh cigarette coupons there was another who started out married life with a china service of ornate and flowered gimcrackery—acquired by some affectionate relative patiently and at great expense, matinee after matinee. Bank nite at the movies gave patrons a crack at a jackpot which might reach an astronomical $800. California movie houses had "tin can shows"—admittance one tin can of food for the needy. The show itself was something of a bargain. For 10¢ a child of Smitty or Skippy's age could see a double feature, three cartoons, one or two serials, previews of coming attractions, possibly a "Pete Smith specialty" and a newsreel. Harold Teen and Lillums could get into a matinee for 15¢, the evening performance for a quarter. As Harold might have remarked, "It was a lot of movie for two bits, lil lamb's lettuce."

Blondie, Tillie the Toiler or Winnie Winkle could buy a really good fur coat for $295. More to the point, they could buy two cotton dresses for a dollar as late as 1938. A three-piece suit, featuring a "sweeping skunk tuxedo" if one was in the market for such a thing, was theirs for $69.95. If Tillie's boy friend Mac had wanted to treat her to a Broadway show they could have sat in the balcony for 55¢ at any time in the Depression. If the more costly seats were vacant—and they usually were—they might be ushered into the front row to encourage the actors.

A six-course dinner with wine could be had for 99¢. Groceries for one with lavish entertaining came to $10 a week. The price of three brands of A & P coffee remained constant throughout the Depression—Bokar at 27¢, Red Circle at 23¢, and Eight O'clock "mild and mellow" for only 19¢.

Dagwood and Blondie Bumstead could start married life in "7 rooms, private bathrooms, hot water, fire-retarded halls" for $35 a month. The buyers' market in real estate was reflected in hardsell advertising prose: "Murphy beds . . . housekeeping arrangements . . . placed in efficient array along one wall." The words "relief accepted" appeared often in real estate ads. It was a common practice for landlords to offer a month or two on the cuff so that a tenant could see if he liked his new accommodations.

In 1939 Blondie and Dagwood could have bought for $69 (easy terms of 75¢ a week) fourteen pieces for the bedroom or sixteen for the living room. Some of the items which accompanied the basic four-piece "suite"—Vanity Lites, Bed Lites, scatter rugs "in a popular waterfall design," and a mysterious entity called a "smoker" —qualified as "pieces" only with some slight gilding of the lily.

When one became the parent of a teenager, it was possible to get him to high school without buying a Mustang. A newspaper ad in 1937, only one of a pageful, proclaimed that "over 200 cars at our open-air showroom must be sold at half price." Among them

1929 BUICK SEDAN $23
1928 PACKARD SEDAN $29
1931 ESSEX FOUR-DOOR SEDAN $36
1932 GRAHAM SEDAN $71

. . . and so on through an almost new '37 Dodge for $550. Clearly the automotive industry had yet to hit on its greatest technological discovery—that it was better not to build 'em to last.

The editorial tone of the papers which chronicled Funnyland's highjinks changed over the years. So neatly did the Thirties fall into different periods that it is possible to pinpoint the year in which an editorial was written almost without looking at the dateline. In the early days of black depression, nearly everyone felt that the country was due for a change. Militarism and unpaid war debts were stock editorial page cartoon figures. William Randolph Hearst supported Roosevelt in 1932. After the 1933 bank holiday, even the McCormick-Patterson papers were swept along in the excitement of the first hundred days. The New York *Daily News* sympathized with the bonus marchers, supported the anti-child-labor laws, and turned a kindly eye on the insurance of bank savings.

By 1935 the majority of the press was dead set against FDR. The names of such New Dealers as Harold Ickes, Raymond Moley, Harry Hopkins, Rexford Tugwell, and the first woman cabinet member, Frances Perkins, were almost as well known as those of the Katzenjammers.

The friendly climate of the New Deal would cause union membership to rise from three million or less in 1933 to nearly nine million by the end of the decade. The businessman saw his relationship to the government in the strokes of a 1935 Dowling cartoon wherein a man labeled "utility companies" was treed atop a telegraph pole by a mad dog, "White House Legislation."

The Hearst press was particularly exercised over the threats to the American Way of Life. After reading Barney Google, one might turn to a cartoon showing a baloney-making machine labeled "Brain Trust." Manning it were "Servile Senator" and "Servile Representative," both grinding out the tainted meat of "must" legislation.

Hearst editorial pages denounced "confiscatory taxes." "Soak the Thrifty. Loot Industry! And Spread Poverty!"

Letters to the Editor complained of "Social Security's Bookkeeping Burden on Businessman" or warned against "Conceit Fostered in Plain Man by New Deal." The Pattersons, the McCormicks, the Hearsts, and Mrs. Ogden Reid might protest all they wanted. As the 1936 elections showed, all their combined efforts could not give Alfred Landon a mandate from the people.

In the late Thirties the editorial and front pages were changing and Spain, Munich, Poland, Finland, Dunkirk, and the Battle of Britain brought the outside world a little closer to the Sugar Bowl and Gasoline Alley. But Harold Teen and Skeezix were not political beings like the members of the pacifist Communist American Youth Congress.

Their preoccupations were much more universal. For years the Sugar Bowl had echoed with timely colloquialism: "Izzat so?" just after the Crash, in 1934 "Little Man What Now—Gedunk," in 1938 "Slug down a shag." By 1939 the movie *Dead End* had added a new phrase to Harold's current up-to-the-minute glossary ("Gum bye" "You cur, sir"). "Ahoy," he now greeted the group, "any of you Dead End Kids seen Shadow?"

Around the time Neville Chamberlain proclaimed the possibility of peace in our time, Harold had fallen with his customary enthusiasm under the influence of the King of Swing. His appearance had at last changed from that of a sheik to a jitterbug. The Sugar Bowl had become The Sugar Bowl Swing Club and Harold and

Lillums had jazzed up the language of love. "In the groove," said Harold, guiding Lillums through a complicated maneuver. "Now bank on the turns," Lillums responded, "I hear you talkin', rug cutter."

While all this was going on Skeezix had emerged from knickers. He had such marks of a man's estate as long pants, a motorcycle, and a jalopy. He was overtaking Harold, who had ridden a motorcycle in the early Thirties and who had been menacing the countryside in a car named Leapin' Lena—wittily embellished with such phrases as "Call me a taxi," "Squad car," "Capacity 5 Gals."

Skeezix and Harold might have been considered average children among the denizens of Funnyland. But just how average were they? A 1940 *March of Time* on "America's Youth" indicated that most funny-paper characters were well up on the social pyramid. Little Orphan Annie was one of the few who endured actual want. One could always be sure that a period of privation would be followed by a year or so of Oriental luxury.

The Winkles, the Wallets, the Mullinses, the Lovewells and Teens may not have fallen into the opulent $10,000-a-year-and-plus with a fortunate 250,000 Americans. Shadow, Harold, and J. Beelzebub Binks did not belong to the intellectual elite of nineteen million young people who were in college by 1940, many of them working their way through. But Harold, Skeezix, and Lillums were not thrust prematurely into the semiskilled labor pool to make a meager $18 a week, with 10¢ taken out for Social Security. Poor Smitty was the only one snatched from a pram into an office job. A white collar boy pulled down $15 to $20 a week, most of which was eaten up by room and board and keeping his collar white. Skeezix, just prior to the war, went on the road as a traveling salesman. He never fell—along with a quarter of his generation—into the ranks of the unemployed. The landscape of Funnyland was rural but not so rural that any comic strip character shared the lot of five million depression farm kids who labored fifty-four hours a week for less than $9. To these the *March of Time* held out cold consolation. "Into their keeping is passing a rich heritage—that of the healthy U.S. soil." In 1940, forty thousand youngsters like Skeezix and Harold were doing time, but the names of Winkle, Binks, Wallet, and Smart never graced a police blotter. The bulk of the malefactors were between eighteen and twenty-four years old. Perry Winkle, Jimmie Dugan, and Skippy would not have been considered potential criminals. Society had yet to come to grips with the ten-year-old who sets his parents on fire in an argument over a bad report card.

The parents of Funnyland were able to take care of their children better than their real-life counterparts. Skeezix, on graduation from Snapper Elementary School, attended a prep school called Bunker. If the educational experience was marred by a roommate named Sissy Bly, it may have helped him land that job as a salesman. Maids and other status symbols were not uncommon in Funnyland. "Mr. and Mrs.," Joe and Vi Green, had their faithful Zobelia. Uncle Walt Wallet took a trip to Europe in the Thirties. It marked him as a person of substance as did the air of determined good sportsmanship with which Auntie Blossom did the dishes on cook's night out.

On the other hand, Harold and Skeezix belonged to that generation of teenagers who, despite their jalopies, had to earn small amounts of money on paper routes. They probably had friends who got down on their knees when they wanted to borrow the family cars. Advertisers did not woo them as a multimillion dollar source of purchasing power. There was almost nothing Shadow Smart wouldn't do for a dime. Harold, in the course of one of his recurrent Christmas crises, reflected: "45 berries! I didn't know there was that much money in the world." And his mother responded to requests for an advance on his allowance with an incredulous "Are you mad?"

Before Pearl Harbor the New York *Daily News*—a publication as staunchly isolationist as it was anti-New Deal—stood squarely with Senators Wheeler and Nye. "This war will end when the Allied statesmen abandon all hope of luring another AEF (American Expeditionary Force) to Europe." After Pearl Harbor the McCormicks and the Pattersons exulted over a shellacking administered by the Russians to Hitler's armies.

A post-Pearl Harbor *News* cartoon shows Miss Liberty perched on a pedestal marked Army, Air Force, Navy, showing cornerstones marked Bricklayer, Writer, Mason, Carpenter, Publisher,

Dancer, Musician, symbolizing national unity by showing that these were comrades in arms.

Of all the denizens of Funnyland, trusty old Skeezix heeded the call to arms. Skeezix had become infected with the editorial enthusiasm ("Why wait for the draft?"). Thus were all the soul searchings resolved, the pacifist fervor forgotten. As Skeezix is about to turn twenty-one, he meets a buddy already in uniform and announces his plans to go into the army. "I've got other plans but I suppose I'll have to scrap them. Take it as it comes and do your best." One sector of Funnyland was at last a part of the carnage on the front page. Skeezix's triumph over Harold was now complete. Harold was in quarantine for the measles.

Where are they now? Odd that nobody bothers to keep up anymore. Moon Mullins looks much the same, as does Smilin' Jack. Terry Lee, having defended us from the Dragon Lady and the Herrenvolk, is still operating East of Suez, but Milton Caniff has abandoned him to draw a Hearst strip called *Steve Canyon*. Terry is today a square-jawed young man drawn since 1946 by George Wunder.

Terry around the late Thirties was partially eclipsed by Hotshot Charlie (full name—Charles Charles Charles), who came on strong throughout World War II—to disappear mysteriously during the late Fifties—to reappear briefly in the fight against the Commies and finally to vanish once and for all—or has he? The Dragon Lady still does her evil work. The whole strip takes what Dwight D. Eisenhower used to describe as a strong "posture" in the battle against Communism. ("By day, the hamlet seems as usual, sir," Terry says to his superior. "At night the Viet Cong move in.")

Harold Teen is defunct. Smitty, a youthful-looking married man after more than forty years, is still plugging away at that office. Perry Winkle is also a young married. Caspar Milquetoast died with his creator. Jimmie Dugan and Puddinhead Duffy are also no more—having dragged the *Herald Tribune* comic section and the New York *Sun* down with them to the Happy Hunting Ground.

Subjects for obituaries at the Hearst shop are *Skippy, Tillie the Toiler* (who served her country honorably as a WAC), *Toots and Casper,* and the *Katzenjammers* (who have turned up as far afield as Mexico City). *Barney Google* is still a familiar face, Maggie

Jiggs is still *Bringing Up Father* with the aid of two new artists; Olive Oyl is still engaged to Popeye. Prince Valiant is as square as ever. Blondie looks perennially young, having been some years ago heroine of a series of Grade B movies and a TV series. Unlike most flesh-and-blood stars, she has remained faithful to the same old mate. In some cities—like Chicago and New York—the Hearst papers themselves are among the missing.

Little Orphan Annie looks almost as she did during Daddy Warbucks' ill-fated alliance with Trixie. (Annie's creator, Harold Grey, claimed in an interview to have added a few inches to her stature.) It has been suggested by critics that the dress she has worn since 1924 might be due for a trip to the cleaner. Oliver Warbucks is still the Rough Diamond's Darling. ("That Daddy of yours is the bravest, toughest, grandest, decentest old son of a gun I ever knowed. But the best guys can't win 'em *all*. I sure hope he gets back here safe.")

Recently Daddy Warbucks was in disguise once more. A strip showed him vanishing around a mountain pass with a long white beard. (In 1931 the beard was black.) And again his sanity has been challenged. Annie was working in an insane asylum. (Those soft-headed Child Labor Laws be damned!) Gingerly she pushed a dinner in to a glowering "homicidal maniac," who turned out to be—Guess who? He was unjustly confined to one of the country's least enlightened mental institutions (run by an evil Dr. Le Quaque). In view of Daddy's social philosophy it was fitting that Dr. Le Quaque had never heard of tranquilizing drugs or outpatient care. Not long ago Daddy Warbucks had gotten wind of trouble in a banana republic—where the American flag was torn down and a fifty-million-dollar American plant nationalized. With a righteousness born of the Big Stick era of American diplomacy, Warbucks set off, nuts or not, to take the Number One Boy to task for his theft "in terms even he can understand."

Down the gentle slopes of *Gasoline Alley* the outside world came to Funnyland. Skeezix has been through the common wartime experience—letters written to APO addresses, announcements of a baby's birth brought by mail to a Pacific jungle. Nina, his boyhood sweetheart and wife, struggled with baby-sitters and wolves at the USO dances. The child who was born while he was out in the

Pacific is now a teenager who wanders over the same idealized landscape where Skeezix played as a boy. He has members of his household who refer to him as "Pop." Of all the characters in Funnyland, Skeezix alone has accepted the lot of middle age. He is beginning to have a weight problem that may one day rival Uncle Walt's.

Junior Tracy's boyish head has been superimposed on a body clad in long pants. He has recently married, and one can only hope that the union does not run into too cosmic a clash of cultures. His wife—Moon Maid—comes, as her name suggests, from the moon. She has horns equipped with deadly rays which have been turned to good advantage in the battle against crime. The scene has shifted from the speakeasy to outer space.

A new generation of real-life gangsters has grown up since Tracy and Junior chased after Dr. Hump and Larceny Lu. In Pompano Beach, Florida, Edward G. Bremer died recently. He was the survivor of a 1934 kidnaping by the Barker-Karpis gang. (It was a year in which kidnaping threats were uppermost in Funnyland minds.) He was held, blindfolded, for three weeks and eventually released after payment of $200,000 ransom. Alvin "Creepy" Karpis who masterminded the crime is still paying his debt to society. In the spring of 1965 Owney Madden succumbed to emphysema. Time had mellowed Public Enemy Number 2. The "policy racket," the "bootleg booze" were behind him. He was a big contributor to charity and a big brother to youth. He died in the hometown of his 1934 bride—Hot Springs, Arkansas. The last half of his obituary reads like that of any distinguished senior citizen. One is loathe to admit remembering their heyday. One is loathe to admit remembering Skeezix's knickers, Perry Winkle's velvet suits, the long-abandoned format of the newspapers of one's childhood, or the day when every "Leapin' Lena" had a running board. The reaction is too apt to be like that of Skeezix's daughter when he told her he was born in 1921. "A.D.?" she asked. It was never the same after Skeezix, like many average boys, left the peace of his hometown to join in the carnage on Page 1.

If you haven't changed much, Junior Tracy, we have.

Chapter 2

The Country Cousin
and the City Mouse
Celebrate Sunday at Home

Sunday at home in the Thirties was the day for the funnies. In other respects it varied considerably, depending on where home happened to be. For contrast, take two extremes—a country cousin living in a small Fundamentalist town in the Midwest and a city mouse living in New York City. Both city mouse and country cousin, with all their relatives of Suburbia in between, were children of a great change—the first leisure of the New World. There was more time to spare, and more places to go. There is much talk in the 1960s about the leisure use ahead. The greatest discovery about Sunday at home in the Thirties was that you didn't have to spend it at home at all.

America began to become a nation on wheels. Many families took to the road on Sunday, headed for togetherness on the golf course or the beach.

In the ten years between 1925 and 1935, the number of public bathing beaches, golf courses, ice-skating rinks, and swimming pools had doubled. While the Depression had hit private golf clubs hard, there had been an enormous increase in municipal links. Outside New York, the new Jones Beach could accommodate 100,000 bathers on a sunny midsummer afternoon. All this had bred a new and frightening type of motorist, the Sunday driver. The city mouse might take to the turnpike over the weekend, braving horrendous homecoming crowds on Sunday night. Country mice in the wide open spaces fled the Depression in a movable cottage. In 1930 the first house trailer had been previewed at the Detroit Automobile Show. By the summer of 1936, there were an estimated 160,000 of them on the road. For many of those who could scare up the price of a trailer, it offered not only housing but a means of pursuing hard-to-come-by work. Those compact little vehicles were the spiritual ancestors of today's monster-size "mobile homes" and of the smaller units which throng the highways of the West and obstruct the view of the bears in Yellowstone Park. The communal plumbing of the first trailer camps wasn't exactly on a par with the Ritz. But to its inhabitants it offered a freedom from one's creditors, the local tax collector, and the bank that held the mortgage.

For those without a trailer or car, the wheels were smaller. Bicycling and rollerskating enjoyed minor booms in the Thirties because they were cheap. Bicycling, which reached its zenith in the Hollywood area in 1932–33, gave California girls an excuse for putting on "trousers like Dietrich's."

The revolution in communication which had begun in the Twenties could make a fad travel like wildfire. In 1929–30 a mild game of miniature golf had been the order of the day. In 1932 the family might be huddled over a jigsaw puzzle.

In the mid-Thirties, Monopoly was the national game. Monopoly was invented by an unemployed heating engineer in 1932. Eventually it fell into the hands of the Parker Game Company. Monopoly was to outstrip such other Parker staples as *The Lone Ranger Board Game, The Boake Carter Star Reporter Game, The Lowell Thomas World Cruise,* and *Van Loon's Wide World Travel Game.* By 1935 Monopoly achieved its greatest impact— keeping weekend parties going from Friday till Monday. The game took so long that one could spend days at it, pausing only to eat, sleep, and gather strength to corner the railroads, build hotels on

Ventnor Avenue, or make subtle plans to buy up the Boardwalk and Park Place. Its creator Mr. Charles Darrow died a rich man in August 1967 in that Park Place of Exurbia, Bucks County.

A Sunday in 1934 might have found either the city mice or their country cousins hopefully sending out a chain letter. ("Scratch out the top name and send a dime.") In 1937 rival teams, fluttering quotation marks and syllable counts, would be playing an elaborate version of charades known as The Game. Depending on the intellectualism of the locale, they could be acting out anything from "hell, said the duchess" to "all mimsy were the borogroves" or "the ineluctable modality of the visible." On a Sunday in 1937 either family might have been surrounded by reference books—in the thick of the Old Gold Contest. The contest brought an outstanding ninety answers apiece from two million people. Average entrants spent about eighty hours on ninety cartoon puzzles each accompanied by a list of names. Contestants were to pick out the name represented by the objects, action, or dialogue in the cartoon. When several rounds of tiebreakers narrowed the field to 8160 aspirants for $200,000 worth of prizes, Old Gold required the survivors to complete an essay on "The Increased Popularity of Old Golds in My Community as a Result of the Old Gold Contest." The result in every town was gratifying, especially to the cigarette men—a 70 percent jump in sales over 1936.

People told each other "knock knock" or Little Audrey jokes. Facial muscles were grimly arranged for the dutiful laughter which followed the answer to "Knock knock, who's there?" When Little Audrey "laughed and laughed and laughed because she knew . . ." other sufferers snickered conscientiously on cue.

In 1939 the more athletically oriented in the rural areas might have turned out to watch the local softball team.

Skiing was a fad which owed its rise directly to the five-day week. The Winter Olympics held in Lake Placid in 1932 did much to publicize it. The Boston and Maine ran "snow trains" into northerly areas with such success that, by 1937, ski trains and buses were departing from New York, Pittsburgh, Chicago, Portland, San Francisco, and Los Angeles. Conversation of a Sunday night might revolve around how the snow was at North Conway or St. Sauveur; the Glüwein at Pecketts-on-Sugar-Hill in New Hampshire;

the "ukulele artist," or the marshmallow "lady kisses" at Stowe, Vermont.

From westerly metropolises one could ski at ranches in Missoula, Montana; Sun Valley, Yosemite, or Reno. In the Far West there was, starting each May, glacier skiing on Mount Baker near Seattle.

Prices by today's standards were dirt cheap. The rooms at New England inns were a dollar a night in 1939. It was possible to take a Friday to Monday excursion from New York to the Laurentians for $42. This included transportation, meals, hotel room and private bath, everything except the hot buttered rum.

Grand Central Station in New York posted temperatures and snow data on a dozen skiing centers. Department stores hired Scandinavian ski experts. In 1936 one could take lessons on a borax slide at Saks Fifth Avenue, though too enthusiastic a telemark might land one in a display of men's socks.

Skiing was becoming popular but bridge was king—providing a footnote to the declining influence of the Protestant sects with injunctions against card playing, gambling, and dancing. Frederick Lewis Allen points out that between 1930 and 1931—two of the worst years of the Depression—the sale of playing cards rose to a peak which it would never hit again during the decade. After the Lenz-Culbertson match in 1931 Culbertson's books became best sellers, branding a whole generation with a telltale habit which has survived into the Goren age, of totting up hands in terms of "honor tricks" instead of "points."

The Lynds reported that in Middletown more bridge was played in 1935 than in 1925, that there was more playing for money, and that the habit was spreading from the idle rich to the working class where, through the intervention of the women, it was gradually displacing pinochle and poker.

The churches, which were having a rough time anyway in the Depression, found the Sunday competition a bit tough. Sunday is the traditional day of Remorse. A country cousin in 1931 might be recovering from roosting too long in a tree and breaking a rib. In 1937 or 1938 a city youth might come home from college to recuperate from the after-effects of swallowing a live goldfish. Allen quotes the findings of the Lynds on their return to *Middletown*. There were still some imposing churches left over from the Twenties. The congregation, however, looked older, and sermons generally dealt with the failure of the Depression to bring about a religious resurgence. "Here scattered through the pews is the same serious and numerically sparse Gideon's band, two thirds of them women, and few of them under thirty, with the same stark ring of empty pews down front."

For the country cousin in the Fundamentalist small town, however, the church was still the focal point of activities, social as well as spiritual. There were significant reasons.

Country people had profited less than city people from the increased leisure time which accompanied the New Deal. The ill wind of the Depression had blown in one great good for urbanites—the five-day week. In 1931 and 1932 many businesses had "spread the work" by reducing the work week. The NRA codes had extended the reduction. By 1937 most city dwellers could take off on Friday night for a two-day weekend. It was a rare Daddy who still went in to the office on Saturday. In the small towns of the Midwest and mid-South, bastions of the small businessman, the 5½- and 6-day week still prevailed until after the war. Even today many small-towners spend five and a half days in "the salt mines." Businesses close at noon on Wednesday or Thursday, stay open Saturday when the farmers come to town, with everything building up to the grand climax of the week on Sunday.

Sunday in a small town in Missouri began, fittingly, with Sunday School. Everyone went. There was a men's class and a women's class, a Beginners' Class (usually coeds of 6–9 years), a Junior Class, aged 10–12, and a Senior Class designed to get one through the fleshly temptations of high school. Each denomination had a Sunday School, Bible stories were the point of departure, and the classroom discussion was to be guided by the International Sunday School Lessons.

The young pupils might trace Paul's journeys on a map, indicating in the margin of Acts where he was when he prepared his various epistles. They read from supplementary sources: *Paul's Companions, Paul's Campaigns, Paul's Letters, Paul the Dauntless,* or *Egermeier's Bible Story Book*.

Topics for discussion on a Sunday in May: "What false Messiahs have come in modern days to draw people away?" "Could Solomon have prevented the division of his kingdom or was he helpless in his surroundings?" "Was Jonathan less faithful than he should have been to Saul because of his love for David?" or "What friends do you know who have been aided by adversity?"

More advanced lessons were based on *The Bible Expositor and Illuminator*, a quarterly whose cover looked a bit like *The Illustrated London News* and which advertised in the *Christian Herald* as being "Scriptural, Spiritual, Sound and Sane, Premillennial, Practical, Pointed and Pure."

After this came the eleven-o'clock service. Children came to church with their mothers. Baby-sitting services were largely unknown. "Infant care" consisted of removing the child from the premises when the decibel count got too high. Most sermons in small-town churches were punctuated with baby cries. Meanwhile, back at home, the $5-a-week cook was whipping up the midday meal. Friends generally dropped in for Sunday dinner. A product of such a small-town upbringing recalls that she spent most of Sunday afternoon driving around in cars taking pictures of friends. The fruits of many such Sunday afternoons are immortalized in albums of snapshots all dutifully marked "Betty Jane" and "Martha Sue." In such a town the emphasis was on inspiration but the opportunities for gloom were endless. The handsomest boy might be a Baptist—forbidden to dance.

Less rigorously brought up people sometimes took in a movie. More than one local entrepreneur owned both the movie house and the restaurant next door, both of which he called The Palace.

The restaurant offered fried chicken, roast beef, pork. The movie house offered pictures of popular appeal. It did much better than a nearby competitor who offered highbrow programs such as *A Midsummer Night's Dream*.

After supper came the young people's meeting—held under the auspices of the Methodists' Epworth League, the Christian Board of Education, the Baptist Young People's Union (BYPU).

Parish publications included suggestions for organizing a Mother Goose bazaar or commemorating special events, the Fourth of July, Lincoln's birthday, or Valentine's Day. Sometimes they suggested that the invitees "Come back to the Little Red Schoolhouse for Lincoln's birthday . . .

"There's sure to be rail splitting and a spelling bee.

"Bell rings at 8 P.M.

"You'll be sorry if you play hookey."

or

"You are heartily invited to investigate the Valentine Fun, featuring Tea for Two; Very Miniature Golf, Ping Pong and Table Croquet; Throwing Dart at Target with Red Heart as Center; Furnishing the cleverest last line to a limerick."

The religious were not entirely filmless. Sometimes on Sunday night a film would be shown in the parish house. "Seth Parker in Story and Pictures" told the story of a family living in "The Little Village of Jonesport," featuring Down East Folks, Neighbors at the Cottage, and pictures of the ship in which Seth took a world cruise.

Seth and his Jonesport neighbors were also heroes of a radio program described by Sam Slate and Joe Cook as the highlight of the American Sunday night. Seth Parker—the protagonist—was in real life a minister's son named Phillips H. Lord. Each week the Parkers would forgather to sing hymns and to undergo some homely triumph or tribulation. There was always a prayer led by Seth himself and—throughout the Bible belt—the sequel was general conversation over spongecake.

Seth's cruise ship—sponsored by Frigidaire—was dogged by "Lady Bad Luck," tossed by two hurricanes and eventually rescued in a dramatic scene—said by some of Seth's detractors to have been a publicity stunt.

"Just have faith in God, and by His grace you'll reach the Promised Land," said Mr. Lord. He was not one to spurn earthly treasure completely, however, being also the producer of *Gangbusters*. God's work was peppily endorsed by ministers.

The Sunday evening meetings always had some inspirational topic as a theme. Arguments were martialed by such groups as The Christian Board of Publication, the Epworth League or The Moody Bible Institute—"the West Point of Christian Service."

A boy or girl would expound on "What Do I Know About God?" "Wanted, Youth for the Kingdom," "What the Bible Says about

Temptation and Sin," "The Art of Making a Happy Home," "What Shall We Do About Social Injustices?" "How to Conquer Anger," "Why Is Gossip Harmful?" "What Makes a Nation Great?"

Small-town young people were bombarded on all sides by advice. Parish publications told them how much happier youth had been in the good old days. They were urged on Easter "to take flowers to some sick-a-bed person" or to "find out what birds nest near you." "Humane Sunday is April 19th. Read about it in the Land of Play and see what you can do to help in your own circle of friends and neighbors." Some of the attitudes which were pushed most strongly were those concerning Prohibition.

Before the repeal of Prohibition in 1933 young people in the hinterland were enlisted in a holy war. The handwriting was on the wall for the drys as early as 1931. The Wickersham Report published in that year had contained evidence that Prohibition wasn't working. Two of the eleven-member commission were for Repeal, four for modification, and five for further trial of the Noble Experiment. Despite the fact that the jury wasn't really even hung, with the Janus-like behavior of fact-finding committees the group came out as a whole for a last college try.

In the dry areas of the country "Flying Squadron Clubs" were formed for Prohibition enforcement. There were editorials against "The Wet Stampede" . . . "The Home Is Against the Saloon" . . . "The drys are now in a position to take the offensive in a struggle that never ends."

In 1933 the heat was being put on the half-million young Americans reported to be wearing the Allied Youth Pin. Allied Youth was a Prohibitionist group. It was constantly stressed that the young people had thrown themselves into the battle against strong waters completely of their own accord. A Detroit boy led seven thousand of his contemporaries to the state capital to protest Repeal. One story recounted the shame of a lad who was stripped of his pin. "Jim's hand crept up to his lapel. Slowly he began to unfasten the clasp. The stillness chanted madly in his ears. He could see again the great dim room, the flowers, the silken flags, the joyous flare of the initiation torch when he had received his pin." Jim was reinstated by Allied Youth after blurting out the fact that he was the son of the local bootlegger. "I may have to run errands in a speak-easy as long as my father needs me, but sometime I'm going to hit this thing hard."

Allied Youth leaders clapped him on the back in manly understanding that blood is thicker than water.

The fathers were the villains of the piece. Another youth was reported by the *Christian Herald* to have defied his father, a crusader against the 18th Amendment. The boy hit him where he lived by bringing up an argument in favor of personal liberty. He wanted "personal liberty and the car . . . to go down to the Allied Youth meeting tonight."

Lest Allied Youth be considered corny they had a marching song to disprove the charge:

> *Hey, hey, look us over and say*
> *Don't you want to join us today, day*
> *We're some crowd, you bet*
> *   peppy and gay*
> *Come on our way*
> *Happy? You said it and snappy.*

The furor over Prohibition was all but forgotten by 1937, though the WCTU was instrumental in having a book burned that year for proclaiming that "it has been proved that we cannot abolish drinking by legislation, nor frighten a person into sobriety."

The city mouse's attitude toward Prohibition was likewise a result of early conditioning. Sunday morning might be spent amid the remains of applejack cocktails and the dregs of Bronxes consumed the night before. The issue that inspired such militant feelings west of the Mississippi was airily dismissed by parents on the East Coast. "Prohibition is a bad law, dear, which was passed by women while all the men were away at war. Therefore Daddy and I have a right to disobey it."

If the family owned a car it was likely to be embellished with a sign saying "Repeal the 18th Amendment" in blue letters on an orange background. The city mouse's parents were likely to be among the first to read the ad in *Esquire* in 1934 and rush down to take advantage of National Distillers' "last roundup from our pre-Prohibition casks."

In the city they got off fairly lightly when it came to church-going. Whatever else it may have been in a large city, the church was not the center of social life. Church suppers for all denominations, Bingo parties and Catholic Youth Organization dances were more widely attended in the suburbs. A Protestant city mouse might have the same Church-and-Sunday-School program as his country counterpart, but he usually quit Sunday School much earlier and attended church only sporadically. A Catholic usually had a 45-minute Low Mass already behind him at the time the country cousin was going in to eleven-o'clock service. If he were Jewish, city or country, he had celebrated the Sabbath on Saturday and his Sundays were wide open.

If Dick Tracy and the Katzenjammers loomed large on the city child's Sunday agenda, radio had its place, too. Uncle Don had a late afternoon program punctuated with commentary about birthday boys and girls who would find surprises awaiting them under the radiator or behind the sofa pillow. "Good night, little friends, good night," he usually chirruped. The program's most stunning surprise awaited him one time after he discovered that he had been on the air when he followed the theme song up with "I guess that'll hold the little bastards. . . ." The next surprise—he was finished with network radio.

The city child poring over the New York *American* (later the *Journal-American*) was exposed to a lot of zippy Broadway commentary. Arthur ("Bugs") Baer gave capsule descriptions of Brazil's Vargas, Anna Sten, Jack Dempsey's wife, or Joe Kennedy, "the Administration's Trouble Shooter." The paper featured O. O. McIntyre and a short, embittered story by Mark Hellinger delivered in Damon Runyon gangsterese. Typical was one about a gangster's moll who lies gallantly to save her man—by saying they were both at a movie when a murder was committed. "Ain't it funny what a dame will do when she's in love with a guy?" muses a hard-bitten policeman. Tessie, the moll, is later heard in conversation with another Guys and Dolls character named Maisie. "He breaks a date with me and I gotta call you to go to the movies with me," she says unflatteringly to Maisie. "He had no right to break a date with me just 'cause them guys come for him to go to Callahan's Club with them."

It was a typical ending of the Broadway O. Henry. Tessie is well aware that her boy friend *was* with the boys at Callahan's Club and that in saying he was at the movies she has shattered his alibi, and that he is very likely headed for Death Row. Such is the wrath of a woman spurned.

The appetite for the bizarre might be whetted on *Believe It or Not* by Ripley (King Features—daily and Sunday throughout the Hearst empire). Robert Ripley had roamed the four corners of the earth in search of curiosa, and the fruits of his research were reprinted in cartoons from coast to coast and brought in flesh-and-blood form to viewers of the traveling road show, Ripley's "Odditorium."

If the Chinese marched past us four abreast, so Ripley told us, they would *never* stop marching (our first contact with the concept of infinity). There were people turning to stone . . . men who popped their eyeballs out of their heads . . . belles of Somaliland who put up their hair with coffee beans . . . sufferers from mysterious digestive disturbances which caused them to hiccough without respite for decades.

All this was little more than a warm-up to the treat vouchsafed to everyone who lived in a city large enough to have a Hearst paper. This treat was *The American Weekly*. It arrived every Sunday with a cover in full color showing something grimly cultural—a reproduction of Trumbull's "Battle of Bunker Hill," a scene from Wagner's *Götterdämmerung*. Long after other papers had abandoned it, *The American Weekly* clung to a typeface with a black capital—the rest of the sentence in gray—and endless headings and subheadings in script, all punctuated by a most erratic hand. No branch of human knowledge was omitted. City mice were taken on excursions into history: "The Glamorous Career of the Notorious 'Turf Caroline' a vamp of the 80s . . . delighted to pose occasionally sporting a monocle and a cigar."

Or a little further back: "30,000 years ago a Sacrilegious Stone Age Genius Broke the Most Sacred Taboo and Carved the First Human Portrait"; "Who was the Prehistoric Model—Maid, Wife or Priestess Who Inspired This Leonardo da Vinci of the Mammoth Hunters?"

The occult was covered by messages coming through on spirit

typewriters; cataleptics, thought dead, brought back to life; "Born Again the Year After She Died."

Zoology: "A Two Headed Rattlesnake" or "Newest Proof That Beavers Are Bright."

Cultural Anthropology: "Why the Eskimos Can't Understand Christianity."

Biology: "Science Discovers That the Nose, Mouth and Ears Keep on Growing Year After Year and Thus Change the Balance and Relations of the Features."

This was illustrated with youthful portraits of John Barrymore, Ganna Walska, and Queen Victoria in youth and old age. A dropsical study of Queen Wilhelmina showed how her mouth, nose, and ears had grown over the years. Another shot showed Father Time's ravages to the "rosebud mouth and small nose of Madame Schumann-Heink."

Falling loosely into the science field were two children raised by wolves.

True Crime was an *American Weekly* staple. "The Secrets of the Sûreté—French Detective Police" was a recurrent feature. More unusual was the one-shot: "How Death Came to the Wedding Disguised as a Roast Pig." "The Mystery of Room No. 304" was a marvelous example of the Hearst juxtaposition of headlines, subheadlines, and art work. A line drawing of a shrouded skeleton peered out of Room 304. The nonstop headline:

An Attractive Young Woman Registers at a Birmingham Ala. Hotel Changes into Sports Clothes Destroys All Means of Identification and Swallows Poison—and a Sympathetic Undertaker Provides a Casket, a Cemetery, a Shop Sends a Dress to Be Buried In and Florists Offer Bushels of Flowers

Illustrations of the dead woman's effects were individually captioned "One of the White Tennis Shoes Found in the Room," "The Unhappy Woman's Pocketbook, Hairband, Buttonhook and Combination Note Pad and Mirror."

After all this it seemed hardly necessary to read the story.

The American Weekly achieved its distinctive heights in accounts of debutante orgies on yachts anchored outside of Newport, in tragedies connected with the Hope Diamond, in the marital misfortunes of John Jacob Astor and Evalyn Walsh McLean. The doings of high society included "The Coat That Won Rose Zell a $10,000 a Year Husband." "It Was Not Mink Nor Ermine But Just a Coat of Gilt Radiator Paint All Over Her Girlish Body That Promoted the $3.00 a Day Burlesque Dancer to Wife of Baron Empain, World's Richest Bachelor—But Magic Was Mixed In." The gilded girl, Rose Zell, had a rival, "Baby Knudson," and both of them were dosing the Baron with Love Philtres. The efficacy of Rose's brew was proven by a shot of "Baron Empain and Rose Zell While on the African Safari Which Began Their Romance and Ended in the Budapest Hospital Marriage."

To illuminate the story, there were drawings of cannibals whipping up magic potions—there was a picture of Reject "Baby Knudson"—and there was, naturally, a naked photograph of Rose Zell triumphant in her radiator paint.

"Romance of a Modern Cinderella" might have been the headline for any one of twenty articles. One such romance involved Olive Hamilton whose voice-with-a-smile captivated scion Billy Leeds. "How the Very Rich Young Billy Leeds Made Life Pleasant for the Poor Little Hotel Telephone Girl and Then Surprised His Friends by Marrying Her." There were pictures of Leeds' First Wife, Princess Xenia. The scene shifted to Atlantic City to "Olive in Her Bathing Suit on the Beach in Front of the Hotel Where She Once Worked as a Telephone Girl." The story climaxed, naturally, on a yacht: "William B. Leeds Ocean Going Yacht *Moana* From Whose Wireless Antennae Suddenly Came the Announcement That Young Leeds Was Going to Marry Within Ten Days One of His Guests on Board."

The lowly born floozy, the spurned wife, the multimillionaire husband were a trio which, with the aid of radiator paint, yachts, and black magic played out a drama every Sunday that always had the same conclusion.

The American Weekly could make an exotic locale live with a capital L. It periodically ran articles on the wickedest cities in the world—with top honors generally going to Marseille. The roulette wheels of Monte Carlo were popular. "Behind the Scenes at Monte Carlo" was once illustrated with a picture of a jaded-looking woman staring into space . . . living with who knows what memories.

The usual glittering array of socialites was on hand: "The Promiscuous Mlle. Yvette Laurent With Her Huge Great Dane on the Beach at Deauville." An untrustworthy-looking man was labeled "The Notorious Mr. Zogoraphos, Head of the Famous Greek Gambling Syndicate on the Deauville Golf Course with Princess Philippi de Bourbon." Also present—the inevitable *arriviste*—"The Princess Fahmy Bey, Formerly Maggie Miller, a Paris Street Gamin of the Slums, Shown in Some of the Jewelry Presented to Her by Her Egyptian Husband Whom She Killed."

All were party to the "Secrets of the Famous Gambling Den," "Tricks of Thieving Croupiers—Daring Schemes to Break the Bank."

It was a liberal education.

Aside from such flashes in the pan as chain letters and tree-sitting, the country cousin and the city mouse had certain passionate enthusiasms in common despite differences in their frame of reference. Both liked to bask in the sun, whether at the local lake or on Jones Beach. Both followed avidly the doings of Clark Gable, Spencer Tracy, and Jean Harlow, whether in the Palace Theatre or the Paramount on Broadway. Both liked to listen to the *Lucky Strike Hit Parade* and to click the shutter of a camera. One curious phenomenon of the Depression was the candid camera craze. Families all over owned Eastman Brownies, which were easy to use, cheap, and made excellent photographs.

Between 1928 and 1936 the importation of German cameras—archetypal luxury items of the period—increased fivefold. The years 1936 and 1938 saw business booming among camera manufacturers and photographic supply stores. *U. S. Camera*—a photograph annual—became a national best seller. Between 1935 and 1937 the production of cameras jumped 157 percent.

The tiny foreign camera which took postage-stamp-size pictures could function in a dim light, and so the candid camera addict could ply his trade in a night club or at intermission in the aisle of a theater. Erich Solomon in *Fortune* was the first to give candid camera glimpses of businessmen at work behind heavy oak-paneled doors.

Frederick Lewis Allen has remarked on the influence of photographers such as Margaret Bourke-White, Walker Evans, and Dorothea Lange of the Farm Security Administration. Amateurs were following their lead, turning their attention from photogenic sunsets to scenes of social realism—slum life and sad-eyed farm women. The city mouse often had a row of ashcans as well as a row of classmates in his Leica portfolio.

After the movies the city family might stop in for dinner at Childs or go for a fudge sundae at Schrafft's. These large chain restaurants purveyed a brand of food which was wholesome and moderately priced, but whose culinary level was little better than the rural restaurant's chicken.

In the course of a weekend in the sticks, the city mouse might observe a couple on a rustic sleigh or hay ride and realize that country pastimes had a certain charm. It came as something of a shock to many city mice in later life to discover that when it came to actual erotic experience their country cousins were generally at least two or three years ahead of them. Bus lines, trolley cars, and sidewalks were a tremendous handicap to doing what comes naturally. Charles Boyer pouring subtitled sweet talk into the ear of some French actress was no substitute for (in the phrase of a later generation) do-it-yourself.

It was the car, in the last analysis, which had shaken things up. The automobile made it difficult for the Reverend Lord to compete with that stream of Middletown traffic headed for the golf links or the line on a Los Angeles Boulevard turning off for the beach. The tipoff among country boys and girls and the operative sentence was: "We spent most of the day driving around." Not every sixteen-year-old who borrowed the family Ford used it to attend the Allied Youth Meeting.

Years later the child of the city might reflect how much his innocence had been preserved by a dependence on public transportation. He or she could look back with a special nostalgia on that poor second best—a secondhand view of what one was missing as provided by William Randolph Hearst.

Chapter 3

Portrait of the Stone Age, or How We Lived Before TV

A little theme music, please . . .

As you twirl the dial of the early Thirties, you will hear snatches of song: "By a Waterfall" . . . "Carolina Moon" . . . "Let's Turn Out the Lights and Go to Sleep," most of it still familiar, but not all of it, perhaps . . . "You-go-home-and-get-your-scanties, I'll go home and get my panties and away we'll go . . ."

The music is issuing from the round, wafflelike speaker of the Atwater Kent. The front of the speaker is black and gold. There is a separate box beside it which contains the works. The controls consist of a round black dial with station numbers and a black knob with an arrow which turns up the volume. Later there will be the cathedral-like models—the Philco, shaped like a stained glass window. Another standard model was the fussing, sputtering Emerson. The status symbol was the stand-up console. When a family had a Stromberg-Carlson console one knew they had arrived.

Early console station-finders are marked "Standard Broadcast." Other bands include Weather, Police, Amateur, and Ship. When Rudy Vallee becomes boring it is possible with a quick flick of the wrist to tune in on squad cars stalking public enemies. Not only the programs are entertainment; in the early Thirties dialing itself is something of an adventure. Instructions: "Where to set dials." WABC is 349 meters, WJZ 394 meters. There is a certain hit or miss quality to the whole thing—the family hunting around on the dial of an evening for WEAF (454 meters) cannot be sure if it will come in at that setting, and quite sure it will not if there happens to be an electrical storm overhead. One of the omnipresent background noises in any program of the Thirties is the crackle, wheezing, hissing, and occasional roar of static.

Radio has not completely outgrown its nine-day-wonder period. In 1934 you can still hear a heartbeat and a kiss broadcast over KDKA, an egg fried on the sidewalk over WOR. De Wolf Hopper declaims from the top of the Empire State Building. One day Amelia Earhart and Ted Husing cruise over Manhattan chatting with theater and night club performers. Stoopnagle and Budd broadcast from the sky with Stoop in one plane and Budd in the other. CBS brings its listeners the first airborne two-piano concert. Scores of marriages are performed in the air with the principals speaking their vows into a microphone. The roar of rushing water comes into one's living room, tactfully drowning out the coos of honeymooners in Niagara Falls.

There are complicated connections between the radio audience and the men who are pushing back the frontiers of the unknown. General Foods has kept listeners in touch with Admiral Byrd's Antarctic expedition over CBS station KFZ. A Seattle telephone company has arranged a momentous conversation between the Byrd group and Robert Flagler in the Arctic Circle. From pole to pole flashes a stimulating discussion of the weather. Mr. Flagler says, "Hello everybody," in Eskimo while announcer Harry von Zell stands by to fill awkward pauses with messages for Grape Nuts.

Floyd Gibbons—the most popular news broadcaster of the early Thirties—is forever on location with his microphone. He is a romantic figure, handsome, rugged, with a white patch always worn over his left eye. (He had lost the eye at the battle of Belleau Wood during World War I.) He pioneered in on-the-spot remote broadcasting—217 words a minute at the scene of fire, or earthquake, and in 1932, dramatically, from the battlefields of Manchuria. Later he did a series called *Headlines* about his adventures.

Another, whose technical or emotional equipment is not quite up to the job of doing remotes at the raging waters of the flood, broadcasts from a comfortable hotel room in Cincinnati, while an assistant makes splashing noises in the tub beside him.

Even after its nine-day-wonder period was outgrown, radio keeps listeners abreast of current trivia—in contact with the *Normandie* as it steams into New York Harbor on its maiden voyage—with the Dionne quintuplets as they emit a gurgle heard around the world.

Russ Columbo wails soulfully, "You Call It Madness But I Call It Love." George Jessel, Harry Richman, Ruth Etting, and the Boswell Sisters all have their legions of fans. "The Perfect Song" introduces *Amos 'n' Andy*. . . . In a minute Bill Hays will synopsize the latest misadventures of the Fresh Air Taxicab Company and introduce the babel of minstrel-show accents with the words "Heah they are." The listener will match the theme to the program *Smiles* with the Ipana Troubadors, "Two Guitars" with Harry Horlick and the A & P Gypsies. The strains of "My Time Is Your Time" serve notice that it is our time to hear R. Vallee singing the praises of Fleischmann's Yeast. Alexander Woollcott's influential *Bookworm* program is peppered with egghead references to "old Dr. Freud."

G.E. brings you Floyd Gibbons' *Adventures in Science*—laying special stress on adventures pioneered by G.E. *The Maxwell House Showboat*, introduced with "Let's Have Another Cup of Coffee," combines music and enlightenment. A short talk on ancient superstition devotes much time to dispelling the particular superstition that coffee keeps people awake.

As radio became a more powerful medium the Hooper and Crossley ratings began to strike fear into the hearts of programmers. Mighty were the struggles of broadcasters to have their offerings make it into the top ten.

Around the mid-Thirties a change began to be noticeable in the makeup of the country's favorite listening fare. In the "variety" show of the early Vallee era the celebrity carried the ball alone. By the mid-Thirties, however, he was generally aided by an orchestra and guest stars. With the comparative affluence of the mid-decade, he was usually on for an hour. The new pattern was embodied by

Phil Baker—on stage with a big assist from Ted Weems—or Fred Allen with Peter Van Steeden.

Sometimes the music was the major attraction. Sweetness and light were provided by *Lady Esther Serenade* with Wayne King and the Sweetest Music This Side of Heaven; by the *Kate Smith Hour;* by the *Voice of Firestone,* with its mandatory theme music composed by the Relative of the Management, Ida Bell Firestone. Bandleader Ozzie Nelson and wife, singer Harriet Hilliard, were a team; Horace Heidt and his Alemite Brigadiers served up danceable music that offended no one. Singer Frances Langford starred on *Hollywood Hotel*—an hour-long variety show with Dick Powell as emcee. The program featured twenty-minute dramatic productions with Hollywood stars introduced by gossip columnist Louella Parsons. *Manhattan Merry Go Round* offered more of the same, as did Maxwell House's *Showboat* which in the late Thirties gave way to *Good News* of 1938 and 1939. Among the musical stand-bys of this period were many blood brothers of Lawrence Welk.

It is the comedians that we remember best, especially the married comedians who came out of the ark two by two—George Burns and Gracie Allen, Jack Benny and Mary Livingston, Fred Allen and Portland Hoffa, as well as the Aces and Fibber McGee and Molly. Each of the comics had his own gimmick. Lew Holtz had his "Sam Lapidus." Jimmy Durante had his famed "schnozzola," Eddie Cantor had his wife Ida and his five daughters. Fannie Brice as "Baby Snooks" had her baby brother Robespierre. Included among famous siblings was Gracie Allen's long-lost brother. Jack Benny had his Maxwell, his stooge Rochester ("Yass-s-s, Boss . . ."), the underground vault where he counted his money, his earsplitting violin and his pathological thrift—a quality also attributed to Rudy Vallee who perhaps had a more bona fide patent on it. Ed Wynn was on Broadway when a group of Texaco executives went to see him. To double check how he would project, they sat through the show with their eyes shut. When they opened them, Ed was the leading light of the *Texaco Star Theatre.* As Texaco's Fire Chief he sported a red fireman's hat. He also affected other disguises such as a bullfighter's regalia. So that the listening audience could fancy how funny he looked, he devised the idea of canned laughter. As his fellow comedian Fred Allen pointed out later, he had a lot to answer for.

Comedians of the Thirties depended heavily on the running gag. One such sure-fire device was the intramural feud. Among the most famous were the battles between Walter Winchell and Ben Bernie, Jack Benny and Fred Allen, Bob Hope and Bing Crosby, W. C. Fields and Charlie McCarthy.

Fred Allen was a true comedian's comedian. He took up radio in the early Thirties after a Broadway appearance with Clifton Webb and Libby Holman in *Three's a Crowd*. He wrote his own material and could, with his flat nasality, get a laugh out of reading *Fanny Farmer's Cookbook*. His first show—*The Linit Bath Club Revue*—made its debut on October 23, 1932. In the Thirties one particularly associates him with *Town Hall Tonight*. Compounded of wry news bulletins and offbeat features, *Town Hall Tonight* brought to the microphone such People You Didn't Expect to Meet as a lady blacksmith, a goldfish doctor, a sausage stuffer, and a worm salesman.

He was engaged throughout the Thirties in two feuds. The first was his cosmic battle with Jack (Pinch) Benny. When the two met on Benny's show on March 14, 1937, (ostensibly to do physical battle with each other) only one of FDR's fireside chats—according to contemporary radio surveys—ever commanded a larger audience.

A more serious feud was with the network, which cut him off the air periodically for his nonconformist sentiments, or for running overtime. One such bit of business in which his wife Portland queries him about the reasons for a cutoff, shows Allen's irreverent view of the radio Establishment.

ALLEN: The main thing in radio is to come out on time. If people laugh, the program is longer. The thing to do is to get a nice dull half-hour. Nobody will laugh or applaud. Then you'll always be right on time, and all of the little emaciated radio executives can dance around their desks in interoffice abandon.

PORTLAND: Radio sure is funny.

ALLEN: All except the comedy programs. Our program has been cut off so many times the last page of the script is a Band-Aid.

PORTLAND: What does the network do with all the time it saves cutting off the ends of programs?

ALLEN: Well, there is a big executive here at the network. He is the vice-president in charge of "Ah! Ah! You're running too long." He sits in a little glass closet with his mother-of-pearl gong. When your program runs overtime he thumps his gong with a marshmallow he has tied to the end of a xylophone stick. Bong! You're off the air. Then he marks down how much time he's saved.

PORTLAND: What does he do with all this time?

ALLEN: He adds it all up—ten seconds here, twenty seconds there—and when he has saved up enough seconds, minutes, and hours to make two weeks, the network lets the vice-president use the two weeks of *your* time for *his* vacation.

PORTLAND: He's living on borrowed time.

ALLEN: And enjoying every minute of it. . . .

Small wonder that the little emaciated radio executives winced. Allen and his arch-rival Benny each had a finest hour.

For Fred Allen the finest hour came in the early Forties, for if *Town Hall Tonight* was a funny show, the cast of *Allen's Alley* was even better. The Early Forties Follies would certainly include the foghorn voice of Kenny Delmar as Senator Claghorn, the Yiddisha Mama accents of Minerva Pious as Mrs. Nussbaum, the "Howdy Bub" of Titus Moody, the roar of a brannigan going on at the home of Ajax Cassidy.

Jack Benny's finest moment came in that tense moment on the show when a burglar said, "Mr. Benny, your money or your life." The clock ticked on for an eternity. At last Jack was able to choke out the words, "I'm thinking it over."

Edgar Bergen and Charlie McCarthy's *Chase and Sanborn Hour* was the most popular show of the late Thirties. Bergen's audacious puppet was part of a program package which included Dorothy Lamour, Don Ameche (now graduated from *The First Nighter*) the Canovas: Judy, Zeke, and Annie, and at one point Nelson Eddy. After losing Eddie Cantor to Pebeco toothpaste and Major Bowes to Chrysler, Chase and Sanborn Coffee had ridden into the top ten on Charlie's coattails.

Charlie was a fast man with an insult. Once he tangled with W. C. Fields:

FIELDS: Well, well, the woodpecker's pin-up boy! Is it true your father was a gateleg table?

CHARLIE: If he was, your father was under it.

FIELDS: Quiet, Wormwood, or I'll whittle you down to a coat-hanger!

(A storm of protest broke when Mae West appeared on the Chase and Sanborn Hour on December 12, 1937, and made to Charlie suggestions of quite a different sort.)

In connection with comedians we also remember the stooges. Bing Crosby's *Kraft Music Hall* had Bob Burns. Bob Hope had Jerry Colonna. Colonna contributed to the national scene a scourge on a par with "The Music Goes Round and Round." He was the non-man Yehudi. Yehudi's identity was a mystery. When asked who Yehudi was, Colonna would reply, "Ask Yehudi's cutie." He was equally evasive about Yehudi's cutie—saying simply, "Ask Yehudi." NBC employees were plagued by theories about Yehudi. Some offerings were reprinted in a 1940 issue of *Life*. "Yehudi's the fellow who turns off the radio when you ride under a bridge in your automobile." "Yehudi's the man who makes rimless glasses with invisible lenses for the little man who wasn't there, so he can read between the lines of the unwritten law." Yehudi was "the guy who holds up strapless bathing suits and evening gowns. Down with Yehudi."

The mid- and late-Thirties medley sounded a little different from the heyday of "My Time Is Your Time." Prominent among the voices . . . the yowsah . . . yowsah . . . yowsah of the old Maestro Ben Bernie . . . George Burns prodding his bird-brain wife Gracie Allen to "Say good night, Gracie" . . . Jack Pearl as Baron Munchausen repeated over and over the question "Vos you dere, Sharlie?" while Joe Penner derived many a "yuch, yuch, yuch" seemingly unwarranted by the inquiry, "Wanna buy a duck?" or the contumelious "You n-a-asty man." The peace of the hearth was shattered periodically by the sound of the fire engine which heralded the approach of Ed Wynn the Texaco Fire Chief—the rat-a-tat-tat of gunfire prefacing a "true-life" episode of *Gangbusters*. Among the hardy perennials were Kate Smith introducing her hour show with the theme song, "When the Moon Comes Over the Mountain," Morton Downey, the Cliquot Club Eskimos, the midget

Johnny whose "Call for Philip Morris" was a long-running master-piece of what advertising men would call product identification.

Today the unexpected appearance of an old favorite stirs memories of drying dishes or of listening to car radios queued up for ferryboats waiting to take us across rivers on Sunday nights after the weekend.

We never even asked what had happened to Ed Wynn until his poignant performances in the TV drama *Requiem for a Heavyweight* and his movie role in *The Great Man* . . . or when he made an eloquent commentary on the fleeting rewards of fame, walking along the street, doffing his hat to a casual passer-by—who after all those years actually recognized him.

In the mid-Thirties a new sound began to be heard over the airwaves—the sound of audience participation. The voice of Gabriel Heatter solemnly announced that "We the People Speak . . ." Clarence Shaw of Gig Harbor, Washington, watched his leghorn sprinter win a rooster race on *Hobby Lobby*. A young contestant on *You Sell Me* over Chicago's WBBM agreed to take two dollars for every pint of milk he could wrest from a cow named Lucky. . . . A gentleman who muffed a question on *Truth or Consequences* was told to lie on a bed and pretend he was making love to a seal, while at his side, accompanied by a roar of delight from the studio audience, there materialized a blubbery partner—flippers twitching and barking with coy ecstasy.

It had all begun with *Major Bowes' Amateur Hour*. Major Bowes was the forefather of contemporary television's ferreter-out-of talent, Ted Mack. To New York—the Wonder City—the contestants flocked to be discovered: the divas from Timbuktu zing-zing-zing-a-linging their hymn of hope, the one-man bands, the players of concertos on combs, the legions of imitators of FDR (how many times would we hear the words "My friends . . . and you are my friends," "I hate wah, Eleanor hates wah, Sistie and Buzzie hate wah, Fala hates wah"), the artfully artless rustic comics ("I sort of figured, Major, that I could make more money playing this thing than I could laying eggs") (laughter).

Ten thousand applications poured in weekly. And though Amateur Hour contestants were supposed to be native New Yorkers, they arrived by the trainloads, like would-be divorcees establishing residence in Reno.

From this horde the Major selected twenty acts a week, of which only fifteen were used. The other five were On Call, with the standard Depression radio reward for their patience—a ten-dollar bill. When the Sunday evening show was over the station's switchboards were clogged with some thirty thousand fans casting votes for their favorite acts.

For this frail straw many who were drowning in debt were willing to leave their homes, thumb their way east, gamble the savings of a lifetime. When a contestant failed to make good, he had to slink back home at his own expense. The famous gong spelled death to a contestant's hopes. A strong-armed man stood ready to grab him in case the realization should cause him to utter language unfit for the ears of little old ladies from Dubuque. Not all the talent was live, but the show was.

The contestant could quickly measure his success or failure. "All right, all right," was Major Bowes' signal that applause for a contestant had gone on for too long—the wheel of fortune revolved as Major Bowes intoned, "Round and round she goes, and where she stops nobody knows." To a very lucky few came the news that a night club was interested in signing a contract for the contestant's duck call or solo on the sweet patootie.

Major Bowes made $5000 a week for thus breathing life into the Cinderella story. Harried New York relief officials faced with thousands who didn't make the grade had often to find accommodations and supervise the care and feeding of whole brass bands. *Newsweek* interviewed one contestant who had ended up on the reject pile. Married at seventeen, going on twenty-nine, he had been in the army and had emerged into civilian life at a time when employers had taken to firing instead of hiring. Dependent on him were a wife and a daughter who "hears a song just once over the radio and sings it perfect and only eleven years old."

"Duncan's the name, Jewell Duncan," he told the reporter. "Hitch-hiked up here to New York last July to get on Major Bowes' Amateur Show. I hate this town. I'll sure be glad to get back to Tulsa, Oklahoma. Yeah, I been on relief ever since I got here. Lost all of my clothes hopping a freight. They been darned nice, the relief people—got me a room and all. But it's still bad. I mean *bad*. The other night I just paced up and down my room, looking at the window. Only four stories but that would end it."

He was going back to Tulsa to start at the bottom—and glad of it.

Major Bowes' special appeal was for the lowest-income groups and in particular for Negroes who cherished some wan hope that their national reputation for singin', dancin', and eatin' watermelon might be turned to gold by this amateur's alchemist. The city was filled with shining promise. A boat was always leaving soon for New York. The Jewell Duncans learned all too slowly that New York most often had the cruel show business cliché, "Don't call us, we'll call you," for the "fine tenor baritone" who had wowed the Boston Avenue Methodist Church.

Three or four winners were selected. These fortunate souls made up Major Bowes' units, troops of strolling players who toured the country from Augusta to San Diego. (Minimum pay $50 a week plus transportation; maximum $150 plus transportation.)

But the Major Bowes program did produce some lackluster success stories. The year 1941's Current Biography lists Clyde Barrie, talented Negro baritone, signed by CBS for tri-weekly morning song recitals. Lucille Browning's voice "was heard" (evidently not very loud) at the Metropolitan Opera.

Delineator in December 1935 described "personable, seductively toned torch singer" Doris Wester, a Bowes graduate who became a featured soloist at the Rockefeller skytop retreat, the Rainbow Room. Raymond Kretser—a hen-clucker—could reproduce by the deft placing of tongue in cheek, authentic barnyard noises. He was added to the staff of sound-effect boys at Radio City. A New Jersey roadhouse claimed that Joseph Rogato was the "most lyrical garbage man in the Bronx."

Some performers had already arrived—among them mouth organist Frank W. Smith, a Con Ed president, and Mayor William McNair of Pittsburgh, a fiddler. Dr. Marie Charlotte de Golier Davenport, a 110-year-old pianiste, brought down the house with "an unpublished composition by Liszt, her teacher."

Audience participation took many forms. If Major Bowes offered contestants a chance to pursue the chimera of fame in public, John J. Anthony gave them the opportunity to achieve emotional catharsis by washing their dirty linen over a nationwide hookup. The Elijah of pop sociology, however, was *The Voice of Experience*. Broadcast over a special mutual network, sponsored by Lydia Pinkham's Compound—a specific remedy for unspecified female disorders—it was often suggested that a more appropriate title for the program would be "The Voice of Sexperience."

The agony program was of mixed ancestry. A. L. Alexander's *Court of Good Will* had dispensed free legal advice over WMCA in New York to a parade of selected wretches who had been taken by bogus correspondence schools, had their annulment papers impounded by unpaid lawyers, defaulted on their payments, or whose amatory "mistakes" were unclaimed at the age of six months by either their husbands or their lovers.

During an interregnum between Major Bowes and Charlie McCarthy, Chase and Sanborn briefly sponsored the court. The coffee company dropped it like a hot potato after protests from the Chicago Bar Association and after the Appellate Division of the New York State Supreme Court urged lawyers not to dispense this particular form of legal aid.

Offering himself to WMCA as a substitute for Alexander was a man named Lester Kroll, who was well qualified to give advice on emotional problems. He was a Bronx cab driver who had twice been sent to jail for nonpayment of alimony.

From his *Marital Relations Institute*, which he had presided over at $5 per troubled couple, he graduated to become John J. Anthony of the *Good Will Hour*. His advice was emotional rather than legal.

Mr. Anthony's suppliant hordes laid their grief at the feet of the aural Good Shepherd. The opening plaint became classic: "My problem, Mr. Anthony, is . . ." Then the unctuous voice would soon give wise, dispassionate counsel—the boys in the control room standing by lest someone blurt out a problem with unsuitable overtones. There were many high (or low) moments: "My family doesn't approve of my girl friend because she wiggles her rear end." (The young lady in question was suffering from some rare orthopedic disease.) People on the program would often break down at the very thought of the unwanted baby, the unhappy marriage, the unpaid balance. Mr. Anthony's program offered a field day to parodists. ("My problem, Mr. Anthony, is that I have no problem.") Mr. Anthony demanded of his poor wretches a Spartan self-control in the face of adversity. The leitmotif of the mid-decade was Mr. Anthony's ministerial admonition, "Please try to calm yourself." The program had one iron-clad rule—"No names, please!"

A race unto themselves in those golden days were the radio announcers: Milton Cross, Mel Allen, Norman Brokenshire, Nils T. Granlund, Jimmy Wallington, André Baruch, Harry Von Zell, Ken Niles, Don McNeill. These impresarios got a fast $50 a week or thereabouts during the Depression as opposed to the $50,000 to $100,000 a year similar worthies may pull down now on TV. They did, however, have the satisfaction of being well-known personalities. Today one is usually unaware of the identity of the man who brings us a message from the sponsor. One is certainly unaware of his marital status or other choice bits of information. In the Thirties the most indifferent radio listener knew that announcer André Baruch was that-a-way about Larry Clinton's singer Bea Wain.

Announcer Jimmy Wallington took a part in the proceedings on the Eddie Cantor hour. Eddie would sometimes impersonate "Edwina" and Jimmy a friend called "Jeanette." Together they might go to laundry and card party. Soon other characters were accompanying them on their homely rounds, one a figure of fun who became something of a personality in his own right—namely Parkyakarkus.

"How *do* you *do,* ladies and gentlemen, how *do* you *do.*" This was the trademark of a dashing announcer with a trim mustache, Norman Brokenshire, long associated with the *Chesterfield Show.* His nickname was "Broke" and alcoholism eventually made it grimly appropriate. Newspaper writers were quick to seize upon the phrase "Broke goes broke" when he dropped from a salary of $1300 a week to apply for work with the WPA. (In the Forties, Broke had a comeback, landing jobs with such top shows as NBC's *Theater Guild of the Air* and CBS's *Hollywood Star Playhouse.* He recalled his bad period with typical charm and grace. "I was an alcoholic," he said cheerfully, "but I was never anonymous.")

Many went on to better things. Graham McNamee was announcer for early *Fleischmann Hour* broadcasts. Sometimes an announcer might achieve fame as a summer replacement. *Good Gulf*

Summer Stars, a musical with Harry Von Zell, substituted during the dog days of 1937 for Phil Baker. The boy who really made good was announcer Don McNeill, who graduated to become the emcee of a breakfast club.

The breakfast club was an outgrowth of a variety show for early risers. In the Thirties it usually had some audience participation. To be an emcee one needed to be a very special sort of person. McNeill was qualified as "a righteous family man, God-fearing, orthodox in every way. He is not at all slick, and could never be a sharpy." His audience consisted of "the great middle class, the solid citizens, the churchgoers, the 'squares,' the butcher, baker, and candlestick maker, the Eds and Ednas."

"Hi ya, suckers," McNeill would cry in jovial greeting to the Eds and Ednas, who could look forward from that moment on to an interlude of good clean fun. ("Turn and tickle the person beside you.") Following the tickles came Inspiration Time, Prayer Time, March Time (round and round the breakfast table). The only mildly sexy note struck by the "king of corn" was provided by torch singer Jack Owens. ABC assured Ed and Edna that they were in no danger of becoming inflamed by his musical offerings on Cruiser Crooning Time. "It's in the sugary post office tradition and not remotely connected with adult passion."

Audiences who might a decade or two later have been found among legionnaires of Liberace flocked in the late Thirties to hear Tom Brenneman presiding over *Breakfast at Sardi's.* Brenneman was a veteran of NBC's *Laugh Club, What's On Your Mind, Feminine Fancies,* and the *Spelling Beeliner.*

His manner made him the favorite of Midwestern soda jerks, the inmates of Folsom Prison, and the old girls who paraded up to the microphone to have orchids pinned on them for being the Good Neighbor of the Day. ("I have made Mrs. Ellis the Good Neighbor for today, as she is a steadfast, loyal nurse from World War I and has nursed her invalid husband for more than twenty years.")

Wishing-ring ceremonies gave the girls a chance to see their modest dreams occasionally realized. One such wisher's heart's desire was to see her tenants move out, for example, and, as they were fortuitously listening to the program, they took the hint.

Mr. Brenneman delivered hilarious Homer and Jethroisms

through the mouth of a character named Uncle Corny: "I have just heard of a man who switched from bourbon to scotch, and in the morning, instead of a coat on his tongue, he found kilts."

Sniping in the Benny-Allen tradition went on between Brenneman and the "king of corn."

"You're smart," said Brenneman to a senior citizen.

"I'm not smart."

"Ever listen to Don McNeill?" asked Brenneman.

"No," said the lady.

"Now I know you're smart," said Brenneman.

Mr. Brenneman also showed a sporting tendency to be on the receiving end of the interchange. He could take it as well as dish it out and had no compunction about making a fool of himself. He often put on the senior citizen's hat with humorous asides to the audience about what it reminded him of. He brought down the house with such leading questions as, "Is your husband a good kisser?"

Brenneman's fan mail indicated that he inspired his audience to an occasional *mot juste* of their own: "I'll be glad to use your coffee [Alpine] if it's anything like your master of ceremonies, because I always use drip."

In the 1930s roughly two out of five families owned a radio. What fare was dished up to them by the advertisers and how did they react to it? Behind the top ten favorites, the participating audiences, the breakfast club personality boys, were certain hard facts of economics. Network programming after 1930 offered drama, comedy, music, and news in about equal doses timed down to the split second—quarter, half, or full hour. Sheer volume demand made the networks take the easy way out. They relied heavily on the packaging of shows and the syndication of scripts. "Show packaging," where talent, script, sound effects, and production were all delivered complete to advertising agencies and sold to clients, caused the networks to lose almost complete control over what went over their wires. This, along with the reverence for ratings and the omniscience of advertisers, resulted in an all too familiar reliance on the tried and true, which is the curse of contemporary television. Radio, like television to a large extent, bore the assembly-line stamp.

As a mass medium, radio was prey to all the ills which the advertising industry can inflict on a long-suffering public. Herbert Hoover in the early Thirties had expressed a wan hope that the advertiser's pitch could be kept to a minimum and inserted at some point where it would not interfere with the program. History handed him one of those typical Hoover rewards, the singing commercial. A little product identification music, please . . .

"Don't despair, use your head, save your hair, use Fitch Shampoo." To the mid-Thirties medley were added the chant of the vintner spelling out "C-R-E-S-T-A B-L-A-N-C-A."

It had all begun with the lone bard who had first strung together the immortal words:

> *Pepsi-Cola hits the spot*
> *Twelve full ounces*
> *That's a lot*
> *Twice as much for a nickel too*
> *Pepsi-Cola is the drink for you!*

These days of debates over mediums and messages lose sight of the fact that every medium has its big day. Not necessarily its best day—but there's a time of unique and maximum impact. The impact of television has yet to be assessed. And the impact of radio has never been properly assessed by social scientists. But it is clear that radio had certain special effects. It did not invent but it encouraged and tremendously broadened audience participation. It was no accident that one program eventually came to be the *Town Hall of the Air*. It helped to spread national gags and to reinforce a national accent. (Radio announcers with strong regional accents were frowned upon. The search was for a man with a good neutral sound.)

Radio, like TV, demanded some effort on the part of the listener. It *was* possible to move around the room while listening to *Easy Aces*. One did not need to remain glued to the set. It was possible to read and still hear Benny Goodman in the background—and though it was a point on which we went to the mat with our parents, it was also possible to listen to him and do our homework.

But because it demanded that the listener create his own images—with the assistance of a special breed of writers like Arch Oboler and Irwin Shaw—it created not only writers but also an audience with special skills. The writers emerged from the script mills of the Thirties with an ability to plot and to project pictures through the air. Whatever else they may have been, they were pros. Listeners emerged with an ability to see the pictures. And we came out of it with certain images engraved in our minds forever.

Today radio is rigidly compartmentalized. It is possible to turn to a station which offers an unremitting flow of either rock and roll, popular, or classical music or news. In the Thirties it was all paraded before you like a big vaudeville show and perhaps drove the final nail into the coffin of vaudeville. Whatever our intentions may have been, we got some of the Abyssinian situation sandwiched in between our English assignment and Mr. Keen.

Even today the parent who tries to restrict his child's viewing hours in front of the magic box is often forced to eat his words. The child will come out with some abstruse fact which the parent hopefully attributes to an improvement in the nation's school system—to be told as often as not "I saw it on TV." Radio in the Thirties had a similar effect. Despite the banality of the mass product, some things on radio were remarkably good. Many shows could cause the parent of the Thirties to ask himself even as we often do, "How come the kids today are so much smarter than we were?"

Hark, from the distance comes an unexpected note, the note that the pundits had said would instantly be tuned out. Can it be (to borrow a title) that "I Hear a Symphony"?

The culture boom, phase one, had begun. The first network broadcast by a symphony orchestra was made in 1926; the first sponsored one in 1929—by Philco. The Metropolitan Opera was put on the air in 1931 on Saturday afternoon over NBC with a cigarette company and a mouthwash company following Philco's lead. CBS broadcast the Sunday performances of the New York Philharmonic. Atwater Kent popularized the classics. Dr. Serge Koussevitsky conducted rehearsals of the Boston Symphony, while Bruno Walter carried the torch of culture for General Motors. By 1938 seven million children heard the music appreciation hour conducted by Walter Damrosch. Other highbrow treats were provided by Heifetz, Ponselle, Nino Martini, Lawrence Tibbett, Richard Crooks, Lily Pons, Margaret Speaks, Alfred Wallenstein. Flagstad and Melchior doing a scene from *Siegfried* and Toscanini conducting the NBC Symphony Orchestra were almost as much of a draw as Jack Benny scraping away at his violin.

The music buff was passionately dedicated to his favorite performers. A woman named Jessica Dragonette was the coloratura of Palmolive Soap, Pet Milk, Ford Motor Company, and Cities Service. When she came to Minneapolis on a concert tour fifteen thousand citizens braved a blizzard and a taxi strike to see her. When she was a soloist at Chicago's Grant Park 150,000 people poured in. The concert was free. In the late Thirties, a financial disagreement with her sponsors caused her to retire from the air. Irate fan clubs announced that they would boycott radio until the return of "The Jenny Lind of the Air."

It should be said that some of the purveyors of "good" music served up a diet that could only loosely be described as classical. The Ford and General Motors hours in the late Thirties faced stiff competition on Sunday nights from Charlie McCarthy. General Motors found it expedient to stick safely to light opera. The Detroit Symphony Orchestra, which alternated with homilies in praise of free enterprise on the Ford hour, struck up "Pizzicata Polka," "Poet and Peasant," and occasionally even "Home Sweet Home." It was asking too much of the public who could switch over to Edgar Bergen to put the heavy pedal on Ludwig van Beethoven.

Second only to the symphonic was the dramatic. Dramatic shows came in all sizes and shapes—*Lux Radio Theatre* and *The First Nighter,* the spate of crime shows which filled the air of the early Thirties with thuds and shrieks, the erudite dramaturgy of Norman Corwin, Orson Welles, and the Mercury Players, and the blank verse of Archibald MacLeish. One had but to touch the dial of a Philco to find oneself on the front row of a Broadway play.

There was a great deal of original drama on radio. Arch Oboler began his career in Chicago in the early Thirties, doing horror stories for NBC's *Lights Out.* Later he became a one-man script mill churning out scripts like *Money, Money, Money, Mr. Whiskers, Nero's Wife.* Nazimova starred in an Oboler drama describing

Tchaikovsky's relationship to his patroness. There was much accompaniment of boldly experimental effects—filtered voices, portentous fading out of words.

NBC and CBS battled to bestow the cape of the network Hamlet. CBS offered Burgess Meredith a contract to do Shakespearean drama while John Barrymore was signed to interpret the Bard over NBC. Barrymore's slight bottle problem caused NBC to take certain precautions. His performance was a sensation, aided by a waist-high railing constructed in the studio, lest Hamlet feel Elsinore slipping away from under his feet.

On October 30, 1938, most of Charlie McCarthy's Chase and Sanborn drinkers were for some abstruse reason tuned to Orson Welles' *Mercury Theatre of the Air*. The program was identified but the announcement was followed by a weather report.

An announcement followed: "From the Meridian Room of the Park Plaza in New York City we bring you the music of Ramon Raquello and his orchestra. With a touch of Spanish, Ramon leads off with 'La Cumparsita.'"

An announcer breaks in on "La Cumparsita" with a special bulletin: "At twenty minutes before eight o'clock Central Time, Professor Farrell of Mt. Jennings Observatory, Chicago, reports observing several explosions of incandescent gas, occurring at regular intervals on the planet Mars."

More dance music, further bulletins about disturbances on Mars followed by news of a meteor landing in Princeton, killing fifteen hundred people. Finally after more of Ramon Raquello, terrifying news that the meteor had been a metal cylinder containing Martians armed with death rays.

By this time two members of the Princeton geology department had set out to locate the meteors. In one Newark block people covered their faces with handkerchiefs to protect themselves against "gas." CBS switchboards were swamped with calls by listeners who had ignored or not heard three announcements made during the broadcast emphasizing its fictional nature. Nor did the Pittsburgh woman who contemplated taking poison or the hysterical high school girls interviewed in Pennsylvania associate the invaders with the newspaper listing "Today: 8:00 to 9:00—Play H. G. Wells's War of the Worlds."

It may not have proved, as many people argued at the time, that gullible America was ripe for dictatorship, but it was certainly effective theater.

Radio had its share of men who proved that one could be funny though literate. Alexander Woollcott reached a mass audience with the "Hear ye, hear ye, hear ye," which heralded his approach as the Town Crier. Among weightier programs were *Invitation to Learning, CBS School of the Air, University of Chicago Round Table, The American School of the Air, College Bull Session, Backgrounds of Literature,* and *Capitol Cloakroom.* The most popular of all egghead programs was, of course, *Information Please.*

There had been other quiz programs, such as *Professor Quiz.* Phil Baker on *Take It or Leave It* had coined the expression, "The sixty-four-dollar question."

The regular panelists of *Information Please* were the *New Yorker* book critic Clifton Fadiman, newspaper columnist Franklin P. Adams, pianist Oscar Levant, and New York *Times* sports editor John Kieran. Mr. Kieran combined an encyclopedic knowledge of such matters as the Dodgers' lineup in 1907 with an ability to define such terms as "librocubilarist" (a fellow who reads in bed).

Contestants submitted questions to this panel who appeared with visiting savants—John Erskine, Hendrik Willem Van Loon, Stuart Chase, John Gunther, and Harpo Marx. Any question which they failed to field netted its author a princely sum of ten dollars and an Encyclopaedia Britannica. Sometimes a maverick authority would answer a question while the presumed expert would drop the ball. Stuart Chase, the economist, didn't know that "multiple shops" was British for "chain stores." George S. Kaufman was unable to mention the only distinctive thing about his own play *Deep Tangled Wildwood* until Clifton Fadiman gently reminded him: "George, it flopped." Foreign affairs expert Quincy Howe supplied a verse of a poem which ended:

> *And you each gentle animal*
> *To you for life may bind*
> *And make it follow at your call*
> *If you are always kind.*

None of the literati knew that it was the last stanza of "Mary's Lamb," that nursery favorite whose fleece was white as snow. Paul De Kruif, internationally known writer on medical subjects, muffed the question "Which of the following names doesn't apply to a flower? Arbutus, Coreopsis, Rubeola, Phlox, Wisteria?" Rubeola was the exception as any mother very well knew if she had a pretentious pediatrician and a child with measles.

The charm of the program lay in the fact that the boys were very fast on their feet. Harpo Marx appeared as a guest star and did brilliantly without ever uttering a word. He answered every question by whistling a fragment of a popular tune.

"Gentlemen, who is Reza Pahlavi?" Fadiman inquired.

"Reza Pahlavi is the ruler of Persia," John Gunther supplied promptly.

"Are you shah?" Fadiman riposted.

"Sultanly," said Gunther.

Soon Larchmont dentists and Seattle businessmen were forming Information Please Clubs, pitting their own resident intellectuals against the experts. Sponsors were bidding each other up for this "hot property" which had been sustaining, i.e., unsponsored, a few months before. *Dr. IQ* never achieved the same popularity as *Information Please* but the quiz craze gave rise to another panel, this time with pint-sized Kierans and Levants. The original *Quiz Kids,* Cynthia Cline, Gerard Darrow, and Van Dyke Tiers were a bunch of Chicago high-IQs who held their own when pitted against four Senators (Ball, Hart, Hatch, and Burton). They were followed by Joel Kupperman, and, though we didn't know it, Seymour Glass. An hour between the Kids and Supreme Court Justice Douglas was pronounced to be a draw. Along with their erudition, the kids could make a funny as briskly as Fadiman. Little Van Dyke Tiers once defined a sarong as "Dorothy Lamour's mainstay." By decade's end the intellectual arsenals of myriads of radio listeners were freshly equipped with information. The Island of Reil is located in the brain . . . It is possible for an airplane to go backward . . . The proper song to dedicate to Walter Winchell is "Little Bo Peep."

If *Information Please* gave John Doe a chance to stump the experts, America's *Town Meeting of the Air* gave Mr. Doe a chance to heckle them. A particularly lively evening was supplied in 1939 when Harold Ickes and General Hugh Johnson faced each other over opposite sides of the New Deal fence. Allocation of wartime powers became a lively subject of debate between two didactic, opinionated, and highly articulate figures. Ickes favored giving such powers to the Federal Government. Johnson, who had by then turned on FDR, replied, "I would as soon turn over control of the Army and Navy to a couple of chiropodists."

Johnson was asked from the floor whether he agreed that no one had done more for the American people than the Roosevelt Administration. The general did not. Except for Herbert Hoover, "everyone back to George Washington" had, in his opinion.

The two debaters had the general air of two lawyers who villify one another in the courtroom and then walk out arm in arm to lunch.

"General Johnson," said Mr. Ickes, "thinks I am eccentric in my political and social theories and I am positive he is. I am fond of Old Ironpants. He can be, I am bound to say, generous in his attitude, even if he is cockeyed as to many of his ideas."

From Johnson: "Harold, I am afraid we are going to disappoint the customers. This sounds more like a necking party than a scrap or even a debate. Let's see what we can do to stop the audience from singing, 'Waltz Me Around Again, Willie.'"

How much of the culture of the 1930s has stuck is another question. *Information Please* spawned a horrendous crop of quiz programs of the "Who-was-the-author-of-Shakespeare's-Romeo-and-Juliet?" variety with the end not yet in sight.

The record has its bright side. Historian Frederick Lewis Allen attributes the gains in music appreciation in America over the past half century partly to the impetus of WPA music classes during the Depression, but to an even greater extent to radio.

In the summer of 1965, through the bounty of Schlitz beer, a crowd of seventy thousand assembled under the stars throughout New York City's park system to hear the music of the New York Philharmonic. (A grateful listener bristled at the occasional sight of a can of Ballantine's.) How many members of that intelligent and beautifully mannered crowd (one literally could hear a pin drop) may have come in contact with the Mozart concerto that was played—because some member of the family heard it for the first time while trying to get the *Goldbergs?*

Also destined to have a lasting influence in their curious way were the Depression's rustics of radioland. Between town cats and country cousins, tastes varied. It was not unusual to find a popular attraction such as the *Lux Radio Theatre* big in the city and not making it in the Midwestern Marches. The reverse was true of two programs which went great guns in rural areas but had little appeal on what would now be the art house circuit. The *National Farm and Home Hour* offered a diet of news, entertainment, and folksy advice. There would occasionally be a high point—for example a Bang Board championship. For those groping for a definition of a "bangboard," it was a backstop against which rival corn shuckers tossed the stripped corn—with NBC giving an ear by ear account of every golden bantam moment of it.

Chicago's WLS as well as the Red Network NBC were responsible for the *National Barn Dance*—a hoedown interspersed with stock reports and old-time religion. The program—which was first produced in 1925—was a fixture at the outset of the Thirties. It was the springboard for the talents of Gene Autry, who was a *Barn Dance* regular before going to Hollywood, and for early radio appearances by Amos 'n' Andy, Homer and Jethro, Lum and Abner, Fibber McGee and Molly—even George Gobel. The barn dance was presided over by a (how-'bout-that-by-cracky-scat-my-dogs-and-durn-your-time) character named Uncle Ezra.

Also known as the Arkansas Wood Chopper, Uncle Ezra came complete with nightshirt, lamp, and store whiskers. Assisting him were the Hoosier Hot Shots and a staff preacher whose ecumenical duties in marrying religion and radio included baptizing a baby on the air. The godmother was radio's oldest living actress—Aunt Em Lanning, who held up her end valiantly, though she was a trifle antiquated to dance the Roger de Coverly.

The *National Barn Dance* capitalized on the national passion for audience participation by roving through grange country, with hayloft microphones transmitting Man on the Farm talent shows. This talent laid heavy stress on rooster crowing and hog calling. Romantic interest was supplied by Red Foley, "the cactus crooner."

Many an ol' cowhand joined his voice to the chorus. Cowboy

Tom and others like him sang mournful laments about perfidious fancy women and decent misguided kids who died on lonely plains by the ranger's gun. Nashville became one of the foremost music publishing centers in America, thanks to a program called *Grand Old Op'ry*. The Rex Cole Mountaineers brought Ozark twangs to children who had never seen a cow—or an Ozark. Juxtaposed among disillusioned, bittersweet songs about two cigarettes or lonely diners at tables for two was an undertone like the persistent buzzing of flies: the sound of hillbillys blowing into their sweet potatoes.

Country music is, if anything, more popular than it was in the Thirties. There are still vast sections of the Republic—far from Broadway, Michigan Avenue, or Sunset Boulevard—where it emanates from loudspeakers twenty-four hours a day and where there are endless paeans to that most popular belle of the public domain, "Jeannie with the Light Brown Hair."

Country music got a shot in the arm at the end of the decade from an unexpected source: the clash between ASCAP and the radio networks, which gave birth to Broadcast Music Inc. (BMI).

ASCAP (the American Society of Composers, Authors and Publishers) was organized in 1914, by, of all people, Victor Herbert, to see that the copyright law as to public performances was enforced, and to make it as easy and as cheap as possible for retailers to acquire the right to the wholesale product represented by popular music. The fight over copyright infringement had led to a number of turbulent court battles—to allegations on the part of cabaret, hotel, restaurant, and theater managers that musical performances in public places were not done for profit, since no admission was charged. In 1917 a decision of Judge Learned Hand, was reversed in favor of ASCAP by Justice Oliver Wendell Holmes, who said, in part, "if music did not pay, it would be given up."

After many more legal battles, hotels, restaurants, and cabarets signed up with ASCAP, paying an annual fee through special licenses. Movies became licensees in 1924, radio half a dozen years later.

ASCAP's big rival BMI came into being in 1940 during a bitter battle over renewal of these licensing agreements. During negotiations for a new five-year contract, ASCAP made demands which the networks regarded as outrageous—and whose outrageousness depended to some degree on where you happened to be sitting. ASCAP withdrew the music of all its affiliated members from the airwaves.

The boycott lasted about a year. No more Victor Herbert, John Philip Sousa, Gershwin, Friml, Kern, Rodgers and Hart, Ethelbert Nevin, Sigmund Romberg, Vincent Youmans, Cole Porter, or Irving Berlin. No more "Kiss Me Again," "St. Louis Blues," "Donkey Serenade," "Star Dust," "Ol' Man River," "Stars and Stripes Forever," or "Road to Mandalay." As Glenn Miller's theme song, "Moonlight Serenade," was licensed through ASCAP, Miller had to substitute "Slumber Song," which became the band's radio signature until the new ASCAP contract was negotiated.

In 1941, networks signed a new five-year contract (renewable for an additional five years) for a far smaller percentage of the gross than ASCAP had originally demanded. Truce was reached on Tin Pan Alley. "The Donkey Serenade" once again resounded throughout the land and "Jeannie with the Light Brown Hair" could take a well-earned rest.

Broadcast Music Inc., which was a creature of the radio networks, exercised a powerful influence in bringing ASCAP to heel. In its initial year BMI produced a number of hit songs, among them "The Breeze and I," "I Hear a Rhapsody," "It's a Big Wide, Wonderful World," Meredith Wilson's "You and I," and "You Are My Sunshine" by the composer-statesman Jimmie Davis, who acted sporadically as governor of Louisiana.

The BMI catalogue also included other works by Aaron Copland, Alan Lerner, and Benny Goodman. Sometimes considered to be BMI's best song of this period was "Practice Makes Perfect" by a young Viennese refugee named Ernest Gold.

The formation of BMI did in effect create an open market in music, for ASCAP and BMI had need of each other. Alone, either one of them would risk running afoul of the government monopoly laws.

Today BMI and ASCAP ranks contain a total of over 35,000 titles and almost as many publishers. However, Rome was not built in a day and much of BMI's first musical roundup was from the rustic musicians who worked out of Nashville.

Whether the ban had anything to do with the later popularity of country music is open to question. During the boycott this art form certainly got a lot of what PR men refer to as "exposure" among those who normally would have been tuned in on Cole Porter or Irving Berlin. The dispute reflected the breakneck development of the gadget which in a decade had become a mighty force. Between 1931 and 1939 the stepchild of the communications industry had come of age and payments to composers were up 900 percent. Broadcasters' efforts to get off the hook showed that the exact nature of this lusty new medium had yet to be defined. When radio's poker-faced representatives claimed that radio "does not broadcast music, but emanates electrical energy," they were operating hopefully in the same uncharted legalistic waters as those idealistic restaurateurs who played music for motives that had nothing to do with money.

Everything bad that is said today about TV was said in the Thirties about radio. The public had a twelve-year-old mentality. Toscanini and *Information Please* were far above the average listener's head. Too much violence was bad for the young. *Buck Rogers* and *The Shadow* were seducing the innocents. An example of a "good" children's program was *The Singing Lady*. (When Irene Wicker, who played this role, was accused during the McCarthy era of red affiliations it was a bit like hearing that Lassie was guilty of a Trotskyite deviation.) Yet for better or worse the men from Mars had demonstrated radio's appalling power.

The hillbilly music that was heard during the ASCAP-BMI dispute came to the fore at an ironical time. Hard times had added millions to the radio audience—and the real Jeeter Lester was becoming as obsolete as the brontosaurus. Radio reached deep into remote pockets of the Blue Ridge Mountains and the Rockies. It penetrated to Idaho ranches and fishing shacks in Maine. The voice of Jack Benny was heard in areas which hitherto had reverberated with Elizabethan English. Homes where not long before the occupants had read by kerosene lamp, had an aerial on the roof. A radio was inside many houses at a time when much of the plumbing was still outside. The radio and the automobile brought Jeeter Lester into the mainstream of American culture.

World War II continued the cross-fertilization of city and town. It introduced America to a newly itinerant populace of soldiers and their wives, defense workers and camp followers. Country music would be heard with the music of the Negro as a lesser but audible voice. It would reach a huge audience, thanks to the revolution in the record business brought about by the mass production and distribution of high fidelity tape. Jeeter Lester's strummings would eventually become part of the rock 'n' roll "image." (Who in the Thirties would ever know the meaning of *that* term?)

Radio was but one powerful factor in bringing about the decline of provincialism. Later on the jet airplane would force Frenchmen to look with less disdain upon the lowly hamburger—and cause American suburban housewives to discover that the casserole tasted better when it was slugged with a presumptuous little Beaujolais. And if country music still emanates from Nashville in its more or less pristine form, certain parodies of provincialism have come a long way from the Grange. Hip San Francisco teenagers listen, on car radios, to singers who, in the accounts of a mountain lament lament the fact that the "dealer" has failed to show up. The selections which the children of proper Bostonians are strumming on their guitars sound as if they had come from *The Connection*—scored jointly by some mod from Carnaby Street, a Negro blues singer, and the composer of *Turkey in the Straw*.

Upon the topmost step was a crouched figure. . . . The Shadow's
eyes . . . glinted as they saw the menace . . .

Chapter 4

The Soaps, the Serials, the Pulps

"Tune in on Monday" . . . "To be continued" . . . "A novelette complete in this issue." How the youthful appetite for adventure was whetted by these words! Would Amos beat his murder rap? Who was the mysterious figure who materialized so eerily in the photograph taken by *Chandu, the Magician*? What ghastly practice was Dr. Metzger up to when he said, "I am not to be disturbed for the next six weeks." *The Shadow* might know, but, most of the time, we didn't.

Chicago was the lodestar of our universe. Some of our most thrilling hours came to us through the courtesy of Proctor and Gamble and Ovaltine. *Black Mask* and *Horror Stories* were printed there. While many radio serials eventually succumbed to the magnetic pull of Hollywood or New York, they often originated in the Merchandise Mart. *Ma Perkins, Bachelor's Children, Portia Faces Life, The First Nighter, The Guiding Light, Against the Storm, The Right to Happiness, Fibber McGee and Molly, Little Orphan Annie, Tom Mix,* and *Amos 'n' Andy* all got their start in Chicago.

One genre flourished, reached its apogee in the Thirties. By 1938 there were seventy-eight serials devoted to the activities of the sudsy Griseldas who were the fictional counterparts of the unfortunates on John J. Anthony's *Good Will Hour*. The term "soap opera" came into being because so many of those fifteen-minute shows were sponsored by makers of soap and cleansing agents. Six manu-

facturers bought up more than two-thirds of soap opera time—
Proctor and Gamble leading the field. Breakfast foods and drug
sponsors accounted for a far smaller percentage of "washboard
weepers." Soap opera throve on hard times. In the seven years before 1933, the combined income from NBC and CBS daytime
radio amounted to $8,400,000. By 1940 it had hit $26,700,000.
Fifty million letters were received by one network in answer to
premium offers. A reasonably attractive household gadget or piece
of costume jewelry would reap harvests of 250,000 to 600,000
letters complete with boxtop and cash. When the process was made
easier, listener mail might pass the million mark. Advertisers came
to respect those denizens of soapland—the dedicated nurses, picturesque rustics, status-hungry girls from the wrong side of the
track. There was gold in their ills—the omnipresent blindness and
amnesia, the mysterious "island fevers" and "mountain rashes" to
which they were so peculiarly susceptible, the temperatures of 106
from which they recovered miraculously over the weekend. The
cash register rang up its gratifying total as mortgages were fore-
closed, babies torn from their mothers' breasts, and kindly old
codgers were victimized by scheming loan sharks.

Their woes launched a wave of tears and a number of big names
on future careers. Among those who dwelt briefly in that matriar-
chal world were John Hodiak, Macdonald Carey, Helen Mencken,
Richard Widmark, Red Skelton, Mercedes McCambridge, and Art
Carney. Don Ameche got his start in *The First Nighter,* and played
the lead in four serials. Sandy Becker—the Dorian Gray of today's
kiddie cartoon field—looks hardly old enough to have supplied the
vocal effects for *Young Doctor Malone.* One program in particular
was a show business prep school. Van Heflin and Joseph Cotten
were both on *The Goldbergs* serial as romantic leads. Marjorie
Main and George Tobias were Goldberg grads. Jan Peerce sang
for the Yom Kippur and Passover Goldberg programs. Madame
Schumann-Heink favored the Goldbergs with Brahms' "Lullaby."
A three-year-old neighbor of the Goldbergs was actually a twenty-
six-year-old named Garson Kanin, who remembers "Socratic dia-
logues between 'Mr. Washing Machine' and 'Miss Soap.' "

It has been said that, unlike television which does all the work
for the viewer, radio made the audience work. The marble stair-

cases of soap opera were grander than anything on TV because imaginations were not limited by anything as tangible as a stage set. The mind's eye suffers from no production budget. Aiding the audience was the omnipresent sound-effects man. Ununionized in the early Thirties, an astonishing number of writers, directors, and actors supplied sound effects to cut corners in the Depression radio budgets. Irna Phillips, one of the most highly paid soap opera writers of the mid-Thirties, spent her salad days swishing water around and barking like a dog. James and Marian Jordan, who later were immortalized as Fibber McGee and Molly, used to make shouts, murmurs, street cries, and crowd voices, pulling down fifty dollars a week between them. Gertrude Berg was a purist about do-it-yourself sound effects, and insisted that the cast tinkle its own cups, saucers, and spoons. When shampooing Daughter Rosie's hair, Molly appeared with a tin bowl and a bar of soap. Staats Cottsworth—a hero from *Rosemary*—defied soap opera convention, anticipated the Method and relieved the sound-effects man by kissing his own wrist during scenes of passion. This type of threat to an already overcrowded profession became less common after 1937 when the American Federation of Radio Artists abolished multiple characterization kickbacks and the like, and established thirty to fifty dollars as a minimum fee for a fifteen-minute broadcast.

The water must have swished realistically, the wrists were kissed with conviction, for producers of soap operas were frequently embarrassed by the extent to which the readers identified with the characters. Truckloads of wedding presents arrived when Dr. John Wayne married the heroine of *Big Sister*. When Mrs. Kerry Donovan of *Just Plain Bill* had her first child, the network received hundreds of bonnets, dresses, bootees, porringers. Messages of sympathy poured in when the child was killed later in an accident. An actor who appeared in one serial respectably married was lured to the altar in another. A deluge of letters accused him of bigamy.

When *Pepper Young's Family* lost their house on Union Street the resultant audience reaction gave a poignant view of the times. Mr. Young, after a desperate search for work, was unable to find it. The furniture was moved out. Pepper and Peggy—the children—were faced with quitting school. Letters poured in from listeners who had been through the same thing and who pleaded with Elaine

Carrington, Pepper's creator, "Please let the Youngs get their home back." On Christmas Day she did. Sociologists might wring their hands—advertisers merely rubbed theirs.

What sort of heroes and heroines inspired this passionate loyalty? First there were the homely philosophers: *Just Plain Bill, Ma Perkins,* and *David Harum.* Doctors and nurses were included in *Women in White, Road of Life, Joyce Jordan MD, Young Doctor Malone,* and Rinso's *Big Sister.* There were the career girls dedicated to the avoidance of marriage: tearoom proprietress Ellen Brown; Portia, the lady lawyer of *Portia Faces Life;* and Helen Trent, the Edith Head of soap opera who "proved what so many women long to prove in their own lives . . . that romance can live in life at thirty-five . . . and even beyond." There were also the uneasy Cinderellas—simple creatures like *Our Gal Sunday* faced with an unfamiliar world of diamond tiaras and presentations at Buckingham Palace. Leering in-laws bothered *The Romance of Helen Trent,* and *Our Gal Sunday* confronted the audience with a perpetually unanswered question. "Our . . . Gal . . . Sunday! The story of an orphan girl named Sunday from the little mining town of Silver Creek, Colorado, who in young womanhood married England's richest, most handsome lord, Lord Henry Brinthrope. The story asks: *Can* this girl from a mining town in the West find happiness as the wife of a wealthy and *titled* Englishman?" The question was settled for the ages when she divorced him in 1958. Other uneasy Cinderellas included the humbly born and misallied Laurel (daughter of Stella Dallas) and Kitty Foyle whose digressions from "daytime morality" of the Thirties were explained away by the fact that "it was based on a book."

Soapland was peopled by strong women and sniveling men. In *The Story of Mary Marlin* a mother guided the destinies of a republic all but devoid of male officials. One of Helen Trent's male entourage protests, "I'm not strong, incorruptible, stalwart. I'm weak." It fell to Helen's lot to put on the brass knucks and shape him up.

In *Trouble House* of the Heinz Magazine of the Air, another creation by the author of *Pepper Young,* a strong woman named Martha readies her spare room for weak brother John and his family who had "lost everything." A salty female servant named Phoebe warns Martha that she is making a mistake. John & Co. intend to swarm down "like a horde of locusts and eat up what little you've got left."

John is, as Phoebe has foreseen, indeed a weakling. He has blandly written off the education of his son Ted. "Ted doesn't have to go to college especially these days when, while we're coming out of the Depression, I think jobs for college graduates aren't exactly tumbling over each other yet." One couldn't help thinking that Ted might have made out better with a BA, considering that a college degree was considered a necessary prerequisite for selling blouses at Macy's. John seems happy to palm off this complaining son on poor Martha, along with a nagging wife and a daughter with a habit of falling into quicksand. John settles into Martha's ménage with relish: "Home. I'm home."

As if all this weren't enough, he proceeds to have a heart attack —but once again, good old Martha will see him through. "Your voice," he says, "it's like water rippling over the stones in the brook . . . it's like . . . it's like . . . like the wind in the willows . . . it's like peace." All of which served notice on long-suffering Martha that the pack of ne'er-do-wells was good for at least another year's stay.

Two of soapland's First Families were unique in that they had normal father figures, but here too the woman was the power behind the throne. *The Goldbergs* started out in 1929 with an announcement in the New York *Evening World* of the inception of a radio story: "A cloak and suit operator's rise from a dingy tenement to Park Avenue."

The Goldbergs ran for seventeen years. Selected Goldberg scripts were eventually enshrined as permanent Americana in the Princeton University Library. The author, Gertrude Berg, was also the Ma Goldberg of the show—a generous spirit whose "bosom was big enough for the cares of the whole neighborhood." "Better a crust of bread and enjoy it," said Molly, "than a cake that gives you indigestion."

A philosophy cut across Molly's sectarian lines. She cut the lines herself. A convent of Catholic nuns gave *The Goldbergs* up for

Lent and asked for a synopsis when the period of penance was over. Austere Princeton dons were captivated, along with everyone else, by Molly's salty wit. When daughter Rosie drops a dish, Molly says, "But I'm not complaining, am I, Rosie darlingest?"—pause— "But I *could* have said it was one of my best dishes."

Jake Goldberg considered himself to be master of his house, yet for homely insight one looked to Molly. Jake wants his son Sammy to have "everything money can buy," but it is Molly who sees beyond, wanting Sammy to have "everything money *can't* buy."

The Goldbergs never did make it to Park Avenue. The age of television found them still on 1083 East Tremont Avenue, but they had enhanced their status by moving to the country, and along the way they installed their creator in a ten-room Park Avenue duplex.

En route to their new-found prosperity, they encountered certain interruptions which were the common fate of all of us. In the spring of 1940 the story line of the Goldbergs was briefly interrupted when the time was preempted by the rantings of a European statesman. With the usual salty wit that pervaded the program the announcement was made, "You have heard the concluding remarks of Chancellor Hitler through the courtesy of the Goldbergs."

Gertrude Berg won an Emmy in 1950 for her TV portrayal of Molly, and a Tony in 1959 for her role as Mrs. Jacoby opposite Sir Cedric Hardwicke in *A Majority of One*. She was the author of *The Molly Goldberg Cookbook,* and an autobiography with her son Cherney, *Molly and Me*. She died in September 1966. Permanently enshrined in the Princeton Library, the great lady of Pincus Pines had come a long way from soapland.

One other fine American family dominated the consciousness of the Thirties approximately as the Kennedys held the attention of the Sixties. The Barbours of Carleton E. Morse's *One Man's Family* were unique among denizens of soapland. They came on in the evening. The serial was defined by one observer as "the story of a San Francisco family of comfortable means and unfrenzied existence . . . equidistant between the suds of soap opera and the literary merits of *The Forsyte Saga*."

This hardy perennial was first broadcast over NBC in 1933; on the Pacific coast on Sundays, and on Wednesdays in the east. It was like trying to follow the home life of a baseball team.

Reporting on the program, *Newsweek* had to put out a family tree. Paul, the oldest son, was a World War I ace and secret agent. In 1933 he adopted a boy named Teddy. The oldest daughter, Hazel, married William Herbert and begat twin sons in 1933: "Hank" who became a doctor, and Pinky, characterized by a leading authority on soap opera as "no good."

Claudia ("impetuous") (b. 1912) m. (1931) John Roberts who d. two years later. Claudia had her fling at titled marriage with 13th baronet Nicholas Lacey. To them was b. a daughter, Penny.

Claudia's twin, Clifford, m. Anne Waite (1938). In the same year Anne d.—swelling the Barbour necrology. The youngest boy, lawyer Jack, m. Betty (1938) and became the father of triplets. A potential mate might think twice before marrying into a tribe with such a history of sudden death and multiple birth. (Later, when the family left the ancestral home of radio to go on TV, Jack, by then the audio father of "six beautiful girls," regressed to become a spindly legged video kid with a lifetime of gynecological productivity still ahead of him.)

The paterfamilias belonged to the spare-the-rod-and-spoil-the-child school of child rearing. It was the gentle counsels of sensitive Mother Barbour who softened his image to his children. Eventually Mother Barbour had an effect on her own creator. "Father Barbour used to be at loggerheads with his children," wrote Carleton E. Morse in 1941. "I find myself making him more lenient, more inclined to overlook the little things. He's mellowing with the years." As with Molly it was Mom who pulled the strings. When one of soapland's old curmudgeons acquired a custard heart to match his custard head, the first rule of radio was *cherchez la femme*.

The job of propelling a Molly Goldberg or Father Barbour through a week's activity might be a total labor to a Gertrude Berg or a Carleton E. Morse. Sometimes one extraordinarily prolific writer would become the guiding spirit of a whole empire of soap opera characters. Frank Hummert and Anne Ashenhurst in the early Thirties produced a detective serial called *Betty and Bob*. They thought of branching out. When they married in 1935 they were making close to $150,000 a year. By the early Forties they were producing sixty-seven shows, most of them fifteen-minute soap operas which included *Backstage Wife, Second Husband, Just Plain Bill, Lorenzo Jones, Our Gal Sunday, Stella Dallas, Young Widder Brown,* and *David Harum.*

Motivating much of this immense complex was Robert Hardy Andrews—a one-man script machine whose normal output was 100,000 words a week. This genial spirit made a firm distinction between fun money and eatin' money. For fun money he did historical studies of Defoe, Hamilton, and Buddha. His eatin' money came from *Jack Armstrong, Skippy* and *The Romance of Helen Trent.* He at one time was connected with *Mary Noble, Backstage Wife; Betty and Bob;* and *Front Page Farrell.* Year after year, he ground out *Just Plain Bill* and *Ma Perkins.* When he went to Hollywood for a stint of movie writing in 1936, he finished twenty-seven radio scripts on the train.

Bill, most venerable of soap opera heroes, was a barber bent on transforming his high-spirited daughter into a lady, an obvious case of silk purse and sow's ear. This, plus worrying about her turbulent marriage to one Kerry Donovan, kept Bill so busy (according to James Thurber) that he only had time to shave a dozen customers in a dozen years. Kerry Donovan himself practiced law in an office which he visited three times in eight months. Ma Perkins, one characterized by *Life* as a "backwoods Vesta," helped everyone out of trouble while devoting sporadic attention to a lumber yard.

Andrews was the star writer of what came to be known as "the Hummert mill." The Hummerts applied the techniques of the assembly line to the fifteen-minute drama. The Hummerts would dream up the story line. An episode would be handed to anonymous writers who would fill in the dialogue.

With the Hummerts, too, the secret lay in a single word—output. In the early Thirties, Elaine Carrington sold NBC on a serial about a family of moderate means struggling to raise two children. It was called *Red Davis,* afterward rechristened *Pepper Young's Family.* In 1939 she added *When a Girl Marries* and *Rosemary.* She briefly zeroed in on long-suffering Martha of *Trouble House* on the Heinz Magazine of the Air. Before her death she too had become prosperous enough to hire a stable of authors to propel her characters through the usual one step forward and two steps back in the plot.

In 1937 Irna Phillips gave up barking and turned her entire attention to *Women in White, Right to Happiness, The Guiding Light, Road of Life, Today's Children,* and *Lonely Women.* Though something of a one-woman agony factory herself, she was most contemptuous of the product of "the Hummert mill." Miss Phillips is unique among writers of the Thirties in that her mill is still grinding today.

The big money in soap opera went to these Olympian figures who plotted its tangled interrelationships months in advance. The competent hack who lived from episode to episode never knew as he churned out his breathless daily quota of words what was coming up the following week. Though he might work ahead for a week or so he was as much in the dark as the audience as to the final aftermath of island fever or the fate of the beautiful relationship which flowered when the male lead—paralyzed fortuitously from the waist down—was confined to the care of one of soapland's female Jobs.

Soap opera was a muse who imposed on her devotees a peculiar set of disciplines. For the soap opera actor—since all broadcasts were done live—there was the hazard of getting drunk before the show was done over (at a later time) for California.

For the writer there was the necessity of synopsizing previous episodes for listeners who might have missed them. Thanks to the standard "recap" of previous episodes, it took Bill Davidson four days to shave one of his rare customers. Bill once remarked, "It doesn't seem possible to me that Ralph Wilde arrived here only yesterday." It seemed equally impossible to the audience. Wilde had first turned up on the program thirteen days before. An accident might occur on Monday on *When a Girl Marries.* The following Thursday one might find the leading character still unconscious at the scene of the accident, with the husband moaning over her inert form. When you considered how much ground author Elaine Carrington had to revisit, it was small wonder that the ambulances were late.

"Well, the events of the past few months have left Joan in a turmoil. She is heartbroken over Henry Davis, who she believes has left Stanwood, perhaps for good. And right now, under the pressure of her mother, who is determined that she will go through with her engagement to Phil Stanley, Joan is so upset that she doesn't much care what happens to her. This afternoon, Madison, the old servant who has been with the Fields since Joan was a child, found her sobbing in her room, and immediately drove downtown to her father's office to beg him to come at once. So Mr. Field, who is separated from his wife, and who understands Joan better than her mother does, left an important meeting and started for Mrs. Fields' home to see his daughter. As he and Madison near the house, he turns to Madison, who is driving, and says . . ."

There was also the challenge of working in the premium offer—the photograph of Ma Perkins that brought a flood of a million letters, or the horse given away weekly on *David Harum*. Household gadgets, compacts, costume jewelry, and tested zinnia seeds were among the goodies to be put up on the block. It was not unusual for a couple of actors to interrupt a love scene with a plug for a "resplendent forget-me-not pin."

Sometimes the writer had to manage the disappearance of an actor or actress. A complaint about a headache was almost always followed by a brain tumor, an inevitable indication that a part was about to be written out. When Mary Noble departed for her annual vacation, the script arranged a trip to her sick mother's bedside. Helen Trent always went to New York for a convention of dress designers.

Perhaps the most difficult discipline of all lay in focusing one's moral sights on an America which had not existed since the days of Rutherford B. Hayes.

Today the age of consent has certainly dropped. It has, in fact, been lowered. In the Thirties mothers did not send their thirteen-year-old daughters to the family gynecologist for advice on contraception. College psychiatrists would probably not have dared to prescribe the Pill even had it existed. When telling the young of things to avoid, one would not have headed the list with heroin. But in the Thirties one seems to remember as many scare articles as there are today about girls losing their virginity at Old Siwash.

Repeal brought an upsurge of per capita drinking once one could tipple without threat to the eyesight. The clergy were as upset as they are today about rising divorce rates. There were perhaps even more college students who insisted that for them, at least, God was dead. There were many polls—which crept into print, red-faced college administrators notwithstanding—in which young people insisted that the sexual code of their elders was hypocritical and outworn and smashed at school. The theater in the Thirties gave a better idea of the mores of America than any of the mass media. But soap opera listeners demanded of their favorites moral standards as remote from reality as those dictated to Clark Gable and Norma Shearer by the Legion of Decency.

The serving of a glass of beer or the substitution of a new actor in the master bedroom were sufficient to put the *Pepper Young* home under interdict. From the first episode of *Just Plain Bill* in 1932, the main characters consumed in moments of great stress hundreds of gallons of iced tea. When a character from *The Second Mrs. Burton* remarked, "Some part of me wants you to fall in love with me," listener mail demanded that the suitor who had inspired this obscene outburst be banished from the show.

Each of the large producers of soap opera adjusted to "daytime morality" in his own way. Elaine Carrington was such a romantic that bodily lust hardly seemed to enter the picture.

Robert Hardy Andrews obligingly turned out scripts in which the good girls were markedly different from the bad ones. Julie Stevens, who played the second *Helen Trent,* often rushed over to appear on *Stella Dallas* where she could be a bad girl who smoked and drank. "After all, you have never been in my arms," said one of Helen's luckless horde of suitors who crashed planes into mountains, were slain by gangsters, or who underwent various seizures on the eve of their weddings. While teenagers of the Thirties cheerfully "necked" without benefit of a third party, Helen, at thirty-five and beyond, was under constant surveillance from an omnipresent chaperone named "elderly Agatha Anthony."

Irna Phillips hotly denies that soap opera was shackled by daytime morality or that soapland was peopled by two classes of people —good and bad. She believes that there's so much good in the worst of us and so much bad in the best of us, etc. While the family was the core of every Phillips show, she points proudly to pioneering experiments with illegitimacy on *The Guiding Light* and *Women in White* as early as 1937, a mystery of parentage in *Painted Dream*, an affair with a married woman by one of *Today's Children*. There was indeed no theme which Miss Phillips would have hesitated to tackle except possibly cancer—and as a fellow writer who sat in the Waldorf Towers at her feet much in the manner of Boswell remarked, "Of course we didn't know about the Pap test in the Thirties."

Her departures from daytime morality came under the heading of a public service—letting the ostriches out there know that abortion often ends in infection—or, had we then had the Pap test, that the results often come back positive.

The Goldbergs and *One Man's Family* took their moral convictions from their authors. One simply knew that Rosie, a virtuous Jewish daughter of Molly Goldberg, would never be caught putting out for the boys. Though *One Man's Family* was a nighttime show Carleton Morse practically invented daytime morality.

Henry Barbour was old-fashioned, square, and proud of it. His originator hoped for a national renaissance based on Henry's old-fashioned virtues. In 1941 he expressed the hope in *Better Homes and Gardens* ("The House One Man's Family is Building") that Henry "may not be so far behind the times after all." Happily, in 1941 he could not foresee that in 1949, when the Barbours went on TV, they would bandy about such subjects as the Kinsey Report, unfaithfulness, abortion, and the father's dominant relationship with his daughter. Postwar America had taken six giant steps away from the world of Rutherford B. Hayes. Mother Barbour needed all her diplomacy to guide her children through a world where V was as likely to stand for VD as for Varsity.

Toward the end of the speakeasy era two whites—magician's assistant Freeman Gosden and Peoria bricklayer Charles Correll—appeared in front of a WMAQ microphone in Chicago, and the Fresh Air Taxicab Company was born, and with it the most popular radio show—probably of all time: *Amos 'n' Andy*.

The Fresh Air Taxicab Company numbered in its personnel a bunch of the most outrageous end men ever to perpetrate a "you all" on the public. There was bumptious, shiftless Andy, cautious gravel-voiced Amos, ignorant Lightnin', the scheming Kingfish, vivacious Madame Queen, and Brother Crawford who kept repeating the uxorial lament, "I want you to know that my wife is very unhappy."

Like all Negro characters of the time, Amos and Andy expressed themselves in malapropisms or murdered language. ("I'se regusted.") One picturesque catch phrase—"check and double check" —became the title of a Hollywood movie. Their simple blackface wit so appealed to Calvin Coolidge that he gave instructions that he was not to be bothered by affairs of state while listening to them. Other distinguished fans included Henry Ford, J. Edgar Hoover, Thurber, Vincent Astor, and the Louisiana dictator Huey Long, who took his nickname from the Kingfish. Arthur Brisbane often telephoned after the broadcast to find out what happened next. National telephone traffic dropped off 50 percent between 7:00 and 7:15 P.M. Movie theaters stopped performances to pipe in the show. Newspapers carried accounts of Amos' trial for murder. Car thieves found easy pickings during the program—and were incidentally provided with a built-in alibi. The dialogue from Amos 'n' Andy was so widely quoted that a miscreant could make out a case to the judge for having been quietly at home by quoting something the Kingfish said to Madame Queen on the evening in question. Many a petty larcenist may have gone free because of an interchange like the following:

> ANDY: Say, s'cuse me for protrudin', stranger, but ain't you got a hold of my watch chain?
> KINGFISH: Your watch chain? Well, so I does. How you like dat? One of dese solid gold cufflinks of mine musta hooked on your watch chain dere.

Or the following rueful comment from Madame Queen's breach of promise suit against Andy:

"We was engaged 147 times in one year . . . an' it would been more dan dat if we'd been goin' steady."

Gosden and Correll wrote their own dialogue, but other serials hired writers as furtively as an alcoholic nipped from a bottle in the toilet tank. When Jim and Marian Jordan—two ex-vaudevillians from Peoria—began turning out a fifteen-minute show in Chicago, forty of the two hundred dollars a week which they made was slipped under the counter to writer Don Quinn. The show was the saga of a folksy grocer named Smackout who derived his name from the fact that he was always just "smack out" of everything. Later the folksy grocer ended up on the cutting room floor and became the more universally recognizable Fibber McGee. The locale was shifted from a country crossroads to Peoria. The show was grabbed by a sponsor. The opening performance was broadcast from New York in April 1935. Eventually the Jordans went to Hollywood, where they pulled down $3500 a week from the crises that beset "79 Wistful Vista."

Fibber and Molly's lives followed a workaday routine: trips to the movies, minor clashes with firemen, police, and neighbors. There was the eternal joke of Fibber's unrealized plans to clean out his closet.

At its peak *Fibber McGee and Molly* reached thirty million listeners between 9:30 and 10:00 EWT over NBC every Tuesday. In 1941–42 the Jordans' Crossley rating was higher by a whisker than Jack Benny and Edgar Bergen and Charlie McCarthy.

" 'Tain't funny, McGee" became in the late Thirties what "Check and double check" had been in 1931. It had paid to hire a writer after all. Gabby, well-meaning Fibber had provided the country with a national image. Chuckling wives would remark fondly, "Fibber's just like my husband . . . the old fool."

If McGee was the archetypal husband, America soon had its archetypal teenager. In 1937 George Abbott produced a play by Clifford Goldsmith called *What a Life,* about a high school superintendent. Rudy Vallee suggested that Goldsmith write a short piece around Henry Aldrich, the juvenile protagonist played on the stage by Ezra Stone. Eventually Henry's crack-voiced "Coming, Mother" reached thirty million listeners and brought its writer $3000 a week. Henry's problems were so recognizable to Goldsmith's own children that they once presented him with an itemized bill for plagiarism.

Other comedy serials included *Myrt and Marge* and *Easy Aces,* featuring Goodman and Jane Ace. It was heard in Kansas City, Missouri, as early as 1928 and previewed on network radio in October 1931. In March 1932 *Easy Aces* started a network run that lasted till 1945.

Like the McGees, the Aces were dependent on homely situations. Jane was the eternal patsy. Acting in a little theater production in 1939, for example, she succeeds in turning a tense drama into high comedy which in turn inspired the following bit of dialogue.

Ace claims to have been seized by a dizzy spell during Jane's performance:

JANE: You never got a dizzy spell since I've known you.

ACE: Well, you've never been in a play like that since I've known . . .

JANE: I think it was abdominal of you to walk out.

ACE: Well, yes, it was abdominal, and a dizziness—a combination of ailments, I guess.

"When I get the urge," said Jane, "I'm completely uninhabited."

Clearly, like Amos and Andy, Jane leaned on malapropism for comic effect. In a democracy, there was room for one or two Mrs. Malaprops even among the whites.

Most appealing of all was Paul Rymer's *Vic and Sade* (Monday through Friday, 10:15–10:30 A.M. CWT). Vic and Sade had a son named Rush who had a friend named Bluetooth Johnson. Vic's business associate, Mr. Buller, pulled his own teeth. R. J. Konk was the founder of Vic's Lodge—the Sacred Stars of the Milky Way (Amos 'n' Andy, by the way, belonged to the Mystic Knights of the Sea). Vic and Sade's favorite breakfast food was known as "Brick Mush." They made telephone calls to one Ishigan Fishigan of Sishingan, Michigan. Rymer's most brilliant creation was Uncle Fletcher, whose penchant was reminiscence in depth. Sam Slate and Joe Cook quote a sample in their history of radio, *It Sounds Impossible:* "I wonder sometimes whatever happened to Ardmore Ruler after he sold his buttermilk and cottage cheese store in Blue Haven, Pennsylvania? I know that his brother Harty moved to Walla Walla, Washington, after Ardmore left Blue Haven, married a woman fourteen years of age—later died." It was a program for anyone blessed with total recall.

Among the comic writers of the Thirties as with the producers of soap opera there were frustrated moralists whose creed could be reduced to a single axiom: "The true values are to be found in the small town." After they became successful and moved to the Coast, the Jordans clung proudly to their identity of small-town Americans who refused to go Hollywood. For Henry Aldrich's creator the hope of the future lay in some counterpart of Centerville.

The setting of most soap operas was a living room located in a vacuum variously named Hartville, Dickston, Simpsonville, Three Oaks, Great Falls. Trouble came to these Utopian communities through the intervention of city folk, designing women, unnatural mothers, evil rich men. Against the advice of more stable characters, some—like Starr of *Ma Perkins*, a selfish, restless wife—ran off to New York to a bad end. And the renegade who ran off to the big city was lucky if he did not spend his stay dodging gangsters' bullets.

If soapsuds cleansed a world of moralists, two categories of radio serial were totally devoid of any spiritual content except that the Good Guys won. These were the chillers and the kiddie shows. The audiences very often overlapped. *The Lone Ranger* had something of an adult following, while the little folk might enjoy *Inner Sanctum* and *Gangbusters* too, for its dramatized versions of actual police cases. There were also *Ellery Queen, The Shadow, The Green Hornet, The Blue Beetle, The Thin Man, The Fat Man, Mr. and Mrs. North, Perry Mason, Philo Vance, Bulldog Drummond, Boston Blackie, Mr. Moto, Sherlock Holmes, Buck Rogers, Chandu, the Magician*, and *Little Orphan Annie*.

All the devices of soap opera were utilized to create the necessary aura of realism. The sound-effects man was vital in the background. No expense was spared. As Silver, the Lone Ranger's trusty steed, galloped through the sage, four young men clapped toilet plungers swathed in cheesecloth. Elsewhere a rolled-up bag was dropped on a studio floor—a body fell. Mallets crushed cantaloupes as heads were bashed in. Cleated footsteps clattered on a cement slab, and a detective strolled across the San Francisco waterfront.

Some of the producers of kiddie shows and thrillers were the old reliable writers and soap factories. Assembly-line techniques could be applied to a thriller like *Mr. Keen, Tracer of Lost Persons*. The Hummerts would dream up a story for the show, which would go to a Hummert subsidiary. Faceless writers would grind out the dialogue and the finished product would be kicked back to the subsidiary for production and casting. A Mr. Keen story was a single self-contained story instead of a serial and was followed by a list of actual people who were wanted to cash in on a jackpot in the form of unexpected legacies.

Robert Hardy Andrews of *Helen Trent, Ma Perkins,* and *Just Plain Bill* fame also wrote for the kiddie cabal. For some time he turned out a radio version of Percy Crosby's popular comic strip *Skippy*. He devised the idea of forming a secret society of Skippy's young followers. He got up a code book based on old Gold Bug cryptograms and a secret grip stolen from a national fraternity. All this could be yours for box tops and a signed statement from your mother that you were a Wheaties eater. Big oaks from little acorns. From this modest beginning came art forms: Little Orphan Annie Ovaltine shakers, Ralston revolving coins spelling "Fair and Square," Wheaties grip developers, Post Toasties Junior detective kits. Parents of the Thirties recall with horror larders bulging with boxes of unconsumed breakfast food.

The creator of *Just Plain Bill* was also responsible for *Jack Armstrong, the All American Boy,* who enjoys a posthumous fame among Americans no longer young. Middle-aged eyes moisten at the recollection of the Armstrong theme song:

> *Raise the flag for Hudson High, boys!*
> *Show them how we stand!*
> *Ever challenging the champions*
> *Known throughout the land . . .*

Anyone who can complete this verse or supply the "arfs" correctly in the *Little Orphan Annie* song, and who pretends he doesn't remember Lindbergh, is lying.

The Galsworthy of the West Coast—Carleton Morse—also produced a chiller called *I Love a Mystery.* It was the story of three soldiers of fortune, all recruited from the ranks of *One Man's Family.* Jack, the leader, played Paul on *The Family.* Doc, an easygoing type with a corn-pone delivery, was, in his other incarnation, Claudia's twin Clifford. Reggie, the Britisher, was a Barbour in-law —the titled Nicholas Lacey. The travels of the trio embroiled them with vampires, snakes, raids on pagan temples. Settings were très exotique: Cambodia, the headwaters of the Amazon. Robert Carrington—son of Elaine Carrington and erstwhile *I Love a Mystery* fan—recalls the most famous episode. The trio were on an island complete with bats, an old castle, and a multimillionaire maniac. "Murder after murder occurred . . . and each time Brahms' 'Lullaby' had been first played in the castle chapel on the huge pipe organ. Imagine the horror when Jack and Doc raced into the chapel while the 'Lullaby' was playing and heard the throbbing music and *found the chapel empty!* The organ keys were being played by ghostly hands, or my name isn't Jack Packard."

Tune in tomorrow evening . . .

The hero of double identity was a popular serial figure. Brick Reed was by day "a well-known man about town, publisher of the *Daily Sentinel.*" By night at the wheel of his streamlined "sleek, superpowered" car Black Beauty he hunted "the biggest of all game —public enemies who try to destroy our America." Only his faithful valet, Kato, knew the secret identity of *The Green Hornet.*

The Green Hornet program was a veritable Tower of Babel. Kato lapsed periodically into an all but incomprehensible dialect—possibly with a tagalog root. (Originally Japanese, he became a Filipino cleverly, several months before Pearl Harbor.) Malefactors were recognizable from their tough talk and from names like "Slugger." Comic effects were supplied by Michael Axbridge, "would-be bodyguard and self-appointed reporter," whose accent would have done credit to an Abbey player. "I can see the warm blood tricklin' out of me side," he says, unaware that he has spilled his second breakfast over himself.

The listener enjoyed many an innocent joke at Axbridge's expense. At the end of one episode he assured Reed: "If I'd been in your shoes, Reed, I'd af turned the tables on him somehow and brat him in alive—that I would. My one ambition is to take that Haarnet by the arm and lead him into the central office and collect that reward."

"Take my arm, Axbridge, and help me up," says the Hornet. "I'm still a little shaky."

"Who knows what evil lurks in the hearts of men." (Maniacal laughter courtesy of Orson Welles.) *The Shadow* knows . . . Lamont Cranston's true identity, like that of *The Green Hornet,* is known to one person. Only lovely Margo Lane is aware of his handy talent for becoming invisible. "You stay here, Margo . . ."

Much of the Shadow's energies were spent in pursuit of mad doctors. *The Nursery Rhyme Murders,* for example, take place in a private sanitarium in "a densely wooded area in the suburbs." At first blamed on a childish inmate who liked to hear Mother Goose rhymes before retiring, the murders prove to be the work of a deranged psychiatrist called Dr. Foster, unsuspected denizen of "a complete juvenile world." Another distraught MD creates untold havoc with a chemical solution which brings the dead back to life. His grisly assembly line must be constantly replenished by sneak raids on the city morgue. The Shadow remarks to a reconstructed corpse who has difficulty adjusting: "How much better to have left you untouched after death had claimed you the first time."

In 1933 George W. Trendle, a Detroit businessman, devised a means of teaching patriotism, tolerance, fairness, and a sympathetic understanding of fellow men and their rights and privileges. The vehicle for instilling these homely virtues was *The Lone Ranger.* Longest lived of all radio serials, it was described by C. B. Boutell as "a horse opera with overtones of *Pilgrim's Progress.*"

This equine morality play also upped the sales of the products of seventeen bakeries, one oil company, and seventy-one organizations dedicated to the sale of Lone Ranger pistols, cowboy suits, wallets, games, spoons, and bubble gum. Lone Ranger comics were syndicated in eighty-four newspapers. Lone Ranger safety clubs were formed all over the country. Everyone, it seemed, profited from the cry of "Hi—Yo—Silver," the thunder of hooves, and the laconic grunt of the faithful Tonto.

The Lone Ranger's code was a stern one as set forth by his creator. He might save Widow Jones, Widow Smith, or Widow Brown from the rustlers, but he must never touch her. However, antiseptic romances were permitted to the minor members of the cast. Smoking, profanity, and intoxicating beverages were out. Saloons, those landmarks of the Western landscape, became, where possible, cafés. Sloppy syntax was also verboten, Mr. Trendle insisted. "He must make proper use of 'who' and 'whom,' 'shall,' 'I' and 'me.'" Gunplay was as severely circumscribed as loveplay. The Ranger was forbidden to kill. "He aims to maim as painlessly as possible." "He is the man who can fight great odds, yet take time to treat a bird with a broken wing." Among other unexpected topics which were touched on by the Ranger's credo—the "sacred American heritage . . . that every individual has the right to worship God as he desires." The moral, as drawn by *Newsweek* magazine in a writeup of *The Lone Ranger:* "Purity Pays."

The world of the comics overlapped the cereal serials in the persons of the Lone Ranger, Orphan Annie, Don Winslow, Mandrake, Tom Mix, and Skippy. Other characters who moved between two worlds were the heroes of the pulps. But a vast number of pulp people, to be sure, could never make it in radio; there were just too many of them. The Frank A. Munsey Company, which published the New York *Sun,* had a string of pulps, including *Black Mask, Dime Detective, Western Ranger, Dime Sports, Horror Stories, Adventure, Love Novels, Love Book, All Story, The Spider, Daredevil Aces,* and *Fighting Aces,* which took young readers back to the intrapersonal aerial combat of World War I.

The largest producer of pulps was a firm called Street and Smith. As soap opera had its "Hummert mill," so pulp publishing had what Quentin Reynolds called its Fiction Factory. Street and Smith came out with *Western Story Magazine* in 1919, the *Frank Merriwell Series* in 1921, *Love Story Magazine* in 1921, *True Western* and *Far West* in 1925, *Wild West* in 1927, *Air Trails Magazine* in 1928, *Best Detective* in 1929, *Sport Story, Nick Carter Magazine, Cowboy Stories, Astounding Stories* and *Doc Savage* in 1933, *Dynamic Adventures* and *Romantic Range* in 1935, *The Feds, Pocket Detective,* and *Sport Pictorial* in 1936, *Pocket Love, Pocket Western, Crime Busters,* and *Mystery* in 1937, *The Avengers* in 1939, *Western Adventures* in 1940.

Romance, Detective, Adventure, Western, were the main subdivisions of the world of pulp, though there were other overtones to some of the entries in the "detective" class. An advertisement for *True Detective* which ran in 1931 asked, "Why Is Vivian Gordon's Murderer Free?" and carried the following provocative copy: "The slaughtered woman's intimate diaries revealed her vicious trafficking with prominent businessmen, notorious criminals, political big shots, and one lawyer of whom she wrote, 'If anything happens to me, he is to blame!' What became of the murdered harpy's wrist watch, her diamond ring, her $2000 mink coat . . . What 'daddy' had paid for them?" Other offerings in this issue included "William J. Burns Trails Dynamiters to Tacoma's Free-Love Colony" and "Asbury Park's Most Foul Child Murder." *Spicy Detective,* making no particular pretensions to being "True," did for the adolescent male in its day what *Playboy* does today. One difference was in the rag content of the paper.

In 1931 Street and Smith launched a magazine devoted exclusively to the adventures of the black-cloaked crime fighter, *The Shadow. The Shadow* conferred the following Good Housekeeping Seal of Approval upon his creator Maxwell Grant: "This is to certify that I have made careful examination of the manuscript known as *The Living Shadow,* as set down by Mr. Maxwell Grant, my raconteur, and do find it a true account of my activities upon that occasion. I have therefore arranged that Mr. Grant shall have exclusive privilege to such further of my exploits as may be considered of interest to the American public. (signed) The Shadow." (Mr. Grant was more fortunate than one of The Shadow's other biographers. Henry E. Charlot, who chronicled The Shadow's doings on radio, died of poison under appropriately mysterious circumstances.

The variety of the "black clad avenger's" adventures was reflected in the magazine's art work. In those economy-minded days, the art director, Bill Lawlor, had a heavy black cape and mask hanging by his desk. He would summon an artist and pose as "a bluish streak eavesdropping on a conversation," clipping an Ashanti warrior with a shot from his revolver, being jumped by one of those subhuman gorillas who peopled the underworld of pulp, or swinging from a rope over a crime-ridden city.

Pulp hero Doc Savage had a brief career on radio, but it is through *The Doc Savage Magazine* that he will go down in history. "To the world at large Doc Savage is a strange, mysterious figure of bronze skin and golden eyes. To his amazing co-adventurers, the five greatest men ever assembled in one group, he is a man of superhuman strength and protean genius whose life is dedicated to the destruction of evildoers." Doc took the pledge to fight evil in the March 1933 issue on the eighty-sixth floor of one of New York's tallest buildings, "a gleaming spike of steel and brick." Circulation shortly thereafter hit 200,000. To describe his five associates as amazing was a masterpiece of understatement. They included William Harper Littlejohn, the world's greatest living expert on geology and archeology, Colonel John Renwick ("Renny") whose favorite sport was pounding his massive fists through heavy paneled doors, Major Thomas J. Roberts ("Long Tom"), a physical weakling but an electrical genius, and Brigadier General Theodore Marley Brooks ("Ham"), never without his "ominous black sword cane."

Most amazing of all was Lieutenant Colonel Andrew Blodgett of Mayfair ("Monk") whose brutish exterior concealed the mind of a great scientist. The simian sidekick was covered with short hair. He had a Piltdown forehead. "Monk" was a few inches over five feet tall, yet weighed 260 pounds. His unnaturally long arms enabled him to run with "unbelievable speed." He simply doubled over and traveled by bounds, balancing himself with his long arms when he stumbled. The strange crew was rounded out by Monk's pet pig, "Habeas Corpus."

The quest for justice took the group to eerie locales—to London's Chinatown where they were surrounded by Britishers of the "right-o, old chap" variety and hissing Orientals given to such verbal chinoiserie as "velly solly, no can tell. Me likee splickee Doc Savage." They might find themselves in the Valley of the Vanished in Hidalgo, Central America, where they were surrounded by Mayan artifacts, sacrificial wells, and stone likenesses of the pagan deity Kukulkan.

Lost tribes were omnipresent. The displaced Tibetans who peopled the jungles of Antofagasta, Chile, were possessors of the accursed blue meteor. Or there were the weird inhabitants of the Pagoda of the Hands. (These worshipers of the Thousand Headed Man sported pet cobras who exuded a deadly venom that vaporized in the form of noxious gas.) None of these evildoers was a match for Doc, whose preternatural powers rivaled those of Superman.

Each story had a dénouement involving some ghastly mixup of identity. Sometimes the evil genius of a Doc Savage story proved to be as ephemeral as the Wizard of Oz. "There is no Thousand Headed Man," Copeland muttered. "That is only the name of their hideous mythical deity."

More often the surprise came with the tearing off of a mask. The serpentlike disguise of Morning Breeze, snake man of Hidalgo, revealed none other than Don Rubio Gorro who had earlier extended the welcome mat to Doc as Hidalgo's respectable Secretary of State. The evil Mo-Gwei of *Meteor Menace,* behind his purple devil mask, was actually Professor Stanley, whom Doc had first encountered as one of the accursed blue meteor's victims. (The alert reader might have been tipped off by his "beardless yellow visage" devoid of "cranial hirsuteness.")

Doc Savage's morals were as impeccable as the Lone Ranger's or of the heroines of the romantic pulps, who rarely lost their most precious possession though they had some titillatingly close calls.

In *Meteor Menace* Doc blushes when he is kissed. The Mayan Princess Monja has something of a yen for Doc in *The Man of Bronze,* but Monk discourages her. "There won't be any woman in Doc's life. If there was, you'd be the one. Doc has come nearer to falling for you than for any other girl. And some pippins have tried to snare Doc."

Poor Princess Monja, poor Mayan Maidens of the Valley of the Vanished, attractive in their shoulder mantles and knee-length girdles! If only they could have looked ahead a few years they might have saved themselves for 007.

What became of them all? With the war the temper of America changed. All of Doc Savage's magic availed him nothing against the comic book. Street and Smith put out comic versions of *Doc Savage* and *The Shadow* but they were fighting a trend. Batman was the leader of the New Breed. The last Street and Smith pulp was killed off in 1949. In the Forties *The Shadow* for the first time in his career became invisible against his will.

In the cultural cutoff that followed Pearl Harbor, it was the serial that sometimes gave one the feeling that nothing had changed. Soap opera favorites and thriller heroes were still around—acting like creatures of the Thirties—even as Harold Teen acted like a creature of the Twenties—years after the Crash.

The Lone Ranger, long visible on TV in re-runs, outlived two masked men. Earle Graser and Brace Beemer, who followed George Seaton, have both been summoned to the Last Roundup. Three Henry Aldriches were drafted.

The two leading dialect serials, *Amos 'n' Andy* and *The Goldbergs,* made it for a while on TV. For *Amos 'n' Andy* the trouble began as far back as 1942. Its Crossley rating at that time was surpassed by sixty nighttime programs. Campbell's Soup, whose output was halved during the war, was unwilling to spend $18,000,000 to sponsor the pair. Rinso picked them up in a scarcely recognizable complete-in-one-adventure form. On TV it became an all-Negro show and after 1954 the boys had to share time with guest stars on the *Amos 'n' Andy Music Hall.* More than any other radio show of the Thirties, *Amos 'n' Andy* seems as anachronistic as a burnt-cork comedian. One can hardly read the old scripts without the uneasy feeling that James Farmer is watching.

Some of Irna Phillips' serials are still visible but soap opera popularity never again achieved the popularity it enjoyed during the Depression and early Forties. Updated as it was by abortion and Dr. Kinsey, the TV version of *One Man's Family* was too pokey for the jet age.

To revisit the serials and the novelettes of the Thirties, with their hoked-up settings and their purple metaphors, is to appreciate the technical gloss of *The Twilight Zone* and *Alfred Hitchcock Presents.* The low-comedy Irish, the shuffling Negroes, the picturesque Asiatics with their impenetrable dialects sound strange to more sensitive ears.

Yet something has been lost—the whole thrilling world that opened up the sagebrush, the limehouse, the city hospital, the private nursing home One could revel in the sufferings of good women or the forbidden secrets of a slut's diary. What could rival the delights waiting between lurid covers or just a dial's distance away? They were ours for a whole day or maybe even a week as the deliverer bent over us with a stethoscope and a tongue depresser and pronounced the magic words, "You'll have to keep that child home from school, Mrs. Smith. I'm afraid it might develop into mastoid."

Chapter 5

Happy Days Are Here Again

The music of the 1930s was not one sound but many. To a housewife cooking supper and listening to the radio it might be Horace
Heidt's band playing "Ti-Pi-Tin." To a Broadway playgoer it would
be a Noel Coward character singing "Ziguener." A patron of the
old Cotton Club might remember Cab Calloway doing "Minnie
the Moocher" (and her "diamond car with the platinum wheels").
The ex-teenager out of the Thirties—middle-aged and balding today—recalls the Big Apple, Cro-Magnon version of the Watusi and
the Frug.

The sound of the early Thirties owed much to the bumpety-
bump of the Twenties. Many of the Twenties' celebrities continued
as big moneymakers throughout the decade following. Paul Whiteman's Greater Orchestra in 1928 had listed as luminaries Tom
Dorsey, Jimmy Dorsey, Henry Busse, Bing Crosby, Ferde Grofé.
Later, the Whiteman band continued in popularity despite the defection of Crosby and his Rhythm Boys. Like Whiteman, Vincent
Lopez and Leo Reisman had been around for a long time. Lopez
dated back to the days—or nights—when he could pack them into
the Grill Room of the Hotel Pennsylvania with the lure of putting
on a live radio broadcast. Reisman was well established in Boston
in the Twenties about the same time that Fred Waring had been
making a name for himself in Detroit. Reisman later moved to New

York and one of his most tangible assets was his piano player, Eddy Duchin.

Jazzmen lump Lopez, Lombardo, Reisman, and Duchin together as Mickey Mouse bands. Put more charitably, they were satisfying. The "East Side style," the "hotel sound" is dominated by the tenor sax, the romantic ballad, and the 64-bar show tune and it is still played. Danceable, unchanging, the hotel sound is guaranteed to keep the boys working. It is to be heard in hotel grills, and at debutante parties (with the occasional addition of a string section depending on how much the girl's father is willing to pay). The durability of the hotel sound may be gauged from the fact that not since the 1920s has Vincent Lopez ever been out of a job. If Guy Lombardo sounds to a jazzman like someone "drooling into a kazoo," such distinctions were not apparent to the ear of the early Thirties. Paul Whiteman, Vincent Lopez, and Leo Reisman were then all classified as leaders of "jazz bands," a definition typical of the semantic looseness of the period.

Around 1929 something new had replaced the frenetic St. Vitus dance delivery of the old-style jazz singer—the androgynous wail of the romantic tenor. This something was the "crooner." His archetype was Rudy Vallee. Romance was written on his person—trim white flannels, brown-and-white saddle shoes, and the deft maneuvering of megaphone and "sax."

Martha Gellhorn recalls the electric effect of Rudy in person at the Brooklyn Paramount. In a setting whose "riot of gilt scroll and gimcrack" shamed "the Champs de Mars," Rudy and the band were attired as doughboys. (The band was always getting into costume. At the drop or donning of a hat they obligingly traded their clean white flannels for clean gray knickers or clean blue overalls.) Suddenly Rudy picked up a megaphone, stood quietly at the corner of the stage and began to sing. The audience held its breath, adoring, as he sang democratically to the girl in the front row, to the housewife in the balcony, "I Kiss Your Hand, Madame."

"His voice," said Miss Gellhorn, "is low, pleasant, natural. It slides along. He misses the beat of the orchestra and drops into a slower tempo."

Saxophone at side, megaphone at mouth, the words drifted through the air like a caress—"I'll Get By," "Honey," "You Are the

Girl of My Dreams," "Deep Night"—"a billet doux for each gasping female in the vast theater."

Rudy Vallee appeared in department stores, jamming the aisles at 10:30 A.M. with customers who would stay on after the serenade for the white sale. He inspired literary and musical tributes: "I've heard so much of Rudy Vallee that I think he's more wonderful than Beethoven's sonatas."

The two others in the triumvirate of crooners were Russ Columbo and Bing Crosby. Columbo's "feud" with Crosby was actually a feud of the radio networks. CBS had lured Crosby away from NBC by offering him a screen test with Paramount. When John Royal of NBC learned that Crosby had a throat irritation and could not appear until Thursday of his first week, he started Russ Columbo off on Monday. This had the side effect of curing Crosby. The singing styles of Crosby and Columbo were so similar that listeners frequently couldn't tell which one of them was on the air. Columbo's death in 1934 cleared up the confusion and left the field open to the Old Groaner, who merrily whistled the bridges of his songs and whose "boo-boo-boo" added a new mating call to the language of love.

Crosby had the gift of turning all to gold. When he went to California with Paul Whiteman he was released from his contract with little regret. The amiable California climate had accentuated the proverbial Crosby laziness. Yet with *The Big Broadcast of 1932*, Bing was to emerge as a full-fledged movie personality. He parlayed the nodule on his vocal chord into a $3500-a-week radio contract and developed a distinctive singing style with a "bay-bub-do-ee-do-dee-do" beat. It was described by one critic as a "lad with his voice changing singing into a rain barrel," by another as a "glottal whoofle."

There were those who even began to suspect the authenticity of the Crosby laziness. Once his brother Everett had bought off all the people who owned a piece of Bing, the singer emerged as one of the nation's hottest properties. He cut records, poured liquid love songs into the air, ran an employment agency, a gold mine, a music publishing company, co-managed two prizefighters and a girl's baseball team, and saw to the care and feeding of the race horses which were as much of a boon to Depression humorists as the suit with two pairs of pants. Skeptics might well be tempted to ask, "What price torpor?"

The female counterpart of the crooner was known as a torch singer, and two of the best known, Helen Morgan and Ruth Etting, were holdovers from the Twenties. Helen Morgan sang ballads of thwarted love from the top of a piano—a measure necessitated by the size of her speakeasy, The House of Morgan, which was so small that there just wasn't any other place to sit. The delicate quality of her "Bill" or the little-known "Who Cares What You Have Been?" loosened the tear ducts of all around the piano.

Libby Holman was a torch singer and, like Bing Crosby, owed her good fortune to glottal mischance.

She acquired her famed huskiness when the knife slipped and slit her soft palate during the course of a tonsillectomy. Thereafter, Miss Holman carried the torch of unrequited love through the Broadway productions of *The Little Show, Three's a Crowd,* and *Great Day.* Her great numbers, "Something to Remember You By," "More Than You Know," "Body and Soul," and "Can't We Be Friends?" take one back to a bygone age of "heart balm" suits and variations on the theme of he-done-her-wrong. But Libby's major performance was to sing on the witness stand.

In November 1931 she married Smith Reynolds, heir to the $20,000,000 Reynolds tobacco fortune. On July 7, 1932, at Reynolda in Winston-Salem, North Carolina, young Reynolds was found dead on a sleeping porch, climaxing what the tabloids described as a "whoopee party." Though left-handed, he was shot through the right temple. Bloody fingerprints were found on Libby's bathroom door, and the presence of a blood-soaked towel cast some doubt on the singer's recollection of having seen him commit suicide. Libby was the victim of a lapse of memory described at the coroner's inquest as "retrograde hysterical amnesia."

Also on hand at the party had been actress Blanche Yurka, who had been teaching dramatics to Libby, and a childhood chum of Reynolds' named Albert Walker. Rumors ran rife—that both twenty-year-old Reynolds and his twenty-six-year-old wife were abnormal people, that colored blood flowed in Libby's veins, that Reynolds had a suicide mania. Franchot Tone, Howard Dietz, and other celebrities rushed forward to the singer's defense. Clifton Webb's mother said that Libby had married the suicidal scion out of pity. Tallulah Bankhead said Libby must be innocent because she was too nearsighted to hit him.

If the Reynolds trial was not exactly the house of good taste, it was certainly the scene of good theater. Libby described the brief flash of consciousness when she saw the pistol pressed against her husband's head, when she felt "the crash of the Universe falling all around me." In the improvised room where the coroner's inquest took place, Libby, a shaking, white-clad figure with rich brown skin showing through a network of lace, fainted repeatedly in her parents' arms, to be revived by smelling salts proffered by an accommodating friend.

The tabloids ran lurid headlines on some of Miss Holman's more intimate revelations. Reynolds had been a "Mate in Name Only." The marriage was apparently a duet of nobility. Libby's high-minded attitude toward carnality ("I said that's only a small part of our love. The rest of our love is so great and so big.") was matched by the equally selfless attitude of her husband. He had urged her to have an affair. "The only way for you to be happy is for me to get out of your life."

The jury probe began on August 4, 1932. Libby Holman was indicted with Mr. "Ab" Walker on suspicion of murder. It was discovered that the singer was pregnant and she took the stand in maternity widow's weeds.

As both the coroner's inquest and the actual trial were conducted as high drama, cries of "Oh, it's agony! Oh, I can't brace up. Oh, I can't, oh God!" punctuated the testimony. On November 16, 1932, the charges against both Mrs. Reynolds and Mr. Walker were dropped because of insufficient evidence. She had contributed a true-life torch ballad. The New York *Daily News* implied that the whole thing needed only orchestration. "The famous voice ended in a wail that sent a shiver down the spine. It might have been a savage cry in a colored song." Teaching dramatics to Libby Holman had been a case of bringing coals to Newcastle. One could imagine her rewriting the Frankie and Johnny saga with Frankie hiring herself a good lawyer and an "alienist" and suing Johnny for breach of promise. Libby Holman had also contributed something to the annals of unsolved crime. Before he was eclipsed by another Walker, the colorful Beau James, Ab Walker was alleged to have said, "There's some secret about this matter that I'm going to carry to my grave."

If Libby Holman sobbed of the fickle ways of men, many songwriters, baffled by the collapse of the economic system, were still musically dedicated to the economic Couéism of the Twenties. Tin Pan Alley in the early Thirties kept asserting in the face of breadlines and falling sales curves that day by day in every way things were getting better and better. Smiles and sunshine pervaded such ballads as "The Sunny Side of the Street," "Happy Days Are Here Again," and "Let a Smile Be Your Umbrella." Catchiest of all, perhaps, was "Let's Have Another Cup o' Coffee." This Irving Berlin tune was first introduced in *Face the Music,* with the cast in tea gowns and cutaways in the Automat. It served as the Maxwell House Coffee commercial in the early Depression years. Mr. Hoover's panacea for the Depression offered in song ("Mr. Herbert Hoover tells us now's the time to buy") and its effect on his political career are now a matter of melancholy history.

The true state of the country's finances was more accurately reflected in the ditty "Potatoes Are Cheaper," in Rodgers and Hart's "Ten Cents a Dance," and in the tribute to a deflated currency from a Princeton Triangle Show "Love on a Dime," which became a hit tune in 1935. There was more than poetic license to such titles in view of those newspaper ads offering $5 and $6 items for sale at 25¢ a week.

One song in particular sums up the mood of the blackest days of the Depression. Written by Jay Gorney and Yip Harburg and introduced in *Americana* in 1932, it could have been the theme of the Bonus Army marching that year on Washington. It could have expressed the sentiments of Jimmy Walker sojourning on the Riviera with Betty Compton when he got the overdue bill for his wife's shoes. It could have been written about Samuel Insull. The song: "Brother, Can You Spare a Dime."

One happy by-product of Prohibition: some of the best jazz in the world was served up along with cut alcohol and cut-rate social life. Three types of *sub-rosa* drinking opportunities flourished during Prohibition—the speakeasy, the bottle party, and the rent party. The speakeasy might be an old brownstone in New York's West Fifties where vintage scotch was brought in by truck from Long Island's Montauk Point. It might be a joint on Chicago's Rush Street or on Chicago's West Side where one could hear Louis Armstrong singing "Big Butter and Egg Man from the West" or Jimmy Noone doing "Four or Five Times."

On Chicago's South Side and in New York's Harlem interracial night life flourished. Libby Holman and her husband would start out at Tony's West Side, a speakeasy. In the wee hours they would end up somewhere in Harlem listening to a singer wailing "Stacka Lee."

The bottle party was about what its name suggests. Everybody brought their own. The rent party was a more complicated phenomenon. Rent party hosts provided cut alcohol doctored into "gin" with a grapefruit camouflage. For a two-dollar entrance fee you got all of this that you could drink, the only other outlay being (in New York) the ten-cent round-trip fare on the subway. If twenty people showed up the host would gross forty dollars, minus the gallon of alcohol which he furnished for eight dollars and cut three ways. There was usually a five-dollar fee to the piano player. (In Chicago he would play Chicago-style jazz; in the East stride or ragtime piano.) The janitor got five dollars not to relay complaints.

Some rent parties, unlicensed and extralegal, went on like a permanent crap game. The locale might be a dance studio or rehearsal hall. The host's overhead in this case included payoffs to the local policeman. Most famous of these was Jimmy Daniels' Bronze Studio in Harlem, where the jet set of the Thirties met. It was open on Fridays and Saturdays, and there one might meet such luminaries as Louise Helstrom (heroine of Carl Van Vechten's last novel, *Parties*), Kirk and Constance Askew, Fulco di Verdura (the designer of jewelry), Lorna Lindsay, Philip La Salle, who set beds afire in a succession of hotels from the Plaza to Chelsea, Philip Johnson, Douglas Parmentier, a Knopf editor, Princess Murat, Virgil Thompson (last of the expatriates to come home), the painter Eugene McCowan, and Jimmy's helper, the beautiful Blanche Dunn. There was a large English contingent headed by the then Harlem resident the Hon. Olivia Wyndham, the Negro intellectual Harold Jackman, and Stretch Johnson who danced at the Cotton Club. This glittering crowd would assemble at 11:00 CPT (Colored People's Time, which meant if you got there at 1 A.M. you were early).

Another favorite haunt was the private apartment of Clinton Moore, who was known as the Archbishop of Harlem because of his Episcopal manner. One trudged up five flights to a typical Harlem apartment. A look through a peephole, the door would swing open, and Clinton's voice would declaim, "Come in, come in. Cole's here. Nicky's coming." (Cole in this case being Porter and Nicky being Baron Nicolas de Gunzburg.)

Come 3 or 4 A.M., on to the Red Rooster, where Mae Barnes entertained and where a female impersonator named Phil did his famous number "Stop It, Joe."

Harlem in the Twenties had fostered a variety of talent—Fats Waller, Duke Ellington, and Fletcher Henderson, for example. In 1930 Duke Ellington left the Cotton Club (a favorite 1920s haunt of George Gershwin and Otto Kahn) to participate in the Amos 'n' Andy movie *Check and Double Check*. In 1931 the management was looking for a replacement. Cab Calloway had first broken into the big time at the New Regal Theatre on Chicago's South Side and had played at the Savoy Ballroom and Connie's Inn in New York. He replaced Ellington at the Cotton Club and prepared a new Cotton Club theme song, "Minnie the Moocher." He also became the inventor of a distinctive style later called "scat singing." Black hair tumbling over his eyes, he delivered a galvanic series of "hi-di-his" and "hi-di-hos." If the jazz singers of the Twenties seemed to owe their distinctive style to St. Vitus dance, Calloway appeared to be in the throes of perpetual epileptic seizure.

Calloway was the author of the "Hepster's Dictionary" which defined a girl friend as a "barbecue" and an "icky" as one who "can't collar the jive." The term "jitterbug" was said to have originated at the Cotton Club. The club's trombonist was dependent for inspiration on a mysterious nerve tonic, and when he showed up for the evening Calloway's boys would call out, "Here comes Father with his jittersauce," later shortened to "Here comes the jitterbug."

Another popular Harlem haunt of the Depression was operated

by Dickie Wells. Billie Holiday sang there and it boasted a kazoo band known as "Dickie Wells' Shim Shammers." Strange sounds emanated from metal-stringed ukuleles or "tipples." Chocolate Williams had a tipple band at the Gee Haw Stables on 132d Street. But the novelty music was outshone by the genuinely brilliant. The Savoy Ballroom had one of the best house bands of the Thirties—the Savoy Sultans. Chick Webb played there and "Stompin' at the Savoy" written by one of Webb's arrangers later soared in the repertoire of Benny Goodman. Leroy's, Connors, the Lafayette and Lincoln, the Sunday breakfast dances at Small's and the Lenox Club, remained as monuments to Harlem's golden age. Harlem spawned dances, the Lindy Hop, the Susie-Q and Truckin'. But the parade of socialites "doing" Harlem in ermine and mink was to subside with the end of Prohibition and availability of 3.2 beer.

Many of the larger clubs were forced to close after the repeal of Prohibition. Calloway's Cotton Club moved downtown and was unable to survive on Broadway and Forty-eighth Street. Slowly the focus shifted to West Fifty-second Street—to Helbocks and the Onyx, to the Club Napoleon, the Famous Door, the Three Deuces, Kelly's Stable, Leon and Eddie's, and the Hickory House. Lucky Luciano was a regular patron of the Club Napoleon, as were Ray Bolger, Morton Downey, and Fred Astaire. At the Hickory House one might meet Polly Adler, the author who would one day reminisce about another house that was not a home. The ascendancy of West Fifty-second Street continued through World War II. Small's Sunday morning breakfast dances would eventually be replaced by the Sunday afternoon Jam Sessions at Jimmy Ryan's.

Through the night life of Harlem and the West Fifties paraded great names: Jelly Roll Morton, Louis Armstrong, Sidney Bechet, Red McKenzie, Eddie Condon, Wingy Manone, Louis Prima, Count Basie, Red Norvo, Mildred Bailey, Maxine Sullivan, Ella Logan, Art Tatum, Jay C. Higginbotham, and Charlie Barnet. The future giants of swing were growing up. The Dorsey brothers (Paul Whiteman's Tom and James) were now side men. Bob Crosby, Glen Gray, and Artie Shaw were habitués, of "the Street."

On the Fifty-second Street periphery was Martin Block who, as emcee of WNEW's record program, *Make Believe Ballroom*, was just beginning to invite audiences to dance "in a mansion or small room." Later he became the most highly paid and granddaddy of all disc jockeys. Between 1935 and 1954 WNEW listeners were lured by Block into buying a reported $750,000,000 worth of products. What an obituary writer described as his "sable-smooth voice" netted his shows an estimated $10,000,000 in revenues. Club "21," which today provides the ultimate in expense-account dining, was once just another West Fifties speakeasy with a collapsible bar run by Charlie Berns and "Two Trigger" Jack Kriendler.

Among the outstanding vocalists was Jimmy Rushing, who sang with the Basie band, and the inimitable Billie Holiday who made a legendary musical career out of telling the world that she hated its guts. Waiting in the wings to sing in the Club Epicure was a lissome creature named Dorothy Lamour. Like Lana Turner's sweater, Miss Lamour's sarong brought curves unfettered by a brassiere within the limits of Breen Office morality. (She also brought to Hollywood a jungle innocence which stood her in good stead in many a tropical rock pool when the male lead explained to her that, "In land across the sea, this is how we say 'kiss.'")

The music which came out of the speakeasies and rent parties of Harlem or the Loop, and from the dives of West Fifty-second Street, might have launched a variety of styles from ragtime to swing. But it was the hills of Kentucky and the jails and cotton-fields of Louisiana which bred some of the most original spirits of all. Jimmie Rodgers—whose name is all but unknown to provincials from New York—laid the groundwork for the commercialization of country music. Woody Guthrie—himself a major influence on a later generation of rebellious young folk singers—told in a Library of Congress record how Okies and Arkies clustered around local record stores to hear Jimmie extol the California water that was sweeter than wine. Such a troubadour of the country store may have started many a flesh-and-blood Joad family on the long pilgrimage to the coast. Huddie Ledbetter ("Leadbelly")—known in the idiom of the Thirties as a "bad nigger"—also had the stuff of which legends were made.

Born in Louisiana swampland before the turn of the century, he spent his youth bumming through Texas, displaying the prowess with women which had made him a father out of wedlock at fifteen. Equipped with a pistol and twelve-string guitar he toured the country square dance circuit and acquired a repertoire of Devils Ditties, songs of exploited black workers. These were the angry outcries of men with wonderful names: Iron Jaw, Black Rider, Spark Plug, Goat Face, Breadline.

In an unpleasantness over a girl in 1917, he shot a man and was sentenced to a Texas jail. He was never out of trouble for long. Following a stabbing, he was sentenced to a Louisiana State Prison for assault and murder. John A. Lomax, a collector of folk music, was looking for material to record for the Library of Congress. (He also recorded Pete Seeger, another folk singer whose interest was sparked by those country square dances.) According to a story—considered apocryphal by Leonard Feather's *The Encyclopedia of Jazz*—Lomax recorded Leadbelly's second petition for amnesty and dispatched it to Governor O. K. Allen. In due time, once again Leadbelly was a free man.

Leadbelly's benefactor took his protégé around the country. Leadbelly chauffeured for Lomax and helped with the recording machine. Their travels together give an interesting picture of one phase of Depression social history.

Lomax had written ahead to a penitentiary in Columbia, South Carolina, for permission to record the earthy prison songs within, no matter how violent or obscene. He and Leadbelly arrived to discover that the letter had precipitated a near prison riot. The prisoners had learned through the grapevine that a man from Washington was on his way. They hoped he might cast a critical eye on the Southern prison system. They waited eagerly with long lists of injustices, in the mistaken notion that the benefits of the New Deal were about to be extended to them.

Lomax asked one convict if there was any white man he would trust. "I put a lot of money in one of their banks," the man replied, "and they shut the doors in my face." The man's mistrust extended to members of his own race.

Neither the riot nor the reforms took place.

After Leadbelly's discharge the pair visited prisons whose very names sound romantic. From places like the Redlands and Opelika, in Alabama, and Yazoo City, Mississippi, came such songs as "Shorty George," "Old Riley," "Leaving Blues," "The Rock Island Line":

*(The train left Memphis at half past nine
It made it back to Little Rock at eight forty-nine)*

Cooperative officials met them at all turns. One explained why Leadbelly, when incarcerated in Parchman, Mississippi, slept with a blinding light in his face. Mr. Lomax describes the conversation wryly. " 'The brighter the lights, the fewer guards are necessary,' said our genial host."

"Do you really whip convicts or do you use these straps only as threats?" Lomax asked.

This precipitated another obliging sociological note. "The broad strap burns but does not cut the flesh. We don't hurt the man so that he cannot at once go back to work. We need all our field hands."

Leadbelly just did not have the temperament to become an American institution. At Columbia, South Carolina, his presence was considered too inflammatory to come in contact with the already restive mob within. He was left to sulk out in the car, ill at ease among "the laws." He dedicated this unexpected interlude of leisure to an ill-fated experiment in dentistry. Lomax came back to discover the car covered with blood. Leadbelly had attempted to extract an offending molar with a pair of automobile pliers. "I couldn't get a good holt," he explained.

Things were not too much better in the enlightened North. The visiting lion of the lecture platform—Leadbelly performed at Ivy League colleges—developed a touch of schizophrenia at the discovery that he was just a nigger again when he climbed into the chauffeur's seat. He was as difficult a charge as Dylan Thomas. Lomax was disquieted by his periodic forays into the bushes in search of a likely bit of quail.

Fame went to Leadbelly's head. He and Lomax parted in bitterness. Leadbelly went back to Louisiana with a new wife but was soon back in New York—broke—seeking fame and fortune on radio.

He enjoyed something of a coterie success. (His place at Lomax's recording machine was pre-empted by another original named Iron Head.) Leadbelly played his guitar in night clubs, toured France, and swung his cane down New York streets speaking a Louisiana version of Harlem jive. He died in 1949 in New York City. He was one of those rare cosmopolites like Josephine Baker and Sidney Bechet, and from the sophistication achieved in the Southern prison system he lived to call Washington, D.C., "that bourgeois town."

To the millions of Americans who would never set foot inside the Famous Door or the Cotton Club, the sound of the Thirties was the sound of radio. Nineteen-thirties radio offered a far more varied musical diet than much of the transistorized fare which issues from today's AM sets. Anything you wanted, from Glen Gray's Casa Loma Orchestra to Shep Fields' Rippling Rhythm. A must for every big band was a radio tie-up. In 1932 Ted Weems was signed by Johnson's Wax. In 1933 Glen Gray's Casa Loma Orchestra jumped aboard the *Camel Caravan,* to be followed three years later by Benny Goodman. Lucky Strike became Kay Kyser's sponsor in 1937. With the quiz program *Kay Kyser's College of Musical Knowledge,* it was a rare radio listener who escaped the sound of that Southern accent crying, "Students!" Raleigh cigarettes signed Tommy Dorsey in 1938. Old Gold had had old dependable Fred Waring since 1933 until they switched to a faster tempo in 1938 with Artie Shaw. Chesterfield's choice was Bob Crosby, and later on Glenn Miller. The hand that waved the baton was to a large extent dependent on the hand that waved the butt.

A wide variety of musical styles made up the Atwater Kent overture. After catching Rudy Vallee on WEAF in 1933 one might tune in at 10 P.M. to Paul Whiteman. In 1934, over WEAF at 9:30, Eddy Duchin provided a musical accompaniment to Ed Wynn. At 9:00 over WJZ a note of variety was provided from the rockpile with Warden Lawes' Sing Sing Band. Nor was music confined to the late evening hours. For a Sunday afternoon *thé dansante,* there was Guy Lombardo over WABC going on to Ozzie Nelson at 7:30 over WJZ.

On a Friday night in 1937 Alice Faye was accompanied by Hal Kemp's orchestra over WABC. Later Raymond Scott might oblige with "In an Eighteenth Century Drawing Room," "Boy Scout in Switzerland," and "Toy Trumpet." In 1939 one could hear a revival of a 1917 favorite; Wee Bonnie Baker and Orrin Tucker constantly reiterated their tribute to Johnny's capacity to love, "Oh Johnny, Oh Johnny, Oh!"

At any time during the decade you might tune in unexpectedly on Clyde McCoy's "Sugar Blues." His was one of the more fortunate orchestras—like Orrin Tucker's—which could have saved itself the trouble of recording more than one tune.

The musicality of the Thirties, especially its pop tune consciousness, was exemplified in one program.

How artfully the tension was built up! On Friday afternoon a Brinks armored car would collect from three or four key sources information culled from vendors of records, sheet music, and—after 1939—"automatic coin machines" (jukeboxes, in the vernacular). The highly classified data was held in secrecy until the show by the august accounting firm of Price Waterhouse & Co. Then, at last, the Lucky Strike Hit Parade was introduced by the theme music "Happy Days Are Here Again," rendered in the businessman's bounce tempo so dear to the heart of American Tobacco's George Washington Hill. There was a mélange of lesser beer hit tunes with No. 8, No. 15, and No. 6 scrambled in random progression. A couple of Lucky Strike "extras" would be played and soon the gibberish of the Lucky Strike tobacco auctioneer, climaxing in the cry "Sold American!"

Then a roll of drums: "And now the top three tunes in the nation . . ." The whole family would sit tuned to WABC waiting breathlessly for the unveiling of No. 1. We waited through No. 3, then No. 2 . . . and at last . . . "Here it is, the top song in the country. Number one on your Lucky Strike Hit Parade."

After all this the result generally came as no surprise to anyone. "The seventeenth straight week on the Hit Parade . . . eighth week in first place . . . 'Deep Purple.'" Indeed the unfortunate script writers had a challenge far knottier than any set down to Shakespeare or Chaucer: to impart an air of tingling anticipation to the endless reappearance of "The Merry-Go-Round Broke Down."

The radio bands of the Thirties were generous to a fault in materializing in the flesh. A 1940 issue of *Downbeat* listed approximately eight hundred dance bands playing hotels and ballrooms—Denver's Rainbow Gardens, Chicago's Aragon, or any of the Trianon ballrooms in Cleveland, Los Angeles, or Seattle. Horace Heidt, Phil Harris, Ray Noble, and the ubiquitous Dorothy Lamour turned up on hotel roofs all over the country. As Vincent Lopez and his boys played gamely in bathing suits at Atlantic City on a half-submerged raft their cheerful expressions implied that it was all in the day's work. When Frank Sinatra severed his relations with Tommy Dorsey, he had been on the road so long that he had to be reintroduced to his family.

On certain northerly islands the young male seal does battle with the old male seal to see who will emerge as Chief of the Rock. The showdown between Crosby and Vallee came with the 1935 *World-Telegram* Radio Poll. The poll named Bing Crosby as the top male singer. Rudy Vallee ranked third among "favorite programs," coming after Jack Benny and Fred Allen. Significantly, nobody in 1935 mentioned Rudy's singing.

In 1932 Vallee had inaugurated a new art form, the variety show. His hour-long broadcasts over WEAF became a regular feature of the Depression scene. He conducted interviews with Freddy Bartholomew, Mae West, Grace Moore, Lupe Velez, Dr. Allan Dafoe, Bea Lillie, Marie Dressler, the Grand Duchess Marie of Russia, Max Baer, and Heywood Broun. He launched such talents as Edgar Bergen and Charlie McCarthy, Ed Wynn, Alice Faye, and a comer from the stage version of *Roberta* named Bob Hope. The old seal had wisely realized that his days as a singing sex menace were numbered.

Bing Crosby had also diversified. When he laid "laughing siege" (according to *Collier's*) to the heart of one Wilma Winifred Wyatt, she would at first have none of him because she considered him an incorrigible playboy. She relented after brother Everett's adroit management of Bing's financial affairs imbued the Groaner with a hitherto lacking sense of direction. "Dixie Lee," as she called herself, was still a bigger name than Bing at the time of their marriage. A newspaper account of the event was headlined: "Well-Known Fox Movie Star Marries Bing Croveny." The relative billings were soon reversed. Dixie gave up her career to bear Crosby four sons.

If Dixie had once felt that they could not live on laughs alone she was soon to change her mind. As a screen personality Bing was evolving. His early roles had been those of a romantic collegian— complete with wide pants, snappy roadsters, snappy chatter, and the inevitable sax. He had co-starred with Marion Davies in *Going Hollywood,* which introduced the hit song "Temptation." He appeared in *College Humor* and *Too Much Harmony*. Vis-à-vis Carole Lombard in *We're Not Dressing* in 1934, the new Bing began to emerge. Carole played a spoiled heiress in a story based loosely (very) upon J. M. Barrie's *The Admirable Crichton*. It had a hit song, "She Walks Like You."

The dialogue was what we remember, perhaps erroneously, as crisp.

"I want to marry you, but first I want to have a drink."

"What are you going to do with it, have it stuffed?"

"No, I want to marry it. Then I'll divorce it and marry you."

If lines like this made poor Barrie cringe in his grave, Bing's performance established him as a comedian.

Later came *Mississippi* (1935), *Rhythm on the Range* (1936), and *Pennies from Heaven* (1936). *Waikiki Wedding* (1937) introduced a song called "Sweet Leilani"—and that Club Epicure veteran, Dorothy Lamour. *Sing You Sinners* (1938) presented what was coming to be Bing's public face—"a lazy, happy-go-lucky, undependable, but good-hearted fellow who is mad about horses."

He began to dress the part: Hawaiian shirts open at the collar, battered felt hat worn outdoors and in, slacks that had never felt the touch of an iron, and always a generous mouthful of gum. His singing style for a time seemed to consist of shifting the gum.

Not content with this, he out-Valleed Vallee with a variety program of his own. On the *Kraft Music Hall,* he interviewed Leopold Stokowski, Lotte Lehmann, José Iturbi, Pat O'Brien, and, yes, Dorothy Lamour. He clowned it up with bazooka-playing Bob Burns and displayed a gift for the ad lib which stood him in good stead—as when guest star Jackie Cooper dropped his drumsticks on the floor. "Hold the phone," said Bing, "there's been a nasty accident."

As an emcee he had an easier manner than Rudy Vallee, who took his mission hard. "I saw courage and pettiness and laughter," Vallee reminisced, "and tears and embarrassment. I even saw the beginning of a romance, and once on an unforgettable night the end of a life." To turn Rudy into a wit, gag writers were forced to play largely upon his parsimony. The need for their services was apparent when Mr. Vallee discussed his life goals in *Pictorial Review* in 1930. An article, "Did College Help Me?" gave his revealing view of the aims of higher education: "My biology has helped me in my mode of living through the knowledge and understanding of my physical self which it gave me." Spanish, too, had come in handy, helping the singer "in the vocal rendition of several tangoes."

He was no match for Bing, who, according to J. C. Furnas, combined something "from the dead pan school of slapstick comic and something from the insouciant ogle of the professional masher, to produce an effect of being congenitally at home and sure of himself everywhere. Bing's language became a marvel of prolixity, a polysyllabic parfait."

Someone less sure of himself would have hesitated to play opposite such a veteran ad-libber as Bob Hope. Yet he was a perfect foil for Hope in a series of delightful pictures of which *Road to Singapore* and *Road to Zanzibar* were the first. The latter found Hope as Fearless Frazier, a carnival performer who was constantly called upon to wrestle an octopus or get shot out of a cannon. Their companion on the safari was, of course, Miss Lamour. Their progress through the jungle was illustrated with an animated map, through which the voice of a commentator spoke. "Week after week they plod onward with nothing to guide them but the stars by night and the sun by day . . . And so our safari is forced to rest hoping to regain their strength with generous helpings of wart hog stew."

Hope demurs as Crosby urges him to wrestle an octopus. "I'm trying to make you famous," Crosby explains. "People will write books about you." Hope retorts, "Well I know three words that won't be in 'em: 'ripe old age.'"

There was one other mover and shaker who, perhaps more than anyone else, embodied the spirit of the Thirties, the polished jazz age.

In the early years the bandleader Benny Goodman was principally noted for his rendition of "The Japanese Sandman" and for his appearances on National Biscuit Company's *Let's Dance* show. He did one-night stands across the country and often was plagued by the words "What's the matter, can't you boys play any waltzes?" The breakthrough occurred in the Palomar Ballroom in Los Angeles on August 21, 1935, where he deafened himself to the "Tales from the Vienna Woods" faction and used Fletcher Henderson arrangements. The crowd went wild, and from then on Benny went places. There were similar triumphs in the Congress Hotel in Chicago and in the Mad-hatten Room of the Hotel Pennsylvania in New York. In the winter of 1937–38 in New York's Paramount Theatre a crowd formed at 6 A.M. At eight the doors opened to admit 3634 youngsters given to such expletives as "in the groove," "killer diller," "solid sender," "spank the skin," and "swing it, Benny, feed it to me." Next time it was necessary to play al fresco. Twenty-three thousand young fans expressed a similar ardor at Randall's Island. Adolph Zukor, who had been responsible for the Paramount's $17,000,000 domed lobby, veined marble colonnades, its story-high Hall of Nations, its walnut-paneled Elizabethan Room, its Tea Gallery, its Marie Antoinette Room and its Peacock Promenade, might have thanked his lucky stars that Benny's second coming took place out of doors.

The talent arrayed beneath the Goodman baton was formidable. The band's arrangements were done by Fletcher Henderson, Horace Henderson, and Benny Carter. There were solos by Goodman, Bunny Berigan, and Jess Stacy, as well as Gene Krupa's drumming, and vocals at various times by Helen Forest, Helen Ward, Martha Tilton, and Maxine Sullivan.

Others in the Goodman *Who's Who* included Harry James, Ziggy Elman, Cootie Williams, Vernon Brown, Billy Butterfield, Claude Thornhill, Dave Barbour, Slam Stewart, and Joe Bushkin.

The Benny Goodman trio, consisting of Goodman, Krupa, and Teddy Wilson, was expanded to a quartet in 1936 with the addition of Lionel Hampton. In October 1939 the quartet became a sextet. By this time there were teenagers jitterbugging on tabletops, the ultimate cachet of a Carnegie Hall concert. The defection of many Goodman personnel was almost inevitable; they had become such celebrities in their own right that they flew the nest to try their wings. Lionel Hampton, Teddy Wilson, Gene Krupa, and Harry James formed their own bands with varying degrees of success.

Goodman was a mover and a shaker for many reasons. He made swing respectable—selections from his 1937–38 Carnegie Hall Concerts have become classic on LP. He was the first to incorporate Negro artists into his group. He inspired a whole new school of "swing" musicians. The Fletcher Henderson band had paved the way for Goodman. Now a whole array of leaders and vocalists followed in his footsteps. There were Jimmy Dorsey and Helen O'Connell. There were Larry Clinton and Bea Wain. There were the Woody Herman band and the Jan Savitt band. Benny's chief competitor was Tommy Dorsey, "Sentimental Gentleman of Swing," known best for his great records "Who" and "Marie." Artie Shaw was once a serious contender for the Goodman crown with "Nightmare," "Begin the Beguine," and "Lover Come Back to Me." Shaw —briefly with "Summit Ridge Drive" and "Pompton Turnpike"—was, like Glenn Miller, a producer of the "log cabin sound" (a sound which issued from Frank Daily's Meadowbrook and other roadhouses in New Jersey). In December 1939, confused by an excess of success, he abandoned his band and fled to Mexico. Later he tried to outdo the Philharmonic with a huge orchestra, complete with strings. Then followed a series of disastrous marriages and a career as a Hollywood intellectual.

With Benny Goodman, popular music of the Thirties moved out of the speakeasy age forever. Gone were the throbbing-voiced torch singers, the white-flanneled megaphoned practitioners of the varsity drag. In the minds of an entire generation there would be the vivid memories of Goodman hits: "Christopher Columbus," "The Organ Grinder's Swing," "Sing, Sing, Sing," "Stompin' at the Savoy," "Clarinet Marmalade," "Bugle Call Rag," "And the Angels Sing," "I Hadn't Anyone 'Til You." The man who looked like someone's friendly tailor had a quality possessed by few popular entertainers. He could sit in as comfortably at the Philharmonic as with his own sextet. In 1940 he recorded (with the composer on piano and Josef Szigeti on violin) Bartok's "Contrasts for Violin, Clarinet, and Piano," now a collectors' prize. (A cat really had to watch himself. If he wasn't careful this Pied Piper might lead him to Bach and, to paraphrase Helen Trent, even beyond.) On wind-up record players on beaches and in rumpus rooms from Maine to California the golden clarinet was heard over and over until its tones were drowned out at last by a roar of surface scratch. The scratches reached a crescendo on one of the best swing records ever made. The A-side was "Don't Be That Way"; the B-side, "One O'Clock

Jump." It was probably the greatest bargain in history—the sound of the Thirties in a nutshell for thirty-five cents.

The King of Swing didn't have it all his own way. Pitted against him were such reliable producers of the hotel sound as Sammy Kaye, Horace Heidt and his Musical Knights, Jan Garber, Kay Kyser, and Wayne King, and the indestructible Lombardo still purveying the "sweetest music this side of heaven." But in the battle between the swing bands and the sweet bands, the King of Swing had the edge. There was at least one notable capitulation in the enemy camp. A mid-Thirties recording of "Tumbling Tumbleweeds" and "Diane" showed a new face of a man whose group suddenly became "Vincent Lopez and his Suave Swing Orchestra."

Into the sweet-swing controversy of the late Thirties the flag of truce was finally raised by a musician who would dominate the early Forties. Glenn Miller was an amiable young man who had played and arranged for Red Nichols in 1929–30, for the Dorsey brothers in 1934, and for Ray Noble in 1935. While with Noble he had discovered the style which made him famous, described by Leonard Feather in the *Encyclopedia of Jazz* as "reed section voicing," the clarinet playing the melody over four saxes. In 1938 Miller began making records for Bluebird with a group that included Hal McIntyre, Tex Beneke, and vocalists Ray Eberle and Marion Hutton. The group reached vast popularity with "Sunrise Serenade," "Moonlight Serenade," "Stairway to the Stars," "Tuxedo Junction," "In the Mood," and "Little Brown Jug."

With the lead clarinet as his trademark, he added brasses with derbies, and repetitive riffs. The resulting sound which emanated from Frank Daily's Meadowbrook and the Glen Island Casino was as rich and liquid as an ice-cream soda. It brought the curtain down on the Thirties. Glenn Miller volunteered for the Army, disappeared on a flight from England to France, and was never seen again. He had enjoyed a tremendous vogue among those who three years before might have jitterbugged to the music of Benny. Yet in 1940–41 he had won the *Downbeat* award for the top sweet band. The *Encyclopedia of Jazz* says, "In later years . . . his main interest was the achievement of the widest possible public appeal for his orchestra." For Leonard Feather the difference between a dance band arrangement and a jazz arrangement of the same tune lay in the rhythmic interpretation and the passages left over for improvisation. Glenn Miller left precious little room for improvisation. Not only were his arrangements unchanging, he sometimes even played pieces in the same order night after night. When you latched onto a good thing, stick with it, was the Miller idea, and little was to be gained by giving the alto sax his head. Yet the Miller band had shown that it was possible to be sweet without being square, that there might be room near The Great Bandstand in the Sky for those who complained, "What's the matter? Can't you boys play a waltz?" Blessed are the peacemakers, and Glenn Miller was the most amiable of all.

Miller, Goodman, et al. had a lot to work with.

A veteran of the 1930s remarks, "We *expected* it—*every year* a new batch of wonderful tunes." If the Thirties was the Goodman era or the Crosby era, it was no less the Gershwin era, the era of Cole Porter, Rodgers and Hart, Jerome Kern, and Irving Berlin, the Ellington era.

Duke Ellington had come a long way since the old rent party days. In the early Thirties he had become a radio personality when Ted Husing introduced him as "Dukie." In the Thirties he hit his stride as a composer with "Mood Indigo" (1930), "Sophisticated Lady" (1933), "Solitude" (1934), "In a Sentimental Mood" (1935), and "I Let a Song Go Out of My Heart" in 1938. The Ellington band provided the composer with a talented group of built-in interpreters: Barney Bigard, Cootie Williams, Johnny Hodges, and vocalist Ivie Anderson. The addition of arranger Billy Strayhorn in 1939 inaugurated one of the band's richest periods. Strayhorn's "Take the A-Train" became the Ellington theme song. Ivie Anderson gave what was considered her best recorded performance, "I Got It Bad and That Ain't Good." "Harlem Airshaft" and "Jack the Bear," original compositions by the Master, struck more of a chord with jazz people than his more popular works. Unlike the Goodman band, members of the Ellington group rarely defected for better offers. Ellington had a marvelous talent for keeping the help happy.

Ellington's unique arrangements were due to a blend of tonal colors, with members of the band contributing individual improvisations, and with the timbre of each instrument essential to the overall effect. Ellington was also the inventor of the "jungle sound" achieved through the use of mutes. Even in the hands of a Freddy Martin, these sultry roulades (sometimes achieved with toilet plungers) spelled just one thing—S-E-X.

Ellington's early training at the Cotton Club had seemingly prepared him for anything that might come up. It had been his function to furnish background music for lurid production numbers in which American heiresses were abducted by sheiks, and white goddesses ruled African tribes with bullwhips. Cutting his teeth on such sophisticated subject matter might account for the impression of poise he still gives in later life. It would seem that there is no situation extant or imaginable that would find Edward Kennedy Ellington not in control.

George and Ira Gershwin introduced Ethel Merman to Broadway in 1930 in *Girl Crazy* with a song perfectly suited to her boisterous talents—"I Got Rhythm." They turned their hands to political satire in 1931 in *Of Thee I Sing*, with "Love Is Sweeping the Country" and a parody of a hopeful Hooverism, "Posterity Is Just Around the Corner." The high point of George Gershwin's career came in 1935 with *Porgy and Bess,* but even between this time and his death from a brain tumor in 1937, he turned out such solid hits as "Love Walked In," "They Can't Take That Away From Me," and "Let's Call the Whole Thing Off."

The latter two songs were composed for those dazzlers, Rogers and Astaire. Gershwin was not the only one who aided their fancy footwork.

Jerome Kern had been known in the Twenties for *Show Boat;* for *The Cat and the Fiddle* in 1931. *Music in the Air* seemed in 1932 like a fresh and charming story of love-in-the-edelweiss, though a revival some twenty-odd years later showed those Alps to be capped with the purest saccharine. The show did have some pretty tunes: "In Egern on the Tegern See" and "I've Told Ev'ry Little Star." In the late Thirties he contributed "All the Things You Are" to the Kern-Hammerstein hit *Very Warm for May.* However, it was for *Roberta* that he is best remembered. The film version featuring Rogers and Astaire had a delightful Fred Astaire specialty, "I Won't Dance," and "Lovely to Look At" written with the aid of Dorothy Fields and Jimmy McHugh. "Smoke Gets in Your Eyes" from *Roberta* is described by Sigmund Spaeth as a technically perfect piece of popular music. "Yesterdays," from the same show, is also a classic—having found its way into the repertoire of Billie Holiday, a singer many light years removed from Egern on the Tegern See.

Irving Berlin produced the music for *As Thousands Cheer* in 1933, before taking off for Hollywood. He contributed the popular "Easter Parade" and in "Heat Wave" succeeded in making Ethel Waters' seat wave.* In Hollywood he did some of his best work for Rogers and Astaire: "Cheek to Cheek" and "Isn't This a Lovely Day —to Be Caught in the Rain?" for *Top Hat* (1935); "Let's Face the Music and Dance" for *Follow the Fleet* (1936). "Get Thee Behind Me Satan" from the latter picture was sung by a newcomer called Harriet Hilliard. She was introduced to the movie public in the familiar role of the ugly duckling transformed into a lovely swan by the simple act of removing her eyeglasses. Later, presumably, she removed them regularly for Ozzie Nelson—for she became in rapid succession his singer, his wife, and parent of David and Ricky who appeared in the Fifties and Sixties on TV in *Ozzie and Harriet*.

Berlin's 1937 hits included "This Year's Kisses" and "I've Got My Love to Keep Me Warm." By this time Fred Astaire was indelibly typed as a pencil-slim figure in top hat and tails. As a down-and-out gambler in *Swingtime* (1936) he effected what surely must have been the most elegant of Depression economies—wandering around for a week through the streets of New York in white tie, quite unnoticed in midafternoon. Another Depression measure effected in this picture was the gambit of asking strangers for change and walking away without handing over the quarter or the ten-dollar-bill. On celluloid, at least, this proved effective in doubling one's money.

In "This Can't Be Love," the emotion which for so long had

---

* At the beginning of the 1930s the Negro entertainer stopped making race records and appearing in all-Negro shows off Broadway. Among the pioneering Negro performers who appeared *on* Broadway in the company of whites were Adelaide Hall and Ethel Waters. Among the pioneering integrated shows was *As Thousands Cheer* in 1933, starring besides Ethel Waters, Marilyn Miller and Clifton Webb. When Miss Waters started that heat wave she made history in more ways than one.

rhymed with dove was introduced without the usual medical symptoms—"no sobs, no sorrows, no sighs." Other Rodgers and Hart hits included "Where or When?", the title song from *I Married an Angel*, and "I Didn't Know What Time It Was." In 1939 there were three Rodgers and Hart hits on Broadway—*I Married an Angel*, *Too Many Girls*, and *The Boys from Syracuse*. The pair seemed to have a complete monopoly on the Great White Way. At least one of their tunes has survived into the yeah, yeah, yeah. "Dancing on the Ceiling," originally written for the Jack Buchanan-Jessie Matthews movie *Evergreen*, is currently being served up on records.

The Kit Marlowe of the music world was Cole Porter. Porter had contributed such works as "Night and Day," "Easy to Love," "I've Got You Under My Skin," and two classics from *Anything Goes*: "I Get a Kick Out of You," and "You're the Top." In 1938, in *Leave It to Me*, a new star was launched when Mary Martin in fur jacket and little else came out before the footlights and sang Cole Porter's "My Heart Belongs to Daddy." Porter's mighty line was a compound of unexpected rhyme and sly innuendo, as in the big number from *Red, Hot and Blue* in 1936, "A Little Skipper from Heaven Above."

> *I'm about to become a mother*
> *I'm only a girl not a boy*
> *Years ago I dressed up as my brother*
> *And went rolling down to Rio, ship ahoy.*
>
> *Though it hurts me to leave you me hearties*
> *Still you must understand, it was love*
> *And I'm about to give birth*
> *   to the sweetest thing on earth*
> *A little skipper from Heaven above. . . .*

If these lyrics seem among lesser examples of Porter they seem so only to those who never heard them served up by history's unlikeliest maternity case—Jimmy Durante, or the duet sung by Bert Lahr and Ethel Merman in *Du Barry Was a Lady* (1939):

> *Do you use the breast stroke dear?*
> *Kindly tell me so*
> *Yes, I use the breast stroke, dear*
> *But in the morning, no!*

Johnny Mercer was another personable and witty lyricist— author of "Jeepers Creepers" and the Goodman 1939 hit "And the Angels Sing." "I'm an Old Cowhand" from the film *Rhythm on the Range* presented a cowpoke whose "legs ain't bowed" and whose "cheeks ain't tanned" a "riding fool who is up to date" who knows "every trail in the Lone Star State" from riding them all "in a Ford V-8—yippee-yi-yo-ki-yay."

Billy Hill in "The Last Round-Up" hit upon an extraordinarily catchy melody. His view of such institutions as Buffalo Bill, General Custer, and the Boss in the Sky was reverent.

There was Harold Rome's typical topical type song, "F.D.R. Jones," and from the Garment Workers' show *Pins and Needles,* his two witty tributes to the secular religion of the Depression: "Sing Me a Song with Social Significance" and "One Big Union for Two."

Exotic imports included Kurt Weill with his haunting "September Song" from *Knickerbocker Holiday* and Noel Coward with delightful musical hits to accompany such crisp bits of dialogue as "Women should be struck regularly—like gongs," or as Elyot (with a *y*) said to Amanda (with three a's), "There isn't an inch of you I don't know, remember—and want."

There was—one regrets to admit—a darker side of the coin. Periodically the Thirties produced the nuisance song—"The Music Goes 'Round and Around" in 1935, "The Flat Foot Floogie" in 1938, and "Three Little Fishies" in 1939—which will live forever in infamy—

> *Three little fiddies in the itty bitty poo*
> *Three little fiddies and the mama fishie too*
> *"Fwim" said the mama fish,*
> *"Fwim if you can."*
> *And they fwam and they fwam right over the dam.* *

Yet it was only fair, if only for balance. There was such an embarrassment of riches: "Stormy Weather" by Ted Koehler and Harold Arlen in 1933; "Georgia on My Mind" by Stuart Gorrell and Hoagy Carmichael in 1930, "Rockin' Chair" by Carmichael in

* "Three Little Fishies (Itty Bitty Poo)," by Saxie Dowell. Copyright © 1939 by Joy Music, Inc. Reprinted by permission.

1930, and "Lazybones" by Johnny Mercer and Hoagy Carmichael in 1933; the Astaire dancing special of 1934, "The Continental," by Herb Magidson and Con Conrad; Sammy Cahn and Saul Chaplin's "Shoe Shine Boy" in 1936. Besides such magnificent miscellany, there was the yearly output of George and Irving and Jerome and Noel and Kurt and Cole and the Duke. And it never even occurred to us that there was anything unusual in the fact that they all just happened to be around at once.

Most of the vocalists who delivered the hit tunes of the Thirties played second fiddle to the band. There were exceptions. The endless sister acts, for instance: the Boswell Sisters, the Pickens Sisters, the Andrews Sisters. Ella Fitzgerald may have been considered more of a draw than Chick Webb. Mildred Bailey may have dominated Red Norvo. One could not imagine Hal Kemp's band divorced from Skinnay Ennis, the engaging vocalist who always sounded perpetually in need of oxygen. But when Ivie Anderson, Martha Tilton, or Maxine Sullivan, Ella Logan, Bob Eberly, or Ray Eberle got up to sing they were listened to and liked, but it was clear that the cash customers had come primarily to hear Ellington, Goodman, Lombardo, Dorsey, or Glenn Miller.

Then along came the mover and shaker who would change all this. At first Frank Sinatra was part of the system. When Harry James broke away from Benny Goodman his roster of talent included Connie Haines and the wraithlike Sinatra. The James band struggled to stay afloat. Soon, James gave the boy his freedom to go over to Tommy Dorsey, an error of judgment which both Dorsey and James would joke about later.

Sinatra, born in Hoboken, New Jersey, had been playing the ukulele when Rudy Vallee was still The Vagabond Lover and when Crosby was still in his "boo-boo-boo" period. Sinatra took up singing because Crosby made it look so easy.

When he worked for Tommy Dorsey, Sinatra inhabited the special hell of the featured vocalist. *Life* described him as "one of a group of young men who sat up on the bandstand with their arms folded, until, at a signal from Dorsey, they would suddenly rise like trained seals and walk to the center of the stage. Locking arms and grinning inanely at the cash customers, they would make with the doleful prediction that they would never smile again."

"We were like puppets and Tommy was the guy who pulled the strings," Sinatra told *Life*'s interviewer. Soon, however, the Pied Pipers were piping as background to Sinatra's solos. It was not long before the soloist yearned to solo without benefit of Dorsey. He quit Dorsey in November 1942. The scrappy young boxer (whose proudest possession was a gold identification tag bearing the name of a heavyweight fighter named Tami Mauriello) was not one to have someone else pull the strings for long.

To Dorsey, he owed his unique styling. Sinatra had heard the Sentimental Gentleman at the Roseland Ballroom. Dorsey's phrasing had inspired him to learn to breathe in the middle of a note with his mouth open. "I figured if he could do that phrasing with his horn, I could do it with my voice," said the singer. George Frazier in describing the Sinatra style remarked of Frankie, "He ties the phrases together with moans." The Sinatra style even today reminds one of that bygone era when singers *enunciated*.

Sinatra was a personality in direct apostolic succession to Vallee and Crosby. All three of them shared the quality of sincerity. His goddesses included, of all people, Mabel Mercer—whom he considered to be the mother of us *all*. Sinatra appeared to be utterly convinced that a kiss was still a kiss, a sigh was still a sigh.

The three of them made vocal love with the same admirable impartiality. "Give us this tall slender boy," wrote Martha Gellhorn in 1929, "and this gentle voice that makes love so democratically to everyone." She was speaking of Vallee. Years later the crowd lined up in front of the CBS studio to catch a glimpse of Sinatra rehearsing for the Lucky Strike Hit Parade, and the girls jockeyed for position in front of Benny Goodman's old stamping ground, the Paramount Theatre. Sinatra, like Vallee, had a way of convincing a love-starved teenager that this-number-is-all-for-you-baby—a musical dessert that made the long hours in line worth while.

Like Crosby, Sinatra's dress was casual, but it was different. He affected tousled hair, bulging shirt front, dinner jacket "that would horrify Lucius Beebe." He liked sports jackets, sweaters and Glen Urquart plaid topcoats, large knotted four-in-hands and boyish bow ties. Part of his success came from the fact that he looked and talked like a teenager. Sinatra-isms quoted by *Life:* those kids were *"so* wonderful"—Harry James *"so* sensational." Anything he enjoyed was *"so* terrific."

The "Frank Swoonatra Clubs," the banners bearing the strange device "Semper Sinatra" are beyond the scope of this study, for it was not till the early Forties that Sinatra pulled ahead of Old Seal Crosby in the *Downbeat* and *Metronome* polls to become the nation's No. 1 cause of truancy. He discovered that he had paid dearly for his release from his vows. The horse trader Dorsey had a claim to 33⅓ percent of his earnings. Here Sinatra differed markedly from one of the older seals. There was no record that anyone ever owned a piece of Rudy Vallee.

A final word about Sinatra, the sex menace. There had always been a comic quality to Bing Crosby's oglings. One felt that acquiescence on the girl's part would send him hightailing it back to Dixie and the kids. A mother sensed instinctively that Rudy Vallee was the sort of boy who would kiss her daughter good night at the door. (One could imagine him wrestling manfully with those hormones he learned about at Yale.) No parent in her right mind could look with equanimity on the hollow Sinatra cheeks, sunken eyes, large ears, which gave the wartime adolescent her first taste of the mother-instinct. Even mother herself might suppress the feeling, "I certainly would like to fatten that boy up."

"I look hungry," said Sinatra. "I'm a bedroom singer." If Vallee was the boy who kissed your daughter at the door, Frankie was the boy she would go upstairs with.

With Sinatra the sound of the Thirties blended in with the sound of the Forties. The prosperity which had been just around the corner finally arrived, though not quite as Mr. Hoover had imagined. As Sinatra wowed them at the Riobamba—or sang the hit song from *Casablanca,* "As Time Goes By"—the Thirties were already history, a bygone day when a bass was to be slapped, a trumpet to be muted, and a wine cellar to be entered judiciously when a wall rolled aside at the touch of a straightened-out coat hanger.

Chapter 6

It's Fun to Be Fooled

The magazine and newspaper reader of the Thirties read warnings on all sides. "Wendy was a washout. Men treated her coldly because of her constant colds . . ." "Hired, admired, fired." "Let's face the truth about underarm perspiration odor." "Trust no substitute because it looks like Kotex." Occasionally the ads of the Thirties struck a note of heroism—the woman on a "difficult day" whose face was contorted with pain and indecision: "The calendar said 'Give in.' Midol said 'Go on.'"

They paraded through our consciousness like figures in a morality play. There was the candidate for Iodent #2—"Teeth Hard to Bryten". Iodent #1 for "Teeth Easy to Bryten" was "ideally adapted for the tiny teeth and tender gums of children." There was the woman with a square of film over her mouth which only Pepsodent could eradicate. There was the girl who had never been kissed until she overheard friends discussing her yellow teeth and learned about Kolynos. There was the lissom debutante: "She's lovely. She's engaged. She uses Ponds." Pitted against her were rivals with the Camay complexion, and the Woodbury Soap girl who had "the skin you love to touch." There was the man kicking a cop in the pants in euphoria on "the morning after taking Carter's Little Liver Pills."

Certain campaigns added clichés to the English language. Even today "the pause that refreshes" means Coca-Cola. Yet some gnaw annoyingly at the edges of consciousness, like an old saw which one eventually traces to Shakespeare. Such a saying was "something new has been added." The source in this case was not Shakespeare but a copywriter's reference to the "prized imported tobacco from the Eastern Mediterranean" added to the choice blends in Old Gold cigarettes. The other three of the big four cigarette companies each had a distinctive slogan: "They satisfy" (Chesterfields), "It's toasted" (Lucky Strike), "I'd walk a mile for a Camel" (Camels). There were variations—Chesterfield packages pouring out of a comely cheerleader's megaphone. "Do you smoke the cigarette that satisfies?" the copy would inquire. A picture of a dancing-eyed colleen would be captioned "When Irish eyes are smiling, they satisfy."

Camels made the most energetic departure from the one-line slogan utilizing the comic strip form with a great deal of copy and a plethora of personal endorsements. "Seeing is believing" ran a 1939 Camel ad on the back cover of *Life,* showing daring circus aerialist Everett White discussing the merits of Camels, with special reference to their slow burning and their long ash.

If the gnawing feeling persisted that smoking might be bad for one there was "Larruping Lou Gehrig" to disprove it. Fresh from having hit four home runs in one day, he was lighting up a Camel. "After a good man-sized meal that little phrase 'Camels set you right' covers the way I feel."

Testimonials were elicited from such diverse personalities as "Miss Travis Lander—Cashier," Rose Winslow, Fred Jacoby, the outboard motorboat champion, and golfers Gene Sarazen and Johnny Farrell, who praised Camels' merits as a *digestif.* In those unfiltered pre-carcinoma days, advertisers hinted that smoking might actually be beneficial to the system. "For Digestion's Sake Smoke Camels." Camels were painted as being easier on a mysterious biological enclave known as the T-Zone—as being beneficial to the nerves—as not causing shortness of breath. "It takes healthy nerves to play championship bridge" was one ad showing Camel smokers successfully engaged in various nerve-wracking occupations. Magazine readers were urged to see how their own nerves measured up by testing how long they could point at a spot on the wall without trembling. The ads never suggested what to do when a

Camel smoker took the test and proved to have a bad case of the screaming-meemies.

Endorsements from athletic socialites were highly desirable because they combined in one person blue blood and good wind. Among those who knew "the thrill of playing the game and playing it well" the list was impressive. Sailing, tennis-playing, flying aristocrats listed by city of origin included Mrs. Powell Cabot and Mrs. J. Gardner Coolidge II from Boston, Mrs. Louis Swift, Jr., from Chicago; Mrs. Nicholas Biddle and Mrs. Anthony Drexel III represented the City of Brotherly Love. Mrs. Ogden Hammond, Mrs. Howard F. Whitney, and Mrs. John D. Rockefeller spoke up for New York. In some cases an emolument from the Camel Company meant the difference between cutting one's own zinnias or keeping the gardener, although the latter two hardly seemed to be faced with such decisions.

One Camel campaign featured a series of impressive magic tricks—sawing a girl in half, levitation, and so forth. A diagrammed how-to explanation of the trick followed. The headline for this series might have served as a watchword for the entire advertising industry—"It's fun to be fooled, but it's more fun to know."

As the decade of the Thirties opened, the Lucky Strike Company coined the catch phrase "Reach for a Lucky Instead of a Sweet."

Candy manufacturers cried "foul." A Lucky Strike ad which appeared in the *Literary Digest* on March 8, 1930, gave one of those thinly veiled slaps at a rival product which we see today with "Brand X" and "the 70-cent spread." The art work showed a svelte woman. Behind her was the lumpy silhouette of a figure that could charitably be described as full. An ominous quotation from Thomas Campbell proclaimed: "Coming Events Cast Their Shadows Before."

> Avoid that future shadow by refraining from over-indulgence, if you would maintain the modern figure of fashion.
>
> We do not represent that smoking Lucky Strike cigarettes will bring modern figures or cause the reduction of flesh. We do declare that when tempted to do yourself too well, if you will "reach for a Lucky instead" . . .
>
> You will thus avoid over-indulgence in things that cause excess

weight and, by avoiding over-indulgence, maintain a modern, graceful form.

Note the pregnant pause and the rush of euphemism following that word "instead."

Besides the Big Four one was constantly reminded of Herbert Tareytons, Sanos, Viceroys, and for a short time Debs. The Philip Morris Company concentrated most of its advertising dollar on radio on the midget who intoned portentously, "Call for Philip Mor-ris . . ." The two mentholated cigarettes were Kools and Spuds. Advertisers who were aware that one's initial reaction to a Spud was likely to be adverse, ran pictures of a man grimacing over his first taste of an olive, an exotic treat which—like others in the campaign—he later came to love.

Raleighs were the only cigarette of the Thirties to rely on the giveaway as a merchandising method. To this day it is possible to go into homes where the family furniture was purchased with Raleigh coupons.

The comic strip was a popular device of advertisers. It was utilized by Rinso, Lifebuoy Soap, Alka-Seltzer, Ex-Lax and All-Bran, to mention only a few. Another figure of the Thirties was the comic strip Stella Dallas whose guests go away whispering about her scratchy toilet paper until she switches to Soft-Weve Waldorf.

Colgate and Fleischmann's Yeast were fond of the comic strip featuring an opening photograph with a dialogue-filled balloon. The rest of the action took place in ordinary offset. In the case of Fleischmann's Yeast the faces of teenagers were invariably mottled with coal black pimples.

Cartoon figures throughout the Thirties discussed the merits of Rinso. In the early Thirties some extraordinarily chic types dropped in to Kaffeeklatsch on washday. They wore head-hugging cloche hats and fur-trimmed coats draped in dégagé fashion over their shoulders. Rinso had turned them all into *Vogue* models.

Active vulgarity made the competition stiff, but some of the least tasteful advertising prose extolled the merits of various laxatives. Ex-Lax used the comic strip form with Jefferson Machamer drawing the pictures showing someone's Pilgrim's Progress into the ranks of the "Regular Folks." Ex-Lax also used more dignified approaches, one medical ("Let's See What the Doctor Says About

Laxatives"), another the athletic snob. A picture of one of those tennis players so popular in the Thirties was captioned "Her Tennis Stroke Is Correctly Timed. Too Bad Her Laxative Wasn't."

Jefferson Machamer was not the only cartoonist who pressed his gift into the service of colonic regularity. Kellogg's All-Bran in 1939 had a comic strip based on the Katzenjammers. A pirate is voluntarily walking the plank, preferring Davy Jones' Locker to this "ding blasted constipation!"

Fortunately, Captain Katzenjammer comes to his aid with the heavy echt-Deutsch dialect which caused thigh-slapping among untold thousands of young readers every Sunday: "Chust listen to me! Better you should prevent der trouble instead of trying to cure it after der damage iss done! Eat some Crisp Crunchy Kellogg's All-Bran for breakfast. It's rich in der 'bulk' so many of us need to keep regular. Eat it mit milk or cream effery day. Drink plenty of vater and der whole world seems like a different place."

The pirate follows the Captain's advice and is shortly doing a hornpipe, prompting the Captain to remark, "Ain't he der cholly liddle feller since he choined the All-Bran regulars?"

One laxative ad which entered the Madison Avenue Familiar Quotations volume was Fletcher's Castoria. The headline might vary but somewhere in the body copy was to be the information that "Children Cry for It." One example which appeared in 1931 was guaranteed to rend the heart of any conscientious parent. There was a picture of two children on a kiddie car. "Mother, they're too little!" shrieked the headline. "Don't, don't give them an adult laxative."

Prince Albert Tobacco's kindly old Judge Robbins, benign and seemingly regular, was something of a relief after this peristaltic orgy.

Headaches and minor acidity might be among the less baroque of digestive disturbances, but here again a product came to the rescue. The Alka-Seltzer ads were always in comic strip form. They always showed a couple up in years reciting a little rhyme. In September 1936 they were on the beach.

> *"Oh, dear, my head is aching so*
> *I think I'll hike for home."*
> *"I'd take an Alka-Seltzer, Flo*
> *It always clears my dome."*

A topical note was struck during the Presidential campaign of 1936. An orator was saying:

> *"Upon the question of RELIEF*
> *My plan is simple, plain and brief*
> *Take Alka-Seltzer, tried and true*
> *It's good for colds and headaches too."*

The mule and the elephant were aided by Alka-Seltzer after they suffered the ill-effects of election-night over-indulgence:

> *"And if by chance you celebrate*
> *A victory or defeat,*
> *A glass of Alka-Seltzer's great*
> *To put you on your feet."*

A woman who had just relocated in a suburban home was once asked how she liked her new neighbors. *The New Yorker* reported that she replied, "They're like the people in the Alka-Seltzer ads."

Much of the advertising of the Thirties was aimed at creating a specific bogey in the minds of the public. Minor menaces were "tattle tale gray" (a specter conjured up by Fels Naphtha soap) and grammatical lapses (the bearded Sherwin Cody looked sternly out of newspapers for several generations asking, "Do you make these common mistakes in English?"). There was "athlete's foot" caused by a ringworm germ named "tinea trichophyton" to whom a product called Absorbine Jr. was presumably anathema. Absorbine Jr. ads stressed the fact that you didn't need to be athletic to have athlete's foot. "Her longest walk is from curb to car . . . yet she has athlete's foot." "He 'walks to work' on a streetcar yet he has athlete's foot."

Others included posture condition induced by an improper foundation garment. "Sh-h-h. She has Lordosis." There was the man standing in the washroom immobilized with a hat covering a gaping fly because he had settled for something less than a Talon zipper. "Rough red hands" presented a minor threat to romance which could be abolished by Hinds Honey and Almond Cream. An advertisement for this product, which appeared in 1933, showed a picture of a woman washing out a garbage pail. "Her gown said 'ballroom belle' but her hands cried 'backyard drudge.'" It was never explained in the copy why she had chosen to attire herself for this homely task in full evening dress.

In the case of "pink toothbrush" a new public bogey was created as the product of endless time and expense.

As early as 1932 the Ipana Company depicted a misguided young woman who spent "Hours on Creams and Powders—Not a Minute for Her Gums, and She Has 'Pink Toothbrush.'"

In 1933 pictures of a socialite and a truckdriver appeared side by side:

> *She rides a horse*
> *He drives a truck*
> *Pink toothbrush threatens them both!*

Toward the end of the Thirties the notion of pink toothbrush was effectively dramatized by pictures of soignée-looking women tearing at bloody hunks of meat.

In one of them "A Hostess and a Dentist Battle Over a T-bone."

"'Barbarous,' says the hostess.

"'Intelligent,' says the dentist.

"Hostess: 'Your picture is disgraceful. No girl with a spark of intelligence or breeding would ever eat like that.'

"(But your dentist disagrees emphatically.)

"Dentist: 'That picture is a perfect lesson in the proper exercise of teeth and gums. I hope millions of people see it. If more people chewed as vigorously, there would be far fewer gum disorders— fewer evidences of that dental warning "pink toothbrush."'"

Both the hostess and the dentist could have their way. "Ipana plus massage is the dentist's ablest assistant in the home care of your teeth and gums." It was all right to cook the carcass after all.

Forhan's Toothpaste took a more direct approach. In trains, buses, and trolleys there were ghastly pictures of receding gums and rotting teeth. The specter of "Pyorrhea" awaited all who let "pink toothbrush" get out of hand.

Colgate's bogeyman had already been discovered by Listerine; from an obscure medical textbook an enterprising soul had disinterred the word "halitosis."

The miseries of halitosis were vividly portrayed by a copywriter who should have turned a hand to the novel. A woman is shown walking into a psychiatrist's office. "I want gaiety, friends, love," she sobbed.

"'And you shall have them,' I (the psychiatrist) promised her.

"Into a psychiatrist's chambers streams an endless tide of life's misfits—the lonely . . . the bitter . . . the repressed . . . the misunderstood.

"And now before me stood yet another. I was certain, and later examination proved me right that there was nothing organically wrong with her. Her face, her body, bloomed with beauty and vitality. Yet emotionally she was at the breaking point.

"Gently, I probed for her history. She was 28, single, college bred, lived in a good home with parents of some means, but was definitely the recluse type.

"'Men friends?'

"Her lips quivered as she leaned close to me. The flood tide of her emotions burst through the gates of her control.

"'You've hit on it, Doctor. I'm lonely . . . desperately lonely,' she sobbed. 'Every girl I know is married, but no man seems to want me. They come. They go. I cannot hold them. Even my women friends seem to avoid me. I go nowhere . . . see no one. And oh, Doctor, I want gaiety, friends, admiration, love . . . love . . . love.'

"She had risen, her face was almost against mine. In that instant I knew I had spotted the cause of her trouble. It was obvious."

Instead of therapy, the psychiatrist stepped back a pace or two and recommended Listerine. Soon the suppliant was engaged to marry "a well-to-do Easterner who simply adores her."

The comic strip generally dealt with somebody whose breath Telegraphed a Message.

Twin sisters Margie and Mary were "alike as two peas but it's a cinch to tell them apart." Another unwitting offender laments, "I pay the check and Tom takes her home . . ." Or there is the small boy who, recognizing a familiar evil aroma, says to Santa Claus, "Aw heck. You're Uncle Louie."

Some kind soul tells Mary or Uncle Louie, "You ought to see a dentist about your breath." The dentist recommended Colgate's and one social triumph after another ensued.

Listerine was still beleaguering readers with melancholy case histories ("You couldn't blame her for writing him 'no.'"). Listerine barely took notice that Colgate was poaching on previously staked-out territory. There was enough scare value so that everyone could show a profit out of what "Even Your Best Friend Won't Tell You."

"Mr. Coffee Nerves" was, by comparison, a rather genial sort of villain. He appeared in a full-color comic strip in the Sunday supplements—perennially dressed in a silk hat and soup and fish. You knew it was him because the legend "Mr. Coffee Nerves" was written across the front of his dress shirt. As the homes of coffee-drinking couples tottered on the brink of divorce he would twirl his evil black mustache gleefully. At this point a tiresome old codger named "Professor Kindly" would appear on the scene and tip the troubled household off to the existence of Instant Postum. Coffee renounced, domestic harmony restored, "Mr. Coffee Nerves" would retreat, muttering, "Curses, foiled again" . . . foiled at least until the following Sunday.

The most omnipresent bogey of all was B.O. (body odor). It was invented by Lifebuoy Soap, a powerfully carbolic product which imbued the user with the wholesome antiseptic aura of a dog and cat hospital. Hardly an issue of a magazine or newspaper came out without a new B.O. comic strip drama. One was headlined "Wise Words from Her Baby Sister."

"Oh, Sis, you are a lovely bride," says Baby Sister.

Babs: "I'm so happy. Ted and I adore each other."

Five years later Baby Sister comes across Babs—now one of those household drudges who has yet to be exposed to the wonders of Rinso. But in this case it is not Rinso that is called for.

"But Sis, why so serious? Aren't you glad I'm engaged? Don't you like my Phil?"

Babs: "Of course I do. But marriage can be so different from what one expects. Romance fades so soon. Look at Ted and me."

"Sis, it's partly your fault. Ted has changed because you've let yourself become . . . unromantic . . . a little careless about how you look . . . Sometimes even about B.O."

Babs takes a Lifebuoy bath. "B.O. gone. Romance Returns."

Ted turns adoringly to Babs after Baby Sister's wedding. "She was a pretty bride, but the real hit of the wedding was—my wife."

Later in the Thirties, with people presumably cleaning up more and more, "Nervous B.O." became a variation on the familiar theme. The comic strips dealt with teenagers who found their dates recoiling from them because of nervous tension during the monster picture.

The rise of the deodorant habit found Lifebuoy becoming something of an anachronism. Deodorant manufacturers were quick to point out that a bath only took away *yesterday's* perspiration and that "hours after your bath, Mum still keeps you sweet." Mum's arch-rival, Odorono, featured an armpit test showing a woman sniffing at the armhole of her dress with obvious distaste.

When one departed from the general magazines such as *Time,* the *American,* or the *Saturday Evening Post,* advertising took on the slant of the special market. *Esquire* leaned to virile sportswear and whiskey ads, which were forbidden in media more susceptible to the criteria of Mrs. Grundy.

Advertisements in two classes of magazines had a flavor all their own. These were the movie magazines and the pulps.

In a general family magazine one might see a confirmed spinster who had never heard of Lux: "23 and no sign of middle aisling." The fact that she was going into her dotage in a celibate state was in this case due to "undie odor." A more glamorous approach to the problem was provided by *Silver Screen* and *Photoplay:* "Romantic Grace Moore is practical too. She adores Luxables—*insists* on Lux care." The star was pictured holding tennis racquets, displaying the dress she was to wear in *The King Steps Out,* and giving the inevitable plug for good old Lux. "For cottons, linens, washable silks and rayons, Lux has no equal," said this Columbia Star.

Lux Toilet Soap was plugged as an aid to complexion loveliness. Its properties were endorsed by the stars as a spur to the tired businessman. "Don't let love grow hum-drum," said Helen Twelvetrees on behalf of Lux. "When a man begins to take you for granted watch out."

For those who believed along with soap opera heroine Helen Trent that a woman could find romance after thirty-five—and even beyond—Lux Toilet Soap was like a magic elixir.

"Actually over 40"—a double spread in *Photoplay*—ran in 1932.

"But these lovely stars know the secret of keeping youthful charm."

Three girlish pictures were shown.

" 'I'm over 40!'—Mary Boland.

" 'I'm over 45!'—Nance O'Neill.

" 'I'm over 40!' says Nazimova." One wonders how much Lux had to shell out to wring out admissions like *that*.

The fan magazine reader was responsive to a torrid type of copy. "Your lips as he desires them . . ." so went some lipstick copy in *Silver Screen*. He desired them "savagely red, warmly moist, tenderly soft."

For those who wanted to play it coy there was always Tangee.

Tangee was a girl's first lipstick. In the case it looked bright orange. It was alleged to turn to "blush rose" on the lips. Tangee ads showed three cupid's bows. The first granular pair of lips was labeled "untouched." The second was harsh and greasy. "Don't risk the painted look, Men don't like it." The third cupid's bow featured "Tangee lovable lips," which in *Silver Screen* received the following accolade:

"Her lovely lips appealed to me instantly," said Edmund Lowe. "Suave film star picks most kissable lips in unique test . . . We presented three girls to Edmund Lowe. One wore ordinary lipstick . . . One no lipstick . . . The third Tangee. 'Her lips look kissable,' he said of the Tangee girl. 'They look natural.'"

The ad went on to warn purchasers: "Beware of substitutes . . . when you buy. Don't let some sharp sales person switch you to an imitation. Be sure to ask for Tangee Natural. There is another shade of Tangee called Tangee Theatrical, but it is only for those who insist on vivid color and for professional use." Obviously Mr. Lowe would never want to kiss some fast theatrical type whose lips were "savagely red" or "warmly moist."

Bust developers were widely advertised in the fan magazines. Small ads packed with copy urged the underdeveloped to:

"Be feminine. Develop Alluring Form.

"If you are thin, flat-chested, let me show you how to acquire the firm, well-rounded bust and appealing feminine curves so in vogue today. Try Conform Cream and see results in 15 days." Conform Cream—like most bust developers—came in plain wrapper with money back guarantee and cost $1.00 a jar. The same 1934 issue of *Picture Play* pushed a Special Massaging Cream and a Peerless Wonder Cream. Massage, it seemed, could work two ways. If you were burdened by a full, oversized bust, that could be reduced by practically the same method with the aid of Slimcream. Given the tender age of many movie fans, nature was the ally of these advertisers. Purchasers of the enlarging creams were far less likely to demand their money back.

The November 1934 *Picture Play* also had "Your Marriage Forecast as Told by Your Stars" and contained the reassuring news that "Your Face Can Be Changed."

"Dr. Stotter, a graduate of the University of Vienna with many years of experience in plastic surgery, reconstructs unshapely noses, protruding and large ears, lips, wrinkles around the eyes and eyelids, face and neck, etc. by methods as perfected in the Great Vienna Polyclinic. Moderate fees. Free Booklet 'Facial Reconstruction.'"

There were endless reducing regimens, most famous of which was Mme. Sylvia's 9-Day Diet. For those who didn't want to diet there were pills. "Personal to fat girls: 'Now you can slim down your face and figure without strict dieting or back-breaking exercises. Just eat sensibly and take 4 Marmola Prescription Tablets a day until you have lost enough weight. Then stop.'"

Some of the diets of the Thirties were said to have had terrible after-effects. There were stories of girls who had dieted themselves to death, or taken pills which contained unadvertised tapeworms, which caused them to waste away to shadows. The nostrums of the fan magazines generally promised far more than they delivered. Mme. Sylvia, for instance, invited the reader to bypass Dr. Stotter, claiming that noses could be remodeled by simple massage, like pieces of clay. She pointed to lovely Ruth Chatterton as the *summa cum laude* graduate of home nose sculpture.

Most famous beautician of the Thirties was Edna Wallace Hopper. She was one of the five wives of De Wolfe Hopper.

"Does This Picture Look Like a Woman of Sixty?" ran the caption under a girlish study of Edna.

"I am past sixty, yet people tell me I look like a girl. College boys often flirt with me. I've been booked from one big theater to another as 'The One Woman in the World Who Never Grew Old.'

At a grandmother's age I enjoy the admiration and thrills of youth."

Her secret—theoretically guaranteed to take "ten years from the face in ten minutes" was "the discovery of a great French scientist" . . .

"It supplies the skin with the natural oils that keep it young and free of wrinkles and age lines. With those oils in your skin you are young. Without them in your skin you are old. This puts them in every day.

"It shows results first time you use it. Takes years away, starts to bring back the pulsing charm of youth."

The name of the miracle preparation: "Edna Wallace Hopper's Special Restorative Cream." As its manufacturer claimed modestly, "It may change your whole viewpoint of life."

It was unfortunate for those who looked forward to regaining the "pulsing charm of youth" that the New York *World-Telegram* was unchivalrous enough in 1940 to print a picture of Miss Hopper before and after face-lifting. *Before,* no college boy would have laid a hand on her.

The motives of fan magazine readers were crystal clear. It was more difficult to make out what audience or age level the pulp advertiser was aiming at. Preparations which brought "new hope to prostate sufferers" appeared side by side with cures for adolescent pimples. High school equivalency courses and Wiel Belts to hold up sagging stomachs competed for attention with magic rings and itching powder.

In every pulp directed at a male audience there was a page devoted to Charles Atlas' Dynamic Tension Course. In the August 15, 1933, issue of *Dime Detective* there was a comic strip, now classic, story of "The Insult That Made a Man Out of Mac." Mac, a scrawny scarecrow, is sitting on the beach with his girl when a well-built bully comes by and kicks sand in his face. The bully adds insult to injury. "I'd smash your face—only you're so skinny you might dry up and blow away."

Mac takes the Dynamic Tension Course, comes back to the beach with muscles bulging, beats up the bully and gets the girl. In this strip he was merely following in the footsteps of Charles Atlas (a muscular figure always portrayed in a leopard-skin *cache sexe*), "the 97-pound weakling who became The World's Most Perfectly Developed Man."

"I'll prove to you in seven days that you too can be this new man," Mr. Atlas promised his young readers. It was to be hoped that the credentials of "The World's Most Perfectly Developed Man" were at least as authentic as those of "The One Woman in the World Who Never Grew Old."

A lesser Charles Atlas was George F. Jowett who had "Nerves of Steel, Muscles of Iron" and who promised 97-pound weaklings "a mighty arm and a 16-inch bicep." His book was advertised with a picture of that bicep swelling and breaking a chain.

Another staple ad displayed the diversified wares of the Johnson-Smith Company. In blue ink on a type-crowded page the offerings from Dept. 957 were legion. "Boys! Throw Your Voice." The "Ventrilo" was illustrated with a hilarious picture of a ventriloquist with a midget screaming in a box strapped to his back. There were the aforementioned itching powder and magic ring—a midget Bible, serpent eggs, and a method of learning to play the piano in one hour. An unusual item was the "anarchist bomb": "One of these glass vials dropped in a room full of people will cause more consternation than a limburger cheese." Best of all was their massive, pulp paper catalogue of wonders.

The Imperial Novelty Company catered to slightly more adult tastes:

"New Stuff!" "For Men Only, Tillie and Mac, Toots and Caspar, Boss and Bubbles, Fannie Hill, Harold Teen and Lillums, Boob McNutt and Pearl, The Vampire, The End of Helen, What Tommy Saw Under the Parlor Door, Twelve Gay Love Letters Read Two Ways, Gay Life in Paris; also 50 Rare and Daring French type pictures of beautiful girls in thrilling, snappy, artistic poses with their fellows."

In addition to correspondence courses in accountancy, one might learn more exciting trades.

"Arrest him officer!

"I'll have complete facts on the other fellow tonight!"

". . . Secret Operator No. 38 is on the job . . . follow him through all the excitement of his chase after the counterfeit gang. See how a crafty operator works. Tell-tale fingerprints in the murdered girl's bedroom that help him solve the great mystery! Better than fiction because every word is true.

"FREE—the confidential reports No. 38 made to his chief."

"May open your eyes to the great opportunity for *you* as a well-paid Finger Print expert. This is a young, fast-growing profession."

It was certainly a young profession although, thanks to such organizations as the Post Toasties Junior Detectives, already hopelessly overcrowded.

Sex Harmony and Eugenics in plain sealed wrapper had an obvious appeal for all ages.

The man and the woman locked in an embrace never changed. Nor did the list of benefits which one could derive from the book:

Banish Fear	Stop Worrying
Prevent Disease	Conquer Ignorance
End Self Denial	Overcome Shame

THE FORBIDDEN SECRETS OF SEX ARE
DARINGLY REVEALED

The list of the daring secrets was always the same. There was always a line cut of a troubled couple standing in front of a judge who claimed that "most divorces are caused by sex ignorance." There was the picture of the distraught wife whose husband was obviously leaving her bed and board forever. "Is sex ignorance driving the one you love into the arms of another?" The reader would never fall into either of these traps with courageous Dr. Rubin lifting the veil of prudery. "Away with false modesty! At last a famous doctor has told *all*. The secrets of sex in frank daring language. No prudish beating about the bush. No veiled hints, but TRUTH blazing through 576 pages of straightforward facts." It was a big package. Plus the 576 daring pages there were 106 vivid pictures. And many a young reader hoped—furtively awaiting the arrival of the plain sealed wrapper—that *Sex Harmony and Eugenics* might shed some light on what those Lysol ads meant when they talked about "intimate feminine hygiene."

While Fleischmann's Yeast advertised in more generalized media, those coal black pimples also apparently troubled many readers of *Dime Detective, Love Story, The Shadow,* and *Dime Sports.*

The Colgate-type lead-in was utilized in countless pictures of adolescents lamenting their hideous suppurating sores.

"Nix on parties with my crop of pimples," said one youngster.

"I can't hope to be the heroine with this face," said another.

Another youth who was job hunting while in the throes of a ghastly eruption asked: "Wish I knew why they all turn me down."

All of these dramas ended happily. "Aw quit it, can't you just tell the fellows I'm staying home?"

"Why'd you turn down Judy's invite?" a friend asks. "We had a swell time."

"Just take a squint at these blossoms," replied Ned.

"For cryin' out loud. Is that all that stopped you? Say, don't you know that Fleischmann's Yeast is the way to finish off those hickies?"

When next we see Ned he is sporting a bag of golf clubs and confidently approaching a Tin Lizzie emblazoned with such Harold Teenisms as "No Turns on Red," "Throw Out the Lifeline," "Pony Express," and "Caution, Air Brakes."

"Hi there, Judy," cries the friend. "Look what I've got in tow— old Ned."

"Fleischmann's Yeast clears the skin by clearing skin irritants out of the blood," or such was the thinking when this mass onslaught on adolescent acne took place in 1936. In 1933 "Dr. Bruno of Paris" had recommended Fleischmann's Yeast to a patient who had been suffering needlessly from constipation. By 1941 this miracle panacea had become "one of the richest natural sources of the amazing Vitamin B Complex."

To discover the miraculous properties of this and other products, advertisers were forced to depend on the intercession of that familiar advertising figure—the blunt friend.

"Pardon us, Sally. We all have dates with *another* girl," chorused three boorish swains in a 1938 Mum ad. One of the Fleischmann teenagers was to remark, "It fixed up Bob and he looked even worse than you do." The same sort of friend was forever hustling potential Colgate users off to see their dentists, or making remarks like "Why, Mary, your arm feels like a man's chin." There was in the Thirties a swelling and inescapable chorus of blunt friends telling the malodorous, the blotchy, the insecure, and the rough of hand home truths for their own good. It would have been amazing in real life if the advice had been accepted so philosophically. As one advertising character said meekly, "You ruined my day, but thanks."

The blunt friends' admonitions paid big dividends for the blunt advertiser, coupled as they often were with enormous advertising outlays on radio.

Rinso could also depend on the soap opera heroine *Rinso's Big Sister*. Lucky Strike had *The Lucky Strike Hit Parade. Amos 'n' Andy* were out there plugging for Pepsodent. Fleischmann's Yeast had Rudy Vallee; Lux, the *Lux Radio Theatre*. The formidable baton of Benny Goodman was raised on *The Camel Caravan*. Camels had *Jack Oakie's College* over the Columbia Network in addition to endorsements from Larruping Lou Gehrig.

It added up to a formidable force. Advertising in the best of times is a brass-knucks industry. In the desperate scramble for business in the 1930s, no holds were barred. The advertising industry had a disreputable cousin—the rumor industry. Trained "sentiment spreaders" on a few hours' notice would start a whispering campaign about a product. Cab drivers, door to door salesmen were employed to spread the word that Brand X cigarette company had a leper at work in its factory. One cola was said to contain cocaine.

In the early days of radio advertising Herbert Hoover had wistfully hoped advertisers might stick to a soft-sell approach. By the "Hoover Method" the sponsor was to announce briefly at the beginning of the program that he was providing the entertainment in question as a public service. The announcement might be made again at the end of the show with no interruptions in between.

Soon the air waves would be resounding with the strains of the first singing commercial, "Pepsi-Cola Hits the Spot." Hoover's brave dream had as much effect on advertisers as a Hoover pronouncement on any other subject.

Without drawing morals, it is perhaps better to let the advertising industry speak for itself as it did through three advertisements which appeared in the grim early days of the Depression.

The first appeared in the *Christian Herald* in 1931. It was couched in that stark type-face devoid of frivolous or distracting artwork. It conjured up visions of Sound Finance, the Varied Portfolio, the Rock of Ages, or possibly a funeral parlor—which in a sense was closer to the truth.

These companies were created to acquire and hold as investments enough of the securities of the Insull Group of Public Utilities Properties to insure continuity of policy and management throughout the Group. As stated by Samuel Insull, their founder, they were organized to establish some rallying point of ownership and friendship for the various companies with which my name is associated.

Insull Utility Investments, Inc.
Corporation Securities Co.
72 West Adams Street
Chicago Illinois

The second advertisement appeared two years later, also in the *Christian Herald*. It was a plea for funds for New York's Bowery Mission—and was possibly run at a reduced rate by the magazine as a public service. Headlined "What a dollar can do for a man without a cent", it gave case histories of various people who had applied for help. One was named Joseph:

Never before had this man realized the narrow line separating the citizen in good standing from the down-and-outer. Without money, he too would be without a home, and in order to live he would have to beg for food or get it somehow. Beggars were bums to him; people who lacked ambition and the will to work. For 18 years Joseph —— had worked for Jones and Co. . . . Three months ago this long established firm had gone into bankruptcy. At the age of 60 Joseph found himself with a few dollars in the bank and with no prospect of getting work.

The ad went on to portray the odd jobs gotten by the mission which enabled Joseph to "keep his own little room in a cheap boarding house. . . ." the nightly meal "after the Brotherhood Meeting" which gave him nourishment beyond the "food he is able to get himself."

Other applicants described by the Bowery Mission advertisement were men who ten years before would have been horrified to think of themselves as charity cases. All had, through no fault of their own, crossed that "narrow line between the citizen in good standing and the down-and-outer."

The third advertisement was a comic strip which appeared—also in 1933—in *Photoplay:*

NO JOB, WAS THIS THE REASON?

LIBRARIAN: Another book! You read this one in no time.

WOMAN: Oh, I haven't much else to do. I'm still out of a job. Can't seem to get one.

LIBRARIAN: How did you enjoy this book?

WOMAN: Very much. But look, isn't this unusual? When it says the heroine takes a bath, it actually tells what kind of soap she used—Lifebuoy.

LIBRARIAN: Well, I can read between the lines, can't you? She wasn't taking any chances with B.O. Too bad everyone doesn't follow her example! You'd be surprised how many offend, and probably never realize it.

WOMAN (*thinking out loud*): Could that be a hint for me? Perhaps I ought to get Lifebuoy.

(*In the shower*): My, Lifebuoy's grand! Such wonderful lather. I never felt so gloriously clean.

(*B.O. Gone—a fine job landed!*)

WOMAN: Just dashed in to return this book. It's way overdue. Haven't had much time to read lately. I'm working now and I'm so happy.

. . . and the moral: Don't let B.O. (body odor) stand between you and your job.

Applicants are many, positions scarce, employers critical. Don't miss out on the job you're seeking. Don't risk the job you have by carelessness about B.O.

About the most all-pervasive popular art of the Thirties, it says best in quotation what needs to be said.

Chapter 7

They Don't Make 'Em
That Way Anymore

In an age of "planned obsolescence" the phrase "more car for the money" has a strange, archaic sound. It is difficult to recall that the life span of a car was ever as long as eight years, that the trading in was once a novelty, that car manufacturers in a buyer's market gave bonuses in quality rather than chrome.

In the Depression search for cheap transportation the junkyards yielded up their dead at a price that was right. A well-heeled boy or girl in 1933 could have the satisfaction of driving along the highway and sailing past an old-timer whose exact counterpart had rolled off the assembly line in 1915.

The automotive picture of the early 1900s had been dominated by a single man—he was a production genius, and bleak, ruthless, opinionated—nurtured on prejudices, bromides, and folk medicine. At one time or another he had the Boston Post Road rerouted to preserve the tranquility of Longfellow's Wayside Inn. He banned automobiles from Greenfield Village near his plant at River Rouge. He attempted to revive square dancing and was willing to lay out vast amounts of cash for causes in which he believed, such as America First or making an offer to save Muscle Shoals from the depredations of "That Man."

Wall Street to Henry Ford was "misguided, inefficient, destructive." Bankers were "a lot of Jews sitting around and smoking cigars." His paper, the Dearborn *Independent,* was openly anti-Semitic until 1927. His bogeymen had aquiline noses, greedy eyes, foreign accents, and wrung their hands as they plotted secretly to take over the world. In the first World War, Ford had dispatched an ill-fated Peace Ship (armies and navies were—like Eastern discount rates—the hellish spawn of Wall Street). He once collected damages of six cents after a long wrangle with the Chicago *Tribune,* which had called him an anarchist. Henry was in some respects the archetypal peasant, and God help the city slicker who tried to get the better of him in a business deal. This peasant had been put on earth for a single purpose: to bring cheap transportation to the average man. His instruments were the first assembly line, the $5-a-day wage, and the archetypal peasant's car, the Tin Lizzie.

If Ford had battled the bankers to keep Lizzie's earnings for himself, he had fought a bitter battle to put her on the streets. For nearly a decade in the early 1900s he warred with George Selden, holder of the basic patent on the automobile. One mute but effective witness in the long legal battle was a car designed according to Selden's specifications which started only with enormous difficulty. The upshot of the decision in Ford's favor: Selden's patent was held to be invalid. The way was open to the Model T, Ford's "universal car."

After doing battle with the ravening wolves of Wall Street, he had come through the crash with his fortune nearly intact. During the last ten years of Lizzie's life more than half the cars in America had been those Model T's. Twelve million Lizzies had been made by 1925. In 1924 the car had sold for an all-time low of $290. Lizzie's virtues in this halcyon era had been the virtues of a frugal rural society. Lizzie may not have looked like much but she was a cheap date and you could take her anywhere.

Lizzie's high-rumped undercarriage rattled about the countryside, neatly clearing the mud and stumps of the rural road, leaving trails of lunch boxes and pop bottles in her wake. She ruled the highways until 1927, when Ford switched to the Model A.

In 1931 Ford drove the twenty-millionth Model A down the street. Thanks to the Depression, Lizzie was still around in the mid-Thirties, transporting families to their Sunday amusements. These amusing interludes included cranking up for the start and patching tires after the breakdown. But ownership of a Lizzie was rapidly becoming a confession of failure, like the possession of a hand-me-down pair of high button shoes. The Model T was hopelessly anachronistic. Car radios and foot-controlled dimmer switches had come in 1929. Studebaker had introduced "free-wheeling" in 1930. By 1933 the use of the accelerator pedal as a self-starter was common place. Chevrolet and Plymouth had challenged Ford's sole claim to producing the "universal" car. They forced Ford into acceptance of the annual style change, an invention of the devil on a par with England or the reading habit.

Chevy surpassed Ford in 1931 and maintained its lead throughout the Depression, except for the year 1935. Ford retooled in 1932, this time producing the V-8 engine. In 1933 the V-8 went through what was becoming a yearly metamorphosis, emerging bigger and better in time for the Chicago automobile show. Competition from Ford conversely kept Chrysler and General Motors on their toes. In 1933 Chrysler's poor relation, the Plymouth, changed from a "4" to a "6."

Whatever the sales figures, the nostalgic fantasy highways of the middle-aged are peopled with Fords. "There's a Ford in your future," said the ads, and there were Fords in our past. There were smart 1931 Ford Model A Cabriolets with rumble seats occupied traditionally either by small children or by couples who had their love to keep them warm. (A rumble in those days had an element of violent encounter but it involved affection, too.) There were snub-nosed Ford station wagons with twin antennae on the steering wheel marked "spark" and "throttle." To those of us who learned to drive in such a vehicle, it has been an adjustment to cope with latter-day steering wheels that turn corners meekly without putting up a fight.

Lizzie's mechanical failures were not too far behind us in the Thirties. Three-speed transmission was as recent as 1927 and the Model A was the first Ford to have a single-plate clutch. Many motorists still remember the experiences described by erstwhile Lizzie-owner Lee Strout White. As he wrote: even in neutral, Lizzie trembled with a "deep imperative" and tended to inch slowly forward. Lizzie needed endless supplementary paraphernalia. Thousands of dealers in accessories contributed to her hope chest. There were tire-patching outfits with nutmeg graters to roughen the tube before applying the goo, a radiator compound to stop leaks, a clamp-on dashboard light, antirattlers and a fan belt guide (to keep the fan belt from slipping off the pulley). The rearview mirror was an extra installed by suspicious drivers who liked to know what was sneaking up on them from behind. Filling up Lizzie involved removing the driver from his perch over the gas tank. A stick immersed in the tank gave a clue to the level of the gas, for the dashboard was innocent of gas gauge—and speedometer. Oiling the engine was accomplished by a combination of splash and gravitational pull. Starting up was what we might now speak of as a happening—a crank activated Lizzie into a few scattered explosions. The trick was to get back into the car before she ran over the driver. Lizzie was held at bay by a sturdy shoulder prior to the plunge to leap aboard. "I can still feel my old Ford," said Mr. White, "nuzzling me at the curb as though looking for an apple in my pocket."

The Tin Lizzie appealed to the low man on the status totem pole, the man who patched his own tires. Some of the handsomest cars ever made transported those at the top, men who could maintain an Olympian detachment to what went on under the hood. Some of the small independent manufacturers made magnificent luxury cars which have joined the extinctive brontosauruses of the automotive industry.

The Stutz, of course, was dear to the heart of Fitzgerald's hip flask group. Originally producers of a racing car, the Stutz people made a handsome Lady's Town Car in 1929–30. The superb DV-32 Stutz was a hit at the Commodore and Rake Hotel salons in 1931, 1932, and 1933. Other classic cars were the Safety Stutz, the Bearcat, and Super Bearcat. The latter two were roadsters guaranteed to do more than a hundred—which appealed to sporty types who considered safety a trifle square. Stutz lingered on until 1936. Its fatal mistake may have been trying to woo the laprobe rather than the coonskin trade.

Fred Duesenberg was a celebrated race track driver and pioneer automotive engineer. In the 1930s he turned out roadsters, sedans, four-door convertibles consisting of a basic chassis and whatever body the customer wanted. Duesenberg trademarks were the sweeping fenders, twenty-inch freestanding headlights, and solid-nickel radiator, which it retained despite the vagaries of automotive fashion up to its demise.

The Duesenberg's speed record has been subject to bloodthirsty argument. The "Marmon Meteor," specially rebuilt by two Salt Lake City boys, was clocked at over 130 miles per hour. Similar claims were made for the 1931–32 S-J—a model with a supercharged engine. In 1931 a Duesenberg owned by Douglas Fairbanks, Jr., without benefit of supercharger, trimmed the tar out of an imported Mercedes S.S. racer owned by Zeppo Marx.

The final postproduction Duesenberg was completed in 1939 and delivered in 1940. It had a landau-style body, convertible in several different ways. It boasted lavender-lensed running lights. It was the only model completed without the traditional radiator. This magnificent car provided a fitting finale for a mighty line.

Mr. Duesenberg, father of the supercharger and the four-wheel hydraulically controlled brake, was killed in an automobile accident in 1932. He left behind him a brother, Augie, who labored unsuccessfully to perpetuate production of a grand old car.

His Duesenberg Company had been bought by the Auburn Automobile Company in 1926. Under the management of E. L. Cord, the organization's net profits in nadir-year 1931 surpassed those of jazz-gin-and-bull-market year 1929.

The first car named after Mr. Cord—and distinguished by the front-wheel drive—appeared in 1929. After various delays and bottlenecks the revolutionary Cord 810 was the sensation of the 1935 New York Automobile Show. It was to be one of the world's classic cars. It had a smooth, chromeless body, a radiator of horizontal bands, and headlights which disappeared into the fenders. In 1937 Model 810 became 812 and set a speed record which was unsurpassed for fifteen years. Cord's low-slung lines, huge instrument panel, chrome exhaust pipes coming off the hood and coffin nose are—even by Thunderbird standards—cool.

Cord and Duesenberg were doomed. No one could seriously challenge their worth—except, perhaps, the mass of car buyers who were being created by mass production. The Cord went out of business a year after its dramatic debut. The Duesenberg made its final bow in 1937: a town car with a basketwork body. Moviegoers of the Thirties may cherish the memory of Mae West stepping out of such a vehicle, photographed from an angle which did justice to the salient points of star and car. Suffice it to say that the car looked as long as a city block.

The Cord and the Duesenberg have gone to the automotive hunting ground along with the Marmon, the Oakland, the Essex, the Franklin, the Hupmobile, and the Graham-Paige. Yet they linger on in fond memory with automobile collectors. Even today one searches a Duesenberg chassis in vain for a hint of cheapness or short-cut. The Auburn-Cord-Duesenberg Club bought up stocks after the companies' demise and still supplies parts for surviving cars. A fair percentage of the Cords made in the Thirties are still in operation. The Cord itself can be sent back periodically for complete remanufacture. The Cord took a prize from the Museum of Modern Art as one of ten outstanding automobile designs. *Fortune* chose the Cord as one of a hundred best-designed products, twenty years after its first appearance on the showroom floor.

The Auburn Company lost its ability to ride out bad Depression weather. Erret Cord went to England in 1934 pending some SEC unpleasantness involving Checker Cab stock. In April 1937 he repaired to a Chicago hospital for a "needed rest" and resolved his personality conflicts by unloading his Cord holdings. The splendid cars for which he was justly famous live on as a monument to the days when they built 'em to last.

Pierce Arrow deserves a place in the hall of fame, too. The 1933 Pierce Silver Arrow was one of the first examples of streamlining. Its rear wheel was discreetly hooded. It had gracefully tapered front fenders and power brakes. Years before anyone else thought of it, Pierce dared dispense with its running board. Ten Pierce Silver Arrows were designed as the Car of the Future at the 1933 World's Fair; they were a limited edition, planned to be sold for $10,000 apiece. Car No. 7 worked its way from a gangster's garage, via the D. Cameron Reed Collection, into the Long Island Automotive Museum. Its raffish past was obliterated when its interior was done over in broadcloth, its radio controls and speaker set into working order, and its bird's-eye maple refinished. It is now the spotless delight of the type who not only could but, one suspects, does eat his dinner off the carburetor.

Packard's jutting radiator was a badge of respectability. Packards—as *Fortune* reminded its readers in 1937—carried rich invalids to their airings, diplomats to embassies, stars to their studios, warlords through Chinese dust, heroes through ticker tape, heiresses across Long Island and Grosse Pointe. There was a blemish on the character of the Packard. When gangsters took their victims for the "ride" which ended up in the bottom of a river, the deceased generally rode that last mile in a black Packard sedan. Many a gangster conferred respectability upon his own last ride with this ultimate symbol of status.

The first Packard had seen the light of day on November 6, 1899, in a world of tree-shaded streets where ladies rocked in chairs on the porch. It was advertised as "a gentleman's car made by gentlemen." Somehow this image had remained until the mid-Thirties when the economic pinch caused Packard to try to invade the medium-priced field. In the post-mortems which followed the demise of the Packard in 1958, some dated the beginning of the end to the smashing of Packard's image as a quality car. For the time being—in 1937—Hugh Ferry's bold gesture brought results. As the disgruntled competition was to remark of the *haute bourgeois* Packard, "The new virgin is always the busiest girl in the harem—for a while. Sooner or later she will have to take her chances with the rest of us."

Between the Packard or Duesenberg owner and the nimble operator of a Tin Lizzie were the vast majority of car owners. Ninety percent of this group in 1939 owned a car which was made by General Motors, Ford, or Chrysler. The giants were in brisk competition. Chevrolet was by 1935 the world's largest producer of motorcars and trucks. Plymouth, Chrysler's contender in the American family car sweepstakes, had taken after its rich relation, the Chrysler Airflow, and was offering new directional water circulation and an air-cooled clutch. Chrysler itself had "floating power" and was one of the first cars to offer automatic overdrive. The bards of advertising sang of Fisher bodies, Fisher No-Draft Ventilation, of

Chevrolet's freewheeling, of Oldsmobiles and Pontiacs with Turret Tops.

In the case of General Motors' sturdy workhorse, the Chevrolet, a vacuum power shift with steering wheel control was an option in 1939 and standard equipment in 1940. "Floating power," which had graced the high-priced Chrysler in the early Thirties, drifted down to the humbler Dodge, which in 1940 was equipped with a "full floating ride."

While General Motors had its class products—the La Salle and the Cadillac—and while Ford was to turn out one of the ultimate luxury cars, the great profits were in the mass. The Davids of Detroit all tried to fell the three Goliaths with a cheap car—Graham, Nash, Hudson, Hupp, Studebaker, and Willys. The lower-priced car field was as thick with insecure newcomers as the cocktail bar in Tourist Third.

The business picture of the Depression automobile industry was a dreary patchwork of receiverships, proxy battles, and ousters. A company would go temporarily bankrupt and would be taken over in receivership, frequently by the executive who had brought it down to disaster in the first place. Or a new dynamo would come in with new financing and some dubious record with a defunct company such as Marmon or Locomobile. In 1937 the Hupp Motor Car Company got a brief shot in the arm from Thomas Bradley, who threw out Archie Moulton Andrews and began turning out Hupmobiles again. A 1936 proxy battle led to an attempt to "revitalize" the moribund Reo Company after the felicitous retirement of Oldsmobile's founder Ransom Eli Olds. Reo retired from the production of passenger cars and devotes itself to this day to production of trucks. John Willys dropped dead while trying to reorganize the Willys Overland Company, and Ward C. Canady tried to launch a new Willys pegged at a price bracket somewhere between the Chevrolet and the jalopy. Nash's entry was another blue baby—the Lafayette. Perhaps the most distinguished low-price car was the Studebaker Champion—introduced in 1939. It was cheap, though not as cheap as Plymouth, Chevy, or Ford. It had offered a light frame which by some suspension system incomprehensible to the layman didn't bounce around the road. It had the first overdrive on a low-priced car. Raymond Loewy by 1940 was designing its silhouette in best World of Tomorrow fashion. It had one of the earlier gearshifts under the wheel rather than on the floor.

The Willys, the Lafayette, the Graham Six, the Crosley all were Tourist entries which never quite made the grade. Yet the hopeful dream lingered on . . . "If we can just get control . . ." "If we can grab a slice of Ford's market . . ." "If we can get enough signatures maybe we can get the Old Boy out."

The most radical change in the looks of the 1930s car took place in 1934. Streamlining made the square radiator an additional cross to the upwardly mobile Lizzie owner. Streamlining made the woman who dreamed of mink turn her thoughts to the Chrysler airflow. And streamlining brought about the demise of the Model A. Streamlining inspired *Vogue* copywriters to purple prose. *Vogue* wrote an obituary: "The vertical line has gone the way of the benzine buggy."

Showrooms were filled with the slithery rounded radiator of the new Chryslers, the goldfish-shaped taillights of the Pierce Arrow. The spare tire, habitually located on the running board or the rear of the trunk, began its descent into inner darkness. The true Detroit revolutionary pulled his fenders down over the rear wheel like a missionary covering a wayward native with a Mother Hubbard.

In 1935 the Duesenberg opera brougham made one of the most distinguished marriages of old and new. It had old-fashioned pillar lamps, a basket-weave body, and a sharp, graceful, contemporary sweep to the fenders. The chauffeur, meanwhile, froze up front in the great outdoors, though he had the solace of collapsible roof curtains. The final *e pluribus unum* touch: the running board had been eliminated in favor of steps to the front and rear compartments.

Duesenberg resisted the wilder excesses of streamlining. Some of Mr. Duesenberg's racing background rubbed off on the lowlier Auburn speedster. This middle-income model was supercharged and, like the Duesenberg, running-boardless. The Cadillac inspired *Esquire* to emulate *Vogue*'s purple passion. It had a rounded top sitting close to the frame "like elegant, low-crowned derbies poised over a well-groomed face."

The Ford, the Chevy, the Graham, and the Lafayette contented themselves with rounded radiators.

The Buick avoided the square-nosed effect, while refusing to truck with streamlined excess. *Esquire* considered the 1935 Buick the ideal middle-of-the-road car for "the solid citizen who keeps up with the times."

Among the founders of streamlining were the designers of the 1930 Reo. The 1934 Nash was another groundbreaker. (The 1935 model was anthropomorphized as taking off with "head flung back and hair flying.")

The Nash's designer, Count Alexis de Sakhnoffsky, did throughout the Thirties an illustrated column for *Esquire* in which he applied the streamline technique to speedboats, radios, beer barrels, fountain pens, gas stoves—even golf bags. Some of his adaptations led Sakhnoffsky himself to wonder whether America was ripe for the Visigoths. One such offering was a horizontal clock whose transparent dial flashed the time onto the ceiling—at heaven knows what an emotional price to insomniacs who slept on their backs.

Sakhnoffsky never quite got to the man in the street. His column might offer wish fulfillments to twenty-year-olds who dreamed Sakhnoffsky and drove jalopy; the car *buyer* was more likely a well-heeled Buick type who kept up with the times. Out of deference to him Chrysler had, by 1937, quietly abandoned the airflow line. The Chrysler owner of that year presumably was far less impressed by what happened when the throttle was let out than by the statement of a fellow businessman quoted in the ads: "I see no reason why the family limousine should be less safe than my son's coupé."

After 1934 and streamlining, car designers got cold feet and never came up with anything quite so dramatic. There was, however, a solid technological advance. The rumble seat finally closed for good around 1936. In 1937 that pace setter, Cord, produced a phaeton with "a cloth top that can be lowered and, when raised, provide a complete closed auto." This convertible was the child of the coupé.

The hard-top was also a product of the late Thirties. The Chrysler Thunderbolt—1939–40—"dream car" had a steel top that retracted into the trunk. It was the father of that hard-topped status symbol whose outlines conjured up (according to latter-day Motivational Researchers) a comforting composite vision of a man's mistress (the jazzy convertible) and his wife (the four-door sedan). The Thirties needed no motivational research organization to hit on the truth that that loving couple in the rumble seat would prefer to be indoors for plebiscites on whether the top should go up or down, and other questions.

The automobiles of 1940 and 1941 reflected a decade of change. Cars were roomier and safer, and had gone through the evolutionary process. In 1930 one could still buy a "self starter" as an extra for the Tin Lizzie. By 1940 headlights were set into the fender, the spare was in the trunk, and buttons were raising and lowering the windows of Packards and Lincoln Custom Sedans—as they raised and lowered the top on the Mercury convertible. A few early revolutionaries had dared to strip off the running board. Now running boards were going the way of the prehensile tail. They were optional on the 1940 Plymouth. Chevy did away with them completely in 1941.

The Hudson came out in 1935 with an Electric Hand which enabled the driver to pick his gear in advance. When the time arrived, the hand did the job for him. The 1940 Ford had a fingertip gearshift mounted on the steering column and the 1940 Oldsmobile had the first automatic shift—known as the Hydra-matic. At least one of the early shifts seemed to work at the flick of a finger, with the little control knob set into a column on the wheel; the maladroit driver could easily flick while accelerating rapidly from second into reverse, giving him and the automobile a rude shock and an excellent chance of leaving the transmission behind on the highway. Still, driving was getting to be as effortless as looking at one of Count Sakhnoffsky's horizontal clocks.

By today's standards the most advanced cars of 1940 have a solid, matronly look. Bodies were pleasingly plump. Not till after the war were they mounted on a flat fender like the turret of a tank. As one hunches into a present-day taxi one longs for the spaciousness of the big-bottomed 1930s Mercury, or of the roomy Hudson you could step down into as into a Tishman living room.

The year 1940 was many light years removed from the days

when Chevrolet proudly advertised its "gasoline meter on the dashboard." It was a long way from Lizzie to Loewy, from the crank to the Hydra-matic, from the rumble seat to the Jeep.

As those hopeful directors met in the early Thirties to discuss the "revitalizing" of the Graham, the Studebaker, or the Reo, the specter of the used car hovered over the proceedings like Banquo's ghost. America might be broke but she was still mobile. The number of road miles traveled increased between 1929 and 1933. In 1936 five and a half million families not actually on relief but with incomes of under $750 per year owned cars. Some car owners had annual incomes as low as $250. In this "third of a nation" category it was difficult, even at deflated Depression prices, to afford anything new.

In 1938 *Fortune* gave the life history of the car which was the answer to a pauper's prayer. It was a Ford which was sold new in 1930, "reconditioned" for the first time in 1933 after being taken as a trade-in on a Plymouth. Its speedometer was set back from 41,000 to 23,000, and it was bought by a schoolteacher who drove it west to Los Angeles in 1935, sold it to a dealer, and took a boat back home. Once again it was "reconditioned": the tires were regrooved and the speedometer set back to 27,000 miles. Almost "as good as new," it was sold to a carpenter who traded it in in 1936 for a Studebaker. It was briefly the property of a soda jerker who lost his job before he could meet all the payments. It was bought up by a used car auctioneer who knocked it off for $50 to a reconditioning "specialist." The "specialist" repainted it for $10, patched its weary brake linings with shims from the fabric of an old tire, and "let it go cheap" to a dentist's assistant for $95. It went through two other incarnations before it was finally sold back to Henry Ford for junk. Taken to River Rouge to the Ford demolition plant, it was pressed and fused. Finally it rose like a phoenix as a '38 Ford.

This was the car that was the specter of every dealer who was trying to sell a new Chevrolet, Dodge, or Auburn. It piled up in used car lots. It commanded too big a price as a trade-in. Its repeated encores were anathema to Detroit. When the designers failed, as they did in 1938, to come up with any real improvement over 1937, they added a year to the life of every '37 model on the road. The reputable dealer was caught in a bind between demands from the factory that he sell more new cars and demands from the potential purchaser of the new car for ever more generous trade-ins. The only people who ever made money on it were the aforementioned specialists. Their ethical level may be surmised by the fact that some states required that they be fingerprinted.

The spare parts of the jalopy were a delight to high-school boys. One hybrid was referred to by its creator as a 1925–35 Amrad (short for American Radiator). Originally a 1925 Chevy, the car acquired a Stutz radiator in 1929, along with a De Soto body and Auburn brakes. In 1934 came a Chrysler frame and motor, and in 1935 a Plymouth drive shaft. It did eighty easily, transported countless teenagers to the beach, and generally turned up after school started in the fall—*O tempora, O mores*—as a trade-in.

Small wonder that that poor Auburn dealer grew prematurely gray. Yet sympathy may be reserved. It never must be forgotten that the *new* car market operated in the Thirties by the standards of the Oriental bazaar. One could forgive the more reputable used car "specialists" when they turned the speedometer back to zero for the purpose of "avoiding discussion."

When Henry Ford accepted the annual style change he had little idea that worse was yet to come. A prelude had been provided by the Ford Hunger March of 1932 which brought idle workers from Detroit to Dearborn. On March 7, 1932, workers poured into downtown Detroit to protest Ford layoffs of fifty thousand men during the previous year. Police first used tear gas against the crowd —and finally fired on them. Four were killed, fifty were wounded, another fifty were hospitalized. Red coffins were lowered into a common grave to the singing of the "Internationale."

On October 9, 1935, Sidney Hillman of International Garment Workers, Charles P. Howard of the International Typographers Union, and David Dubinsky of the International Ladies' Garment Workers met in unholy alliance to form the Committee on Industrial Organizations—a militant wing of the AF of L which read them out of its ranks in 1936. The bulldog visage of John L. Lewis became familiar to every newspaper reader from that day on. To

Henry Ford the CIO hierarchy was as welcome as the legions of Lucifer.

Discontent was particularly widespread in the automotive industry. Workers chafed at the inhuman speed-up of the assembly line, and at the company spies, a budgetary item that cost General Motors nearly a million dollars between January 1, 1934, and July 31, 1936.

The bitter "sit-down" strikes against General Motors in 1937 erupted into a state of near civil war in the state of Michigan. A cordon was formed around the Chevrolet plant. Police with buckshot and tear gas faced union leaders armed with pop bottles and metal pipes. Governor Frank Murphy called out the National Guard. At the eleventh hour General Motors' William Knudsen was induced to negotiate. After a costly forty-four days which had paralyzed sixty plants in fourteen states, General Motors recognized the United Automobile Workers as its exclusive bargaining agency and resigned itself to negotiating a contract. Pax Flintana lasted for about a year, until General Motors once again fell out with UAW over the closed shop. Meanwhile, in another part of the forest, the old fox Henry Ford was girding his loins for battle, with the words, "I'll never recognize any union."

The defenders of Fordism were an unsavory crew. Charles E. Sorenson was engaged to "put the fear of God into labor." Henry Herbert Bennett built the Ford Service Department into a private militia. Espionage, labor baiting, terrorism, the employment of racketeers Joe Adonis and Chester La Mare, all did their bit of God's work. An attempt of Walter Reuther and Richard T. Frankensteen to distribute UAW leaflets resulted in sluggings and beatings, a feature of the old company's concept of "service."

The description of labor relations of this era reads like an account of a Napoleonic campaign. Frankensteen was known as the hero of the "Battle of the Overpass." Labor union members went into battle with a marching song: "Solidarity Forever." Bennett's head was cracked open outside the Rouge plant in '32. Norman Smith, who helped organize the River Rouge strike in 1941, had gotten his scars in an earlier campaign when he had been beaten up by Ford goons in Memphis. Nor was all peace and harmony in the ranks of labor itself. Labor's Napoleon, John L. Lewis, head of the United Mine Workers, had had the ultimate compliment conferred upon him by the Kingfish, who called him "the Huey Long of Labor." There were those even in his own union who found the image distasteful. Lewis broke with the White House over the unionization of the steel industry and said he would leave the CIO if FDR was re-elected. In 1936, faced with eating his words, he chose Elba. Another labor leader who got too big for his britches was Homer Martin, head of UAW, known as the "Leaping Parson." The Parson had purged from UAW ranks such worthies as Robert Kanter and Victor Reuther. Some of the rejects visited Martin in his Detroit hotel room. In a melodramatic gesture, which later seemed a bit foolish, he met them with drawn pistols. To the Battle of the Overpass was added the Ambush in the Hotel Eddystone.

Ford had his regional commanders—among them "Fats" Perry, head of the Service Department in Dallas. Perry's boys had a long list of tarrings, featherings, beatings, to their credit. Among those who succumbed to their gentle persuasions in 1937 were two CIO organizers en route to start a unionization drive in Kansas City. One was knocked down, the other beaten up. Two other employees made pro-union remarks while on a fishing trip. The Service Department had them kidnaped. Others suspected of union sympathies were ambushed and beaten at the home of a stool pigeon. An attack was made on W. J. Houston, attorney for UAW. A traveling salesman was roughed up, though it later turned out that the miscreant with union sympathies was his twin brother. The most thorough job of the Service Department involved one George Baer who was not even an automobile worker. This official of United Hatters Cap and Millinery Workers was rendered unconscious by the boys. One member of the Department sat on his stomach on the floor of a car. Another perched on his head. His face was covered with blood. His nose was broken, his teeth knocked out. An eye dangled out of its socket. The Service Department debated tossing him in the river, but settled instead for the public highway, as a reminder to passing cars of the merits of bargaining individually.

The tide of history, however, was running against Ford. The good fight, in the first place, was expensive, and capitulations were taking place on other fronts. Little Steel, for example, had also refused to sign with the CIO. Picketers in South Chicago had been fired on. The strike was broken but the working classes did not take kindly to massacre. Four were killed, six fatally injured, and ninety wounded. Republic Steel, as a result, had ended up with vastly decreased profits, and damage suits amounting to $220,000. As a result of the sit-downs General Motors' profits were down from $140,000,000 for the first half of 1936 to $110,000,000 in the first half of 1937. U.S. Steel signed with the CIO in 1937, preferring graceful capitulation to blood-red ink.

Many businessmen had hoped that the National Labor Relations Board would go the way of the NRA. Yet the Supreme Court surprised everyone by upholding the Wagner Act. (In 1941 the justices dealt a further body blow to Ford by refusing to allow him to appeal a decision requiring the company to reinstate twenty-three employees discharged for union activity.)

When war broke out between England and Germany, Ford's attitude was: A plague on both their houses. Here again he was out of the mainstream. Packard borrowed money from the RFC to build an airplane plant. General Motors turned to production of airplane and submarine motors and machine guns. Chrysler began to manufacture tanks. Dodge trucks were the backbone of army transport. (It may have been reasoned that the Wehrmacht could hold no terrors for any company that was the leading supplier of New York taxicabs.)

Ford finally leaped on the bandwagon with the production of "blitz buggies" and Pratt and Whitney engines. It was a measure of Ford's parochialism that he turned down a contract for making Rolls-Royce Merlin engines because six thousand of them were going to England. Packard got the contract and turned out more engines than Britain itself. The Laprobe Set always had been given to Anglophilia.

In 1941, as another bitter strike threatened the Ford plant at River Rouge, Mr. Bennett tried to invoke the forces of patriotism.

"Those former sit-downers whose acts of terror make Jean Valtin's revelations in *Out of the Night* seem like Mother Goose stories would now sabotage the Defense program of the nation to satisfy their greed for dues and more dues."

When the NLRB forced Ford to hold an election, Mr. Bennett said: "CIO will win it, of course, because it always wins these farcical elections. . . . We will bargain until Hell freezes over, but they won't get anything."

Mr. Bennett's crystal ball was clouded.

The Rouge strike ended with a smashing victory for the CIO, with Ford granting far more than the union demanded. The war effort was another force bringing Ford to heel. The government with its fat defense contracts was in a position to tell Ford to shape up or ship out.

Ford the industrialist was one of a dying breed, a subscriber to a sort of puritan ethic. Among the homilies by which he lived: "If you study the history of almost any criminal you will find he is an inveterate cigarette smoker." "I do nothing because it gives me pleasure." "Salt is one of the best things for the teeth and also for the hair." "The great majority of women who work do so in order to buy fancy clothes." "A man learns something even by being hanged."

On economics: "There is something sacred about wages." "I want the whole organization dominated by a just, generous and humane policy." The workers who had once subsisted on his revolutionary five dollars a day had had a Sociological Department to guide them in justice and humanity and to make sure that the money went for milk, vegetables, and salt rather than booze or the ponies.

In 1941, however, Ford's ninety cents an hour had been surpassed by Chrysler and General Motors. The Ford image was anathema to the *Nation,* which referred to the "Ford Reich" and castigated the Sage of Dearborn for his failure to perceive that Marxism was "the greatest social adventure of modern times." *Time* magazine, from another part of the political forest, drily characterized the Service Department with its broken heads and loosened teeth as "far from prissy." Both were agreed that Ford methods were a little behind the times. And not only Ford. It was a measure of the age that paid vacations were still a point of issue during one of General Motors' later-day go-rounds with the CIO. Yet a day was dawning when the worker could spend his hourly wage without any assistance from any Sociology Department—thank you.

The admen and decorators who flourished on the output of Detroit gave not a clue to the blood that was shed during these nights of the broken heads.

Ford's Sunday evening hour beat the drums for what the *Nation* called "industrial fundamentalism." When General Motors' radio program was content to deal with problems in construction and automobile safety Ford offered his listeners a philosophy of life. Mr. W. C. Cameron piously indicted "money-minded business" which operated industry for profit rather than—like Ford—for the general good. Mr. Cameron was against government interference, since industry had not been responsible for "one iota of harm to this country. The errors of human economics are continually canceled by the unfailing balance and supply of the economics of God."

That endearing Scottie of billboard fame who counseled motorists to "Watch the Fords Go By" gave no hint that they would go by bodies thrown out on the highway.

The higher-priced cars held out to the average man the prospect of knighthood. Car ownership in a democracy took the place of a lion couchant. "Those glistening chrome exhaust pipes of the supercharged Cord are the coat of arms of motoring royalty."

Cadillac and La Salle custom interiors in 1932 offered "soft, rich, deep-textured materials of the rarest beauty," "wood panelling . . . of the finest grained walnut," "accessory fitments such as vanity sets, cigarette lighters and clock cases . . . done with the faultless taste of a jeweler's setting." Packard held out to the young Plymouth owner the possibility of being a member of the elect. A young couple in a 1934 Packard ad gazed at a white-walled tire on the side of a car which tapered off to that famous pointed radiator. The first car they had owned had been small and inexpensive, and yet "even while they were buying it, he told her 'Some day I'm going to buy you a Packard.'" The ad gave a glowing picture of a family fulfillment on "the day that was years in the making."

Packard's "Ask the Man Who Owns One" was one of the most inspired advertising slogans of all time. The man who owned one was a creature for whom the skins-of-a-dozen-hand-picked-virgin-alpacas was not too good, as a 1935 Packard ad testified:

Just as only a few acres in the world produce the rare bouquet of old Burgundy, so too, only a single county grows wool that is fine enough to upholster the new Packard Twelve. The fleeces' pick from three choice flocks grazed in the lush pasturage of a tiny Texas area, are required for a single car.

Packard advertising was as handsome as the Packard itself. Steichen's photographs, Helck's paintings, Horter's etchings, and Cooper's lettering had made their distinguished appeal to a conservative clientele. On one occasion, at least, the ads had been capable of jazzier moments. In 1913 Harry K. Thaw had escaped in a Packard Six from the Mattawan State Asylum for the Criminally Insane. Packard ads describing his feat concluded with a word to the wise: "When high speed is necessary, when a fast getaway is absolutely imperative, Ask the Man Who Owns One." John Dillinger once conferred a similar compliment upon the Ford. Advertising executives being as timorous as they are, the pickup of his testimonial was a good deal slower than the pickup of the car.

Packard advertising in the Thirties reflects the malaise with which the company made its first halting advance toward the proletariat. In 1934 Walter Damrosch and the NBC Symphony were offered up as a Tuesday night treat. Lawrence Tibbett was substituted for Mr. Damrosch and *Fortune* reported that he was soon singing fewer arias and more Carrie Jacobs Bond. President Alvan McCauley shuddered when Young and Rubicam suggested a variety hour emceed by the fantastically popular and suitably gentlemanly Fred Astaire. When the name of Jack Benny was mentioned the distasteful grimace became an apoplectic paroxysm. Packard's Friday-Philharmonic standards caused radio executives to reflect unhappily, "We have an Episcopalian reputation and we want to do business with the Methodists."

The handmaiden of the adman, the decorator, furnished interior and exterior with the Dorothy Draper touch. Cords came in "cigarette cream," "desert tan," "carmine red." Light bodies had dark interiors, light beading and trim—a typical 1930s study in bold contrast. Other decorator touches: the La Salle radiator whose vents were balls, the gunmetal Cord with chartreuse seats, the chartreuse Cord with gunmetal seats, the cream-colored Auburn convertible with red seats, the Pontiac in gunmetal with lemon seats; the Packard and Buick in cream or red.

The Alexis de Sakhnoffsky dream cars offered interesting examples of transportation in evolution. In 1938 he designed a station wagon "with the swank of a town car." Some features later filtered down to the Chevrolet level. Its spare tire was prophetically hidden inside the chassis. Its bulging front fender was inconveniently bisected by the front door. Still, Sakhnoffsky's idealized station wagon—like the town car—exiled the driver to the out-of-doors. The idea died hard that one couldn't aspire to chic (or on a lower economic level to youthful *élan vital*) unless someone in the car wrote an epilogue to the ride in an oxygen tent with double pneumonia.

To read the magazines of the Thirties was to be taken into an automotive Eden peopled by snappy suburbanites and sybarites on safari. Society women scribbled bread and butter letters on built-in writing tables while shouting over speaking tubes at the chauffeur for on-the-spot weather reports or for advice on how to spell. As some of Sakhnoffsky's dreams became reality in the low-priced three, the shipping clerk who read *Esquire* did not need to buy a Cadillac to achieve blue and beige fabrics, walnut-grained moldings. He could get all those William Pahlmann overtones in Plymouth's 1941 Fashion Tone Special De Luxe.

The Depression had really wreaked havoc with the economics of God. Though Henry Ford might long for a return to Lizzie's standardized heyday, he had a marked ability to roll with the punches in a world he never made.

In 1922 Ford bought up the Lincoln Company. He introduced the 12-cylinder Lincoln in 1932, and the Lincoln Zephyr in 1935. The Mercury joined the family in 1938. The Lincoln was a 12-cylinder job which sold—after 1933—for $5000. The Lincoln Continental, introduced in 1939, was a car magnificent enough—as far as design went—to make the Packard and the Cadillac look to their laurels. The Duesenberg, the Cord, and the Stutz, which had the edge on it in the matter of workmanship, had gone the way of the good little dressmaker whose most exquisite stitching was to be found on the inside. The whole Ford line had been subtly upgraded. Something about the V-8 appealed to the blueblood who wouldn't have been caught dead in a Chevrolet. By 1940 the "universal car" had become, as Nancy Mitford might put it, "U."

At the same time there had been a downgrading of the class

product. Like the little seamstress, compromise had hit that old-world craftsman. Few car models from the post-World War II era will survive in the automotive museums of the twenty-first century. Those CIO vacations with pay were expensive. Something had to give and adroit Detroit hit on quality.

The Willys never caught on in the Thirties even with the so-called common man, because it looked tinny. Yet even the rich today are accustomed to cars whose spare parts rattle around in the rear because someone has forgotten to assemble them. Fortunately the leveling process has helped those at the bottom of the social scale as well. The less-than-wealthy no longer have to hold their cars still before they can leap behind the wheel.

Behind the chichi of the ad copy were the bitter, bloody upheavals of an industry which was part of a world in flux. Henry Ford died in 1947. He had already lived to see the CIO in his shop and his engines exported to perfidious Albion. He had seen his competitor, the Willys Company, with its production of the jeep, become the wartime world's only universal car. He had dimly sensed the narrowing gap between the owner of Ford and Cord.

Had he lived a bit longer, anti-Semite Ford would have heard Henry Ford II getting in a plug for the Great Society at a meeting of the United Jewish Appeal. Whatever old Henry's reaction to the platform, he might have approved his grandson's phraseology, which recalled his own reasoning. "The poor simply are not very good customers for our sort of products."

He would not have been as pleased to see what had happened to the frugal virtues. The sons of men who battled the Ford militia now demanded Michelin tires and custom paint jobs on their own automobiles. The grandsons of Model T owners are dropouts who roar around the countryside in Stingrays, Lincolns, and Cadillac coupés. They munch Double Bubba Burgers with little girls who tease their hair, and work (at God knows what) in order to buy fancy, tiny clothes.

Once in a while one of the brontosauruses tries to walk the earth again. The '32 Ford is a contemporary hot rod favorite. There have been to-dos about reviving the Duesenberg and the Cord. They just don't quite belong.

In March 1966 a new Duesenberg was unveiled. It sold for a

mere $19,500, whereas a particularly fetching old-timer might to-
day bring close to $40,000. Somehow the newcomer looked out of
place. It was a shiny monster whose old-fashioned radiator superimposed on chrome bumpers gave it a menacing leer. Where were
the graceful fenders, the wire wheels, the spare tire set aristocrati-
cally on the side? And it was *black*. A Duesenberg had no business
coming in any color but yellow. They really can't *afford* to make
'em like the Duesenberg. As for the Ford, where's the challenge?
It's just too easy to get it to start.

Chapter 8

Joseph Invictus

> Why is it that each is the last to find
> That his legs are gone—that his eyes are bad,
> That the quicker reflexes have left his mind,
> That he hasn't the stuff that he one day had,
> That lost youth mocks, and he doesn't see
> The ghost of the fellow that he used to be?

Grantland Rice's poetry is typical of the efforts of the sportswriter *qua* bard. Many lines in the same meter were written throughout the Thirties in recollection of the great names of the Golden Age of Sport. The big ballyhoo of the Twenties had been responsible for making nine-day wonders of everyone from Gertrude Ederle to Charles A. Lindbergh. Babe Ruth, Knute Rockne, Red Grange, Jack Dempsey had all been given the treatment, and emerged with halos, Golden People. Many of them were still around as the next decade went through its growing pains. The crowds in Madison Square Garden had to sit through many a six-day bicycle race and dull prizefight as the heavyweight crown was tossed around by a collection of tyros before the Thirties finally produced an authentic folk hero, a man named Louis. Meanwhile, the dactyls and spondees were dedicated to the Champs of the Twenties as they checked out one by one.

Some of the Golden People were still on their way up. Some were on their way down. Some were in retirement. Some were making a last college try. The name of Helen Wills Moody had been heard in the Twenties but it was in the early Thirties that her fabled white eyeshade became a fixture. Her running grudge match against Helen Jacobs had begun in 1927 when she had mopped the court with her opponent, and in six successive years when Miss Jacobs failed to take a single set from her. On August 27, 1934, Mrs. Moody defaulted to Miss Jacobs. "I felt as if I were going to faint because of a pain in my back and hip and a complete numbness of my right leg." The numbness vanished by 1935 at Wimbledon when Miss Jacobs once again thought she had Mrs. Moody on the ropes. Mrs. Moody suddenly put sting in her strokes, ran for points instead of watching them wearily from the baseline, and reeled off five straight games to take set and match.

The girls gave the fans their money's worth. Miss Jacobs once hit the ball so hard that she knocked the racquet out of Mrs. Moody's hand. She in turn showed the effects of her exertions to the extent of forgetting that she was serving. Helen Wills Moody, however, had that mark of champions. She cared. It was all in the training. Once after dancing for hours with Paul Gallico at El Morocco, she remarked to him, "You know, Paul, this is awfully good for my footwork."

Bobby Jones in 1930 won the four major golf events of America and Great Britain, the so-called Grand Slam which earned for him the equivalent of a Roman triumph—a ticker tape parade and an accolade from Grover Whalen.

Bill Tilden had turned pro and could thumb his nose at the Nice Nellyism about the sanctity of the amateur in sports by giving out testimonials for Camels. Tommy Hitchcock, minor deity of the Twenties, was still one of the group that defeated the British polo team in 1939. Gene Tunney had unseated Jack Dempsey from the world's heavyweight championship in 1926 and had retired to a wealthy marriage; Ty Cobb—"the Georgia Peach"—had left the diamond in 1929, baseball's only millionaire. Johnny Weissmuller, after a glorious swimming career in the Twenties, had settled down to a swinging movie life as Tarzan.*

* The role demanded an ability to go from vines and to murmur to Maureen O'Sullivan the lines, "Me Tarzan, you Jane." Off screen, with a cast that included actress Lupe Velez, dancer Bobbe Arnst, society girl Beryl Scott, and golf champion Arlene Gates, life in the connubial tree house proceeded somewhat less amicably.

Babe Ruth had been in slow decline since the banner year of 1927 when he hit sixty home runs. He fell from 49 in 1930 to 22 in 1934. His golden moment did occur in the Thirties. In 1932 in a World Series game against the Chicago Cubs, he had two strikes on him. Before he swung for the third time he pointed to the bleachers to show the crowd where the ball was going to land. It did. And a legend marked the spot. In 1935 he was released from his contract with the New York Yankees and signed as assistant manager and president of the Boston Braves.

Ruth wound up his career signing his name to articles which had been ghost written for him. (There had never been any ambiguity about his professional status.) Nor had the confidence and color gone with advancing age. Graham McNamee and Grantland Rice once had the Babe on a national radio hookup. He had been instructed to make the usual allusion to the Duke of Wellington and the playing fields of Eton. The Babe paid homage as follows: "As Duke Ellington once said, the Battle of Waterloo was won on the playing fields of Elkton." (The last named being the scene, in Maryland, of Ruth's marriage to his first wife.)

Mrs. Walter Lippmann once queried the Babe on his great feat of 1932. Grantland Rice recalled his cheerful reply.

"Root's still in there," the Babe obliged. "He breezes the first two pitches by—both strikes! The mob's tearing down Wrigley Field. I shake my fist after that first strike. After the second I point my bat at these bellerin' bleachers—right where I aim to park the ball. Root throws it, and I hit that (censored) ball on the nose—right over the (censored) fence for two (censored) runs.

"'How do you like those apples, you (censored) (censored) (censored)?' I yell at Root as I head towards first. By the time I reach home I'm almost fallin' down I'm laughin' so (censored) hard—and that's how it happened."

Mrs. Lippmann, accustomed as she was to hearing the aftermath of Versailles described in polished phrases, was so unnerved that she left the party after her all-too-successful attempt to draw out the Babe.

Red Grange was working in a night club and the last legendary figure of the Twenties, Knute Rockne, the Notre Dame coach, had been killed on a flight from Kansas City to the Coast in 1931, after dilating on the safety of air travel. Even the normally restrained New York *Times* lapsed into the lachrymose idiom of the sports world after this event:

> And yesterday Knute Rockne went West. He intended to fly to Los Angeles, but tragedy intervened, and Rock went over the Great Divide, beyond the night, across the day to where beyond these voices there is peace.

Some athletes might die and some might fade away. Certain fixed stars throughout the Thirties were simply there. First were Joe McCarthy's Yankees. The Sultan of Swat might have gone off but Lou Gehrig was waiting in the wings. In 1932 he was photographed congratulating the Bambino on his tour de force. Yet the Iron Man was even then trying to duplicate it. Gehrig never quite matched Ruth's record but he hit 46 home runs in 1931, 49 in 1934, and 49 once again in 1936. Before his retirement in 1939 he set a record for having played 2130 straight games. At the time of his retirement Hank Greenberg, who but for Gehrig might have been playing first base for the Yankees rather than the Detroit Tigers, remarked hopefully, "Maybe that Yankee dynasty is beginning to crumble."

He was not only rueful, he was wrong. By the time "Iron Man" Gehrig died in 1941, the Yankees had another great star, "Jolting Joe" DiMaggio, who connected in fifty-six straight games the year of Pearl Harbor. Furthermore, the Yankee team was always more than the sum of its parts. After Ruth's triumph in 1932 the Yankees took the series in 1936, 1937, 1938, and 1939. After a lapse in 1940, they beat the Brooklyn Dodgers in 1941.

Infallibility is not an easy quality to live with. The Bronx Bombers never stirred the passionate loyalties inspired by the teams that never won. The New York Mets of the Thirties were the Brooklyn Dodgers. The Shea Stadium of the Depression was Ebbets Field.

The Dodgers were always in the cellar, scarcely ever lifting the hopes of their legions of fans. But they were nothing if not colorful. A Dodger coach had once smashed a fist through a subway window, felling a guard who dared to stick out his tongue at him. The Dodgers had a genius for the baroque blooper. On October 6, 1941, for example, a victory over the Yanks seemed assured. The Dodgers led 4–3. Tommy Henrich swung and missed for the third time. Suddenly the Dodger catcher, Mickey Owen, let the ball slip out of his hand. Before he could retrieve it, Henrich was safe on first. The final score 7–4 for the Yankees became one more cross to be borne by those who lived at the junction of Flatbush and DeKalb.

Throughout the Thirties there was generally some celebration requiring beer, beer for old Notre Dame. The immortal Rock's last act as coach was to lead the team to a smashing victory over Penn in 1930. Jimmy Walker, New York's lively and light-fingered mayor, generally had reason to be proud of his favorite b'ys. To be sure, there were setbacks. In 1931 he went to South Bend to watch them go down to ignominious defeat at the hands of Southern California. After Rockne's death the National Football College Championship passed to Michigan ('32 and '33), to Minnesota ('34, '36, '40, and '41), to Texas Christian and Texas A & M in 1938 and 1939. The Irish of Notre Dame remained the heroes of the barroom ballads. In 1935, when they were trailing 13–0 against Ohio State with the clock ticking off the last few moments of the final quarter, they suddenly managed a 32-yard run and a touchdown pass, pulling out an eleventh-hour Notre Dame victory and providing restaurateur Toots Shor with a means of remembering his wedding anniversary. (Milestones with Toots are always related to sporting events. Galento's victory over Nova commemorated the signing of the lease on his restaurant in Dr. Shor's Famous Memory Course.)

As the Irish were always with us, so too were the English. Yachtsman Harold Vanderbilt defeated British attempts to capture the America Cup in 1930, 1934, and 1937. Thanks to this gentleman-sportsman the English were never able to avenge the Boston Tea Party.

The sporting world of the Thirties also had its Grand Old Man. Connie Mack (born Cornelius McGillicuddy) played catcher for the Pittsburgh Pirates, midwifed the American League, and founded the Philadelphia Athletics. On his seventy-ninth birthday in 1941 he had occasion to reflect that he was a major leaguer before Bill Tilden was born, that he was one of the few Americans who could remember horsecars and John L. Sullivan, Gentleman Jim Corbett, and Boss Tweed.

Spoken of in almost the same tones as Connie Mack was the sprinter Glenn Cunningham. Fox Movietone showed him year after year crossing the finish line—not always, to be sure, in first place. In the 1932 Olympics he placed fourth in the 1500-meter race. In 1934 he was defeated by "Bounding Bill" Bonthron. In the 1936 Berlin Olympics he was defeated in the same race by Jack Lovelock of New Zealand. Oddly enough, he seemed to pick up speed with age. In 1938 "Galloping Glenn" passed his fellow Kansan Archie San Romani at the mile mark. "How long can it go on?" marveled John Kieran. "Young fellows are bound to catch up with him and pass him some of these days or nights, but in the meanwhile the old gentleman has been setting a marvelous pace." The spry old gaffer in question was at the time a graduate student at NYU.

As the Old Champ checked out a new one was always on his way up. In 1931 a nineteen-year-old tennis player named Ellsworth Vines became champion and was widely hailed as a second Tilden. He and the original went on tour together. Temperamental Tilden kept threatening suicide. Vines, who was still young enough to find nightly awakenings by the self-destructive a novelty, cried, "We gotta stop him." Others wearily told him not to worry, and assured him that nothing would stop Tilden if he had really made up his mind. Vines' reply: "Don't worry, hell. I don't want him to kill our tour."

A few short years later, Vines got his comeuppance. In 1937 a redheaded Donald Budge defeated Baron Gottfried Von Cramm at Wimbledon, and a year later he beat Gene Mako at Forest Hills, taking the Australian, British, French, and American crowns in his own version of the Grand Slam. The verdict: "Better than Tilden and Vines."

No *one* person stepped down to hand the laurel wreath to Mildred "Babe" Didrikson. This one-time typist for the Employers Casualty Company of Dallas entered the Women's National Track and Field Championships in 1931 where she won six firsts. In the 1932 Los Angeles Olympics she won the javelin throw, the 80-meter low hurdles and the heart of sportswriter Grantland Rice.

In a football suit she could hold her own with bruisers from Southern Methodist. She could peg a baseball 296 feet—just like a man. She dived and swam superlatively, boxed with Artie Mc-

Govern, and once split the lip of the light heavyweight champion Bill Stribling. She was an accomplished dancer—ballroom and adagio. As with Mrs. Moody, her first thought may have been for her footwork. She played gin rummy and the harmonica. She cooked like Escoffier and one could imagine her, after going a few rounds in the ring with the boys, inviting them up to her place for divinity fudge. It was one of her greatest regrets that she couldn't meet Grantland Rice for post-mortems of the Big Game in the men's locker room.

In 1935 she put away boyish things and concentrated on golf. She was the first woman to win the British Amateur. She was three-time winner of the world's championship at Tam O'Shanter and won eighty-two golf tournaments between 1935 and her death from cancer in 1953. In 1938 Babe married George Zaharias and in the words of sportswriter Paul Gallico (whom she had once outrun in a friendly race to the seventeenth hole), she became "sis from her head to her toes." She sported lipsticks, compacts, and lace handkerchief and seductive lingerie, telling Gallico, "It's silk and ah like it." Only a few who remembered the old days had trouble getting used to the flower hat perched uneasily on the javelin thrower's brow.

In baseball the names of Ruth and Ty Cobb were replaced on the sports page by those of Hank Greenberg, Carl Hubbell, Lefty Gomez, Lefty Grove, Dixie Walker, and Pee Wee Reese. Mel Ott—a veteran of the Twenties—was still going strong. Baseball's greatest showmen were the two most colorful Cardinals, Dizzy and Daffy Dean.

Dizzy Dean joined the Cardinals in 1932. This great pitcher was known for glazing fastball and blazing temper. When provoked he was known to rip up baseball uniforms. (Leo Durocher, whose name would one day be synonymous with dem bums, was a Cardinal at the same time, giving the team a dangerously low collective boiling point.)

In the 1934 Series the Cards routed the Detroit Tigers. In his first five years with the Cardinals, Dean averaged twenty-four victories a year—with seventeen strikeouts in a single game in 1933. Paul ("Daffy"), a younger brother, joined the team two years after Dizzy. In 1934 Dean boasted that "me 'n' Paul" would win forty-five games for the Cardinals. They won forty-nine. Fond of posing as simple rustics, the Deans were vague about their names and origins. Dizzy was sometimes "Jerome Herman," sometimes "J. Hanna." The family homestead vacillated in locale from Texas to Oklahoma.

Advertisers all over the country were quick to capitalize on their magnetic appeal for the grip-developer and autographed-baseball markets. Known as "a man of a few thousand words," Dean aspired to being a legend in his lifetime. He claimed to have gotten married under floodlights in front of home plate at a Houston ballpark, to have registered once at three St. Louis hotels so that he could flop when the spirit moved him. He redecorated a banquet hall with a banquet in progress. When things really got dull, Dizzy donned Indian headdress, wrapped himself in a blanket, broke into a war dance or built a bonfire in front of the Cardinal dugout. With Dizzy, baseball was a million laughs, and usually good baseball.

In the late Thirties he was traded to the Chicago Cubs for $185,000 and three able-bodied Cubs, every one of them mightier than this fading Cardinal. Dizzy got his walking papers in a way that added little luster to the legend, after nearly scalping himself when the door of an automobile opened, dumping him out on his head.

About the time that the term "white elephant" was beginning to be used in connection with Dean, the youngest pitcher in major league history was riding to high school on the bus in Van Meter, Iowa, wearing his Cleveland Indian cap. Young Bob Feller made his baseball debut in 1936 at seventeen. While in school he was pulling down $10,000 a year, and competing ball clubs were bidding up to $100,000 for his services. In his first major league game Feller struck out fifteen batters—two shy of the record set by Dizzy Dean in 1933. In the third week of play he passed Dean's mark. Four years later Dean would be offered Feller's starting salary and would accept it after declaring to all, "I won't sign for no $10,000."

Sic transit gloria.

By 1940 "Old Dizz" was on his way to the Texas League under option (subject to twenty-four-hour recall). He was unable to pitch overhand and P. K. Wrigley, hoping to recover something on his investment, sent a tutor along to give him pointers on delivering the

1. Mr. J. P. Morgan and midget, 1933

The Acme Newspictures caption accompanying the photograph, taken when he was testifying before a Senate investigating committee, said that it "was engineered by a press agent who caught the financier in an extraordinarily expansive mood. It will be a long, long time before Mr. Morgan is in so obliging a mood again."

2. Labor unrest
Truck drivers strike, Minneapolis, December 1934

3. Labors over
Lou Gehrig retires, Yankee Stadium, December 1939

MORE FUN THAN THE PARTY...
THERE AND BACK IN AN *AIRFLOW*

Chrysler
TOMORROW'S CAR TODAY

*T*HERE'S a new zest . . . an amazing new experience . . . in going places in an Airflow Chrysler.

With all its delightful roominess, the Airflow Chrysler combines a marvelous lightness and smoothness in performance . . . a sensation of floating along in glorious freedom . . . as silent and effortless as sailing before the wind!

Part of the answer is Automatic Overdrive† . . . that marvelous but simple device which cuts engine revolutions a third in country driving. It's a thrilling sensation . . . this flying along with a loafing engine. As you travel 100 miles . . . the engine has turned only the equivalent of 70 miles. You get up to 5 more miles to the gallon . . . and engine life is vastly prolonged.

Then there's the marvel of the Airflow Floating Ride. All jolts banished. No tiny jiggles and jars. Just a long, slow, even glide . . . the most restful you ever experienced.

You'll never know just how much an Airflow Chrysler can mean to you until you get into the car and ride. Your Chrysler dealer

★ *Dashing New Chrysler Six Convertible Coupe* ★

will gladly arrange a trip and show you all the things this amazing car will do.

☆ CHRYSLER SIX . . . 93 horsepower, 118-inch wheelbase, $760 and up.

☆ DE LUXE EIGHT . . . 105 and 110 horsepower, 121 and 133-inch wheelbase, $925 and up.

☆ AIRFLOW EIGHT . . . 115 horsepower, 123-inch wheelbase, All models, $1345.

☆ AIRFLOW IMPERIAL . . . 130 horsepower, 128-inch wheelbase, All models, $1475.

☆ AIRFLOW CUSTOM IMPERIAL . . . 130 horsepower, 137-inch wheelbase, $2475 and up.

†Standard on Airflow Imperial. Available on all 1936 Chryslers at slight additional cost.

All prices list at factory, Detroit; special equipment extra.

Ask for the Official Chrysler Motors-Commercial Credit Company Time Payment plan. Available through all Chrysler Dealers.

Chrysler's on the Air! . . . Big Star Program . . . Every Thursday, 8 P. M., Eastern Daylight Saving Time . . . Columbia Network. You're invited to listen.

6. FDR & Eleanor

7. Nelson & Jeanette

Often a bridesmaid but never a bride

EDNA'S case was really a pathetic one. Like every woman, her primary ambition was to marry. Most of the girls of her set were married—or about to be. Yet not one possessed more grace or charm or loveliness than she.

And as her birthdays crept gradually toward that tragic thirty-mark, marriage seemed farther from her life than ever.

She was often a bridesmaid but never a bride.

* * *

That's the insidious thing about halitosis (unpleasant breath). You, yourself, rarely know when you have it. And even your closest friends won't tell you.

Sometimes, of course, halitosis comes from some deep-seated organic disorder that requires professional advice. But usually—and fortunately—halitosis is only a local condition that yields to the regular use of Listerine as a mouth wash and gargle. It is an interesting thing that this well-known antiseptic that has been in use for years for surgical dressings, possesses these unusual properties as a breath deodorant.

It halts food fermentation in the mouth and leaves the breath sweet, fresh and clean. *Not* by substituting some other odor but by really removing the old one. The Listerine odor itself quickly disappears. So the systematic use of Listerine puts you on the safe and polite side. Lambert Pharmacal Co., St. Louis, Mo.

9. Up from The Depression
Families wash clothes in FSA camp laundry...1939

THIS BIG MONEY-MAKING OUTFIT..

Now Free!

Get Started At Once In Fine Paying COFFEE AGENC

How would you like to have a fine-paying business of your own—a simple-to-run Coffee Agency in which you can start making good money your very first day? Here's your big chance if **you act now.** To an honest, reliable man or woman in any open locality, I will give — FREE — complete business equipment containing absolutely everything needed to run a fine-paying neighborhood Coffee Agency. **You don't send me a penny.** If you want to better yourself—want cash to spend —money to save—the means to live in comfort—let me show you your big chance.

Without any previous experience, you can now own a simple, pleasant, dignified Coffee Agency—a profitable all-year 'round business of your own, in which your home is your headquarters. No training course required.

Be a Food Distributor

The complete valuable Display Outfit which I give you FREE is absolutely all you need to run a fine-paying neighborhood Coffee Agency. And I am willing to extend liberal credit so you can build a splendid business on my capital.

Food Distributors make good money because they handle daily necessities that people simply must buy. You will distribute our guaranteed, uniform high quality products fresh from our own pure food kitchens and laboratories. You will make calls on your list of regular customers, take orders, make deliveries, and pocket a liberal share of every dollar you take in.

Splendid Cash Profits

You owe it to yourself to write and see what wonderful success so many others have enjoyed with this simple money-making Plan. Let me mail you full particulars — then you can judge whether you want to start right in making money at once. You can devote your full time or part time.

Everything You Need— FREE

I will give you FREE a complete valuable Display Outfit, including a big assortment of regular full-size packages. Without your sending me one penny, I will also give you a simple-sure-fire Plan which anyone can

follow. I will give you advertis[ing] material and positively everything you need to make good profits y[our] very first day. I will help you ev[ery] step of the way.

In addition to your fine cash earni[ngs] you can get food products and [over] one hundred other daily househ[old] necessities for your own use at wh[ole] sale prices—so you save money as [well] as **make** money.

Get Full Particulars— NOW!

This is a sincere offer made by a [reliable], old-established company o[perating] from Coast to Coast. Writ[e] once for full particulars. Unless [you] take advantage of my remarkable [Free] Outfit Offer now, you may be miss[ing] the very money-making opportu[nity] you have been looking for. Strike [out] for yourself! Be independent! M[ake] money! Enjoy life! Remember— don't send me a penny. Just fill [in] and send the coupon and I will [send] you full particulars. Do this TOD[AY].

E. J. MILLS, President
7965 Monmouth Ave., Cincinnati[, Ohio]

MAIL COUPON for Full Details of FREE OFFER

E. J. MILLS, President
7965 Monmouth Ave., Cincinnati, Ohio.

Without the slightest obligation on my part, please m[ail] me full particulars about your offer of a Complete Free Out[fit] so that I can start making money at once in a Local Co[ffee] Agency of my own.

Name ....

Address ....

....

(Please print or write plainly)

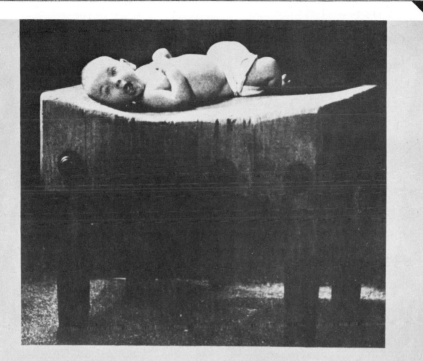

Nice fresh babies . . .79¢ a pound!

SEVERAL of the world's leading nations have put bounties on babies.

They are not hypocritical or evasive about the reason behind this golden impetus to breeding. They want more babies now for bigger armies later . . . babies to be fattened up for sixteen or seventeen years, then delivered on the hoof for slaughter!

So breed, Mother, breed for the glory of your heroic Leaders. Take good care of that cuddly baby, Mother, so he'll grow up big and strong and the butchers will be pleased with him. And be thankful, Mother, for your great privilege of producing a son whose destiny it is to be blown to hell!

.   .   .

This baby-bounty business is one of the more revolting indications of the war insanity that afflicts the world today. We may consider ourselves here in America as removed from it all . . . as determined to stay out . . . as wanting only peace.

But war insanity is a horribly infectious disease. And if war breaks out *any place in the world*, we'll find it terribly difficult to stay out—despite all our present high-sounding talk of neutrality.

That's why an immediate, constant, and aggressive campaign for peace is so essential. We, here at World Peaceways, are conducting such a campaign.

We have made it our job to keep people who want peace as fervently as we do, enlightened on what's going on in world politics. We foster, in every way we know how, the cause of peace. We have plans we hope may help keep us out of war.

But it's a monumental job, that needs the help of all decent people. We'd like your support. We *need* your support. Write to World Peaceways, 103 Park Avenue, New York City.

12. The Scottsboro Boys

13. The Harry James Band

On the pier, Atlantic City, 1939. The male vocalist, to the right of Harry, later made something of a name for himself.

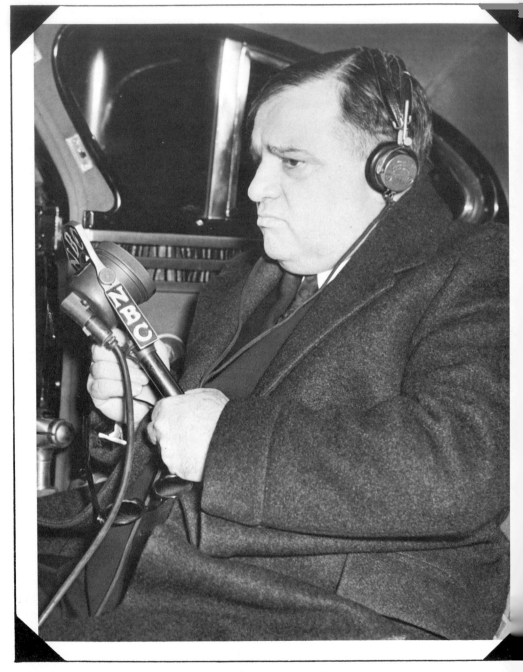

14. La Guardia, Fiorello

15. Corrigan, Wrong-Way

16. U.S. soldiers on parade: the World's Fair, 1939

ball sidearm. At about this time the clown in the war bonnet looked out from the pages of a magazine holding four of a kind and sponsored by a plug from the little woman: "We'll be back—don't forget that." Cynics fluent in the Dean idiom merely grunted, "How?"

The words of the parting champion were often the measure of the man. Bill Tilden had cheated Father Time for nearly a decade. "Why, Bill's an old man," said Ellsworth Vines (Tilden was pushing forty), "but his stamina would kill a horse." When Tilden hit forty he made the mistake of taking on Donald Budge at the Westchester Country Club. He beat Budge in one set. Budge took the next two from him handily. Grantland Rice describes the aftermath. "Bill took one look at the young man. 'Dammit!' he cried, 'just give me your legs . . . no, to hell with your legs . . . just give me your feet and I'll go right back there and whip the daylights out of that Budge! The legs can still carry me. But the feet are heavier than lead.'

"There was nothing left to say," recalled Rice. "I patted Bill on the shoulder, told him he was magnificent, still, and left."

A charming envoi was provided by Gene Sarazen in 1940. In 1922 this ex-caddy had announced that he was going to win America's Number One golf tournament, and he did. Ten years later he won it again. In the 44th U.S. Open in 1940, Sarazen was thirty-eight. The new faces were already in evidence. Jimmy Demaret, Ben Hogan, Sam Snead, Ralph Guldahl, and Byron Nelson were all under twenty-nine. Sarazen plodded along in out-of-style plus fours. Using a forty-year-old putter, Sarazen did eight strokes better than Snead and three better than Hogan, Guldahl, and Nelson. He tied dark horse Lawson Little with a 72-hole total of 287 strokes.

The next day, in an 18-hole playoff, Sarazen lost to Little 73–70. Once again he had called the shot correctly. No golfer over thirty-five, according to Sarazen, would ever win the Open. His victorious opponent was twenty-nine.

Crabbed age gave way to youth even in the equine world. In 1938 at Pimlico an upstart named Seabiscuit challenged War Admiral—Man O' War's proudest son. Seabiscuit, a four to one shot, forged ahead to dethrone the champion. Seabiscuit was but one of the parade of thoroughbreds who galloped through the newsreels of the Thirties—Gallant Fox, Stymie, Alsab, Whirlaway. None had the satisfaction of War Admiral's distinguished father. His beloved trainer Will Harbut had himself photographed with a tear in the eye, looking heavenward with his "baby" who was theoretically readying himself for what sportswriters like to call the Big Sky Sweepstakes. Ironically, it was Harbut who beat Man O' War to that final photo finish.

One field where the new generation improved on the record of the old with terrifying rapidity was in the field of automobile racing. In 1932 Sir Malcolm Campbell set a speed record of 254 mph at Daytona Beach. Campbell bettered his own speed to 301 in 1935, and by the end of the decade John Cobb had run it up to 368.9. Cobb's land speed record stood unchallenged until 1964 when it was broken by Malcolm Campbell's son Donald. With the turbine-powered cars of the future who can tell where it will end? The real hero of the piece is the car itself, and machines are mercifully mute: no statements for the press, no furtive tears. Cobb's Railton could never say pityingly to Campbell's Bluebird, "Champ, honest, you never looked better."

As the Twenties produced Babe Ruth, so did the Thirties bring forth at last one Titan who seemed destined to flout the laws of nature. Heavyweight boxing champion Joe Louis seemed in the Thirties to be truly immortal.

Since the championship went up for grabs after Gene Tunney's retirement in the late Twenties, a parade of fighters blundered into it—and out—in rapid succession. Max Schmeling, Jack Sharkey, Primo Carnera, and Max Baer—largely by happy chance—put up their hands and mumbled their versions of "I did it all for you, Mom."

Then along came James Braddock, hero of a Depression Cinderella story. He was the model of the down-and-out pug. Retired from the ring, he had been on relief. No food, no job, no hope, four mouths to feed and the usual answer: "No Help Wanted."

In despair he had gone back to fighting and had finally gotten a match with Max Baer. The legend of the hare and the tortoise was suddenly re-enacted in Long Island City.

Baer, the clown, had not bothered to train. He paraded about the ring looking contemptuous. He snarled at the referee and tried to frighten Braddock by making faces, a stratagem which had worked on the childlike Carnera. Braddock stumbled through a dull fight, piling up points. At the end of the fifteenth round it was Braddock by a fluke.

Enter the *real* champion. The managers of Braddock watched nervously as the young Negro from the Ford factory landed a smashing right to the face of Primo Carnera. Next, Joe Louis wiped the smirk off the face of Max Baer, prompting sportswriter John Kieran to a flight of poesy:

> And what a poet I would be and Oh! the songs I'd sing
> If I could put the punch in rhyme that Joe puts in the
> ring!

When Louis took on Max Schmeling in 1936, however, he suffered from one of Baer's chronic complaints—overconfidence. In Yankee Stadium in the twelfth round, with the odds eight to one against him, Schmeling knocked out Louis to get another crack at the title he had lost to Jack Sharkey. Louis' manager Joe Jacobs was so dismayed by the outcome of the fight that he rushed into the ring to embrace his boy and lost his pants.

It was Louis' only lapse. James Braddock, nervously watching the gathering whirlwind, refereed, endorsed drinks and health foods, and amassed a nest egg against the inevitable Evil Day.

Louis' autobiography from then on might have been entitled *And Then I Hit*. Out of the hordes of his victims are many who are little more than long-forgotten names. We remember Tommy Farr, but how about Nathan Mann and Harry Thomas? Sacrificial lamb Max Schmeling came back for a return engagement and was polished off in two minutes and four seconds. Then came two more faceless ones—John Henry Lewis and Jack Roper—the first in Madison Square Garden, the second in Los Angeles, both kayoed in the first round.

Number eight was "Two Ton Tony" Galento, a huge, bumbling fighter in the Carnera tradition, almost as broad as he was long. He was turned in midair by a terrific left in the fourth round and was dropped like a lump of hamburger on the canvas. Miraculously he climbed up again, spouting bloody froth at every terrible punch. The fight was stopped by the referee out of simple humanity.

Next, in order, on the Joe Louis hit parade: Bob Pastor in Detroit in the eleventh, Johnny Paycheck in Madison Square Garden in the second, Arturo Godoy in Yankee Stadium in the eighth, Al McCoy in Boston in the second, Red Burman in Madison Square Garden in the fifth, Gus Dorazio in Philadelphia in the second, Abe Simon in Detroit in the thirteenth, Tony Musto in St. Louis in the ninth. A contemporary wit branded them as members of the "Bum of the Month Club."

After this uninterrupted carnage there were signs, as Pearl Harbor approached, that the champion was beginning to slow down. On May 23, 1941, in Washington, D.C., Louis took on Max Baer's brother Buddy. He won the fight on a technicality but meanwhile fans saw Louis on the floor, Louis out of the ring, Louis holding, Louis clinching, Louis bleeding. He was still champ—but no longer in a walkaway.

On June 18, 1941, Billy Conn drove Louis to the ropes in the third round. He pounded his foe around the ring in the tenth and eleventh. He rocked Louis on his heels with a left hook in the twelfth. In the thirteenth, however, nimble Conn made the mistake of coming too close and the fans saw the familiar sight of the challenger's buckling knees. The champion knocked Conn out five years later on a return bout, but justice was meted out more slowly than it had been to Max Schmeling. To finish Conn off for the second time, an older and slower Louis took all of eight rounds.

A partisan observer of the first Louis-Schmeling fight was Adolf Hitler, who saw from far-off Berlin a vindication of some of his favorite theories about the master race. Some of these theories were popular in Berlin when a crowd of 100,000 jammed into the world's largest stadium for the 1936 Olympics. Brown-uniformed storm troopers jammed the streets. Overhead, Junker transports droned along in flying wedges. A million persons gathered along the Via Triumphalis between the Lustgarten and the Stadium to give the Führer a frenzied ovation as he passed. Thunderous applause greeted the *Hindenburg* which cruised overhead trailing the Olympic flag—its crew unaware of the fiery finale which awaited it in the coming year. Racial purity, Caesarism reborn, clean-limbed manhood were woven into an updated Nibelungenlied, dramatized with blasts from distant trumpets, choirs of thousands dressed in white, choruses of heils, batteries of guns. The release of three thousand white doves was a final tour de force of the department of special effects.

The national delegations filed in alphabetical sequence into the stadium. The Olympic salute and the Nazi salute were confusingly similar. Each group was watched for signs of sympathy with the legions of Hellas or the legions of Wotan.

Wotan's hordes whistled their distaste as the American team hove into view. Only the United States refused to lower its flag out of deference to the Führer. The band burst into "Deutschland Über Alles" to put *them* in their place. Turkey and the USA gave non-committal military salutes. The Bulgarian delegation gave the Nazi salutation and goose-stepped to boot. Bolivia, Iceland, and Afghanistan all chose to flatter the Führer. Bermuda gave the Nazi salute —though Der Führer probably did not expect to rely too heavily on future military aid from the denizens of Elbow Beach.

Rose petals and flaxen-haired *Mädchen* were a part of Hitler's pre-Buchenwald public image, and a little girl went up and presented him with a bouquet of roses. Gently the Führer touched her hair, which was bound by a chaplet of flowers—a touching vignette of the man who loved children. She was led up to the notables, including Colonel and Mrs. Charles A. Lindbergh, with the assembly shouting an accompaniment of heils. The tresses of the little girl were, needless to state, fair.

Dr. Lewald of the German Organizing Committee had an unfortunate tendency to German long-windedness. He referred to this stadium "built according to your will and purpose" and to the "strong beauty of these young teams at our feet," to the character-building effects of sport and to the "spiritual bond of fire between our German fatherland and the sacred places of Greece founded nearly four thousand years ago by Nordic immigrants." The Führer by contrast was, for once, admirably terse.

Sailors along the skyline raised the flags of nations—more trumpet fanfare—more distant guns—the doves—and at last the Olympic flame. It was lit on a small black altar by the last runner in a series of relays who had carried it across Europe, lighting up Olympic altars as they went, all the way from the Temple of Zeus.

Rudolf Ismayr, weight-lifting champion of the 1932 Olympics, swore the Olympic oath with one hand on the swastika. A humble sheepherder presented Hitler with an olive branch, accompanied by the hope that "the nations of the world will ever meet solely in such peaceful competition." This nearly broke up the Führer. Finally the Hallelujah Chorus from Handel's *Messiah*—a reminder of the existence of that so-called other Germany. The most unsympathetic liberal had to admit that it beat anything at Radio City Music Hall.

Hero of the day as far as America was concerned was an Ohio State sophomore named Jesse Owens, a sprinter known as the Buckeye Bullet. On August 5, 1936, he won the 200-meter race in a record-shattering 0:20:7. He went on to become the first triple Olympic winner since Paavo Nurmi in 1924. Thanks to him and others the Americans led the Germans by roughly one hundred points in the track and field events. Before "African auxiliary" Owens stepped up to collect his laurel crown, the Reichsführer excused himself. He was driven away from his official box by a providential downpour of rain. Owens did not fit in with the blond Heidis, the picturesque shepherd, or the other Todd A-O touches: he was black.

Prominent among the sportswriting and broadcasting Establishment were Jimmy Cannon, Bill Corum, Red Smith, and Tommy Laird. John Kieran was a sportswriter before he became a pundit on *Information Please*. Many who disliked Pegler the union baiter had a soft spot for the old days of sportswriter "Peg."

Grantland Rice's *Sportlight* had, in the Twenties, presented one-reel movies about the exploits of Big Bill Tilden, Jack Dempsey, and Bobby Jones. In 1932 Rice joined Paramount Pictures with a contract calling for one *Sportlight* a month—covering everything from marble derbies to tennis player Alice Marble.

Others who followed in Rice's footsteps were Graham McNamee, Bill Slater, and Ted Husing. Prominent in the NBC stable was Bill Stern, who reported on football games and fights for MGM's *News of the Day* after 1938, having meanwhile made everyone aware of the virtues of Twenty Grand Cigarettes and Adam Hats.

Also on the NBC payroll was Clem McCarthy, whose machine-gun delivery was equally well adapted to prize fight or horse race. A whole generation will remember with affection the McCarthy account, matching the rise and fall of thundering hooves as they rounded the clubhouse turn, the introduction intoned through the nostrils: "R-r-r-acing fans, they're off!"

Ring Lardner and Gene Fowler were charter members of the Establishment. Some of the fraternity were recruited from other branches of the arts and from writers who had made a splash in the larger pond. Honorary degrees were awarded to actor Pat O'Brien, cartoonist Rube Goldberg, to Quentin Reynolds, Mark Hellinger, and Irwin S. Cobb. Among the beloved originals were Al Schacht, "the clown prince of baseball," and the late Mayor James J. Walker of New York who embodied the group's collective ideal of that indefinable quality called "class."

Many of the group clustered around the figure of restaurateur Toots Shor, in whose ebullient personality the baseball world met the world of the speakeasy. Shor got his start in the Five O'Clock Club owned by Big Frenchy la Mange and Owney Madden. Later Toots moved up through the lost civilization of sliding panels and gin in teacups, incurring the undying enmity of speakeasy czar Sherman Billingsley. He came up via The Ball and Chain, The Maison Royale, Leon and Eddie's, and finally La Hiff's Tavern. At La Hiff's he encountered the celebrities who were to become his bread and butter: Jimmy Walker, Ring Lardner, Heywood Broun, Bill Corum, Mark Hellinger, Gene Fowler, Mike Romanoff, and Walter Winchell.

Shor's cavalier attitude toward money brought La Hiff's down to disaster. In 1939, however, he started his own place, which was completed in 1940 on personality, "palship," and promissory notes. As he took command of his new place of business, Shor threw away his last quarter, dime, and nickel. "I might as well walk in flat pocket," he said. By the standards of the brotherhood it was a classy entrance.

The group at Shor's was dedicated to stag conviviality. Philosophers among them suggested that if the world were to adopt their ethical norms, war, famine, etc. would miraculously disappear. These norms included a willingness to respond to the plea of a brother for funds. Gentlemen with class would give a prompt affirmative answer to the Big Question. An example of the Big Question was put by Shor to a pal: "I gotta have three Gs and I ain't got no time for dialogue. Can you get it up—yes or no?"

An encyclopedic knowledge of sports was also essential.

John Bainbridge, who did a profile of Shor for *The New Yorker*, remarked that a neophyte who was ignorant of the identity of Tinker or Evers or Chance or who didn't know what Brooklyn player ruined Carl Hubbell's near no-hitter on Decoration Day in 1940 was as out of place at Shor's "A.C." as an unfrocked priest at St. Peter's. Grantland Rice's All America was regarded by the group with the awe that an Ivy Leaguer might feel toward Porcellian or Fly.

It was also necessary to survive in the parry-and-thrust of manly insult and practical joke. Members customarily greeted each other with "ya big galoot," "ya fat slob," "you crippled nose son of a bitch."

Drinking patterns were subject to all sorts of unspoken tabus. ("Only faggots eat when they drink.") Prominent among comradely virtues was the ability to handle a skinful with grace. Henry McLemore became a hero to Grantland Rice when he strode through the asparagus in his socks at a function of the San Francisco Press Club with the words "Ladies and gentlemen, I would like to give you my recipe for apple butter."

Alligators under pillows, badger hunts with quite a different animal in the bag were among the merry antics which relieved the monotony of spring training. "Tell Tommy that Ketchel was a lousy bum," a patsy would be encouraged. Or he would be urged over in the direction of a lowering ex-Notre Dame guard: "Why not say a few words to Hunk?" Given the low boiling point of some stars, the hilarious dénouement would generally involve the neophyte's being bounced up and down like a tennis ball. Sometimes the boys would evolve a truly heroic hoax. During the Prohibition days the Washington Senators cooked up an amusing treat. Bucky Harris and Al Schacht had embarked on what Schacht hoped would be carnal relations with two girls whose husbands had "gone North." Bucky, who had been briefed in advance, fell to the floor clutching his stomach and giving Schacht the scare of his life as one of the "husbands" fired a shot at him—with blanks.

John Bainbridge has described the group attitude toward death which was closely allied with their attitude toward liquor. "Drinkin'," said Toots Shor, "that's my way of prayin'." When Shor went around looking glum instead of insulting the customers one knew that Old Mark or Old Jim had "beat us to the finish line," "gone West," or "over the border," or been "called upstairs." Then Pat and Toots and Granny would pour it on. The bar at Shor's would be kept open after hours out of deference to the mourners. Bottles would come out and there would be reminiscences of the good old comrades and the golden days before the Big Fellow started to shuffle the cards. The Big Fellow, who could be either the Deity or Babe Ruth, in this context always referred to the former.

Liquor brought forth many a spontaneous tribute to the deceased.

Toots Shor to Jimmy Walker: "Jimmy, Jimmy, when you walked into the room you brightened up the joint."

Or Grantland Rice to Babe Ruth: "I hope it's an eternity before some youngster, teeing off on today's jet ball, smashes Babe's mark of sixty homers in one season. This I hope for wherever he is, kicking his heels around on some king-sized cloud."

Even comedian George Jessel, who frequently went to the funerals of total strangers, found Shor to be a bit much. Bainbridge recounts that Jessel once said to Toots, "Isn't that tough about losing McKinley?" Shor burst into tears on cue, and cried, "Bring me a bottle!"

Other milestones along Life's Road were uniquely described by the sports fraternity. A veteran of two marriages was a "two-striper." A new arrival might be heralded as "your new shortstop," or as Pat O'Brien once put it, "You finally got a man on third."

The group had certain communal colloquialisms. The feeling prevailed that there was nothing more hilarious than referring to any athlete by his full name—Big Bill Tilden as "William Tatum" or Ol' Dizz as "Jerome Herman." The same went for any Biff or Buck or Rock or Red.

Another propensity of the sportswriter was a tendency to lapse at the slightest provocation into verse. "While sport has been a big part of my life, I must admit that verse has meant even more," said Grantland Rice. Nor was he the only bard who battened off such popular themes as The Big Upset: Schmeling's victory over Louis in 1936, mighty Stanford's Rose Bowl defeat in 1934 at the hands of effete easterners from Columbia, Larry Kelley's touchdown for Yale in the same year, which upset undefeated Princeton. Such events often inspired John Kieran to write two poems—one when he was borne along on the groundswell of acclaim for the favorite, the second when in some "Ballade of Joyous Error" he philosophically ate his hat.

With apologies to Tennyson, Kipling, Sir Arthur Conan Doyle, Dan McGrew, and literacy, reams of poesy were ground out in commemoration of the Old Grad, the Golfer's Battle with Slice and Hook; the Rookie's Spring Song; the Day the Guards Crashed Through. Jack Sharkey's love of flowers was extolled to the meter of "Come into the Garden, Maud." Where, the sporty lyricists would ask, are the great ones—Ring, "Odd" McIntyre, Don Marquis, and the rest—who have gone before? Only one celebrity could say and Grantland Rice for one was aware of His vigilance:

> For when the One Great Scorer comes to mark against my name
> He writes—not that you won or lost—but how you played the game.

John Kieran, who avoided the mucker's pose affected by many of his colleagues, wrote many passages which showed that he was not ashamed of having been exposed to secondary schooling:

> Next came Theodorus Sandwinnus boldly to meet the valorous Cobb yclept Rotundus, great in girth, graceful as the Nubian giraffe, light of foot as the two-horned African black rhinoceros. Down went Theodorus when his opponent smote him as Ajax smote the Trojan. Now lies he low and dreams of verdant hillsides and sweet purling streams, while in his ears there ring the melodious chirrupings of a thousand sweet birds.
>
> Then came Publius Stanislaus Poredius to drive a foeman from the field, whereupon all lesser heroes retired and a weighty snort went up: "Hurrah! Here come the elephants!" (Inveniunt elephantes! Evoe!)

There were other classical references ("Nunc te, Carnera, canam") ("Bellona horrida").

The reader needed a bit of secondary schooling along with an exhaustive knowledge of sports and at least two rereadings of this paragraph to realize that it was a description of the preliminary bouts leading up to the clash between Victorio Campolo of the Argentine and the future heavyweight champion Primo Carnera (yclept Carnera Carnivorus Horribilis).

Red Smith was one sportswriter who was able to describe a sporting event without undue bathos or excessive use of the ablative absolute.

On December 5, 1947, he described a scene which added ten years to the life of every sports fan of the Thirties.

The Brown Bomber was once again taking on a beat-up family man. At the end of fifteen rounds, after ten and a half years as champion, there Louis was, staring out into Madison Square Garden —owlish, grotesque—one eye wide and the other beaten almost shut. The havoc had been wrought by Jersey Joe Walcott, a father of *six*. After sparring inconclusively for fourteen rounds, each fighter had been awarded seven rounds and the fifteenth was up for grabs. Walcott was instructed to avoid a knockout at all costs and spent the fifteenth giving the champion a wide berth. The bell rang. The first ballot was for the champion, the second to Walcott, the third and last to Louis. There was a chorus of boos, when the decision was announced, by those who thought Walcott had been robbed. It was a Louis victory, but hardly in the great tradition. Joe had been battered around the ring, knocked sprawling twice. He had heard the incredible sound of booing. Red Smith said that he looked like a small boy about to cry. There it was in black and white—evidence that the Brown Bomber was only human after all. "So long, Joe."

Not till September 1950 did Louis finally lose his title to Ezzard Charles. The sight of Louis shuffling around the ring had more shock value than the sight of Lou Gehrig walking across the field, a bit off balance, to announce the Yankee lineup; or the news, unnoticed by most Americans, of Tommy Hitchcock's death in a P-51 during World War II. Middle age began when Joe Louis became an underdog.

It was a reminder that there was no exception to the fate of the fading athlete, even to him whose exploits have a full half-page to themselves in the *Information Please Almanac*.

Joe's difficulties were just beginning. He had been badly managed and had gone into some ill-advised business ventures, including an appearance as the hero of a movie. In 1959, after prolonged years of litigation, the United States government agreed to settle a $1,250,000 claim against Louis for back income taxes. Joe was to pay it off at the rate of $20,000 a year. The government also got its hands on a legacy of $687 left to him by his mother and two trust funds amounting to $66,000 set up for his children, despite his attorney's statement that part of the money in the trust had come from Louis' ex-wife Marva Trotter.

The good guys rallied around. The Harlem Globetrotters staged a benefit to help bail out Joe. A group, with Jack Dempsey as chairman, was formed to settle his tax debt. In his heyday it had been his victims who had stirred our sympathies. One awaited a Louis fight with a tremor of physical apprehension for the very life of an opponent like Tony Galento. Only later on was Louis reduced to the human condition as he floundered, along with the rest of us, through deduction and red ink with nothing off for depletion.

In the larger battles that began to occupy people's minds in the Thirties the cardinal virtue of the Twenties disappeared—the absolute purity of the amateur athlete. In the 1930s the sun was beginning to set on such gentlemen yachtsmen as Harold Vanderbilt, on such gentlemen polo players as Tommy Hitchcock and Pete Bostwick, and even to a certain extent on the college football player.

The golden people of the Twenties were not all that golden by the tougher professional standards of today. Bobby Jones' scores ranged between 290 and 296. Today an aspiring champion would have to play ten strokes below that total to be in the running at all.

A sportsman who took money for writing articles was in the Twenties regarded in the same light as the girl who puts out for cash. Big Bill Tilden got into deep trouble for doing a series of articles on tennis. In 1925 he was challenged on a panel on "amateurism and bylines" by the gentleman polo star Devereux Milburn. "I would *like* to have accepted that money to write about my particular sport," said Milburn. "But I simply felt that as an amateur I couldn't accept it."

"It's a matter of taste, not amateurism," Tilden retorted.

As the Depression wore on, fewer could speak like Milburn, with a piety born of a trust fund. The postwar sports fan cynically accepted the fact that sports, like quiz programs, were big business. Tales of fixed basketball games were taken in stride, along with the hiring of college football players to beef up the line. Better football might have been played at the famed Giant-Green Bay Packer game of December 12, 1938, than at the contest between State U and Siwash MM. Yet it was Siwash in the Thirties that packed them in. The day would come when the Giants and the Green Bay Packers would be as much of an attraction as those cheerleaders and fresh-faced coeds. Fans may well have reasoned that if they were going to watch players who took money, they might as well watch players who took it over the counter.

If anyone could doubt that the amateur had lost his virginity, one need only contrast the reaction to Bill Tilden's newspaper articles and the sangfroid of an audience munching its Fritos and watching a professional wrestling match on television. The latter were secure in the knowledge that the fall would occur just in time for the commercial.

And yet if something has been lost it may be that, with the passing of the amateur tradition, America put away childish things. To be a Golden Person is no longer the ambition of every American adolescent, and at least we have outgrown the brand of political naïveté expressed in 1936 by Avery Brundage, president of the United States Olympic Committee. He had taken a look at the black uniforms and the white doves and concluded: "No nation since ancient Greece has captured the true Olympic spirit as has Germany."

It was characteristic of the transitional Thirties that its greatest athlete represented professionalism at its best. Joe Louis defended his title more times than any modern fighter, cheerfully battled anyone with whom his managers chose to pair him. He was probably the hardest hitter that the prize ring has ever known. If a Louis fight was sometimes a dull fight it was because the outcome was predictable in advance. His only weakness was a lack of the ability to play to the grandstands, which often redeems the "Oops, sorry" of the amiable duffer. One could only wish for him that he had at least enjoyed the tax structure of the age of the amateur.

With apologies to Grantland Rice, John Kieran, poetry, et al.:

A PLEA TO THE BIG INTERNAL REVENUE COLLECTOR IN THE SKY

We are experts at playing Where Are They Now
Where are they now, we know
We are dated Father William by a different Tom Wolfe
And an older Killer Joe.
We have seen Dizzy Dean pastured out in the minors
Budge has done our cleaning and pressing,
The Clown Prince of Baseball has served us steak,
    and salad with Roquefort dressing
Whither the racquet of yesteryear
The ball he put a cut on
After Baron Von Cramm became number 6
    in the lineup of Barbara Hut-ton
And far far worse than that first gray hair—is
    Dempsey collecting on his Medicare.
But there was always one who was bigger than life
And year after year we sat
Twirling the dials of the Atwater Kent
As the bodies hit the mat
Down went Schmeling and two little Baers
Galento, Pastor, Godoy
Beat to a pulp by the flying fists
Of boxing's Golden Boy.
We watched the human sacrifices
Being fed to the Bomber's Maw
Would Braddock be wise to go back on relief
Carnera and Louis—there should be a law
Arithmetic was for CPAs
Just give him a jaw and he'd crack it.
He didn't think he was slugging his way
Into a higher surtax bracket.
How they swarmed around with chances to buy in
A movie, a "gold mine" a merchandise tie in.
He was king of the ring with money to burn
In the days before Marva signed a separate return
Now—
A simple riddle for the business men

What percentage of Joe is eleven times ten?
If you're listening Up There, heed this simple plea
Ere he walks his final mile.
You must have a rebate for a champion
Who would rather fight than file.
If he'd only made it in oughty ought
He could have kept the percentage low.
Spare our Bomber, O Big Timekeeper
On the long count—Okay, but on the Long Form no.

Chapter 9

Instant Current Events

In the year 1914 Karl von Wiegand of the United Press cabled 138 words from Berlin to New York on the Austro-Hungarian ultimatum which precipitated the first World War. He was chided by his superiors for wasting cable tolls.

On January 2, 1935, Bruno Richard Hauptmann went on trial in Flemington, New Jersey, for the 1932 kidnaping of Charles Augustus Lindbergh, Jr. Sixty-five transmitters and three foreign cable connections were installed by the telegraph companies. Western Union and Postal Telegraph had seventy-five operators and twenty or more messengers to relay hot copy to the press. A dozen airplanes, using an emergency landing field two miles from the courtroom whisked films, sketches, and photographs to Boston, Philadelphia, and New York. A special teletype connected directly with London to keep our British cousins abreast of developments in "The Most Sensational American Murder Trial of the Century." Kathleen Norris, Alexander Woollcott, Damon Runyon, Arthur Brisbane, and Walter Winchell were all on hand to report the heart-rending high points—as when Lindbergh identified his son's sleeping garment. More correspondents, sob sisters, psychiatrists, and cameramen converged on Flemington than had represented American papers in France during World War I. When, during the judge's charge, an interdict was pronounced on the sending of copy to the press, Emil Visconti, chief of Western Union, tucked batches of "hot news" under his coat and slipped out to the wire room unnoticed.

In the 1930s the country savored to the fullest the dubious delights of rapid news communication. Throughout the Twenties, there had been widespread ballyhooing of all sorts of nine-day wonders. Lindbergh's historic hop from New York to Paris in 1927 had resulted in the most soul-searing publicity build-up in history. But the dawn of a new era had come about with the first world-wide news broadcast in 1930. It presaged a bombardment of facts and opinions from the radio, from magazines, from the newsreel camera, air waves and from the pundits of the press which continues, proliferates, and which we are still trying to assess and manage.

One of the most popular purveyors of instant current events was the *Literary Digest*. It served up a weekly diet of heavy-handed political cartoons and equally heavy-handed witticisms under the heading of "The Spice of Life," bowdlerized quotes lifted from various newspapers. All a writer needed were scissors and tape. . . . "So opines the *Hartford Courant*." "It appears to the *St. Louis Post-Dispatch* . . ."

Through its pages strode the heroes/devils of the decade: John Bull, Marianne, Wheat Surplus, the bearded Old Year, the diapered New Year, "Militarism" with bearskin and sword. Poor Mr. Taxpayer—shown in a barrel, or on state occasions in a suit which could have used the ministrations of a good reweaver. A typical *Literary Digest* cartoon which appeared in 1933 showed Hitler charging in a Napoleonic hat from an edifice marked "Europe's Asylum." In case the hat hadn't gotten the idea across, the helpful caption read "I'm Napoleon."

"The Spice of Life" was equally explicit. A he-she joke, more risqué than most, engaged a man and wife in the following dialogue:

She presents him with an offering. "It's a bottle of hair tonic, dear."

He: "Oh, that's very nice of you, darling."

She: "Yes, I want you to give it to your typist at the office. Her hair is coming out rather badly on your coat."

The New Yorker's one-line caption was to spell the death of the he-she joke. In 1936 the *Literary Digest* was faced, too, with competition from a lusty newcomer to the Luce family. Henry Luce's two major magazines of opinion had been *Time* and *Fortune*. The latter, founded in 1930, had become a standard bit of decor in the offices of more intellectual dentists. Luce bought the name of the old humor magazine *Life,* which had foundered through devotion to the he-she joke. On November 23, 1936, the first issue of *Life* appeared. An advertisement for Ethyl Gasoline in the front cover was phrased in the form of a "knock-knock" joke. "Knock, knock! Who's there? ETHYL. Can't be. Why not? ETHYL stops knock and puts new LIFE in your car."

The rest of the magazine was packed with fast, zippy commentary and not-so-covert editorialization. There was a story on NBC showing its impressive roster of celebrities. Walter Winchell, Gypsy Rose Lee, Jessica Dragonette, Dorothy Thompson, and Rudy Vallee were introduced as "National Bedtime Characters," presumably because they were in action at night. There was a picture story by Margaret Bourke-White on "FDR's Wild West," a Montana reclamation project—as "wide open and as rickety as Hell's Delight, the Red Light suburb of Happy Hollow." Relief workers were shown making whoopee on Saturday night. The not-so-covert editorialization compared Theodore Roosevelt's frontier ("the natural result of the great trek to the Pacific") with FDR's ("the natural result of $110,000,000").

Two natural results of *Life's* appearance were one successful imitator, *Look,* and the death of the *Literary Digest* school of rehash reportage. The Landon defeat of 1936 completed the job. Prior to this event the *Literary Digest* poll had enjoyed a reputation for infallibility. When the poll predicted a Landon victory the reputation went down the drain. The magazine was despondently published in 1937, but a cartoon in that year showed the handwriting on the wall. A despairing GOP was accepting a bowl of gruel from an arm marked "Landon." "Same old soup," GOP was grumbling. "I had hoped for something more nourishing." The editors of the *Literary Digest* might have echoed his cry. That arm marked Landon had given them the Sunday punch.

One magazine which miraculously did not lose its aura of infallibility throughout the Thirties was the *Reader's Digest*. However clouded the crystal ball, it never published its errata. It purported to offer a sampling of the best of the current press. To be seen with a copy was to enjoy a reputation for deep thought.

One might not have time to keep up with all the popular publications: *Saturday Evening Post, Collier's, Liberty, Vanity Fair, The New Yorker, Redbook, Esquire, The American, Cosmopolitan, Pictorial Review,* and the *Delineator.* As a *Digest* reader one could quote from them all, as well as from weightier sources: *The Atlantic Monthly, Harper's, Scribner's, The Survey Graphic, The Outlook and Independent, The Nation,* the *New Republic, The Forum, The Living Age, Current History.*

The first admittedly original *Digest* article was published in 1933. Around the mid-Thirties came the revolution, which was signaled by a sharp swing to the Right. The self-styled "medievalist" Paul Palmer arrived at the *Digest* as an editor from 1935 to 1939. He availed himself at one point of the consulting services of Lawrence Dennis, writer and speaker known as America's No. 1 intellectual fascist. At this period the "planted" *Digest* article made its appearance. This was a piece actually written in the *Digest* shop, planted in a magazine, and eventually "reprinted" in the *Digest.* In one case this produced a literary rarity, a "condensation" which ran 468 words longer than the "original" from which it had been "cut."

In the early Thirties the *Digest* actually did offer a broad cross section of public opinion on a variety of subjects. One could visit the set of *Green Pastures* "Backstage with the Lawd," ponder what might happen "If Beer Returns," read all about Reno, "Tammany Hall," "The Spectre of Russian Wheat," or enjoy a "Preview of the Next War." No one in 1930 could call the *Digest* editors to account for its lineup of the players. The war was to be between the haves and have-nots. The haves included France and Britain, the have-nots were the powers defeated in 1918. A friendly policy on the part of England and America was said by the *Digest* to have kept Japan out of the have-not camp.

The Depression in 1930 was obtruding upon a world which still had a bit of the flavor of the Twenties. One could delight one's dinner partner with excerpts from *The American Mercury* about the gaucheries. For instance, the sermon topic at a Baptist Church in Kansas: "Can a bobbed-haired woman go to Heaven?" Or at a Baptist Church in North Carolina: "Will there be any bootleggers in Heaven?"

Other articles previewed the philosophy of the New Deal. There was a discussion of the revolutionary practice of liberal employers in paying cash indemnities to laid-off workers. The world of 1930 had not even found a name for what the *Digest* picturesquely termed "industrial alimony" and a later generation would term severance pay. It would be written into every union contract, and mount so high that an employee with "tenure" could get away with almost anything short of spitting in the boss's eye.

The 1930s was a time of esoteric panaceas for hard times. Among them were California's Ham and Egg movement, Upton Sinclair's EPIC plan, Huey Long's Share Our Wealth, Father Coughlin's National Union for Social Justice. The oddest of all was the cult of Technocracy.

One month in 1933 the *Reader's Digest* presented the case for Technocracy and the next month the antis had their say. The extent to which the public had lost faith in traditional economics was reflected in the high caliber of the contributors. Simeon Strunsky of the New York *Times,* James S. Thomas of the *Nation's Business,* Dexter S. Kimball of *Science,* and George Soule of the *New Republic* earnestly debated the theme of man vs. machine, and argued why they did or did not believe that the American economy should be handed over to the engineers and the currency replaced by energy units known as "ergs" and "joules."

The true worth of the technocratic idea might be better summed up by a ditty in the counselors' show at a girls' camp in 1933. The counselors turned their hand from rewriting the "Missouri Waltz" and the "Stein Song" to paraphrasing a current hit: "Fit as a Fiddle and Ready for Love." It had a refrain—"hey nonny nonny and a hot cha cha." They crammed current events down their young charges' throats to the tune of "tech nonny nonny and a noccra-cee."

Yet if the contributors to the *Reader's Digest* devoted their time to discussing what was nonsensical, it was potentially dangerous nonsense, of a type that was taking root in other parts of the world. In Germany, pontificated the *Digest* editors, "the great majority of the people will never support such patent foolishness as Hitlerism."

By 1938 an article was reprinted in the *Reader's Digest* in which a travel agent who did business with Germany described his experiences with some of those enlightened people who had rejected the nonsense of Hitlerism. They came to America and expressed the belief that the beacon on Chicago's Palmolive building was for antiaircraft defense, that the Pope was a Freemason, that the New York *Times* was a Bolshevik paper, and that World War I had been started by J. P. Morganstein.

The *Digest* didn't call the shots much better with another future Axis power. The *Living Age* suffered the fate of many an intellectual periodical and went out of business, to be bought in June 1938 by three sub-rosa propagandists for the Japanese government. The *Age* had always been a good source of *Digest* pickups. Under the propagandists' aegis, thirteen pro-Japan *Living Age* articles were reprinted in the *Reader's Digest*. The majority were plants.

Predigestion of current events had the endorsement of such a contemporary god as the author of *The Story of Mankind,* Hendrik Willem Van Loon. "Before the Throne of Coming Events," said Mr. Van Loon, "it will avail you nothing to explain, 'Well, I did not understand,' or 'So many things had happened I just could not keep interested.' For you shall go down into the limbo of those who did not desire to survive . . .

"In the olden days before the machine became our Iron-Man Friday people obeyed the law 'Work or Starve.' Today the slogan is 'Think or Perish.'"

Van Loon did not hold out to the ordinary man the hope of joining him in the major league of "four books a day people." While it was anticlimactic to have his ringing call to the intellectual life end with a low commercial plug, there was at least a ray of hope. To those who preferred to think rather than perish,

"I say read the *Reader's Digest.*"

There was even hope for those who did nothing but listen.

When news of the Lindbergh kidnaping broke in March 1932, it was sent to New York radio stations by the Newark papers which performed this "courtesy service" for a credit line at the end of the bulletin. In view of the later highjinks at the Hauptmann trial it is noteworthy that in 1932 NBC considered the story too sensational to carry.

For many years the newspapers tried to keep the networks from reporting the news. In 1934 they clamped down on the Columbia News Service which gave information to Boake Carter, H. V. Kaltenborn, and Edwin C. Hill. Radio networks decided that Kaltenborn, Lowell Thomas, and Walter Winchell were not "newscasters." From this semantic nicety a new type of pundit, the commentator, was born.

Eventually the wire services realized that they were fighting City Hall. In 1935 INS removed all restrictions, UP a month later, AP not till 1941. A new multiple pickup was begun by CBS with a group of promising young fellows—Bob Trout in New York, William Shirer in London, Pierre Huss in Berlin, Edgar Mowrer in Paris, Edward R. Murrow in Vienna, and Senator Lewis B. Schwellenbach in Washington.

By 1938 broadcasts from these capitals gave a sense of immediacy that the printed word could never quite capture.

No newspaper account could shiver the female timbers as did the voice of Edward VIII when he abdicated the British throne in 1936: "I have found it impossible to carry the heavy burden of responsibility and to discharge my duties as king . . . without the help and support of the woman I love . . ."

—or capture the horror of Herb Morrison reporting for Chicago's WLS on a routine landing of the dirigible *Hindenburg* at Lakehurst, New Jersey, in 1937: "—it's burst into flame! Get this, Charlie! Get this, Charlie! It's crashing!"

—or the incredulity of Great Britain's Prime Minister Neville Chamberlain during the Munich crisis in 1938: "Fantastic, incredible it is that we should be digging trenches and trying on gas masks here because of a quarrel in a faraway country between people of whom we know nothing."

—or shatter the calm of a Labor Day weekend as did the Midwestern voice of Elmer Davis, coming over a car radio in 1939, when he announced the end of the twenty-year armistice: "Great Britain went to war against Germany today."

Radio became a formidable weapon in the hands of a politician who projected. Imitators might have a field day with the "My friends" which introduced FDR's famous Fireside Chats. But from the moment he announced that "the only thing we have to fear is fear itself" it was obvious that he had little to fear from such colorless orators as Herbert Hoover and, later, Alfred M. Landon.

Radio did much to enhance the image of Fiorello La Guardia, scrappy, beloved Mayor of New York, who served notice on every "ward heeler" and "tin horn chiseler" that "I can run on the laundry ticket and beat these political bums."

Radio spread the fame of the Reverend Charles Coughlin. From the Shrine of the Little Flower near Detroit he served up a blend of Populist economics, Papal encyclicals, and anti-Semitism.

There were hordes of experts who rushed to explain what it all meant—the clipped Brahmin accents of Quincy Howe, the balanced analyses of Murrow, Davis, and Kaltenborn. Fulton Lewis, Jr., stormed away against the New Deal. Drew Pearson relayed behind-the-scenes gossip which author Lloyd Morris compared to "the divinations of a tea shop gypsy." Walter Winchell's Sunday night broadcasts addressed to "Mr. and Mrs. America and all the ships at sea" were also recalled by Mr. Morris. Not content to address Mr. and Mrs. America through his syndicated column, he bombarded them in a "rapid fire succession of staccato barks, accompanied by the incessant clicking of a telegraph key." Besides passing along intelligence on what Broadway celebrities had gone "p-h-h-h-t" Mr. Winchell conveyed, according to Morris, "momentous secrets to the President, the Secretary of State, the Attorney General, with urgent suggestions for action."

Sometimes a particular crisis would plummet a pundit to national eminence. The Munich crisis established H. V. Kaltenborn in the monastic simplicity of CBS's Studio Nine, with an old soldier's cot and a pair of earphones. Beginning on September 12, 1938, his vigil lasted for eighteen days. In eighteen extemporaneous broadcasts he brought some of Chamberlain's "faraway" people, Hitler, Beneš, Henlein, Hodža, and Daladier, a little closer to the followers of Rudy Vallee and the Chase and Sanborn Hour.

Gabriel Heatter had been doing a program on behalf of the Modern Industrial Bank until the execution of Bruno Richard Hauptmann in 1936 set him up as the national voice of doom.

Heatter had been sent to the trial at Flemington by Mutual

Broadcasting, which paid him fifty dollars a week. The ordeal of Gabriel Heatter was literally sweated out in three fifteen-minute broadcasts a day. (He was constantly menaced by colds owing to his frenetic and hydraulic delivery.) By the end of the second day his salary had skyrocketed to $800 a week. Soon he had added Tastyeast and Grove's Bromo Quinine to his sponsors. By the time Hauptmann was actually executed, radio no longer considered the story too sensational to report. By an elaborate manipulation of handkerchiefs and a genius for ad lib, Heatter managed to scoop the other networks by a full ten seconds. An eager public waited for the exact moment when Hauptmann fried. The ubiquitous Mr. Van Loon cabled Heatter his congratulations. "Your work tonight stands forth as the one relieving spot of dignity and decency."

Mr. Heatter's portent-ridden delivery caused many of his flock to write fan mail addressed to "the Reverend." He imparted the same significance to the fall of the Low Countries as to an advertised cure for falling hair. Pearl Harbor caught him unawares ("I had reservations for Florida"), but after he rallied, it became his war. He had a bombproof shelter installed in his home, stocked with food, stirrup pumps, and sandbags. "After the fall of France I began to fight back," he said. (He fought more vigorously, perhaps, than the French.) Years later he told Philip Hamburger, who did a profile of him for *The New Yorker,* "My voice came to the people in the dark time." It came bearing the message, "There's good news tonight." The dark time in retrospect had been filled with uncertainty, and not only for nations. "Oh, as I look back, suppose England had fallen and Stalingrad gone down? Heatter would have been a dead duck."

Dean of the newspaper pundits was Walter Lippmann, who went to the New York *Herald Tribune* in 1931 after the closing of the New York *World.* In 1932 Walter Lippmann was considered by the historian Frederick Lewis Allen to be the most influential of all Americans. He was the mainstay of those who might have been tongue-tied and helpless when the conversation at the dinner party should turn from the great Lenz-Culbertson bridge match to the Reconstruction Finance Company and the Gold Standard."

By 1937 Lippmann's place had been pre-empted by Dorothy Thompson, whose ill-starred marriage to Sinclair Lewis was re-created in the 1963 best-seller *Dorothy and Red.* It was Dorothy and Red's tragedy that the masculine interests belonged to Dorothy. The author of *Babbitt, Arrowsmith,* and *Main Street* lived in perpetual fear of becoming "Mr. Dorothy Thompson." When she was considered as a possible Republican candidate against FDR, he said grimly, "Then I can settle down and write a column called 'My Day.'"

Lewis' excellent mind had a more frivolous turn than his wife's. He dabbled in theater. He visited Franklin P. Adams' place in Vermont along with such wits of the 1930s Establishment as "A. Woollcott," "G. Kaufman," and "Mrs. Dorothy Parker whose dachshund was seriously bitten by a butterfly." To FPA's "The Conning Tower," a genial scrapbook column in the New York *Herald Tribune,* Lewis' offerings were decidedly apolitical. Once he contributed a list of unusual establishments featuring the article "ye": "Ye Appetite Luncheon," "Ye Olde Branch of the N. Y. State Association of Retail Meat Directors, Inc."

His wife had little truck with such foolishness. Her first *Herald Tribune* piece in 1936, dealing with "The Corporations Tax Bill," served notice that anyone who wanted feminine froth had better turn to her *Ladies Home Journal* column, "Kirche, Küche, und Kinder." Miss Thompson got her first big break when Hitler threw her out of Germany in 1934, in belated pique over something she wrote about him in 1931. She was so busy awakening America during the Munich crisis that only as an afterthought did she call up to find out if her summer home had been swept away in the 1938 hurricane. In 1940 she switched her allegiance from presidential candidate Wendell Willkie to FDR. It was an act of courage which cost her her job. Though she had occupied a popular niche usually reserved for ball players and movie stars, her contract in 1941 was not renewed. The slant which the paper demanded of its political writers was embodied in cartoons featuring an evil zoo-keeper called FDR holding captive a restive animal named "Free Enterprise."

More than any other American, Dorothy Thompson kept hammering home that fascism should be fought. With the declaration of war in 1941, in Mr. Sheean's opinion, she had fulfilled "the tornado of her destiny."

But living with the tornado had been a bit rough on her husband. Her companions bored him: "Johnny" (Gunther of the *Inside* books), Edgar (Mowrer, writer and radio commentator), Raoul (Roussy de Sales, noted French journalist), "Ham" (Armstrong, editor of *Foreign Affairs*). Lewis wearied of hearing her reciting the Constitution, quoting from Spengler and Ortega y Gasset, or kicking the Balkan situation around night after night, with Johnny, Edgar, Ham, and Raoul. Possibly he may have gotten wind of certain other manly interests confided by Miss Thompson to her diary and reproduced by her good friend Mr. Sheean on the theory that unflinching old Dorothy would have wanted them plastered all over a Crest reprint. Yet this was not what made Lewis jealous. "If I ever divorce Dorothy," he said, and eventually did, "I'll name Adolf Hitler as corespondent."

It was FDR's interventionism which put her into the New Deal camp. She had opposed the President in his 1937 attempt to pack the Supreme Court. There was no room quite large enough to contain two such flowers of feminism as herself and Eleanor Roosevelt. Yet she reversed the usual pattern of the Thirties when at the end of the decade she came to praise Roosevelt rather than to bury him.

Other pundits of the Thirties were immune to the Old Magician's spell. Mark Sullivan led the Greek chorus against the New Deal. H. I. ("Hi") Phillips had an FPA-like column called "The Sun Dial." He saw himself as a lone voice of old-fashioned "hoss sense," crying out in a wilderness of "boondogglers," where if FDR had his way every worker would soon be asking for the whole week off. "All hands at the local flour mill," according to a 1937 Phillips column, "left the plant and went to Washington in gaily decorated buses yesterday. 'Bump' Hayley, owner of the mill, was surprised when he showed up at the plant and found nobody working. As no picnic had been announced, it is assumed the employees decided they didn't like the way the shop was being run and had gone direct to Roosevelt."

The Scripps-Howard columnist, Westbrook Pegler, had started out as an ardent New Dealer. A onetime sportswriter, he had expressed his early admiration for FDR with the embarrassing sort of literary cowlick-tugging popular among patrons of Al Schacht's and

Toots Shor's. "I'm afraid I couldn't be trusted around Mr. Roosevelt," he said in the early Thirties. "For the first time in my life in this business, I might find myself squabbling for a chance to carry the champion's water bucket."

Soon the champ was giving the business to anyone with a five-figure income and with his waxing fortunes Pegler's urge to carry the water bucket waned.

His reputation had been built up at the expense of a number of pet hates. Taking them collectively it was difficult to pinpoint Pegler's ideological position. He could eulogize a San Jose lynch mob in 1933, or deliver with equal fervor a moving plea for Jewish child victims of Nazi persecution. The Newspaper Guild enraged him, as did Adolf Hitler and the German agents he imagined to be streaming up the streets of Hoboken. He was capable of outstanding journalism and of gutter feuding. He won a Pulitzer Prize for his articles on Willie Bioff, corrupt czar of a West Coast motion picture union. The articles also drew the envious calumny of another accomplished hater—Walter Winchell—who referred to him as "Westbore Pigler."

Among the targets of his ire were a fellow Scripps-Howard columnist, Heywood Broun, Tom Mooney who was doing a life stretch in California on perjured evidence, Father Coughlin (the "Mad Monk"), William Randolph Hearst, the "nation's number one fascist." (This view was presumably modified later when he went to work on that fascist's payroll.) Finally it was all focused on a single target—Eleanor Roosevelt—who joined the Scripps-Howard Syndicate in 1935. Her column "My Day" provided a well-bred counterpoint to the Pegler billingsgate.

Their first two meetings, both at picnics, each caused a Peglerian broadside. He blasted what he described with ugly strength as her "Kiss the pillow" hen parties in the White House, her child-raising theories, her activities in connection with the left-wing American Youth Congress. The First Lady philosophically concluded, "I guess he doesn't like picnics."

Mrs. Roosevelt resolutely focused her apolitical gaze on "three little robins outside my bedroom window . . . My little birds have flown this morning into a strange world all by themselves."

Pegler then spoke with the voice of one of those common-sense

Americans, "Mrs. George Spelvin." En route to buy "bread, eggs, soap, cigarettes and gin," Mrs. Spelvin cast out titillating hints about what went on at those youth meetings:

> Well, fun is fun sister, but I don't remember reading where you ever got elected to anything, so if you don't mind I will politely ask you to politely keep out of my affairs, like raising my kids. . . . Because after all, I am the one who gets the headaches and how do I know what goes on at those youth meetings and I notice they are very partial to going out in the country and to be practical about it sister, I was not born yesterday, so how do I know they don't choose up sides—if you know what I mean.

"Having no public position myself, I can be consistent," the journalist had once said. At the time of Pearl Harbor, Pegler once again displayed his contempt for the virtue of small minds. He believed that America First had been correct in stating that Roosevelt had tricked the country into war. Yet in the process Mrs. Roosevelt had somehow become a super Gold Star Mother. "I think," said Pegler, "we can take the wraps off and call her the greatest American woman." The honor must certainly have come as a surprise.

Each pundit had his individual following and role: Dorothy Thompson, the Woman of Destiny; Pegler, the National Counter Irritant; Heatter, the Good Shepherd (who regarded his relationship to his listeners to be part family doctor, teacher, parish priest); Boake Carter, described by *Pictorial Review* in August 1936 as a man of "demon energy" with "the eyes of a watchful animal." It was something of a relief to turn to Lowell Thomas, who felt that his responsibility to his audience ended with reporting the news. Asked what he considered his influence to be he remarked refreshingly, "I try not to think about it at all."

The American desirous of keeping au courant had other allies— Lucius Beebe on gracious living, O. O. McIntyre on Broadway, Dorothy Dix on affairs of the heart. (There was also the sensational one-shot documentary, *The Birth of a Baby,* put out by The American Committee on Maternal Welfare in 1938.)

He also could count on five newsreel companies: Fox Movietone, Pathé, Paramount, Universal, and Hearst News of the Day.

Lowell Thomas was Fox Movietone's "serious" commentator. Jimmie Fidler turned the Hollywood Spotlight on such earth-shaking events as Shirley Temple's taking the wheel of her own tiny auto, or the wedding of Jack Haley's stand-in. Lew Lehr, with the assistance of a staff of monkeys, did light moments in the news: during the Roosevelt-Landon election of 1936 "the Dripplepuss Candidate picks his cabinet," or "our daffy anthropologist gets tangled up with a llama and some baby llamas and takes it on the llama . . ."

Ed Thorgersen and Tom Cummisky covered Movietone sports, offering a montage of the highlights of a football game that was often a good deal more interesting than the game itself. The Broadway beat was covered by a young newspaper columnist, still sporting a Harold Teen, 1920s haircut, named Ed Sullivan.

Graham McNamee worked for Universal. Pathé had an exclusive contract with the Dionne quintuplets. The output of the five newsreel companies—with the occasional exception of Paramount—was a tribute to the philosophy expressed in 1937 by Thomas Sugrue that the average American is frightened or bored by history.

Faced with a breadline, an apple seller, and a flagpole sitter—all common sights in the grim, early days of the Depression—Fox Movietone would photograph only the flagpole sitter. William Fox believed that the man en route to the cashier's cage or the free soup might frighten off moviegoers so that they would stay home from Fox newsreels. When Fox finally wished to show footage of unemployed men selling apples, they had to rent it from Paramount.

When the five companies were asked to name the six newsreels of which they were proudest they drew heavily on events almost totally forgotten today, like "Captain de Pinedo burning to death at Floyd Bennett Field."

The only one of any lasting moment was a Paramount sequence of book burning in Germany. Fox Movietone and News of the Day both chose automobile racing disasters, though it would seem that when you'd seen one car pile up you had seen them all. The Duke of Windsor and Mrs. Simpson were romantic, newsworthy, and noncontroversial. Fox Movietone's "best" showed the royal lovers at Cannes. Paramount caught them peering out of a window at St. James's. Disaster without political overtones was popular—fires, panics, earthquakes, volcanoes, tidal waves, and tornadoes. Pathé named among its greats the sinking of the *Morro Castle* off the Jersey coast in 1934 and a flood in Colorado where two extraordinarily jolly-looking people about to go down forever in the maelstrom smiled genially at the camera from a piece of floating debris.

Gruesome scenes were generally eliminated because of the bad audience reaction. When the G-men ran John Dillinger to earth in 1934 outside a Chicago movie theater, the finale of the event involved one newsreel company in costly litigation. A woman sued— albeit unsuccessfully—on the grounds that the sight of Dillinger stretched out on a slab had induced an abortion.

War was costly and unphotogenic. Spanish Civil War scenes, among the treasures of Fox Movietone's Film Library, were at the time considered to be pictorially a flop. If the newsreel companies showed a fondness for endless parades, it was because goose-stepping legions got across the notion of dictatorship on the march without subjecting talent and equipment to the risk of possible annihilation.

Typical Movietone miscellany included Jimmy Walker at the piano before the process servers closed in, the disappearance of Amelia Earhart Putnam in 1937, sinking of the *Panay* in China in 1937, the sinking of the *Squalus* in 1939, Senator McAdoo's wedding, a fire in an ice plant, the picking of the "Modern Venus" in Coney Island, or Jack Haley's advice to newlyweds: "Don't live with your wife's folks."

Through it all would go the pert fashion commentary of Vyvian Donner—debutantes strolling in sailcloth slacks with their dogs . . . "A spaniel for a stroll and a costume for a swim, rather a coming out party . . ."

Sometimes the newsreels were guilty of sins of other omissions. In the 1937 Memorial Day Massacre near the South Chicago shops of the Republic Steel Company, the police had opened fire on picketing workers, a fact regarded as too "controversial" to mention in the newsreel reports. A more disgraceful misuse of the medium had occurred in 1934 when Upton Sinclair, author of the EPIC plan, had terrified the orthodox burghery of California by running for Governor. The main features of the plan were set forth in a volume entitled *I, Governor of California and How I Ended Poverty*.

Right-wing figures in Hollywood raised half a million dollars for newsreels, described by Arthur Schlesinger, Jr., in *The Politics of Upheaval:* "Substantial community leaders and gentle old widows (played by bit actors) declared for . . . the Republican candidate, while bearded figures with heavy Russian accents explained why they were voting for Sinclair." Sinclair was soon at work on a rueful sequel: *I, Candidate for Governor and How I Got Licked.* It mattered little that some of the scenes of disreputable migrants descending on California were later identified as clips from a Warner Brothers film, *Wild Boys of the Road.*

In the Mad Thirties the *March of Time* marched onto the scene. Westbrook Van Voorhis was *Time*'s portentous Voice. Roy Larsen, circulation manager of Time, Inc., had dreamed of a dramatic newsreel since the first *March of Time* radio broadcast in 1931, Louis de Rochemont of Fox Movietone helped to make the dream a reality. The first two-reel *March of Time* ran for twenty minutes. It was a mixed bag, covering London's traffic rules, New York night clubs, Japanese militarism, war debts, the NRA and Gatti-Casazza's opening of the Met. Later the *March of Time* followed M. de Paris, France's Lord High Executioner, through a grisly day, which began when he set up the guillotine in the morning and ended with his homecoming to his tomblike house full of "damp and decorum" in the suburbs.

The *New Republic,* always critical of the Luce enterprises, chided the *March of Time* for giving contemporary history the same shuddering treatment for the rightist leanings of Mr. de Rochemont, for being too rough on the CCC, for being too kind to the Croix de Feu, for being too impartial in the coverage of ministerial murders in Tokyo, where the editors tried to do the right thing by both murderers and corpses.

Whatever its claim to impartiality, the *March of Time* covered a lot of ground: radio comedians, the WPA Theatre, Leadbelly. It filled audiences in on domestic issues: the split between the AF of L and the CIO which established CIO's Lewis as "labor's man of destiny." The editors urged Mrs. Worthingtons in the hinterlands not to put their daughters on the train, conjuring up awful visions of what happened to "business girls in the big city." The *March of Time* also covered the "Angels"—black and white—who believed that the Negro cult leader—Father Divine—was actually God. What-

ever may be said of his claims to Godhead, his job placement services, his soup kitchens made this controversial figure a force on the
terrestrial plane.

Huey Long, Father Coughlin, and Dr. Francis Townsend were all
the subject of *March of Time* documentaries. High points of the
Long career involved swearing in a pretty typist as Louisiana's
Secretary of State. Later, one could see a somewhat censored version of an occasion at Sands Point, Long Island, when Long was
struck by a man who resented his means of expressing impatience
on line at the urinal. The *March of Time* documentary on Huey
Long, April 19, 1935, came out in the year he was assassinated.
The killing of Long had removed one of the greatest threats to a
Roosevelt victory in the coming 1936 election, the one which Father Coughlin had predicted would be America's last.

In the late Thirties the limelight turned from the would-be domestic dictator to topics such as "The Refugee Today and Tomorrow" or "Japan, Master of the Orient." "Inside France's Maginot
Line" took the moviegoer to "the one fixed boundary in a Europe
of trembling frontiers." There were reassuring glimpses of impreg-
nable pillboxes and concrete caps. Couriers scuttled through Maginot's long catacombs. Soldiers scrambled up and down ladders. A
man in a chef's hat whipped up an excellent dinner, a tribute to the
Gallic habit of putting first things first.

"Only one thing is certain, all this concrete and steel will prevent any such sweeping advance in the early days of a war as was
seen in 1914." Unfortunately audiences could not appraise the
efficiency of Hitler's Siegfried Line, since the Führer did not oblige
the *March of Time* editors with a guided tour.

"Inside Nazi Germany," a 1938 *March of Time* documentary,
gave audiences their first look at various features of the Thousand
Year Reich not stressed in the travel posters. Dorothy Thompson
honored the newsreel with a column. The Chicago Board of Censors banned it. Harry Warner refused to show it. The *New Republic* gave it a grudgingly favorable review, admitting that it was a
good job, but leaving the impression that there were many connected with it whose hearts belonged on the *New Republic* though
their pocketbooks jangled with Luce change.

In July 1940 the *March of Time*'s first full-length feature, "The

Ramparts We Watch," focused on "Sometown in the US," showing how the inhabitants of a small American town between 1914 and 1918 "hoped, argued, worked, fought, lived, died, made war and made peace." It was a thinly disguised interventionist tract. It was evidence of the Luce empire's willingness to battle fascism once it was really clear how the cookie crumbled. It was the first of a genre of wartime pictures which would show hissing Japanese going down in doomed submarines, and seamy-faced Britons gamely taking time out from the blitz to brew a pot of tea. One writer considered the unfavorable depiction of Germany as "an offense to the God of love." A draftee found that it made him "more willing than ever to fight."

It was also evidence of the revolution in public opinion which had taken place since 1935. The limousines pulling up to Number 10 Downing Street . . . The hollow commentary which Mr. Van Voorhis intoned into a voice box were ideally suited to the creation of heroes and villains. It was interesting to look at the changing view of Gallant Little Finland and the Wicked Munitions Maker. In 1937 and 1940 the *March of Time* did two documentaries on Finland. Newspaper headlines proclaimed: FINNS WORK HARD TO PAY WAR DEBT. There were pictures of hardy men in saunas beating themselves "into a healthy glow with birch branches."

When the second newsreel came out, it buttressed the laudatory impression. Finland had just made its plucky stand against the Russians. The *March of Time* marched through a tour of the Washington embassies in 1940. Few of them were in good odor. After the Anschluss, Denmark had leased the Austrian Legation. The Czech and Polish Legations housed diplomats made nationless by Nazi conquests. Most unpopular were the Russian Ambassador, thirty-seven-year-old Constantine Oumansky, and the tenant of the German Embassy. The recall of United States and German ambassadors had left the German Embassy in the hands of the Nazi Chargé d'Affaires, Hans Thomsen, "once," according to the *March of Time,* "well liked and socially popular." (It was later noted in William Shirer's *The Rise and Fall of the Third Reich* that Herr Thomsen took advantage of his social decline, dashing around offering cash emoluments to isolationist senators and congressmen with an eye to keeping America out of war until the Führer had a chance to polish off England.) By contrast the Finnish Minister Hjalmar Procope's telephone was never still. "Every door in Washington" was open to him.

His country was described as the Belgium of the second World War, the Finns as "hardy and rugged as the terrain," toughened by the climate and by their thousand-year-old struggle for survival and for independence. Admiration for the Finns enabled Elmer Davis and Herbert Hoover to meet for once on common ideological ground.

In 1940 audiences might hiss the Russian spokesman's version of the hostilities: "The Finnish army invaded the Soviet Union, is a tool of capitalistic and imperialistic powers and we were forced to counterattack in self-defense." Yet a few years later a good many American moviegoers might have subscribed to such a rereading of history after the hardy Finns had entered the war on the German side and after the heroic defense of Stalingrad by America's Slavic ally. The cold war and the space age have driven the hardy Finn into obscurity. Postwar students of current events nervously zeroed in on Moscow, Peiping, Leopoldville, and Saigon and paid little attention to Who's Who in Helsinki.

On April 19, 1935, the *March of Time* took a familiar cartoon figure to the cleaner—the wicked munitions maker. In 1934 Gerald Nye had launched an investigation of the munitions industry. Nye belonged to a group of Midwestern progressives which included Henrik Shipstead, the La Follettes, and Burton K. Wheeler—all of whom later clapped loudly for Charles Lindbergh when he told America First of the folly of pulling Britain's chestnuts out of the fire.

The Nye investigation put the blame for the Depression and the first World War squarely on the shoulders of the Morgans and Du Ponts. Somewhere in the proceedings someone coined the phrase "merchants of death."

One of these "merchants" was the antihero of a *March of Time* documentary which opened with familiar shots of marching troops. "Today the world is full of talk of war," intoned Mr. Van Voorhis, "but today the man in the street knows a lot more about war than he did twenty years ago."

Enter the villain: eighty-five-year-old Sir Basil Zaharoff, "whose job for fifty years has been to foment wars and supply all nations with weapons of destruction . . . He began life as a poor Greek. He is ending it as one of the richest men in the world."

(Shot of the inevitable limousine driving away from Monte Carlo.)

"It is his secret where he is going . . ."

The camera then focuses on Senator Nye in the midst of a tirade against "international racketeers in hate, fear in the hell that war is." A senator pipes up, giving an alarming picture of munitions makers thoughtlessly at play in the gambling hells of Europe. Charles M. Schwab was quoted as saying roulette was good for his nerves.

(Back to Sir Basil in his wheelchair.)

"Close as he is to making his final peace with his maker, he is still today the chief adviser, the wisest and the richest of the dealers in death."

In November 1941 the *March of Time*'s "Main Street USA" would show an America almost completely converted to a defense economy. Had Sir Basil turned up at the Pearly Gates a month after Pearl Harbor, even Saint Peter might have favored the old boy with a frosty smile.

The communicative arts of the Thirties show the enormous extent to which the best minds of any generation are imprisoned in the framework of their time. Dorothy Thompson may have bored Red to death with her unending reiteration that fascism is a bad thing. Yet *three-quarters* of the people who wrote in to her in 1940 either didn't believe it or didn't believe it strongly enough to go to war.

The invincible Maginot Line, the hardy Finn, the wicked munitions maker were popular stereotypes unwittingly mirrored by the *March of Time*. The munitions man would lose his horns and tail along with the once-fearsome figures of little old ladies hitchhiking to a Townsend Club meeting. They were no longer a menace after Dr. Townsend and Father Coughlin went down to ignominious defeat in an abortive third party movement in 1936.

At the end of the Thirties it was possible to chuckle over the fact that Walter Lippmann had once taken Dr. Townsend seriously, that Dorothy Thompson had looked upon the Technocrats' vision as an unpleasant alternative to the drift "into impossible cynicism and despair."

Hindsight could cause Frederick Lewis Allen in 1939 to cut the creator of Technocracy down to size as "an eccentric, boastful, haphazard young man" given to needling people in Greenwich Village bars, "who claimed to have had an important career in engineering and certainly had conducted a small paint and floor wax business."

Yet the vision of a planned economy had once been an almost universal article of faith. It would come up to haunt Westbrook Pegler after he had come under the influence of John Birch and too much of Mrs. Spelvin's gin. He would damn as "pro-Communist" any statement that a strong central government was a legitimate reaction to "poverty, oppression, and the exploitation of the masses by the few." The source of this heresy—Westbrook Pegler—June 6, 1937.

The insights gleaned from the balcony of the Bijou have, in the long run, been as reliable as any.

Here we watched a circus promoter put a midget in J. P. Morgan's lap. Then we met Anthony Eden, the fair-haired boy, rolling up in one of those endless limousines to 10 Downing Street. Now we see Samuel Insull, an old man hounded through the back streets of Europe, trapped at last behind the bars of a Cook County jail. We heard the distant sputter of guns in far-off China. We listened to the endless debate of the "spineless" League of Nations in Geneva. And, as the photogenic parades goose-stepped to an ever-faster tempo, came an occasional moment of high drama. There was Haile Selassie standing before the League of Nations and the Fox Movietone camera, just after the invasion of Ethiopia, making a last desperate plea for his cause. The Italian delegates cheered as the good guys voted to dismiss sanctions against Italy. The Lion of Judah, majestic in his royal robes, got a big hand from the democracies, and that was all. We would remember it a good deal longer than deaths on the Indianapolis speedway.

We saw it all between the Thelma Todd short and the Pete Smith Specialty—a world that was changing in a way that even the *March of Time* could not foresee—between Vyvian Donner's saddle shoes and dipsy-doodle costumes and Lew Lehr's oft-repeated observation that "Monkeys is the cwaziest people."

Chapter 10

Freedom of the Beach

"The serviceable little messenger boy has given way to a new, essentially feminine creature who is allowed to look elegant and dignified. With cropped hair and an evening dress like a small tight sack, it was impossible to make an 'entrance.' Now any woman can be a Ouida heroine."

So wrote *Vogue* in 1930. And: "No more shall we see calves flattened against a sofa or sagging ankles twisted around a chair leg." In the rebellion against the short-skirted, bosomless Little Boy look of the Twenties *Vogue* rejoiced that "once again little micelike feet peep out from under chiffon flounces."

Others were less jubilant. Two years before Patou had caused a sensation with models cinched in by corsets, hated symbol of woman's thralldom. Chanel, long praised as the apostle of "sheer modernism," had demonstrated to the flapper the unwisdom of trusting the ally who speaks through a mouthful of pins. She had flabbergasted everyone with an evening gown which showed the knees in front while trailing a train like Grandma's on the ground in back. Buyers had pinched themselves. "What they really wanted to do," said *Collier's*, "was to pinch Chanel." Had the rebellion of Flaming Youth been all for nothing? "Will the working woman submit to the fluttering draperies that will catch in the subway door? Will our advanced hygienic standards tolerate bedraggled petticoats?" demanded the New York *World*. "Let's not wear them!" said Fannie Hurst.

Public personalities hedged when asked for comment on this burning issue. The then Prince of Wales said in February 1930, "I don't care whether they wear them long or short. I am going off on another lion hunt." President Hoover refused to express himself, pleading that his administration had been blamed for enough already. Only Bossie Gillis, Mayor of Newburyport, Massachusetts, dared to take a strong stand. "No good American woman should surrender to them frog curryotiers."

For all of this, by 1931 the Paris races looked like a pre-World War I film. The styles of the Second Empire were enjoying a revival. The bumpy tempo of jazz was supplanted by the dulcet compositions of Lehar, Offenbach, and Strauss. Designers were going back to the reign of Louis the Bald for inspiration. Lucien Lelong, who enjoyed a reputation as the "social philosopher of couture," saw the Second Empire styles as "a colorless screen of meaningless fireworks, masking the ennui and monotony which has resulted from a dearth of ideas."

Weary of sterile debate within the French dress industry, M. Lelong journeyed to America in 1931, where such indigenous developments as the "speakeasy dress" gave him renewed faith in the vigor of grassroots design and sent him back to France better able to face the spiritual poverty of his colleagues.

After the first violent wave of resistance—when the Marines were all but called out to keep the peace at fashion shows—the American public followed the designers into the past as if that old designing fellow Merlin had cast a spell over them. Women were even enjoying their new-found bondage, wearing formal kid gloves, managing five separate trains, switching about in materials with strange foreign names: "tchin-sou," "crêpe sumida," "voile redelic."

The forces which had turned intellectuals from expatriation to the Federal Writer's Project had played a part in covering the flapper's knee. Frills and flounces which had disappeared from the stark attire of flaming youth now provided employment for needy garment workers. The passing of the bob, the return to longer, softer hairdos, and the rise of the permanent wave had healthy repercussions upon the hairdressing industry.

Businesses as well as busts were affected by *Vogue*'s 1932 pronouncement: "Spring styles say CURVES." Even Queen Victoria was forgiven her sins as long as she kept the corset department in the black. Economists hoped that women would consume more bread in an effort to restore the grandeur of yesterday's unfashionable mammaries—that in striving after the Rubens look women might tuck into the wheat surplus.

Gloves were a part of the new formality. The final cachet was conferred upon the new look by *Parents' Magazine* in 1932. The August issue showed a girl dressed in a skirt that all but brushed her ankle bone. It was entitled "If I Were That Girl's Mother." The ultimate acceptance of any style came at the moment when it was discovered that you could look like a slut in it.

Vogue took passing note of the contributions of the lingerie department—the "all-in-one" combining bra and panties; the "step-in," a treacherous French pantie with a button closing and a way of falling off in the street (leaving the wearer to step-out as gracefully as possible).

Primarily, though, the hat was the thing in the Thirties. Hats, according to *Vogue* in 1931, broke away from the cloche cliché and developed a sense of occasion. "They threw off the complacency and placidity that had settled upon them and became witty, animated and alert." They were credited with stemming the tide of depression. Readers of the financial pages looked hopefully to musketeer felts, 1900 Canotiers, to the headgear of Watteau shepherdesses and Renaissance pages.

Somewhere en route to the reign of Louis the Bald, an enterprising designer stumbled upon the Empress Eugénie hat—a small feather-trimmed derby which set long-silent wheels of the Danbury millinery factories whirring into gratifying twenty-four-hour-a-day activity.

In 1931—not a year noted for a boom in business—the Danbury hatters' August payroll amounted to $1,000,000, the highest on record till that time. Great was the rejoicing among dyers, hat label manufacturers, blockers, and the purveyors of those unfinished felt shapes suggestively labeled "ladies' bodies." Elderly craftsmen who worked with feathers came out of retirement like Rip Van Winkle.

The columns of the New York *Times* were deluged with letters from irate bird-fanciers. These brought spirited rebuttals by the editor of *The Millinery Trade Review,* who pointed out—with some logic—that most feathers on Empress Eugénie hats came from barnyard fowl whose plight elicited scant sympathy when they turned up on the family dinner table.

While *Vogue* felt that its readers needed no such instruction, more proletarian publications came out with articles on the pronunciation of "Eugénie." That the lesson was lost was indicated by a bit of uncommissioned verse which appeared anonymously in the columns of the *Literary Digest:*

> *The Empress Eugenie*
> *was surely a meanie*
> *for giving us only*
> *three fourths of her beanie.*

The State Window Display Association in Des Moines, Iowa, ticked off its membership for referring to the "U-Jenny" hat. Display men were urged henceforth to refer to the new creation as the "E-zhen-ee." The New York *Times* tartly suggested that the Corn Belt might better give up entirely any efforts to pronounce the language of Louis.

It took more than the Empress Eugénie to bring about that elusive prosperity which always remained just around the corner. In January 1931 the New York *Times* had to leap to the defense of the "ungrateful" poor, who were apparently examining with a critical eye the out-of-date offerings sent to relief stations. New York's Police Commissioner Mulrooney said that the unemployed at the Charles Street Station turned up their noses at high button shoes and other castoffs of the rich which had been lying around in closets for as long as twenty or thirty years.

After the Eugénie craze had spent itself, a new specter arose to haunt the high brass at the Hat Institute. In 1932 the treasurer of that august body estimated that New York had some thirty plants devoted to the rehabilitation of hats thrown into ash barrels. New York turned out some two thousand dozen of these hats a day, Chicago and St. Louis about half as many between them. They were compressed into thousand-pound bales, bid for at central warehouses, and sold by the pound for fifteen or twenty cents. The better discards from stores brought as much as $2.50 to $4.50 a dozen. Factories cleaned the felt, reblocked it, put on new bands and linings, sold them for $1.50 or $2.50 each. If one didn't look too carefully, you might mistake them for new. As a come-on to the purchase of a suit, many chain stores threw a hat in for free, along with the second pair of pants.

While *Vogue* prattled away about Watteau shepherdesses, the grim reality for many people was a pair of somebody's shoes given away for "sweet charity" or a chapeau dragged out by some furtive figure who saw gold lying under them thar coffee grounds and orange peels.

As the worst days of the Depression passed there were compensations—for some. *Vogue*'s college issue in 1935 showed a quintet of extremely matronly-looking undergraduates capering across a page in Statue of Liberty formation. Her sweater might have an "uncombed look," her saddle shoes were "a disgrace"; but, said *Vogue,* the girl "definitely has a flair for clothes."

What strikes the contemporary viewer is the college girl's formality. Two of the five girls wore hats. All had skirts. Revealed in the copy, if not the picture, were Lastex girdles. (Corseting by 1935 had hit a golden mean between the laissez faire of the Twenties and the "steel-ribbed dreadnought" of the Victorian era.) The college girl had a really splendid-looking silk brocade evening wrap among her effects. She dreamed of wearing a knit dress for classroom wear. *Vogue* recommended—rather hesitantly—wide-ribbed Dubonnet stockings, but only for the girl who dared.

Revealing sign of the times: a "Mussolini-inspired" hand-crocheted hat with bulbous tassel. Smith '35 buttoned her cardigan up her back, wore scarves and plaid jackets, and was—also sign of the times—only *"fairly* conscientious about deodorants and in checking perspiration."

By 1940 neatness had gone with the wind. In the spring of that year men's tailors found themselves, to their amazement, taking the measurements of clients from Vassar, Wellesley, and Smith. Men's loafers supplanted the traditional saddle shoes. There was a rash of mannish accessories: flannel slacks, raincoats, gabardine crew hats, boys' rubber boots, loose-fitting sweaters, crew shirts, mittens shaped like boxing gloves, slipper socks, visor caps, and the omni-present blue jeans with shirttails flopping out. Girls were paying fifty-five dollars for sports jackets which with a few obvious dele-tions would have fit their brothers.

The sexes were tending to look more and more alike.

The boys themselves were no longer the gray little mice of yester-year. By today's standards, men, too, had started the decade for-mally. Teenagers who peopled the Fleischmann's Yeast ads in 1936 turned up for a date as often as not in double-breasted suit and fedora. On the *Vogue* level men owned—rather than rented—top hat, white tie and tails. Throughout the Thirties many night clubs demanded formal dress. Yet more and more men began to go waist-coatless, sporting bright-colored playsuits and slacks. Merchandis-ers pushed Norwegian-type shoes for sportswear, patent-leather monk front shoes for evening wear, beach shoes, and lounging slippers from the far corners of the earth. There was a trend toward color and informality—an East Indian madras cummerbund in place of a waistcoat, worn with a white dinner jacket.

By 1937 men were wearing loud slacks on the beaches, gaudily patterned shirts on the tennis courts, bright-colored sweaters for golf. Mixtures of odd coats and trousers became popular for eve-ning wear. The New York *American* came to sound like *Vogue* in describing such fripperies as "a smart novelty belt made of a silk ribbon jacket over a rubber lining." Tailoring firms were besieged with orders for dinner jackets in plum, canary yellow, pastel green, Gulf Stream, blue and bisque. Raymond Godfrey Twyeffort, Chair-man of the National Fashion Committee, decreed sternly, "There is no excuse for drabness in our leisure hours."

The boy whose budget made no allowance for such niceties as Gulf Stream dinner jackets, soon made the discovery that color, like sunlight, was the possession of prince and pauper alike. *Scho-lastic Magazine* was sending out frantic SOS's to high school boys on the unwisdom of combining purplish shirts with yellow and green ties, blue trousers, brown and orange socks, and sweaters with touches of red. While they were at it, they might have thrown in a cautionary word about the porkpie hat, the "action-backed" suit, and the jacket which combined a hound's-tooth-check back with a solid-colored front.

Sports were the great leveling influence. Girls as well as men were participants in the active life. They might not affect golf knickers with gun club check or plaid stockings like those inspired by the Prince of Wales, but it was difficult to tell a man from a woman on horseback or on the ski slopes. Baggy ski pants elasticized at the bottom were standard uniform for fashionable ski-master Hannes Schneider or his hapless if socially impeccable pupil, the Baroness von Arnheim—mercilessly drilled by Schneider in her seventeenth successive day of Stembogens. The slopes of Europe set the pace.

The sports-inspired brown and white spectator pump was a practical and attractive classic. But the ghillies, the golf shoes, the English brogues succeeded in giving women the manly, no-nonsense look of a Red Cross nurse.

As late as 1925 there were city ordinances against one-piece bathing suits and flesh-colored bathing stockings. In the 1930s youth went from one uncontested victory to another in the battle for freedom of the beach. Nudity had come in with hard times. The sunbathing craze of the mid-Thirties would rout the beach censor once and for all. Ina Claire wrote as early as 1930, "Everyone today is dashing out into the sunlight. One look at Antibes, with its white rocks against a glorious blue sky . . . and its beach clotted with brilliant orange mattresses, and its green-blue sea gently tossing little anchored floats, that look like small white rubber bathtubs, in which you may lie and invite the sun. One look at all this, and you forget that you ever knew trouble. You are part of the rollicking crowd that plays all day and a good part of the night . . . and you long for more and brighter beach clothes fittingly to clothe your mounting spirits." Miss Claire clothed her mounting spirits in shantung pajamas "with the English officer air" and a "gay dervish beach suit." On the way home she reported: "I indulged in a regular orgy of buying lounging pajamas. I've decided I am going to wear them to the exclusion of other things."

Americans who were in no position to take a trip to Antibes could enjoy the same voluptuous sensations as Miss Claire at local beaches. The beach pajama went indoors for the cocktail hour and the informal dinner party. Bathing suits became ever skimpier as the public flocked out of doors to frolic under a sun which shone impartially over Juan Les Pins and Coney.

In 1932 *Collier's* wrote of the bathing suit: "Skirtless, backless, legless, all but frontless, these clean-limbed, stripped-for-action little masterpieces gain in chic with every inch of fabric they sacrifice." By 1936 there was scarcely a city in America which still attempted to regulate the measurements of beach and hiking attire. Only an occasional eyebrow was raised at the spectacle of a halter top or bare midriff. The two-piece suit with diaper shorts and halter had replaced the all-in-one bathing suit of the early Thirties with its webbed white belt and perennially rusty buckle. A ban on shorts in Yonkers made nationwide headlines. Even in Yonkers the problem was not one of morals but of esthetics—a protest against the baring of "too fleshy bodies."

Cities with restrictions against white, rubber, or "extreme" suits hastened to repeal them, though many a girl may have yearned secretly to have the ban back when her rubber bathing suit split in half at the crucial point in a swan dive, or when her strapless bathing suit ended up around her waist as she was rolled by a wave.

Men shared in the fruits of revolution. As late as 1937 tops for men's suits were mandatory at Atlantic City. "We'll have no gorillas on our beaches!" proclaimed the good burghers. Yet Atlantic City was bucking a trend. Frederick Lewis Allen reported that when Clark Gable undressed in *It Happened One Night,* revealing that he wore no undershirt, "the knitwear manufacturers reeled from the shock to their sales." Esthetic considerations, in the long run, carried the day. There was little to be said for a gorilla's chest seen through a top—darkly.

If the children of Mrs. Grundy enjoyed a freedom undreamed of by the flapper, it was partly because their parents' attention had strayed from the kneecap to the wallet. Throughout the Thirties the columns of *Parents' Magazine* were filled with advice to families who were struggling with cruel choices between saving for a son's college education and gratifying a daughter's need for a prom dress.

Scholastic Magazine ran a series of articles entitled "Boy Dates Girl." Among other things, the editors dispensed hints on putting life into dilapidated wardrobes—brightening up an elderly dress with buttons in the shape of tennis racquets or footballs, reviving a last-year's sweater by appliquéing a felt heart over the left breast.

The boys and girls of a mythical institution called Central High School peopled the pages of *Scholastic*. Jerry, the most popular girl in the school, was the stock heroine of every teenage column, the one who earns the respect of young men who make passes at her by rebuffing their advances with a merry quip. There was Polly, the girl in straitened circumstances who did all the cooking for five small brothers, and was a whiz with her sewing machine to boot. (The felt heart over the left breast was one of her stylistic inspirations.) Breathy exclamations of admiration from her classmates greeted each homemade creation. The virtuous characters in "Boy Dates Girl" addressed each other in a somewhat stilted idiom: "Oh my, and I meant to get home early so I could dye my dusty pink sweater a deep wine color." "I have to stick to browns a lot, because they're practical, but I do try not to look dullish." Polly's friends were as wits a trifle heavy-handed. As she rushes home to dye the sweater and cook burgers for the five little brothers, a friend remarks, "Well, don't get mixed up and dye the hamburgers."

The villains of the piece, the wealthy Dickens sisters—objects of pity at Central High—were showered with expensive clothing which obsolesced rapidly in their feckless hands. When one of them left a brand-new sweater hanging on a hook in her locker overnight, with disfiguring results, the Central High wags quipped, "How's your carbuncle?"

As symbols of the wasteful ways of the wealthy, the Dickens sisters have paled considerably over the years. In retrospect their wild extravagances offer only a nostalgic reminder of Depression prices. One of the virtuous characters remarks, "I feel sorry for girls like the Dickens sisters. They buy all their dresses at Madame Bonat's, wear $10 shoes and pay $1.35 a pair for hose. But most of the time you can't tell whether they've been sleeping in their clothes or not." They show the shifting emphasis of the Depression moral code. The good girl was the girl who made her own clothes; it was no longer merely enough that she keep them on.

As the hardships of the Depression were somewhat eased in the late Thirties, fashion suddenly became infected with a spirit of madness.

On November 16, 1939, the House of Westmore gave one of the most curious celebrations in Hollywood history. Juliette Marglen, founder of Hollywood's successful "Fingernail Hospital" abstained from manicures for an entire year. Her nails, which ranged from two to three and a half inches in length, were trimmed with a small jigsaw at a "fingernail birthday party." As an admiring circle of Hollywood celebrities looked on, holes were drilled in each nail and the nails were strung into a necklace—a graphic if grisly monument to the virtues of calcimining and massage.

The late Thirties saw the birth of the open-toed shoe—one of the ugliest shoe fashions of all time—against which *Vogue*'s indomitable Edna Woolman Chase crusaded with all the fervor inspired by lost causes. Women's shoes, as Frederick Lewis Allen said in *Since Yesterday,* were equipped with "a small hole in the front which presented a stockinged toe to the eye and offered easy entrance to dust, gravel and snow."

Vogue admitted that the shoes of 1938 were ugly. "Some of them look pretty clumsy you probably say. They do. They should. It's no sin to call a shoe clumsy these days. It's a compliment. If you haven't worn a platform or a wedge sole, do have a pair or two of autumn shoes with this new thick look." When a thick wedgie was combined with an open toe, the compliment was—to put it mildly—backhanded.

There was a rebellion against the much-touted maturity which had prevailed in the worst days of the Depression.

Skirts were shorter and shorter. By 1939 they were back almost up to the knees. "Swing outfits," "girlish ginghams" abounded. The august pages of *Vogue* showed "jitterbug juniors"—on the advertising pages, where everything displayed did not necessarily bear the editors' nihil obstat.

Military motifs were popular. In 1939 there was a rash of hats like a French cadet's kepi with braid trimming, military collars, and cuffs, dress parade hats, epaulets, cockades, American eagle belt buckles, and dresses with double rows of buttons.

Hats sprouted wild little feathers and veils. "Pile it on, the fantasy, the fun," counseled *Vogue* in 1936. "Top your distinguished head with all manner of flora and feathers, tweaks and twists of velvet or lamé." "To be worn with . . ." ". . . orchids on your head" "a peony-laden grandmother's bonnet" "a sail-flying turban" "Dante's beret."

Fashion pundits debated what hat went with the new upswept hair. A woman in a New York tea room in 1938 took the bread basket off the table, put it on her head and attracted no attention whatsoever. One woman, wearing (with wit) a feathered dagger, caused a man to lose the sight of one eye.

As the Twenties had a Flapper, the late Thirties had a Glamour Girl. Café Society had supplied the first one—debutante Brenda Frazier with long bob, strapless evening dress and little girl's bows. Miss Frazier's West Coast repeat was a diminutive ninety-eight pounds of blonde menace named Veronica Lake. She stood five feet tall. Her long yellow hair fell to her shoulders in a series of undulations, one of which nearly obscured her left eye. This new fillip which she added to the standard glamour girl coiffure became known as the peek-a-boo bob.

Dorothy Lamour was another exotic bloom who brought a Hawaiian accent to the age of sun worship. In 1940, resorts blossomed with dinner dresses fashioned after Hawaiian "holokus," flowered evening dresses, lava lava outfits and tiger fish playsuits. Mabs of Hollywood designed a three-piece bathing suit with a hula skirt made of real grass and *Life* magazine felt it necessary to explain the difference between a "sarong" and a "pareo." *Life* attempted to school its readers in the delicate art of draping a sarong—a garment popularized by Miss Lamour—which presented to the unskilled all the hazards of the Roman toga.

Lest one get the notion that the late Thirties were a time of frivolity, there was a grimly alarmist publicity release from 20th Century-Fox to gainsay it. The "Threat of war," according to this source, "has brought Hollywood stylists face to face with their worst dilemma in years. . . . They know that the outbreak of large scale hostilities in Europe will change the fashion picture completely overnight, but at the same time, they are completely helpless to meet the problem. . . . The gowns they are creating for pictures to be released months away may be entirely out of date should war break out in Europe. . . ."

Twentieth Century-Fox went on to do some heavy social theorizing about the relationship between fashion and *Weltanschauung*.

The fashions of the past five years had reflected a world obsessed with the jitters. The cockeyed hats, ludicrous veils, and fantastic costume jewelry expressed turmoil in the world . . .

"Our work necessarily has been geared to this trend, and yet must be in advance . . . should war break out in the meantime," the publicity writer said, "everyone in this profession will find the ground cut out from under our feet . . . Consequently we are a little more fervid in our prayers for peace than most people on this side of the Atlantic." Thus did the fate of Europe obtrude into the thoughts of Sunset Boulevard—an irritating unknown in the costuming of Sonja Henie, Mary Healy, and Edna May Oliver for their roles in *Second Fiddle*.

As the World of Tomorrow was previewed on Flushing Meadows, gathering war clouds did not deter the progress of industrial design. Donald Deskey, Walter Dorwin Teague, Russel Wright and others did a piece in *Vogue* showing the silhouette of the future. All were intoxicated with plastics, air conditioning, and high speed travel. Among the more exotic offerings were Egmond Arens' bridal veil of Goodyear Pliofilm, Russel Wright's spun aluminum coat, and Gilbert Rhodes' disposable socks, pants, and shoes made of a plastic at five cents a throw. You just went to the five-and-ten and asked for "cellulignousamidomethoacrylimine."

Joseph Platt's electrically heated coat would keep a girl toasty while she indulged in a quaint desire for an old-fashioned breath of fresh air. There were devices for imprisoning gamma rays and adjusting body heat. Henry Dreyfuss dreamed of a condensible fabric which could be steamed to life size on arrival in outer space. His girl's bosom was outlined in transparent tubing which contained its own air cooling system. For dashing around the cosmos one needed only a single basic outfit. Donald Deskey's woman of the future was equipped with interchangeable chiffon units. Gilbert Rhodes' man was to have a solo suit ("two zips and it's on"). Vanity would be assuaged by a halo of beryllium copper wire which provided spectrum variations sufficient to turn a drab mouse into a forceful polychrome Titan for the directors' meeting.

Bodies would be scientifically beautiful. Purses would disappear in Donald Deskey's universe because credit would replace money.

Egmond Arens' bride would set off with her lucite jewelry, her belt of traffic reflectors, to some pleasurable experiment in "eugenic selection."

The "futurist" hopefulness of these good men seems quaint in these days of escalation and mushroom clouds. They looked forward to a world that was free of war, draughts, obesity, emaciation, humidity, bad complexions, superfluous leg hair, and the common cold, where everyone was to carry an air conditioner around in his navel.

On October 27, 1938, the first fruit of the World of Tomorrow became a reality. A momentous announcement was made that nylon —history's first completely synthetic fabric—had been developed by the Du Pont Company at a cost of $27,000,000. In October 1939, four thousand pairs of nylon stockings went on sale in Wilmington, Delaware—an offer confined to Wilmington residents. People checked into Wilmington hotels in droves to qualify. It was claimed by some that keeping nylons in the icebox made them runproof, that a Vassar girl had suffered fatal burns while wearing them, that to get a run one would need an acetylene torch.

Nylon, according to the New York *Times,* was actually a corruption of the words "no run." It was not, as another wild and strained rumor went, a contracted form of contumely directed at the Japanese silkworm, "Now You Lousy Old Nipponese."

What were the preoccupations of the lady of fashion as she stood in line for those nylons, blissfully unaware that the Japanese silkworm was about to be avenged? In 1939 *Vogue* put its imprimatur on certain current mannerisms and its anathema on others. One side of a double spread, "Thank You, Mrs. Conway," lauded the *Vogue* reader "for pinning violets on your purse . . . for deciding that Paramount must have been drowsy when it bought the title 'Café Society' from Lucius Beebe, for not being afraid of having your varnish cracked by 'The Yearling' . . . for recognizing the vitality of those five playwrights Sherwood, Anderson, Rice, Behrman, and Howard in their productions about America . . . Thank you for the clarion red of your coat, for being unashamedly fond of your children and for not doing your drawing room in white."

A facing page, "Tut, Tut, Mrs. Conway," ticked Mrs. Conway off for her "sickening admiration for the Glamour Girl" . . . for having enjoyed the movie *Marie Antoinette* "which politely ignored the French Revolution," for joining in the Lambeth Walk, for not knowing the answers to questions on quiz programs, for smoking through her veil, "for sitting way down front and being sprayed by Maurice Evans' all-too-liquid delivery."

One began to have a sneaking sympathy for Mrs. Conway's unfashionable preoccupations. *Vogue* had a nasty way of leading her astray. The magazine had acclaimed "purply cosmetics" as one of the "ten great plays of 1938." Now she was chided for carrying "purple lipstick to funereal lengths." Pile on the fantasy, old girl, they had said a few years before. Now the editors reminded her grimly that "little doll hats" were "merciless" to the face. One could sympathize with her shallow delight in doctor's memoirs and in Norma Shearer, her excitement over Douglas ("Wrong Way") Corrigan. It was difficult to see why she was responsible for the fact that Maurice Evans spat into the front row.

Two years later Mrs. Conway would probably have been found in an Air Raid Warden's helmet. Those 1940 Hawaiian fashions had been a straw in the wind. France had fallen, and for the first time in years the fall collections were not Paris inspired. In 1941 the capitals of the world would scramble for the mantle of Patou and Poiret. Adolf Hitler, like a movie mother propelling a child into a coveted role, would announce that Vienna was henceforth to be the world's new style arbiter. The silhouette of '41, he seemed to think, was to be the lumpy image of the German fraulein.

Then Veronica Lake put up her peek-a-boo bob as an example to lady riveters and won accolades from industrialist Vivien Kellems for her contribution to assembly-line safety. In a new genre of movie she would blow herself up with hand grenades, cause bombers to crash, display the agility of a commando—and face the retribution meted out by the Production Code with an irresistible combination of bravery and bitchery.

Nylons would go to war, along with Lucky Strike Green. Collection centers would be set up to transform discarded stockings into parachutes and fighter plane tires. Mrs. Conway's daughter would go patriotically to her war job (*Vogue* in 1941 decreed that ladies of leisure were passé) in rayons, which by nightfall would so sag about her ankles that she could store her dinner in them.

Vogue introduced 1941's second collection of indigenous American fashions: satin jackets, ostrich hats, bugle beads, "backlog bracelets" (which could be broken into separate clips) as being compatible with "the seriousness of the times." "Come what may we will go on wearing clothes, the prettier the better—for the sake of our morale and our men's. We can keep our chins up better under a new fur jabot. We can go more sure-footedly in good shoes. We can face tomorrow better if tonight's dress is a dream of black lace. Vanity, of course. But vanity is self-preservation."

History did not relate how Mrs. Conway adjusted to the seriousness of the times, but her daughter was pictured in *Vogue* in a boxlike fur jacket, pinning a decoration on a serviceman. Mrs. Conway's sins in 1939 had included not appreciating the Federal Theatre, dropping names from the foreign news while not knowing who her own assemblyman was, and for thinking that Modigliani was "either a cheese or a wine."

When one read what her daughter had been up to in 1941, Mrs. Conway had obviously been improving the species.

Vogue thanked Miss Conway for "using the brightest lipsticks . . . for not looking like Veronica Lake or Deanna Durbin . . . for loving the funny papers and Byron, Woody Herman and Information Please, pale fluffy bedrooms and bright red moccasins . . . for planning to marry—for love only.

"Thank you," said *Vogue,* "for understanding a world beyond dances and schoolrooms, for learning how to wind a bandage, and that sand is better than water for extinguishing incendiary bombs.

"Thanks for the smart tweeds and ravishing evening dresses you buy within a small allowance. Thanks for getting emotional about war."

Miss Conway, unlike her poor mother, presumably *did* know the *Information Please* answers as well as Oscar Levant and FPA. She knew "how to Lindy Hop and when not to." (Recall her mother's disgraceful exhibition with the Lambeth Walk.) One would never have thought feckless Mrs. Conway capable of imparting to her daughter know-how about sand and incendiary bombs. Between that and following the war news, it was small wonder that Mother had lapses about Modigliani Cheese.

Miss Conway, in the war years, would revert to being a "serviceable little messenger boy." For fashion would go full cycle. Those little micelike feet peeping out from under chiffon flounces would give way during the war to regulation L-85, stabilizing skirts just below the knee. Sapphic-looking *Vogue* models were to pose short-skirted, arms akimbo, like Lord Nelson giving orders from a poop deck. When Miss Conway went out to lunch with her co-workers, the massive wartime shoulder pads gave the group a look of a Notre Dame backfield on the move. Later on, when skirts once again caught in the doors of buses and when men formed a League of Broke Husbands to protest the lowering of the hemline, one thought of 1930 and had a feeling of *déjà vu*.

In the 1930s the length of a skirt had become a matter of economics rather than morals. Femininity in fashion had not—as emancipated women feared—presaged a return to pre-World War I hypocrisy or flirtation behind a fan. Miss Conway in the Thirties had steadily gained in freedom—freedom to work, freedom to strip. Morally she was at a halfway house between Queen Victoria and Rudi Gernreich.

In patting her on the back in 1941 *Vogue* thanked Miss Conway for the "balance which justifies your having so many new liberties (you have more freedom than any girls since the Stone Age—so thanks to your parents for the long leash)."

The tut-tuts and thank-yous doled out to Miss Conway were actually directed at her mother. "Thanks for knowing that liquor has nothing to do with sophistication, and for having the Coca-Cola obsession instead. (But also thanks to your mother who serves cocktails to you and your beaux, thus giving you the prerogative of refusing . . .) . . .

"Thank you for choosing to come home at early late hours, and thanks to the mother who lets you choose." It will be seen that Miss Conway was her own woman to a greater extent than she had ever been in the day of the Black Bottom and the boyish bob. Her mother trod an increasingly delicate tightrope. Should Miss Conway have elected to come home at a late, late hour instead of an "early late" one, if she had stretched out a hand for that martini, Mother Conway would have found herself in a fix to challenge the powers of a Metternich.

Fashion in the Thirties and early Forties reflected the changed status of women. It also reflected the changed realities of power. After the Fall of France, Paris never quite regained its throttle hold on couture. French designers had to share the postwar limelight with such upstarts as Emilio Pucci and Cole of California. The frog curryotiers could no longer electrify Seventh Avenue as they once had with the news that Lanvin had gone Cossack, that Patou was monkeying with the Moyen Age waistline, or with such terse orders of the day as "Paris dictates crimson or green hair."

The Paris hat did not regain its pre-Pearl Harbor eminence, either. The Hat Institute might yearn in vain for those days when figures in the Rinso ads had kaffeeklatsched, when quartettes of women in Listerine ads had sat around the bridge table—all in hats —discussing a friend's halitosis.

If progress came to the postwar world, and it did, it was not as it had appeared to such Elijahs as Russel Wright and Walter Dorwin Teague. Round shoulders and postnasal drip are, like death and taxes, still in evidence. One measure of progress is instead the concept of "built-in obsolescence." A whole generation has grown up—to be sure—unaware that "stocking" once connoted only silk or lisle. A whole generation is also unaware that "no run" was once more than a mere shibboleth. On the way back home from a nylon sale in the late Thirties a woman's stockings blew out of her car window. Eight other cars ran over them before she picked them up, yet there was "not a single break in the delicate threads."

When patriotic Miss Conway came home in the evening from her war job, she might stop by periodically at a nylon repair shop. Many Miss Conways wore the same pair of stockings "for the duration." After the war—as any wearer of one of the 83,000,000 dozen pairs of nylons sold in 1964 could testify—the manufacturers never made *that* mistake again. Skirts might rise and fall, hats could come and go, but it was a canard to say that stocking manufacturers were impervious to the lessons of history.

Chapter 11

Late Tubular
and White on White

On October 31, 1965, the New York *Times Magazine* showed a series of living rooms inspired by periods of the past. Bracketed with an Empire lady beside a harp was a room out of the 1930s. Is this really the verdict of the ages of that hopefully "futuristic" era when Mr. Robsjohn-Gibbings' "Modern Sans Epoche" was "not a style, not a period, but a true new philosophy"? Have Le Corbusier and Dorothy Draper been relegated to museums or quaint settings, along with the Empire settee?

Every decorating style is a rebellion against its immediate predecessor. Yet the Thirties, more than most, represented a break with the past. The past, in 1931, was the Taupe Twenties, whose muddy palette still lingered on. Browsing through a 1931 issue of *The American Home* one is confronted with Oriental rugs and wing chairs inspired by Grinling Gibbons.

Yet a better way of life was in the making. There were ironing machines ("mangles") and Venetian blinds. The first air conditioners were inspiring health talk about the effects of humidity on the nasal passages. Color was invading the bathroom for the first time. Polychrome fixtures in such decorator hues as orchid, ivory, and Ming green were replacing the pull chains of yore.

The Century of Progress exhibition had yet to flood the market with plastics. Cellophane and chartreuse were unknown. A decorator's idea of brightening a boy's room was to give him dark oak beds, a dull gold bedspread, a rust-colored rug, pictures of undersea life, jade woodwork, and walls that were a darker variation of the standard Landlord's Cream.

By 1933 the revolt was under way. The battle cry went up: "Don't be afraid of color." Decorating editors waxed lyrical over "texture," "contrast," and "interplay." Pit a mauve rug against white Chippendale. Do the unexpected—scarlet walls and white leather upholstery, black waxed linoleum with white inlaid stars.

The landlord winced as his nice sour cream-colored walls were painted bottle green, navy, or chocolate, or covered with black marbleized paper (dusty rose was at least a little easier to paint over). He usually winced in silence, since he knew he was damn lucky to have rented the place at all . . . Sometimes even the decorating editors shared his misgivings. "But how deft must be the hands that guide the destinies of these spectacular interiors. What assurance and decision must direct each vivid gesture!"

In 1932, at the President's Conference on Home Building, much interest was shown in what was then a novelty known as "modernistic architecture." The "Century of Progress" World's Fair in 1933 in Chicago introduced John and Jane Doe to the architectural *genre* which was going great guns on the Continent. "L'Esprit nouveau" had first been introduced at Le Corbusier's Pavillion at the Paris Exposition of 1925. Concrete vaults, glass walls, open floor plans, and buildings on stilts expressed Le Corbusier's conviction that houses were "machines for living." Working in wood, leather, and tile, he designed furniture and interiors to match.

Traditional Franco-German rivalry was briefly forgotten in Le Corbusier's alliance with the titans of Bauhaus. The Bauhaus school had been established by Walter Gropius in Germany in 1919 to coordinate the decorative arts into structures which revealed rather than concealed their purpose. The school moved to Dessau in 1925. Hitler's mistrust of functional steel and glass caused Gropius and Marcel Breuer to emigrate to the United States in 1937. As a result, the Graduate Center of Harvard University rose to become a monument of New World Bauhaus.

The first architectural exhibition of the Museum of Modern Art was organized in 1932 by Henry Russell Hitchcock and Philip Johnson. At the same time, describing the work of such innovators as Le Corbusier, Oud, Gropius, and Mies Van der Rohe, Hitchcock and Johnson published a book *The International Style: Architecture Since 1922*. As we get it from the horse's mouth in their book, characteristics of the style were emphasis on volume as opposed to mass, regularity as opposed to symmetry, and dependence on the intrinsic elegance of materials as opposed to applied decoration.

Alfred Barr, Director of the Museum of Modern Art, wrote in a preface to their volume that "there exists today a modern style as original, as consistent, as logical, and as widely distributed as any in the past."

The International Style has had its distinguished opponents, such as Frank Lloyd Wright, whose houses recessed into hillsides and one-story Prairie-style dwellings still belong in the mainstream of modern architecture. Perhaps the only parts of the Western World where the International Style has made little headway is in that strangely anachronistic land of massive skyscrapers, shaky balconies, and Victorian dust-catchers—the Soviet Union.

The brave spirit of the newly defined International Style dominated the Century of Progress—though of course there were always those who hampered Progress's wheels with dreams of Pseudo Tudor, Cotswold Charm, or interiors of Ruby Ross Wood Regency. (Miss Wood was a chichi decorator of the day.)

The 1933 Design for Living house at the fair included an exciting new material called "Rostone," a combination of limestone and shale. The circular House of Tomorrow had a second and third floor with walls of a glass specially treated to attract ultraviolet rays. Air conditioning obviated the need for windows. Venetian blinds lined with aluminum were to reflect heat and cold. *House Beautiful* voiced timid objections to some of the more dramatic aspects of Progress. The hexagonal rooms in the brick-and-cantilever job seemed to be "hardly justified." The living room at the Stransteel House "leaked out" on three sides. Guests at the House of Tomorrow might question why all the utilities had been put on the ground floor, so that they walked too easily into one of Daddy's hobbies or Mother's Monday wash.

Gray dominated the Design for Living House as it would dominate the spectrum of the Thirties—mingled here with violet, blue, and peach, and white cotton hangings. Bedazzled viewers would gaze at the wonders of plywood, vinylite, sealex, Masonite, Bakelite, linotile, Carrara glass, Japanese laminated wood, glass blocks, and Merimet—a copper sheathing welded to fabric. The public stared skeptically at vinylite towel racks, chromium tubular standing ashtrays, at the cellophane fabrics in the Masonite House. With mingled claustrophobia and chills they shivered at the air conditioning in the House of Tomorrow and wondered if the air was really as fresh as what came through the open window. Would glass block ever replace white clapboard and gray shingle? Sometimes they would turn in puzzlement from all these marvels to Ripley's Believe It or Not exhibit (where one man was popping an eyeball out of his head and where another unfortunate was slowly turning to stone), or to the Midway where they could witness the more familiar decorative assets of Fan Dancer Sally Rand.

Yet the carnival wonders of Bakelite and cellophane would soon become day-to-day realities. Plastic and prefabs would displace the old-fashioned products of the lumber and brick industries. Indeed, thirty years later good wood had become one of the more expensive building materials. A Century of Progress begat a whole school of industrial designers: Raymond Loewy, Gustav Jensen, Henry Dreyfus, Gilbert Rhode, Walter Dorwin Teague, Norman Bel Geddes (who in turn begat the tubular lavatory basin), Donald Deskey who begat the Bakelite desk, and most famous of all, Russel Wright, who led homely aluminum out of the kitchen.

Mr. Wright, like Rena Rosenthal, was also at home in cork, but it is for his spun aluminum bean pots, hors d'œuvres trays and water carafes that he will—if at all—be remembered. They were the standard decor for those first-year-out-of-Vassar apartments tenanted by Mary McCarthy's Group. (Miss McCarthy had one of the group give as a wedding present a cocktail shaker made of oak and aluminum. It was shaped like a skyscraper and accompanied by a matching tray and twelve little cups. The set was nontarnishable, and alas, one fears, nonreturnable.)

Decorators were quick to pounce on the possibilities of cellophane. It was used for chair upholstery and slipcovers, bedspreads and placemats. When cellophane went Hollywood it appeared in *Swingtime* as a many-tiered night club tablecloth. It inspired Cedric Gibbons' high-style window treatment—a very wide wall with a loop hanging down and a deep cellophane flounce. It was also used for lampshade covers—and perhaps the ultimate in period pieces might be a standing chromium lamp with a black and white shade that warped and twisted and struggled to get out of its cellophane cocoon.

Furniture came in all sorts of odd sizes and shapes. It was the day of the built-in. A 1930s movie short showed a sybarite who had so simplified life with switches, built-in bookshelves, retractable toasters and coffee pots and headboard dials, that it was never necessary to get out of bed. For those who could make it to the living room, the line of Edward Wormley for the Dunbar showroom was bulbous and overstuffed, big on odd hardware and interesting textural interplay.

In the furniture field, the brave manifestoes of International Style were translated into "touch tempting surfaces." Mies van der Rohe—a director of Bauhaus—created the chair with legs of crossed metal on two sides. Marcel Breuer evolved the chair with seats and back sunk into one continuous hunk of tubular chrome.

Alvar Aalto bent plywood into chairs that were displayed at the Museum of Modern Art. Isamu Noguchi created the first amoeboid tables. Eero Saarinen in 1940 developed the "womb chair." Slightly later Charles Eames was the master of the type of chair design which holds that comfort can best be achieved by bringing strategic support to a single vertebra. In his 1944 book, *Good-bye, Mr. Chippendale*, T. H. Robsjohn-Gibbings delivered the *envoi* of the whole group to the past.

If a Century of Progress and the International Style contributed to the overall look of the Thirties, so too did the movers and shakers of the Decorating Industry. It was said of Nancy McClelland that after her predecessors had stripped off the wallpaper, along came Nancy to put it back. Lost civilizations of botanical prints had preceded that wave of cream paint and Miss McClelland covered the whole mess up with wood paneling, tapestry, scenic wallpapers, murals, borders, cornices, and dadoes. She was responsible for the first modern penthouse garden. While it is difficult to remember that John Wanamaker was ever first in anything, the installation of Nancy McClelland's "Au Quatrième" made it the first department store to carry antiques.

Margery Sill Wickware's trademark was interesting color. When she put a bowl of lilacs into a room, according to *House Beautiful,* it didn't just happen. William Pahlmann, who was Lord and Taylor's answer to Nancy McClelland, was noted for drama. It was he who designed a window which slid up and out of sight like a garage door and who first thought of putting feathers on a flesh-pink mirror.

Among the movers and shakers one would have to mention the Crown Prince and Princess—Cedric Gibbons and Dorothy Draper.

Cedric Gibbons was a set designer for MGM. He told readers of the *Ladies Home Journal* in 1933 that "Every Home's a Stage." Thanks to Mr. Gibbons there were many homely stages thereafter from Seattle to Larchmont graced with chromium-legged tables and twin beds joined with a single headboard. There were yards sold of such unfamiliar materials as white sailcloth, denim, seersucker, and cellophane. White pianos were shown in MGM's *Men Must Fight;* inlaid black and white floors with apologies to MGM's *Dancing Daughters.* The bedroom treatment from *Dancing Daughters* was not for the timid: twin beds of modernized Directoire painted black, with ivory panels at head and foot, all mounted on a low black dais, with the heads resting regally in an arch.

Mr. Gibbons was one of the first to suggest that decor should reflect the personality of the owner. Joan Crawford, "a vivid and restless" personality, could stand up to bold backgrounds. Norma Shearer might have worried a little that Mr. Gibbons did not allow her to "sit in a chair with a huge design."

Gibbons dedicated himself to exorcising the last relics of the tauped Twenties. Get rid of those "drapes" over pianos, the "scarfs crushed in the middle of tables are very bad." It may never have occurred to him that a future generation might hold cellophane bows in contempt. His own withering scorn was reserved for the bronze base whose hands held up a clock or vase. "Don't give it away, destroy it (hanging isn't good enough)."

Dorothy Draper, the author of many books, was the Mary Baker Eddy of the cult that anyone can become a good decorator. Prerequisites were "a sense of beauty, a sense of fun, and some common sense." Profitable offshoots of her own mystique were the Arrowhead Springs Hotel in Hollywood, the Camelia House in Chicago's Drake, the Mayflower Hotel in Washington, Hampshire House and the Carlyle in New York; as well as the indigenous stately homes of Mrs. Frank Vanderlip, Mrs. Owen Young, and Mrs. Preston Davies.

She first awakened the public to the potentialities of paint. She once did over an old building by painting it black with white trim and by doing the doors in different striking colors. It was one hundred percent rented in three months. Miss Draper was much in demand after that for remodeling jobs on tenements.

Her own apartment in Hampshire House paid homage to the black and white syndrome. Scattered about were small tables of black mirror. There were black lacquered commodes, dark walls, white damask curtains, and white plaster lamps, as well as antique pieces and family heirlooms. This, in the jargon of the trade, was known as mixing periods with a sure hand.

As many decorators did not fear color, Miss Draper was not one to shy away from pattern. Her drawing-room chairs were slip-covered in a brilliant chintz. A legacy of her stay as a member of the decorating staff of *Good Housekeeping* was an office papered in the cabbage rose design which she had made popular and which pulsated most disquietingly when the staff came back from lunch.

As atomic fission was a product of the joint efforts of many brilliant minds, the same might be said of the two great decorating discoveries of the 1930s. The first discovery was that modern furniture could be combined with motifs from the mysterious East: statuettes of Oriental deities, zebra stripes, lacquered Chinese screens. Mr. Robsjohn-Gibbings mixed walnut furniture with a fresco copied from the Sigiriya rock caves of Ceylon. His Modern Sans Epoche mingled with a yellow block Japanese screen and the head of a Chinese demigod and dispenser of mercy.

Frank Everest Moffat artfully blended zebra stripes in a room that combined twentieth-century civilization and what appeared to *House Beautiful* to be "jungle savagery." It is questionable whether any inhabitant of the game preserves of Tanganyika or Kenya would have recognized the chromium seal with a crystal ball on his nose.

Mr. Moffat was also responsible for hoking up eighteenth-century bootracks with red silk cords and brass hooks and using them as umbrella stands, and for combining green walls with the hues of a British dessert called "raspberry fool." *House Beautiful* described him as "a prankster firmly grounded in tradition."

Other tradition-minded pranksters stumbled on the second great revealed truth of the Thirties—that you could live with Victorian if you didn't rebel against it and make it quite clear to everyone that you knew it was funny. Mr. Bruce Buttfield certainly knew what was what. One had only to consider his lavish use of round mirrors of sapphire glass. Yet he was also capable of taking a Victorian dustcatcher, stripping it of its rust and plum upholstery and putting it in a room with Russel Wright aluminum.

Alfred Kazin recalls visiting the decorator Muriel Draper's house on lower Lexington Avenue. It had an "artful Victorian parlor" and on each stair landing there was an alcove containing a violin tied round with ribbons. The neo-Victorian setting did seem a trifle chichi for a talk on the agony of Spain.

Mr. Tom Murray Baker in 1935 turned his hall floor into a black and white checkerboard and decked his walls with pictures of Queen Victoria's bridesmaids, framed in white molding with black glass mats. Messrs. Baker and Buttfield and Miss Draper were to inspire a whole Noah's ark full of couples of young men. Whatnot cabinets, backbreaking Victorian settees, and other Mauve Decade instruments of torture would one day rank as the ultimate in camp.

The readers of *House Beautiful* suffered from what was described in the 1960s as baroque worries. *American Home* was more likely to come to grips with a belly issue. Royal Baking Powder ads which appeared in its pages in 1935 dealt with housewives who gave their reasons for liking Royal Baking Powder. "I allow myself only a dollar a day for food, so I can't afford to risk failure when I bake," one such testimonial ran. Other variations on the theme: "Just married on an income of $18.00 a week" . . . "Two children, a hungry husband and $10.00 a week for food" . . . "Only $25.00 a month for groceries" . . . "Food for four on $8 a week." By the time the couple who had married on $18 a week got around to saving for a baby, the daily food budget was down to seventy-five cents.

It was a cinch that these housewives were not concerned primarily with what color Dorothy Draper would paint the front door or what Cedric Gibbons had meant when he opted for those dusty pink walls. The less pretentious magazines were concerned with a reader who could not only not afford a decorator, but who in most cases was also unable to afford furniture.

For every home that was a stage there were a hundred where Mother had laid her hands on some crates and was trying to transform them into "simple, dignified bookcases." The paint, according to *American Home,* "creates miracles in moments." "With a little ingenuity"—so Mother was forever being told—"a simple packing box could become a table." An apple barrel and a breadboard could be transformed into a dressing table with a slight assist from Dad. (While he was hammering away Mother would be stitching up the cambric skirt and lining it with cotton cord.)

Even *House Beautiful* went in for high style do it yourself, telling readers how to make their own lampshades and valances. You could, for example, put a valance over a scroll of carved wood, paint it white to look like plaster, and no one would know that it wasn't bona fide Cedric Gibbons. You could finish off a board with glass whirls, or garland a blue-mirrored valance with crystal fruit. Silver and gold lace doilies from Dennison could be pasted on a valance for a feminine effect, as opposed to the stark masculine simplicity of wooden brackets and brass curtain rods. Every era has its share of tat—and much of the tat of the Thirties could be laid to the necessities of doing it yourself. That landlord digging himself out from under the layers of black and navy paint might contemplate with even more understandable horror the walls of the couple who couldn't afford Nancy McClelland, who had a "paint a mural" party and asked the gang to come with brushes and paints.

There was also a lot of nautical tat around. Someone had thought of racking children up against the wall in bunk beds and the temptation was irresistible to turn one's home life into one long shipboard experience. There were lamps with ships under sail, vases with anchors, hemp mats with anchors and ropes; white fish plates and Barnacle Bill chairs of marine blue iron and white cotton rope. A circa 1933 nautical cabaña featured fishnet curtains, rope swung between two white posts, and a bar with a copper anchor where Jack Tar donned his yachting cap for the weekend, and proceeded to dispense Bronxes from a chromium shaker.

The nautical cabaña might also have fallen into the category of fun tat. In this classification were pink elephants, mauve monkeys, cork gameroom accessories and clever ice-cube containers. A *very* period note was struck by the genial cakewalking wooden Rastuses who held up rings of pretzels and generally contributed to fun in the rumpus room.

Under the heading of miscellanous tat were Maxfield Parrish prints, tinted pictures of the Dionne quintuplets, copper ashtrays with a silhouette of a comically knickered golfer taking a wild swing on the third green. The glass ashtrays embedded in a replica of a Firestone tire were handy for smoking in the tub.

The apogee of all 1930s tat was sired by the Scottie. Every household object from engagement pads to playing cards was embellished with cute likenesses of this beloved mammal. Typical of Scottie-inspired accessories was the do-it-yourself valance, pictured in *House Beautiful,* made of plaid buckram and fastened with large wooden buttons. A side effect was the complete extinction of the Scottie as a domestic animal and the ultimate abdication of his niche to the French poodle.

Progressing from tat to cliché there were colors, bibelots, and so forth that were done to death, though in many cases they were as intrinsically attractive as anything that has come along since. These included such combinations as lemon and gray, chartreuse and dubonnet, black and red, black and white, and gray, silver, and gold; black mirror-glass tops on white pedestals; bottle green walls and white woodwork and—after 1935—pickled pine. Everything was mirrored, indirectly lit or flounced with bathrobe cord. Screens were omnipresent: lacquered oriental screens, chromium screens, screens with Napoleonic motifs. A big do-it-yourself item was the screen made of night club match covers, which incidentally subtly got across the notion that the owner got around.

Prominent in the fine arts division were mobiles and any form of abstract painting—Arp, Miró, Calder, Lee, or Kandinsky established you as a swinger. More common were Picasso's *Woman* or *Boy Leading a Horse,* and Van Gogh's *Sunflowers.* (A note to make a painter cut off his other earlobe: *Sunflowers* was available in a choice of decorator colors: yellow, turquoise, or chartreuse.)

The Thirties was certainly the white on white decade. Not that there was anything wrong with white *per se* . . . but . . . furniture was sprayed white, milk-white urns were filled with white ostrich plumes, the white vase on the dining room table was filled with white grapes, mirrored white plaster tables were embellished with white plaster ropes, white Chippendale and white garden furniture was grouped around a glass-topped table. The difference between a Victorian monstrosity and something that shrieked high-style was a coat of white paint.

This was not to mention white leather picture frames and desk sets, white milk glass swans, white tin trays, white iron horse doorstops, white high-pile rugs, white pottery apples. Individually attractive though these things might be, they were somewhat deadly in their collective impact. Entering an up-to-the-minute Thirties apartment, one might suddenly go snow-blind.

If Victoriana was the decorator's Scylla, all-white was his Charybdis. Cedric Gibbons cautioned the *Ladies Home Journal* reader not to go overboard on it. This advice sounded strange from the man who had put Jean Harlow and William Powell down in a world of white pianos, white sailcloth, white telephones, white glass curtains, and white wool fringe.

It was in the brave clichés of furniture designer and architect that the 1930s gave its Nicene creed of a lost faith—the gospel of Progress written in Bakelite, cantilevered tubing, and laminated wood. When Philip Johnson designed a house of glass, when Isamu Noguchi put a table on a stalagmite base, when Marcel Breuer and Walter Gropius, honored refugees in Massachusetts, designed a house with the Venetian blinds *outside* the window they were professing their faith in a clean break with the past. The devil take that poor housewife struggling with ice-encrusted cords and snow-covered slats, or fighting her Victorian inhibitions as the whole block looked into her bedroom.

When "the music of the spheres became the whir of gears" history would not find Gropius or Noguchi wanting. They had produced "controlled clarity," "clean, sparse, masculine line," a way of life that was "meaningful for our time." A chair was no longer merely a chair but a "machine for sitting." As Frank Lloyd Wright said in derogation of some old-hat design, "Machine at the Service of man has summed this up before."

The pity of it is that certain classic examples of this brave new way of life have been lost to future archeologists. At the 1939 New York World's Fair were two model houses. They were financed by the FHA, decorated by Sears, Roebuck, and available for temporary occupancy to typical Americans atypical enough to want to spend a week in a goldfish bowl. One cost $3100 to build, $1200 to furnish—all the trimmings down to the blond lamps and service for six for less than $5000. It was typical of a forward-looking generation that the exterior of one house was described as "American Modern," though there was nothing about its clapboard frame or shingle roof to make Mark Twain feel out of place.

A more snobbish future archeologist might prefer the World's Fair Terrace Club. The terrace was lemon yellow trimmed with white. There were yellow curtains and gray and white awnings, and the furniture was, as one might guess, silver gray.

A "modernized baroque" interior glistened with silver metallic textured wallpaper. A console table had a dark gray antique top and the inevitable white plaster base. Torchères holding up multi-armed candelabra diffused indirect lighting toward the white winged motifs on the ceiling. The whole edifice had come into being in a semimystical fashion, described as "out of wasteland swamp and salt marsh," girdled by parks and an "idyllic lagoon."

Another interesting lighting treatment was to be found in Sloane's 1938 House of Years, which incorporated bleached oak furniture, zebra-striped chairs, and black walls "blued off like a raven's wing." Here the indirect lighting came out of the petals of a fixture shaped like a calla lily.

On the ocean liner *Normandie,* Diana was surrounded by stylized gazelles in inlaid marquetry. The mirrors were copper tinted. The light all came from neither candelabrum nor calla lily, but from circular tubing. It was perhaps the classic example of Marine Modern.

All of these four examples proved to be equally ephemeral. The Terrace Club has gone the way of all those hanging gardens of Babylon which rise periodically from the wasteland swamp and salt marsh of Flushing Meadows. The main branch of E. J. Korvette's stands on the site of Sloane's House of Years. The *Normandie* capsized and was scrapped. The fate of those $5000 model homes is well known to anyone who has sat down to talk turkey recently with an architect, builder, or interior decorator.

These artifacts have disappeared without a trace. They have taken with them the sense of excitement that went with pitching tradition out the window. They have left a certain age group with little more than a vague predilection for mirrored paneling and combinations of gunmetal and yellow.

It is easy to foresee the eclectic possibilities in a revival of this bygone style—rooms done over in Pickled Pine, Century of Progress, Early El Morocco, 1933 Crow's Nest, Dorothy Draper Walkup, Normandie Inlay, Cedric Gibbons Late Show. Antiquarians may soon be walking the streets in search of a genuine Russel Wright skyscraper cocktail shaker, a Stork Club screen or an authentically well-thumbed deck of Scottie playing cards. The *pièce de résistance* may well be that rarity of rarities—a pre-Roy Wilkins pretzel carrier.

The New York *Times Magazine* rooms recapture a bit of the lost splendor. Huzza to Le Corbusier's *chaise longue* in black foalskin, to the black lacquered chest, the white Chippendale chairs, the zebra rug. After all this time it is good to hear that "black and white makes news" again. If you just hang onto a thing long enough . . .

The Bauhaus steel and glass room touches a responsive chord as do the leather lounge chairs by Mies van der Rohe. Yet something is missing. One searches the *Times* in vain for an antique chromium seal. Where, Mr. Tom Britt, are the calla lilies of yesteryear? Your black and white kitchen is a dream, Mr. Edward Zajac. There is one anachronistic detail—that handy sprayer by the cold-water tap. Any member of a generation which squeezed its own oranges will tell you that neither Bauhaus nor l'Esprit Nouveau was equal to getting the pulp and seeds off the side of the sink.

A "patchwork of the past." Don't you know that "past" is the ultimate dirty word? "Jet blue walls and abstract painting place a room in the Sixties?" You boys really ought to sit down and have a good straight talk with a machine. *The Sixties!*

Vas you dere, Sharlie?

Chapter 12

The Expanding "400"

"I will build that and that and that," said J. P. Morgan the Elder, pointing to plans for a new medical school at Harvard. The celerity with which he committed himself to the expenditure of a million dollars was typical of the man who had once ordered his chauffeur to drive up on the sidewalk to avoid a traffic snarl. It was also typical of what has been called the "Astorbilt era," an age of terrapin stew, Saratoga trunks, chaperones and card dances, when Alfred Gwynne Vanderbilt drove his equipage down Fifth Avenue to mark the beginning of the coaching season, and when the Morgans could remain aloof from the sweaty ordeal of the social climb because they were already *there*.

Society as defined by Ward McAllister had been restricted to the four hundred names on Mrs. Astor's visiting list. At the time of the crash there were still about some faces from this age of titans and grand dames. In 1934 the obituary columns marked the passing of the self-styled inheritor of the title *"the* Mrs. Vanderbilt." Once this lady was said to have hurled bonds back into the face of an offending messenger, who had had the effrontery to address her as Mrs. Cornelius Vanderbilt. "I know of no Mrs. Cornelius Vanderbilt. I am Mrs. Vanderbilt." When she died the title passed to her son's wife, who was equipped with a suitably archaic set of brownstone-front-era trappings: beige fox scarves, a diamond stomacher, and a collection of headache bands. By this time there were members of the Vanderbilt clan who were on relief.

The locus of fashion in the Stanford White era had been Newport. Its decline was symbolized in 1933 by the passing of Mrs. Oliver Hazard Perry Belmont. Mr. William K. Vanderbilt, who was her husband in the 1890s, presented her with Marble House, a Newport villa in the great tradition. Situated on Bellevue Avenue, it cost $2,000,000, with $7,000,000 more lavished on the interior. A marble driveway with high marble walls led to a white Italian marble structure reminiscent of the Trianon. Pilasters and Corinthian capitals were scaled to the proportions of an Oriental temple. With Mrs. Belmont's second marriage Marble House was sold in 1933. It had fallen into at least temporary disuse, since it reminded Mr. Belmont of his predecessor. Mrs. Belmont had a French Gothic home in Sands Point, Long Island, which was sold in 1928 to Mrs. William Randolph Hearst, and a château in the Loire Valley. Mrs. B. had the baroque era attitude toward real estate. You could dress it up, dress it down, buy up a block, bring a monastery across the Atlantic stone by stone. Any way you sliced it, it cost a lot.

Mrs. Belmont's other projects included women's suffrage and getting her daughter Consuelo married off to the Duke of Marlborough—a union whose dissolution became something of an ecclesiastical *cause célèbre*. After Mrs. Belmont's death, revenooers discovered bootleggers operating a still on the parquet floor of her Long Island dining room. This huge copper-and-steel apparatus had a 5000-gallon capacity, was meticulously polished, and was a fixture worthy of Marble House.

Besides Mrs. Vanderbilt and Mrs. Belmont, there were other relics of the days when a name still counted for something. There were a few draughty town houses on Fifth Avenue replete with urns, Victorian statues, Bouchers, Greuzes, and Aubusson tapestries. The powder room would have a rosewood toilet table littered with lipsticks, hairpins, and shabby silver brushes. One sat at a dinner table with silver menu holders, turned to one's partner with Swiss-watch precision as the courses changed, and was given the chance to field one remark from the hostess. After dinner the women repaired to one room to discuss clothes, resorts, and servants. The men talked of horses, yachts, and other people's mistresses. The stroke of eleven was the signal for "joining the ladies" for desultory dancing, for a buffet supper on top of the groaning dinner, for conversation with the original "Roosevelt refugees" who had moved to England the day FDR was elected.

Looking back one is struck by the deadliness of Society's amusements. Its most fashionable *faubourgs* had water that was polluted (the North Shore of Long Island), filled with seaweed (Bailey's Beach), ice-cold (Bar Harbor, where the temperature was, significantly, congenial to white seals), and Palm Beach, which became unfashionable the moment the weather got nice. Sybaritic pleasures were looked upon contemptuously with the ice-in-the-water-pitcher stoicism of the British aristocracy. Comfort smacked unfashionably of Grossinger's. The way to success for the social climber involved mastering some violent sport that he hated, or being grilled by some inquisitorial board of governors for a club where the elect spent their days listening to lectures on mulching and antique porcelain, tracing their blood lines, or reading papers in French. Cleveland Amory once explored the question of *Who Killed Society?* Certainly a contributory factor was *ennui*.

As for the actual effects of the Crash, we have the evidence of Maury Paul, William Randolph Hearst's syndicated society snooper. He wrote in 1938 of the social revolution taking its toll from families "Once on the Top Shelf of Affluence." Here "confiscatory taxes" reduced "great fortunes to the vanishing point." "Baker and Pyne Clans Are Among Those Who Have Seen Depletion of Their Riches Via This Route." He gave a dramatic picture of socially prominent fifty-year-olds forced by the Depression to punch time clocks, Union Club Members eking out an existence as floorwalkers, Racquet and Tennis Club members all but panhandling, post-debs holding down jobs as models and press agents. Most dramatic was the case of Andrew McKinney, once the possessor of a town house in the East Seventies who listed himself in the *Social Register* as living at the New York Yacht Club, and whose address was at last revealed to be Welfare Island.

For most of Society's victims of the Crash the workaday reality involved an unobtrusive pulling in of horns. All was not lost. The Depression provided a bonus to him who had held back from plunging from a Wall Street window and who had clung prudently to his A.T. & T. In December 1932, *Fortune* pointed out that in Los Angeles you could have your garden taken care of for a dollar a week; that a dignified couple would run your Commonwealth Avenue house in Boston for eighty dollars a month; that a "shuffle-footed but affable Negro" would fry your chicken and do your washing for eight dollars a month in Virginia. Even in the North in the early Thirties, Bridie might work for keep. In 1938 *Fortune* re-evaluated the "servant problem." By then, in the Northeast, Bridie might average forty dollars or more a month. Wages were lowest in the South and in small towns where the average was under forty dollars. The $70-a-month wage level for New York was in 1938 nearly double that of the rest of the country.

Lest Bridie's employer seem like a Simon Legree, one must bear in mind that the fiscal years had not been too kind to him. Five thousand dollars a year in 1938 was *four times* the national average. Assuming the family paid one thousand dollars for rent and five hundred dollars a car, Bridie's keep left the classic family of four only $2700 for everything else. With only herself to support, Bridie was not too badly off compared with her employer, and a great deal better off than most of the white-collar class. Indeed, among such classic complaints that the mistress had about Bridie—shiftlessness, lack of interest, carelessness, and independence—it is odd to read the mention of "high wages." To Bridie herself the wages were not the worst feature of her condition of servitude. Being treated as a lower form of life was the chief thing which galled her, along with the hours. Bridie and her employer could not get together on the length of the work week. Most of the ladies could have sworn that their maids worked an eight-hour day. Bridie herself put the figure closer to twelve or fourteen. Interestingly enough, the color bar had an effect upon the laws of supply and demand. The "Situations Wanted" ads were placed mainly by colored girls who wanted to do part-time work and to sleep out, while the "Help Wanted" columns were devoted to requests for white girls who would sleep in and put in limitless overtime not stressed in the ad.

There was still a supply of fresh-faced Scotch and Irish Nannies with the experience of steerage a scant generation removed, and of antique Swedes who had a fortune in the mattress saved up for the return to the Old Country.

Beulah might walk into an employment agency and know instinctively why Bridie had gotten the job away from her. Those were the days when Beulah still knew her place. The issue of *Fortune* which dealt with the servant problem also had an ad for the Otis Elevator Company where one of those picturesque shuffle-footed Negroes was saying of the product of a rival firm, "Boss, dese elevators run on de haphazard schedule."

Though there were still eight million unemployed in 1938, there were at least one million families who could afford servants and couldn't find them. The minute that times got a trifle less desperate, Bridie and Beulah began to chafe at unexpected dinner guests, sharing a room with a baby, the mistress's menopause, and the master who wanted to corner them in the laundry room.

As servants in the Thirties came to be described as a "problem," the coming-out party came to be described as a "racket." Gloria "Mimi" Baker, a 1930s glamour girl, described her coming-out party as really a "coming in."

A girl of seventeen with any potential was already the veteran of many balloon nights at the Stork. She was well known to the head-waiters of such hangouts of the *bien élevée* as La Rue, the Nine O'Clock Club, and the *faubourgs:* Tuxedo, Rumson, Bernardsville, Bar Harbor, Newport, or the North Shore. She had attended the "right" finishing schools: Chapin or Miss Hewitt's Classes if she lived in New York; Winsor or Miss May's in Boston; Foxcroft or Fermata, Shipley or St. Timothy's if she "went away." She had consulted the kingmakers, Miss Juliana Cutting, Mrs. Huntington Tappan, and Mrs. William H. Tew, from whose "canned lists" the hostess drafted socially impeccable manpower.

If she lived in New York she had come up through the debutante bush leagues: Miss Robinson's Wednesday Afternoon dancing classes at the Plaza, Miss Benjamin's Wash Your Hands and Go. At subdebutante subscription dances—the Holidays and the Get Togethers, the Metropolitan, the Cosmopolitan and the Colony—she was one of those girls whom stags cut in on, because they knew they would never get "stuck."

For every "Mimi" Baker who couldn't dance two steps with the same male there were ten who shared the fate of the luckless girl described by an unchivalrous youth in 1937 in *Scribner's Magazine*. He wrote, with what appeared to him to be witty resignation, of an interminable interlude spent "with my cheek soaked with perspiration gathered from the adjoining cheek of a stout, vigorously healthy young female and with the lovely thing's bushy hair buried in my right eye, and with my shoulder sagging from the support of a goodly portion of her 145 pounds." Perhaps it never seemed to occur to him that Miss Tub might not be having the time of her life either. After fifty revolutions around the dance floor, her brave, frozen smile at the stagline proclaimed that she was having fun, fun, *fun*. Out of the corner of her eye she could see a pitched battle going on between a violently protesting youth and a member of the Floor Committee who was trying to drag him over to dance with her.

The unpopular girl looked forward to such merrymaking with the emotion that precedes root canal work. More chivalrous boys than the one quoted underwent torments too, like hermits of the middle ages. If they went to a dance and enjoyed it they were not in a state of grace.

The girl who survived and actually took to all this might just have had the makings of a glamour girl. At seventeen she was ready to matriculate socially according to the totems of her native city. If she lived in Washington, she might do the "Eleanor Glide" at the White House. She might attend the Veiled Prophet Ball in St. Louis, where the prophetess was anonymous and in one case pregnant. In Texas she would attend a mass debut at a country club and worry about whether she would have a date for her own party. (At least a girl could always count on *getting* to the dance with one of the dependable mercenaries who peopled the staglines of New York.)

Lavish debuts were still given, but by the late Thirties Publi-ciety wanted something more. The real cachet came to the girl who could satisfy the newspaper readers' insatiable appetite for details of her day, who was approached to lend her name to a Camel testimonial, or who could make the cover of *Life*.

To some there was vouchsafed little more than a case of the flu and a bill for the decorations. To Joan Peabody of Philadelphia, memories of a $100,000 outlay, a ballroom done over to look like

Hialeah Park, a life-size wooden horse and some anticlimactically defective soap bubbles. To Jane Swift and Ellen Orr of Chicago, rueful recollections of $1800 worth of champagne consumed by the Princeton Triangle Club and the decimation of the guest list by debutantes' occupational influenza. Edith Earle Lee of Philadelphia might reminisce as a grandmother of the dimmed lights and throbbing motors of a small silver zeppelin spilling souvenir sailor hats over the guests. Baltimore's Catherine Bond Johnson could make the unique boast that the Alcazar Ballroom was transformed in her honor into an orange grove—with real oranges and an "irrigation ditch" bubbling with authentic champagne. There was the San Francisco Crocker heiress who came out under a tent high enough to cover the trees on the Crocker estate. It was not Thorstein Veblen who killed society. For the debutante's father it was Constance Spry, floral arranger.

Barbara Hutton's coming-out party at the Ritz in 1930 cost sixty thousand dollars, featured four orchestras, a Spanish dancer at the supper break, and live birch trees. Doris Duke's guests in Newport wriggled to the waterfront at dawn in a "snake chain" to Meyer Davis' rendition of "When the Saints Go Marching In." But the "Gold Dust Twins" would go down in history less for their parties than for their ability to make headlines and disastrous marriages. The Glamour Girl era had its female Elijah who paved the way —Barbara Mdivani-Reventlow-Grant-Troubetzkoy-Rubirosa-Von Cramm-Vinh.

Esmé O'Brien was one of the first of the *nouvelle vague* debs. Her coming-out party in the Junior League in 1937 cost a mere five thousand dollars. Yet, of the many called, she was chosen by the editors of *Life*. Several inside pages were devoted to her morning melon, to her activities in connection with a Bicycle Breakfast. She made no secret of the fact that she wouldn't turn down a Hollywood contract or that she longed for a bigger stage than the one that housed the Junior League follies.

The way was paved for all those social career girls, for actress Diana Barrymore, for Halldis Prince, a Winsor School graduate who came out in 1936 in Boston's Somerset Hotel. As a New York model she was photographed by *Life* at a Condé Nast party. In the glittering company of Helen Hayes, Charlie Chaplin, and Lauritz

Melchior, Halldis was swept along in the conversational eddies of the *au courant* "Germany can't win." "There's Sol Rosenblatt." "She was Snow White's body."

Barbara Wall came out in time to make *Life*'s cover the hard way: working from eight-thirty to five-thirty five days a week, walking fifteen miles a day as a guide at the New York World's Fair. Her "pretty, pleasant, and encyclopedic manner" described by *Life* stood her in good stead when little old ladies inquired, "Where is the periscope?" "When does the helicline take off?" "When do they feed the lagoons?"

There was the spate of Society Singers: Eve Symington, Adelaide Moffett, Lois Elliman, Audrey Gray, Anne Francine, Daphne Nelson, Patty Cartwright, and, best known of all, Cobina Wright, Jr. Cobina Wright, Sr., herself a singer, had apparently decided to live through her daughter, who seemed supremely disinterested in her own career. Young Cobina's coming-out year was fraught with accomplishment. She was elected Jewel Queen of the Fair, won one hundred dollars for being the most beautiful young lady at the Stork Club, and appeared in a night club with her mother, both of them wearing matching Daniel Boone hats. A gold cigarette case was presented to her at Fernanda Wanamaker Munn's coming-out party. The Doughnut Industry honored her as a "gracefully correct dunker."

Debutantes who did not actually *do* anything were expected in the late Thirties at least to be good copy. Maury Paul gave the reader a feeling of having been at the Versailles when "Vivi" Fairchild walked in "wearing her maddest red and blue hat—accompanied by Eileen Herrick and a pet monkey." His capsule description of "The Debbies in Brief" could be dropped into casual conversation to convey intimacy with the great. "Vivi" Fairchild was "Snappy and knows all the answers." Eileen Balfe was "Kinda Kute." Mr. Paul attempted to endow the debbies where possible with a talent. "Nancy Van Vleck is a talented sculptress and rides well." "Rosemary Hodges excels at amateur theatricals," " 'Milo' Gray wields a clever pen." Today, we ask Miss America to give her opinions about the Space Age.

But of course the greatest of them all was Brenda. Brenda Frazier's party at the Ritz cost only $25,000. Maury Paul chided her mother the next day for cheese-paring on the decorations. Yet he soon forgave her everything. Brenda's face, submerged in layers of dead white powder, was superbly photogenic. She didn't need to toil or spin; she just adorned.

Brenda's mother had hired a press agent or, as the euphemism went, "a counselor of public relations." He did his work well. Few people in 1938 were unaware that Brenda had ridden down Broadway in a hayrick, that an orchid was named after her, that she and Cobina Wright were the prototypes for the two radio comics "Brenda and Cobina." Walter Winchell described her as a "celebutante." She was selected as one of the eleven most glamorous people of 1938.* The Velvet Ball—a charity event—got her on the cover of *Life*. She was immortalized under a hairdryer, sitting at the Rainbow Room with Douglas Fairbanks, Jr., dining off lettuce leaves and champagne at Armando's. When she took a trip to Nassau the papers re-enacted a farewell scene with one of her beaux which would have done credit to Giacomo Puccini. She was "lost" to the press for twelve hours, an interlude which was treated like a major news blackout from Paris or Rome. The lamentations of Jeremiah wafted up from El Morocco, and it came as a shock to newspaper readers shivering unfashionably in New York to discover that "Life Goes on Without Brenda."

Ward McAllister, who coined the term "400," set up the Edwardian norms for debutantes. These included "a first season at Bar Harbor, a second at Newport with ponies and a pretty trap with a well-dressed groom and Worth to dress them." Mr. McAllister significantly advocated "keeping the young girl well in hand." A girl of this period who had so far forgotten herself as to bare an ankle was exiled to Switzerland. The aristocracy was supposed to shun both the limelight and footlights. Mrs. Stuyvesant Fish had caused headlines and riots by driving in the park with Lillian Russell. In the 1890s when the William H. Crockers gave a breakfast in their home for Sarah Bernhardt, San Francisco's Nob Hill was rocked to its foundations. The *Argonaut* lamented editorially

---

* She shared this honor along with Barbara Hutton, Alice Marble, Orson Welles, Hedy Lamarr, Anthony Eden, and, of all curious choices, Neville Chamberlain.

that the Crocker threshold "should have been polluted by the crossing of this artist."

One wonders what the *Argonaut* would have made of Elsa Maxwell's list of the aging playboys who were most in demand as escorts for glamour girls. These included George Jean Nathan, the drama critic, "any deb's perfect supper partner," Cole Porter and Allaster McIntosh, a one-time husband of Constance Talmadge. As though the aura of greasepaint which hung over this crew were not bad enough, another debutante's delight—the Duc di Verdura—was in trade as a jewelry designer "often called a modern Cellini." Even Lytle Hull, a respectable businessman, had to pander to the glamour girls by saying that he preferred "first nights to first mortgages."

What would Mr. McAllister have thought of Brenda Frazier for allowing her picture to appear with the following plug from Maury Paul?

> Lovelies who go in rigorously for a Woodbury Facial Cocktail at the zero hour of five P.M. are usually the glamour girls who are the toast of the stagline in the romance hours later.

To the girl who took Mr. McAllister seriously, the 1930s held out the dreary prospect of oblivion. Way down on Cholly Knickerbocker's list were some unobtrusive "buds" who did not take milk baths, endorse soaps, or pose with pet ocelots. They were likely to be damned with faint praise like Rosemary Warburton: "Her modesty is refreshing"; given the Judas kiss along with Ruth Bissell, whom he described as "The educational type"; or dismissed like Pat Bull as "just another deb."

As must be apparent, the glamour girl was reflecting an upheaval which had already rocked the world of her elders. Polite society was secretly a little bored with those lectures on mulching. It was the Whitneys who first cast their eyes toward forbidden fields west of Fifth. Jock and Sonny Whitney turned away from their Fifth Avenue dinner partners toward the more sprightly company of Robert Benchley, Brock Pemberton, George S. Kaufman, Dorothy Parker, Donald Ogden Stewart, Neysa McMein, Edna Ferber, Harold Ross, Irving Berlin, and Fred Astaire.

Gertrude Vanderbilt, the artist, married Harry Payne Whitney and started up a *salon* of sorts. She never made the mistake of mixing her crowds. Guests at her studio teas at 17½ Macdougall Alley belonged to one world; the family friends at 871 Fifth Avenue to quite another. East Side was East Side and West Side was West Side and never the twain should meet.

By 1937 the mating of Broadway and Fifth Avenue was no longer frowned upon. Maury Paul had christened the offspring "Café Society." It was prohibition that had originally driven society into the speakeasy, and into such better bred hot spots of the early Thirties as the Place Pigalle, the Casino, the Chapeau Rouge. There were pedigreed faces in the audience for such dance teams as Fontana and Constance, Veloz and Yolanda, the De Marcos, Maurice and Cordoba. There were even bluebloods in the Paradise in Harlem. By 1937, however, *Fortune* noted that the higher one rose in Café Society the less time one spent in cafés. They also noted that Café Society had its Regency Council. Mrs. Margaret Emerson McKim Vanderbilt Baker Amory Emerson was its Delphic Sibyl. (She had paused briefly in this career of misadventure to beget glamour girl Gloria Baker.) The passing of society's tabu against divorce was pointed up by the social ascendency of this much married maiden *

The question of who was "in" or "out" was as much a subject for debate as contemporary nuances of "camp" and the "in-ness" or "out-ness" of Baby Jane Holzer and Sybil Burton. *Fortune* handed out a kind of Michelin fork to such worthies as Mrs. T. Markoe Robinson, Mr. Frazier Jelke, Mr. Jerome Zerbe, Mr. Dwight Fiske, Mr. and Mrs. Louis Bromfield, and Miss Constance Bennett—then currently married to Phil Plant.

Some were cryptically listed as being "in and out" or "in when in town." Asterisks were awarded to those in *Who's Who*. Those not in the Social Register were branded. J. P. Morgan and Toscanini represented voices of society and art respectively who could

---

* Other members of the Regency Council included Mrs. Vincent Astor, Miss Elsa Maxwell, Mr. Charles A. Munn, Mr. Condé Nast, Prince Serge Obolensky, Mrs. Charles Shipman Payson, Mr. and Mrs. William Rhinelander Stewart, Mr. and Mrs. Herbert Bayard Swope, Mrs. Harold E. Talbott, Mr. and Mrs. Cornelius Vanderbilt Whitney, Mr. and Mrs. John Hay Whitney, and Mrs. Harrison Williams.

but didn't want to play. It was typical of how things had slipped that two members of the Regency Council, Miss Elsa Maxwell and Prince Serge Obolensky, weren't even in what has been called The Holy Book.

There was always a party at Elsa's. Society's portly court jester was forever getting herself up in spangles or dungarees. She brought to her task knowledgeability, authority, a lot of *chutzbah,* a marvelous imperviousness to how she looked from the back, and a party for five hundred that would cost any John and Jane Adams $24,000 could be given by Miss Maxwell for $2100. The Starlight Roof of the Waldorf presented her with rent-free quarters. She got the food at cost—$1.25 a head. The liquor was donated and the two best orchestras in town were scraping and tooting away at the $25 union minimum. Among her gayer events were a barnyard party, her Pet Hates Ball in which everyone dressed as his pet abomination. In 1933 her famous scavenger hunt had socialites madly dashing about New York in search of a live monkey, an honest banker, and Jimmy Durante's show. The winners split cash prizes and the honorable mentions got a case of post-Repeal champagne.

If Elsa was God to Café Society, Maury Paul ("Cholly Knickerbocker") was her prophet. He was born in Philadelphia in 1890 and got his start when William Randolph Hearst caught his *como ci ciama* Marion Davies engrossed one day in a rival newspaper. It seemed that she was reading a gossip columnist named Dolly Madison. Dolly was sent for and proved to be a man. Dolly changed his pseudonym to "Cholly" and on the Hearst payroll quickly became a power as formidable as Lolly. Where Louella Parsons' prose style led to widespread speculation as to what she could have on Mr. Hearst, Cholly Knickerbocker's success was more understandable. If a lady novelist had been crossed with a snake charmer, she might have turned out the gospel according to Paul.

What distinguished Maury Paul from other society scribes such as Lucius Beebe, Gloria Braggiotta, Frank Crowninshield, and Nancy Randolph was his ability to create heroines and convey a feeling of cozy intimacy with "Terry" and "Winnie," "Vivi" or Babs. Mona Trader Schlesinger of Milwaukee, for example, had made a good safe marriage to a simple Wall Street boy. She might have

lived out her days in pleasant obscurity had not Cholly Knickerbocker started to refer to her as "the divine Mona." Presto—an
original Knickerbocker creation—Mrs. Harrison Williams, the
world's best-dressed woman and member in good standing of Café
Society's Regency Council.

The "Ritz Regulars," the "Cosy Colonyites," the "glitterbugs,"
the "dance list lads," the "buds," the "lovelies," and the "debbies"
were blended by Mr. Paul into a syndicated shopgirl drama more
exciting than soap opera. "New York Society's Great Tragedies—
Do You Remember Them?" took up such social events as the
suicide pact between Harry Crosby and Josephine Rotch Bigelow
(an event barely touched on in an autobiography which appeared
by Caresse Crosby—Harry's ex-wife). "Cholly Knickerbocker says,"
another regular feature, showed the columnist's encyclopedic knowledge of Society's marriage and divorce structure: "Countess Palffy
Not Only Has Decided to Shelve Second Mate, They Say, But
Has Chosen Austrian for Her Third; Further Indication Seen of
Divorce in Prince Hohenlohe Household." (That day's work ended
on an upbeat note: " 'Braddy' Norman Moved to Doctor's Hospital to Be Near Wife When Their Baby Arrives.")

The Lady Novelist side of Paul warred perpetually with the
snob. One part of Mr. Paul's heart was reserved for the stuffy Old
Guard. In "Don'ts for Debs" he gave Mamma a series of Edwardian caveats:

> Don't invite debutantes your daughter has never met to enter-
> tainments you give.
> Don't allow your daughter to attend ballet or other evening en-
> tertainments minus maid-chaperone.
> Don't allow your daughter to indulge in spectacular stunts even
> in the name of sweet charity.

He loved such grand dames as Mrs. Hermann Oelrichs, Mrs.
Ogden Goelet, and *tutoyed* them constantly in print. "I may write
about Café Society," he once said, "but my heart belongs to Grace,
'Florrie,' Sophia and Helen." The latter—stripped of their first
names—were Mrs. Cornelius Vanderbilt, Mrs. Hamilton Twombly,
Mrs. W. Watts Sherman, and Mrs. Harry Payne Whitney.

Yet the Lady Novelist preferred someone who could get into a good society tragedy, conjure up a bit of bad blood at the gaming table, or provide an occasional corpse on the floor. He found even the divine Mona a little pokey after her canonization as a clothes horse. Sometimes he elevated a person to social leadership who, through no fault of his, proved unworthy of the crown. Then they would become candidates for one of his pieces, "Whatever Became of Mrs. Blank?" Mrs. Blank, as every reader knew, had committed the cardinal sin of dullness. Sometimes he would brew up a good feud like the one which allegedly took place over a bridge debt between Beth Leary and Princess Ketto Mikeladze. This typified Pygmalion's fondness for throwing a couple of his Galateas into the ring and letting them go a few rounds together.

The truth about Café Society was, one suspected, more prosaic. Elsa Maxwell in a moment of candor turned upon the entity she had worked so hard to create. There was no experience undergone by Café Society, according to Miss Maxwell, which could not be described by a vocabulary limited to the words "divine, lousy, okey doke, thrilling, intriguing, sex appeal, colossal, prince, heel, stunner, swell, nuts, simply, complex, gorgeous, devastating, inhibition, belly and bully." The glossary also included several serviceable Anglo-Saxonisms. Miss Maxwell confessed that the twelve-minute lull required by the musicians' union could easily have proved fatal at her parties. There were no members of Café Society capable of twelve minutes' intelligent discourse. Good reason why she always provided *two* bands.

Café Society went on trial in 1934 in the person of Mrs. Reginald Vanderbilt. Cholly Knickerbocker had given Gloria Morgan and her twin sister Thelma a snow job as "the Miraculous Morgans." Gloria was further described as "one of the most beautiful, if not *the* most beautiful woman in the world." Gloria and Thelma both married wealthy sportsmen twice their age. Thelma became Lady Furness. Gloria married Reginald Vanderbilt in 1923 after an engagement party which included at least one judiciously chosen guest—Maury Paul.

Mr. Vanderbilt died in the Twenties after receiving a medical report that he must cut out drinking. "That," Gloria wrote, "was a sentence of almost complete annihilation. It is difficult to break the habit of a lifetime."

In 1932 their child, also named Gloria, recovering from an operation, went to visit her aunt, Mrs. Harry Payne Whitney. Her mother visited her whenever she had one of her sporadic outbursts of familial feeling. Mrs. Whitney showed little desire to send Gloria home. The custody suit which ensued in 1934 was rife with juicy tidbits involving many half-a-fork members of Café Society. Lady Furness, the other "Miraculous Morgan," appeared on the witness stand, an outraged tigress, defending her own and her sister's young. Little Gloria's nurse, Mrs. Emma Sullivan Keislich, described features of Mrs. Vanderbilt's way of life which recalled J. P. Morgan the Elder's warnings about the function of closed doors.

Even the nudes in the Whitney Museum were used against Mrs. W. as mute character witnesses. Gloria was awarded to Mrs. Whitney, while the Surrogates gave her mother an allowance out of the $2,800,000 left to the child by her father. Mrs. Vanderbilt claimed she had been deprived of her daughter without due process of law—whether it was due or not, the process was certainly wordy. The testimony ran to six volumes.

Whatever Mrs. Vanderbilt's moral influence, it was well that someone else had been chosen as custodian of Gloria's nest egg. Gloria *mère* was dogged throughout the late Thirties by lawsuits: by a disgruntled Parisian for breaking a lease, by a chauffeur-bodyguard for back wages, by a dress store which had never been paid for some maternal largesse, by a detective agency for balance due on a private eye.

Mrs. Vanderbilt attempted to go into business for herself with predictably unhappy results. Sonia Gowns, Inc., numbered on its board Mrs. Vanderbilt as President and Lady Furness as Vice President—a fact which should have given pause to Mrs. Sonia Rosenberg and Mr. Abraham Rosenberg, her husband, who served respectively as Secretary and Treasurer. The quartet operated the business at a $50,000 loss, and eventually filed a bankruptcy petition—the classic fate of the gallant little widow who opens a little shop.

The financial problems of another socialite were to rock the throne of a more austere Morgan whose name was synonymous with the Old Guard. J. P. Morgan had already had one *mauvais quart d'heure* in court when at the Pecora hearings of the Senate Banking and Currency Committee a press agent in one of those pointless coups common in public relations circles had put the midget Lya Graf on his knee. Shooing the circus pair away from the Presence was a young man who had temporarily stemmed the 1929 panic by offering to buy steel at 205. Richard Whitney was much in demand thereafter for little talks about the mysteries of short selling and investment trusts. Business honesty was a recurrent theme. He arbitrated disputes between failing companies and their stockholders, and delivered light repartee as toastmaster to the Stock Exchange's employee-athletes. As President of the Exchange in the early Thirties he was regarded by the government as balky. (He once patiently explained his refusal to require Stock Exchange members to answer a Senate Banking and Currency Questionnaire.) Yet he more often affected philosophical resignation. He advised FDR on Stock Exchange reform, tossed bouquets at the Better Business Bureau, and once dumbfounded a brokers' testimonial dinner by saying, "We have today a new boss. It is the Securities and Exchange Commission." He strove tirelessly to awaken his regulatory body to the magnitude of their joint task.

Richard Whitney, like Liberace, had a brother George. George's position in the House of Morgan made it easy for Whitney to get credit. When the credit was overextended, George came to the rescue with $650,000 in 1936 to remedy an "unwholesome condition" in Richard's books and in November 1937 when he coughed up $1,052,000 to replenish the Stock Exchange Employees' Gratuity Fund. Brother Richard had been appointed to reinvest securities for the fund. To get credit from the Corn Exchange Bank he had somewhat cavalierly numbered those Christmas tips in the Fund among the assets of Richard Whitney & Co.

George was in for more surprises. An audit of Whitney's firm was made on February 28, 1937. On February 16 of that year Whitney had set up the Richard Whitney Control Account, to which he transferred securities held for his father-in-law, George Sheldon, the estate of Ella Haggin McKee, Mrs. Mary Stephens Baird, and the New York Yacht Club. Small wonder that George, after reimbursing the Stock Exchange employees, had implored his brother to give up finance.

The *coup de grâce* came when the Exchange sent around another of those dreary questionaires. The answers, received on February 21, 1938, showed that Whitney's firm had a deficiency in working capital amounting to $375,000. The accounting failed to mention a $100,000 loan from the Marine Midland Trust. "I'm afraid," said the Exchange's controller, "we are going to have to go up some dirty alleys."

On March 8, 1938, Whitney was expelled from the Exchange. He was charged with the theft of $105,000 from his father-in-law's trust fund and of $109,000 of securities from the New York Yacht Club.

For sheer ingenuity Whitney couldn't hold a candle to ex-convict Philip Musica, who as "F. Donald Coster" was, at about the same time, milking the crude drug department of McKesson & Robbins. Where Musica's peculations were the work of an imaginative freelance, Whitney's struck at the heart of the Establishment.

The bad news brought in by the accountants caused a fluttering in the fashionable *faubourgs*. Morgan partners, in search of a stay of execution, dashed back and forth between the Links and Metropolitan Clubs, and at last to *faubourg* Glen Cove—to the side of J. P. Morgan himself. Sunday found him passing a quiet day at home. Through the financier's mind may have passed the memory of Mr. Pecora's impertinent questions about the feudal power structure of the House of Morgan, about stocks sold below market price to favorite clients, or about those two years when Morgan hadn't paid a cent of income tax. He may fleetingly have remembered the $474,000 that Whitney still owed him on a $500,000 loan made by the Morgan firm in 1931. The House of Morgan had covered for Dick who had blotted his copybook *that* time by getting an unsecured loan from the Corn Exchange Bank of which he was then a director. J. P. Morgan & Co. had bailed Dick out just once too often. Its head may have recalled his interchange with Lya Graf, and sensed correctly that he would soon be back on the witness stand. In the words of the New York *Times*, Mr. Morgan "made no suggestions." It had become apparent that, however much one might want to help Dick, this time one couldn't get away with it.

Hardheaded tycoons at the trial confessed to what seemed like extraordinary naïveté. Only one broker, Bernard Smith, seemed aware that Whitney had long been "on the cuff" throughout the street.

It was brought out during the questioning that, despite the multimillion-dollar business done by the House of Morgan, its personnel took no interest whatsoever in the regulatory mechanism of the Exchange.

Morgan had voted approval of the loan made by Thomas Lamont and George Whitney to cover up the affair of the Gratuity Fund. Morgan had the air of the Rector of Justin laying down the law to the first form.

"Every man's money is entirely at his own disposal. George told me at that time . . . Let me see, I want to get this right . . . 'Dick got into an awful jam in November and I went to Tom Lamont because you were not here, and he loaned me the money and I want to pay it back.'"

Morgan did not notify the Exchange or inquire what boyish scrape could have cost over a million dollars. "That was George's lookout," Morgan said with a chuckle. "It was his money."

"Did you give any consideration at all to your responsibilities toward the Exchange?"

"No, none at all," said Mr. Morgan amiably.

The old boy was not an unsympathetic figure. "Do you know Richard Whitney?" counsel for the SEC inquired.

"I knew him," said Morgan with such stress on the past tense that a ripple of laughter went through the court.

What did he think Dick's "awful jam" might involve? Could it have had to do with horses or women?

Mr. Morgan having gotten off one good one was tempted to try again. "Oh no," he said. "The sum was too big."

Whitney was found guilty and sent to Sing Sing in April 1938. A day after his arrival his connections were severed with Harvard University. Harvard might have counted itself fortunate that he had never been in charge of the scholarship fund. The fact that he once played baseball there stood him in good stead. The *Times,* reporting on his activities in Ossining, noted that he made two hits in three times at bat. Convicts stepped aside to let him pass in the yard. The prison guards were equally deferential. "All men who came in Thursday, Friday, Saturday, Monday or Tuesday . . . and Mr. Whitney please step out of their cells." As with Little Orphan Annie's Daddy Warbucks, there was just something about him.

Throughout the pronouncements of the Kens and the Toms ran the theme of an unspoken moral code of what was or was not done. They kept reiterating that Dick only owed the money "to his friends." "George Whitney did what any brother would do," said Morgan. "Mr. Lamont did what a friend and partner should have done." There were those who would enter a disclaimer against Morgan's judgment that everyone behaved beautifully.

In 1938 Morgan was sued for a bad Whitney check. Mrs. M. S. Baird and the New York Yacht Club sued the Exchange, apparently concurring with SEC officials that Whitney went undetected because of the "unwritten code of silence." The receivers grubbed about in Dick's funny money investments—the distillery stock, the soured applejack, the patented dishwasher that was ahead of its time—and came up with a bit of fool's gold, a stock called "Florida Humus." Whitney's butler, Ernest Watz, who had a claim of $1723 against his employer, informed the receivers that they were hoping for too much. They would get little out of "Florida Humus" but alligators and rusting machinery. If Society had a servant problem the servants had their problems too, when the master was tempted to take a flier in real estate with their life savings.

No more thenceforth could the Stock Exchange function as a private club where government accountants were welcomed as frostily as the first ladies who invaded the Union Club on cook's night out. The Social Register Association, another administrator of the old school tie code, had its problems with Whitney. Nothing put the Association into a swivet so much as a Sing Sing address. The 1938 edition had carried the legend "Whitney, Richard, Mr. and Mrs. (Sands-Gertrude Sheldon)." They lived at 115 East Seventy-third Street, the most fashionable district in New York. Whitney's club memberships, described in the elaborate speedwriting of the Association included, besides the New York Yacht Club, the Knickerbocker, Essex Fox Hounds, Turf and Field, Racquet and Tennis, Links, and the River Club. By 1939 (Sands-Gertrude

Sheldon), Miss Nancy, and Miss Alice had hied themselves off to 55 East Eighty-sixth Street. Whitney had understandably resigned from Ny (The New York Yacht) and he sensed that prison pallor would be out of place at "K," "Ef," "Tf," "R," "Ln" and "Ri." The gentleman-athlete was passed over in silence along with his creditable performance on first base. Other figures missing from club reading rooms were Insulls. The 1934 Chicago *Social Register* omitted the names of both fallen utility leaders Samuel and Martin J. Insull. Samuel Insull, Jr., was one of those innocents whom the Register kept on the roster, but his club membership had dropped from twenty-five to one.

In the arbitrary manner of English Nannies the *Social Register* handed out its black marks and gold stars. To Richard Whitney's wife came the annual reassurance that we're on your side, Gertrude. Theft, however, had to be grand scale. Mrs. Richard Knight was married to a man whose kittenish antics included standing on his head in front of the Metropolitan Opera House and telling off the New York Bar Association in legal briefs too vituperative to be acceptable to the Surrogate's Court. He was forever up on minor charges, ranging from assault to the theft of two goldfinches and a radio. In 1941 he and Mrs. Knight were both out. It availed Mrs. Knight nothing to be a daughter of the distinguished lawyer Cass Ledyard, partner in an impeccable Wall Street firm. Clemency was more apt to be extended if one's husband had perpetrated grand larceny. There was no joy in heaven for the wife of a mere public nuisance who was fined fifty dollars and pleaded guilty to a charge of disorderly conduct.

Almost worse than going up the river was going on the stage. Hope Williams was bounced in the early Thirties. Irene Castle McLaughlin's name was deleted in 1934, as were those of Mr. and Mrs. Ludlow Ogden Smith, formerly of Philadelphia. Mrs. Smith was known to millions of moviegoers as Katharine Hepburn. Greasepaint was the downfall of Whitney Bourne and Jane Wyatt. Mrs. Phyllis Livingston Potter was dropped for marrying Fred Astaire, Café Society's darling. Mrs. William Gaston (Rosamond Pinchot) got the axe when she appeared in *The Miracle*. Ellin Mackay, Mrs. Irving Berlin, and Mr. Richard Aldrich who married Gertrude

Lawrence, made a double mistake. They married showfolk who were Jewish.

As with other of Nanny's moral judgments it was hard to find a rule of thumb. Jane Wyatt was out in 1934, back in in '37. Ruth Draper and Cornelia Otis Skinner never fell under the interdict though they did monologues. Audrey Gray and Daphne Nelson were permitted to trill away in night clubs with the Association's blessing. Perhaps their high C was held to be symptomatic of nothing more serious than growing pains. One could seemingly be a lady if one's falsetto were high enough or if there were no other people on the stage at the same moment.

Cleveland Amory points out other inconsistencies. One looked in vain for the heroes and heroines of the society columns, the Windsors, Barbara Hutton, and Doris Duke. Of the Roosevelts, John, Franklin, and the late Eleanor were among the elect, while Elliott and James were cast into darkness. Why, one wondered, was Arthur Hays Sulzberger superior to the Howards, the Paleys, and the Sarnoffs? Why was Hearstling Carmel Snow acceptable and Condé Nast's Edna Woolman Chase not? Maury Paul was known to most of society's Old Guard as a "dreadful little man." Yet he was listed in both New York and Philadelphia editions till his death in 1943. Why did the Chief himself never make it? Was Marion Davies the albatross around the neck of the Lord of San Simeon?

John Jacob Astor VI hung on throughout the Thirties while still married to Ellen ("Tuckie") French. After two subsequent marriages to Gertrude ("Gertie" or "Trudie") Gretsch and Dolores ("Dolly") Fullman, young "Jackaster" applied to the New York State Supreme Court to discover who was legally his wife. Eventually the Social Register lost patience with him. Old school ties might often be honored in the breach, but one was supposed to remember whom one had married.

There were those who dared to make sport of Nanny. The irrepressible Huey Long asked to be dropped from the Washington edition when he was listed as Senator from Louisiana. He wished to spare embarrassment to all who had been omitted and who were appalled to find his name listed. Furthermore, he found Washington society woefully lacking when it came to the proper technique of dunking corn pone in pot likker. In 1936 Mr. and Mrs. G. L. K. Morris listed a Junior "Miss Rose" who later turned out to be a Pekingese. The Morrises were dealt with lightly. Mr. Morris was a brother of Newbold and a descendant of a signer of the Declaration of Independence. His wife was a singer and presumably flighty. The couple were in the 1937 and 1938 editions, though Rose had been dropped. The staff may have been mellowed by some of the hair of the dog that bit them.

Nanny had an inexplicable fondness for one of her most wayward girls. Unpaid bills, allegations of parental neglect, Prince Hohenlohe, Lady Milford Haven and Nurse Keislich notwithstanding, Gloria Morgan Vanderbilt was not thrown out until 1942, a year in which she did nothing more spectacular than get robbed at her daughter's wedding. Gloria II married Pasquale ("Pat") di Cicco, an actor's agent who was the heir apparent of a dynasty of successful truck farmers. The homely aroma of the cabbage family was more socially unacceptable than all of Mother's high jinks. One could imagine Nanny handing out that ultimate demerit with a sad shake of the head. "My dear, we've been patient long enough. You should have done something to stop the child."

The Social Register recorded the passing of a way of life. The day before Pearl Harbor, Richard Whitney started out unobtrusively as a beginner in a plant of the National Fireworks Company. One summer edition listed upward of a thousand yachts. By 1940 Cornelius Vanderbilt applied for authority to sell the *Winchester*. In 1941 the furnishings of J. P. Morgan's *Corsair* were sold to raise money for Bundles for Britain. All yachts were out of the 1942 edition. The postwar tabloid reader would have lost interest in Edward T. Stotesbury's *Nedeva* and A. Atwater Kent's *Nor 'easter,* once anchored reassuringly off Bar Harbor. Said reader came to be far more interested in the sea-borne amours, say, of Frank Sinatra and Mia Farrow.

The war between celebrity and aristocracy had its decisive battles in the Thirties. Celebrity won, and when it came to crashing Café Society the secret ingredient was cash. Aristocracy may have scored a late victory when five young Virginia gentlemen tarred and feathered the columnist Igor Cassini in 1939. But unregenerate Esmé O'Brien and unregenerate young Gloria Vanderbilt married Sarnoffs and Stokowskis and Lumets despite all of Nanny's injunctions. Pedigreed brides and benefit chairmen once had a Society section to themselves—not to mention pictures in the roto-gravure. But something grand had been lost. Socialites no longer head the list of "most wanted" names for testimonials. They now often share the second half of the paper with torso murders, zoo stories and school bus accidents. Suzy Knickerbocker, however, still wields a mighty pen as the Maury Paul of the jet set.

Those survivors of Mrs. Twombly's generation blamed FDR, the Groton boy, for whom the school tie was not enough. He and the Internal Revenue Department and the servant problem were accused by Amory of murdering Society in the first degree. Form 1040 is responsible for the fact that the $100,000 debut which launched Charlotte Ford in Detroit in 1959 is today the rarity rather than the rule. Even the Fords in the Fifties didn't go as far as Helen Lee Eames Doherty in the days before the big tax bite, when she gave each guest at her coming-out party a Ford Cabriolet. The hold of Wall Street on the banking system and the divine right of the Old Guard were shaken to the core when Richard Whitney ended up on the rockpile. When Bridie left the maid's room for the wartime assembly line the grande dame suffered a body blow. When Mrs. Hamilton Twombly presided over her coterie, "America's Last Court," she and the other ladies never had to worry about her eyebrows going up in a broiler fire. In the main, there was one culprit, however.

In 1933 the governor of the Society of Mayflower Descendants brought loud applause with the statement that Franklin D. Roosevelt's ancestors had come over on the *Mayflower* and that he was heir to the tradition of the New England conscience. This was shortly after the Bank Holiday, and probably the last time that FDR got a hand from that particular organization. America's conscience had changed between Plymouth Rock and the day when Dick got in his "awful jam." The standards of Social Registerites were more those of the rest of the country than anyone cared to admit, and there were many socialites who were hard to call to account, for they listed their addresses—summer and winter—as Liberty Hall.

Chapter 13

The Celluloid Safety Valve

"When my father was out of a job during the Depression he would often go to the movies and sit through the feature three times."

This simple statement, more than any other, accounts for the curious fact that the movies of the Thirties were such a flop as a source of Communist propaganda. Some studios—notably Warner Brothers—tried to bring Father to grips with social reality. But most of the cinemoguls agreed with Louis B. Mayer that Dad got all the social significance he needed at home. The script writers of Hollywood might take the Spanish Civil War to heart but they were more concerned with a public that preferred Carole Lombard doing secretarial work in a penthouse with a white telephone. Father sitting there in the dark forgot his own plight as he watched the gods and goddesses of the screen sweeping down marble staircases into dining rooms with a footman behind every chair.

Depression movies portrayed an America devoid of economic conflict. It was—after 1934—also an America devoid of sex. In the pre-Code days Miss Mae West strutted brazenly through *Night After Night* (1932), *She Done Him Wrong* and *I'm No Angel* (1933), sinning without the slightest hint of suffering and adding such classic injunctions to the language as "Beulah, peel me a grape."

Not that pre-Code heroines never suffered. Irene Dunne had a rough time of being John Boles' mistress in *Back Street* in 1932.

The wages of sin were visited—in the form of a healthy baby—upon Marlene Dietrich in *Blonde Venus,* and Clara Bow in *Call Her Savage.* Constance Bennett suffered the same fate in *Common Clay* (1930), *Born to Love* (1931), and *Rockabye* (1932)—a record which might have discouraged a lesser girl from illicit dalliance. Before the arrival of the little stranger in such pictures the camera focused long and lovingly on the heroine's preparations for bed.

Before 1930 and 1932 there had been a spate of blood-ridden gangster pictures: *The Big House, Little Caesar, The Public Enemy, The Secret Six, Quick Millions,* and *Scarface.* Prominent among the bad boys were Paul Muni, Edward G. Robinson, George Raft, Wallace Beery, Humphrey Bogart, and James Cagney. In *The Public Enemy,* Cagney achieved eminence among male and female audiences by smashing a grapefruit in one girl's face and clipping another on the jaw. In *Vice Squad* in 1931, Paul Lukas immortalized the infamous stool pigeon, "Chile Acuna, the human spittoona."

There were some who claimed that such high jinks had led to the prosecution of Al Capone and other notorious gangsters. A more straitlaced section of the public cried that something must be done.

In 1933 the bishops of the Roman Catholic Church banded together to form the National Legion of Decency. Jewish and Protestant organizations joined with the Legion in a mass boycott of sex and sensation. The old Production Code of 1927–30 was exhumed and rewritten, and the Breen Office—a branch of the old Hays Office—was set up to enforce the code. Penalties were stiff—a $25,000 fine for transgressors. The bishops were able to make the Code stick because at that time the Motion Picture Association held the movie theater circuits in a death grip.

After 1934, sexual overtures were made principally in sign language and desperadoes had it borne in that crime doesn't pay. In *G-Men,* James Cagney switched over to the side of law and order. The *Literary Digest* in 1935 commended Edward Paley and Barton MacLane in a review of that picture for what was termed their "clean cut portrayals of two vicious killers."

Having opened the gates of larger censorship, they were open to smaller censors, too. Movies after 1934 were subject to secular as well as ecumenical wrath. Glass blowers protested the showing of canned beer. Beer can manufacturers resented bottled drinks. Insurance companies wanted to delete all references to accidents. The National Billiard Association protested low-grade poolrooms. The State Department worried over America's reputation as projected by *The Grapes of Wrath* and *Tobacco Road*. When *Beau Geste* was refilmed in 1939, the villains were given Russian names because the export market to Russia was small. When *Idiot's Delight* was filmed by Hollywood, to avoid offending any ethnic group it was set in a mythical country whose inhabitants spoke Esperanto. Movies were accused by a Senate Investigating Committee of fomenting war. Filming of Sinclair Lewis' *It Can't Happen Here* was scrapped out of deference to the delicate sensibilities of Hitler and Mussolini.

Every serious play or book underwent a metamorphosis when it crossed the Mississippi. It was fumigated to meet Code requirements, peopled with a reliable stable of character actors. The result was often barely recognizable to the author. Sometimes a jarring happy ending was tacked onto a fine picture as with James Hilton's *Lost Horizon* or onto the screen version of the grim Broadway play *Little Man What Now*. Sometimes a gamey rustic was physically and morally deloused . . . the Okies in *The Grapes of Wrath*, the hillbillies of *Tobacco Road*. Grandpa Joad and Jeeter Lester were both played by Charley Grapewin. Of the two, Grandpa traveled better. Enough of the tragedy of the Dust Bowl survived in *The Grapes of Wrath* to win for the picture the New York Film Critics Award for 1940. Jeeter Lester, shorn of his sexual and physical itches, was a straw man. As the harelipped Ellie May— sans harelip—Gene Tierney was cornpone Junior League.

The Primrose Path, which on Broadway had shown a dynasty of loose women having a whale of a lot of fun, was presented by Hollywood as a problem drama. Joel McCrea saved Ginger Rogers from a fate which the Broadway heroine was all too ready to embrace. Miss Rogers did not quite make it as a "pigtailed slum Diana." "As a vehicle for the waxing dramatic talents of Ginger Rogers," *Time* magazine commented wryly, *"The Primrose Path* is something of a tumbril."

Sidney Howard's *Dead End* came to Hollywood almost intact

with the good guys and the bad guys split—as their creator had intended—strictly along class lines. In the movie version of *Winterset* a gangster got his Production Code deserts when he was killed by his henchmen. He had gone scot free on the stage. *The Children's Hour,* a Broadway drama of boarding-school Lesbianism, was played strictly hetero on the coast. Arthur Kober's *Having Wonderful Time*—once a Rosetta Stone of Jewish dialects—was played by a cast who had undergone mass Aryanization.

Only the cute Sunday School cherubim and seraphim of *Green Pastures* made no attempt to "pass." In 1936 Marc Connolly preserved every Uncle Tomism intact: the dusky angels fishing for catfish from fleecy clouds; Noah laying in a keg of whiskey as a precaution against snakebite. Custard which needed more "firmament" was whipped up by a new Lawd (fresh from a triumph as the cannibal chief in *Tarzan of the Apes*).

A man from Mars seeing *Black Legion, Fury, Dead End, I Was a Fugitive from a Chain Gang, The Grapes of Wrath, Of Mice and Men,* or Warner Brothers' *Wild Boys of the Road* might have gotten the impression that Depression America was something less than the land of milk and honey. Yet few realistic pictures presented the free enterprise system in the merciless light of that social satirist Charlie Chaplin.

City Lights in 1931 opened ironically upon the unveiling of a monument to "Peace and Prosperity" where the homeless little tramp had fallen asleep.

His fortunes throughout the film were dependent on a millionaire inebriate who elevated him to untold heights of prosperity during periodic alcoholic reunions, but who had no recollection of the Little Tramp when cold sober.

Modern Times in 1936 was a savage satire on machine age mores. One had to look to Chaplin to see the Little Tramp turned into an automaton by an assembly line speedup, to see Hoovervilles and luxurious department stores, "free" men jobless on the streets—while criminals in jail at least had the guarantee of a square meal. Chaplin the social philosopher had lost much of his following by the late Thirties, when he made his first talking picture, *The Great Dictator*. The public preferred noncontroversial "screwballs" to Charlie as Adolf Hynkel, "Der Phooey," lasciviously eyeing a globe.

Walt Disney to millions of children was simply the creator of Mickey Mouse, Donald Duck, and Snow White. He had, to be sure, won an impressive number of Oscars: for *Three Little Pigs* in 1933, for *Three Orphan Kittens* in 1934, for *Ferdinand the Bull* in 1938. He also produced *Pinocchio,* invented "Fantasound," and made the chase between a bemused cat and a crafty mouse as much a comic cliché as the custard pie.

Like Chaplin, Disney was often accused of profundity. Author Lloyd Morris in *Not So Long Ago* saw significance in the timing of the hit tune from *Three Little Pigs.* Coming on top of Roosevelt's statement that "We have nothing to fear but fear itself," "Who's Afraid of the Big Bad Wolf?" was for Mr. Morris "an anthem of hope for the whole nation."

When Disney peopled his cartoons with talking steam shovels and garrulous rocking chairs, "was he not depicting a world in which scientists would speculate about the analogies between electronic 'thinking machines' and the human brain?" It was the comedians of the Thirties who inspired the thoughtful search for anthill- and machine-age-type parables.

The moviemakers of the Thirties had a Depression tolerance for what Alistair Cooke has called "the vast progressive school on the steppes." As the earnest Communist of *Ninotchka,* Garbo was converted to capitalist fripperies by Melvyn Douglas. The process could work in reverse. In *Tovarich,* Charles Boyer and Claudette Colbert played down-and-out White Russians forced to hire out as a couple. They ended by coughing up the forty million francs left them as a legacy by the Tsar to the commissar who was messing about with oil rights in Baku and Petrovolsk. Basil Rathbone promised to show the gratitude of the Soviet people by removing the mustache from Claudette Colbert's portrait in the Imperial Palace.

Director Frank Capra occasionally injected a nebulous message into such vehicles as *Mr. Smith Goes to Washington.* But many delightful Capra hits, like *It Happened One Night* (1934), *Mr. Deeds Goes to Town* (1936), and *You Can't Take It With You* (1938) were totally devoid of "preach."

Comedy was the forte of the Thirties. There are few Tab Hunters or Tuesday Welds who can match Myrna Loy and William Powell in the Thin Man series, Jean Arthur and Gary Cooper feeding doughnuts to a horse in *Mr. Deeds Goes to Town,* or Hepburn and Cary Grant in *Bringing Up Baby, Holiday,* or *The Philadelphia Story.* The felines of *The Women* were by-products of the Depression. Will Rogers, a wit of a homelier order, has yet to find an opposite number today. Marx Brothers' revivals still pack them in. Delighted audiences to this day flock to see W. C. Fields in bed with a goat in *My Little Chickadee* or as *The Bank Dick* luring the epicene Franklin Pangborn to his downfall in the Black Pussycat Café.

The drawing room comedies of the Thirties dared but never defied the Production Code. The suspected adulteries of the heroine always turned out to be the result of some hilarious misunderstanding. In *It Happened One Night* Claudette Colbert and Clark Gable find themselves, by a hilarious misunderstanding, sharing a room. They bed down on either side of the tremulous Walls of Jericho in a typical bit of Production Code naughty-naughty-naughty, but damn it all, nice.

In *Theodora Goes Wild,* Irene Dunne became the archetype of the screwball heroine. *The Awful Truth* established her in a league with Claudette Colbert and Jean Arthur. *The Awful Truth* promised more to the prurient than it delivered. Cary Grant suspected Irene Dunne of carrying on with her music teacher. In the ensuing divorce Miss Dunne got custody of Mr. Smith (a fox terrier who already pulled down a fat paycheck as the Thin Man's Asta). Mr. Smith involved Miss Dunne in an embarrassing interlude when he played "go find" with what *Time* called "two shriekingly circumstantial" derby hats in her apartment.

In *My Favorite Wife* (1940) she once again had some explaining to do about an interlude she spent as a shipwrecked lady anthropologist on a desert island with Randolph Scott. Gail Patrick, the Society Menace, had meantime married Cary Grant—with lots of Enoch Arden complications—in front of a comically confused judge.

Miss Dunne hired a balding shoe clerk to impersonate the companion of her island odyssey (provocatively nicknamed "Adam"). When the real Adam stood up on the diving board at the local bath club, she had a *quart d'heure* with Cary Grant almost as *mauvais* as the one with the derby hat.

An art form which was dominated by sweetness and light was the musical. The immense popularity of Deanna Durbin and Judy Garland was attributable to their girl-next-door quality. Both had been launched in the mid-Thirties in the MGM short *Every Sunday Afternoon*. Judy remained with MGM. Deanna was driven into the arms of Universal when MGM failed to pick up her option. Twentieth Century-Fox borrowed Judy for *Pigskin Parade* and she made an immediate hit as the leather-lunged hillbilly singing "It's Love I'm After." She went on to triumph as the beloved Dorothy in *The Wizard of Oz;* to career and marital difficulties with David Rose, Vincente Minnelli, Sid Luft, and Mark Herron; and to return trips to the Palace Theatre where middle-aged spectacles fogged up in a Pavlovian reaction to "Over the Rainbow."

Miss Durbin made her first big hit in *Three Smart Girls*. Later cast as a perennially burgeoning adolescent, in *One Hundred Men and a Girl, Mad About Music, That Certain Age, Three Smart Girls Grow Up, It's a Date, Spring Parade,* and *Nice Girl,* she sweetened for the public an unpalatable dose of classical music. When she attempted to act her age (her first marriage was in the offing about the time of her picture *First Love*) the music went sour. She went on to marital difficulties (Vaughan Paul and Felix Jackson), to career difficulties (*It Started With Eve, The Amazing Mrs. Holliday*), to a third marriage, retirement from the screen, and a weight problem.

The talents of Fred Astaire and Ginger Rogers were more durable. Mr. Astaire was an elegant streak of lightning whose sparse hair, nimble feet, Pinocchio profile, and twirling coattails added up to a strange kind of magic. Like Rex Harrison he was a past master at the art of putting a song across without a voice. A whole generation remembers with delight when he and Miss Rogers went *Flying Down to Rio* in 1933, Mr. Astaire doing "I Won't Dance" in *Roberta* (1935), tapping over Venetian bridges in *Top Hat*. He was assisted by a gallery of minor character actors—Eric Blore, Victor Moore, and Edward Everett Horton, and by writers of *dernier cri* dialogue, as from *Swingtime* (1936): "I often talk to myself. I'm my own grandmother and I have to keep the old girl interested."

The cycle of Dick Powell musicals began when he played opposite Ruby Keeler in *Forty-Second Street* in 1933. In *Gold Diggers of 1935* he danced amid Busby Berkeley settings, introduced the "Lullaby of Broadway," surrounded himself with one hundred beauties playing one hundred pianos and with a predictable cast of minor characters: Gloria Stuart, Alice Brady, Glenda Farrell, and Hugh Herbert as a dimwitted millionaire with a passion for snuff boxes. The same personnel was on hand for *Gold Diggers of 1937* —Dick Powell, Glenda Farrell—titillating the sensibilities of Victor Moore who had taken over Hugh Herbert's role of the tycoon— in this case an amusing hypochondriac. In successive *Gold Diggers* and *Broadway Melodies* Busby Berkeley dressed girls in geometric and floral patterns and photographed them from above. His greatest triumph was in *Flying Down to Rio* where a whole chorus did the Carioca on the wing of a plane.

Stars of the Met—like Broadway playwrights—joined the gold rush. Grace Moore went to Hollywood in *One Night of Love* in 1934, Lily Pons in *I Dream Too Much* in 1935, Gladys Swarthout in *Rose of the Rancho,* even Kirsten Flagstad, who emerged from a miasma of fog, complete with spear and horned helmet, in *The Big Broadcast of 1938*—proof that nobody was above making a bargain with Old Nick.

When Jeanette MacDonald breathed her last "I love you" in 1965 her parting words were right in character. She had appeared with Maurice Chevalier as a somewhat lantern-jawed Merry Widow, in an MGM version in 1934. Like all musicals of the day, it had its amiable eccentric, Edward Everett Horton playing a distraught ambassador, George Barbier as a Balkan monarch and Una Merkel —a figure whose diction established her irrevocably as a child of the twentieth century—as Barbier's coquettish consort.

In 1935 Miss MacDonald was paired with Nelson Eddy in *Naughty Marietta.* The team went on to a succession of hits: *Rose Marie, Maytime, Girl of the Golden West, Sweethearts,* and *Bittersweet.* In *Maytime* she was a singer who fled from loveless marriage into the arms of Nelson Eddy. The Code decreed that the star-crossed pair should not meet till ten years later on the stage of the Met where consummation was well nigh impossible. The whole thing ended with a shooting and was graced with an extraordinarily mixed bag of songs: "Carry Me Back to Old Virginny," "Les Filles de Cadiz," and excerpts from Tchaikovsky's *Fifth Symphony*.

Like Fred Astaire, Mr. Eddy occasionally strayed from the straight and narrow to make a picture with Eleanor Powell. Such was *Rosalie*, in 1937. Eddy studied for five weeks with Lieutenant Frederick M. Thompson of West Point to give credibility to scenes where he led a flying wedge of chorus boys in "The Caissons Go Rolling Along." It is not recorded what Lieutenant Thompson thought when Mr. Eddy stood under Eleanor Powell's window and announced, "I'm your dream soldier reporting for duty."

Rosalie pulled a switch on the Balkan prince wandering among his people incognito. Miss Powell was a Balkan princess disguised as a Vassar girl. Eddy hopped a plane for the spring festival in Romanza, knowing only that Rosalie would be wearing a Pierrette costume. The dream soldier was confronted by an entire troupe of Pierrettes, but Miss Powell stood out in any crowd. She danced down a graded pyramid of drums on legs described by *Time* magazine as "animated by a baleful intelligence of their own."

History provided Cecil B. De Mille with material for a number of super-spectacles: *The Sign of the Cross, Cleopatra, The Crusades*. Also in costume but far higher in quality was the output of Irving Thalberg: *The Barretts of Wimpole Street, Mutiny on the Bounty, The Good Earth,* and *Romeo and Juliet*. Studios sought inspiration in the works of Shakespeare, Dumas, Kipling, Victor Hugo, Charles Dickens, Elizabeth Barrett Browning, and Louisa May Alcott. Charles Laughton drifted through history, throwing bones into the rushes in *The Private Life of King Henry VIII*, dogging the footsteps of Fredric March in *Les Misérables*, screaming "Mr. Christian . . ." at Clark Gable in *Mutiny on the Bounty*, and turning a slightly mellower face toward the public in 1936 in *Rembrandt*—always a fine, if unphotogenic performer.

Other character actors perennially lost in the past were George Arliss and Paul Muni. As Richard Griffith and Arthur Mayer pointed out in *The Movies,* Arliss played Disraeli, Voltaire, Richelieu, and Alexander Hamilton as identical "crafty but benevolent old gentlemen who spent most of their time uniting unhappy young lovers." In *The House of Rothschild,* a typical Arliss vehicle, the only accurate date was that of the Battle of Waterloo.

Paul Muni, in *The Life of Emile Zola* (1937) and *Juarez* (1939), played costumed reformers. (Reformers in modern dress carried the suggestion that society might be in need of reform.) Twenty years later the McCarthy era would brand Muni's *Juarez* and *Zola* as Communist propaganda. It was doubtful if they had much influence on the generation which saw history as Bette Davis praying for fertility and who thought that Arliss engineered the purchase of the Suez Canal.

Paul Muni played Louis Pasteur. Gangland's Edward G. Robinson went legit as the discoverer of *Dr. Ehrlich's Magic Bullet* in 1940 with the usual quota of trials which beset the patient researcher. With the assistance of Donald Crisp, Ruth Gordon, and Otto Kruger he pursued truth, despite a racking cough, and kept bursting in with news of ground-breaking discoveries: "The horses have thrown off the effects of the toxin." On glancing at a wiggling spirochete he remarked, "Hardly more than a motion. That motion is a dance of death."

Irving Thalberg produced *Romeo and Juliet* in 1936. Warner Brothers was indebted to the Bard in 1935 for *A Midsummer Night's Dream*. Warner Brothers imported Max Reinhardt to direct an array of somewhat un-Shakespearean types: James Cagney in picturesque Robin Hood costume as Bottom, Joe E. Brown as Flute, Hugh Herbert as Snout, Verree Teasdale as Hippolyta, Dick Powell as Lysander, Mickey Rooney as Puck, and Arthur Treacher an array of somewhat un-Shakespearean types: James Cagney Bottom engineering a prison break, Ninny's Tomb as the perfect butler, passing canapés, Lysander doing a waltz clog with Ruby Keeler, Snout as a tycoon in an MGM musical, and Hippolyta as the wife of the dapper Adolphe Menjou.

There were certain fixed stars in the firmament: Johnny Weissmuller in the Tarzan series, Warner Oland as Charlie Chan, the Bulldog Drummond pictures, Bela Lugosi as Dracula, and Boris Karloff as Frankenstein. There was King Kong chasing Fay Wray up the Empire State Building—which a later generation would classify as "high camp."

There were the Fu Manchu pictures, where Myrna Loy got her start as an Oriental Menace.

The College of Physicians and Surgeons, contemporary division, numbered in its ranks Herbert Marshall, dragging Garbo off to China to cure cholera in *The Painted Veil;* Robert Donat losing his integrity and splitting fees in *The Citadel;* Lionel Barrymore, the brilliant diagnostician Dr. Gillespie, and Lew Ayres as Dr. Kildare; Jean Hersholt as the fanatical surgeon in *Men in White.* Then there were those reporters to whom the Newspaper Guild once took exception: the cast of *The Front Page;* Paul Muni donning contemporary dress for once as the Lonely Hearts editor in *Hi, Nellie!* No roundup of the 1930s cinema would be complete without mention of Rosalind Russell, the career girl. Her employers, like Cary Grant in *His Girl Friday,* liked her for trying to throw things at them. Because of her a whole generation of secretaries got their walking papers for talking tough to the boss when they wanted a raise. Beginning with *Bring 'Em Back Alive,* Frank Buck performed intrepidly in the jungle, surrounded by torpid tigers and superannuated snakes.

Between the Crash and Pearl Harbor there were a dozen or so truly memorable pictures: *Cavalcade* in 1933; three great Selznick offerings: *Gone With the Wind, A Star Is Born,* and *Rebecca.* Claude Rains, Robert Donat, and Robert Montgomery gave marvelous performances; Claude Rains in *The Invisible Man,* Donat in *The Ghost Goes West,* Montgomery in *Night Must Fall.* Luise Rainer will always be remembered for the telephone scene in *The Great Ziegfeld.* Rosalind Russell was unforgettable in *Craig's Wife* ("I still hate her," was a common tribute to her acting). Also in the Memorable Performances Division: Victor McLaglen in *The Informer,* Wendy Hiller and Leslie Howard in *Pygmalion,* Orson Welles as *Citizen Kane,* Laurence Olivier and Merle Oberon in *Wuthering Heights.*

Most amusing to look back on was the avant-garde. Ben Hecht and Charles MacArthur's *Crime Without Passion* was an "experimental" drama about a psychiatrist bent on committing, in the spirit of research, the perfect crime. Characters' thoughts were superimposed by double exposure so that one could watch Claude Rains wrestling with his conscience. Other affectations included stream-of-consciousness dialogue and an opening shot of the Eumenides plunging down the side of a skyscraper.

The Scoundrel, another Hecht-MacArthur offering, presented Noel Coward as the merciless publisher Horace Liveright trading quips with Edith Wharton and rejecting manuscripts with cruel and witty epigrams. Mr. Coward got his comeuppance when he drowned and was doomed to walk the earth forever until someone could be found who would shed a tear for him. Who would do that? Certainly not the victims of those cruel and witty epigrams. At last Julie Haydon shed a tear for him, putting his troubled shade to rest. Audiences who can still catch an occasional art house revival of *The Scoundrel* are somewhat taken aback by the spectacle of Mr. Coward, a distraught revenant, walking into a room clutching a handful of seaweed.

Margo—an actress who had appeared in *Crime Without Passion* —also appeared in Maxwell Anderson's *Winterset.* Mr. Anderson was incapable of saying anything in prose. His *Mary of Scotland* with Katharine Hepburn and Fredric March was cast in blank verse.

Many of Eugene O'Neill's works were transplanted to the screen: *Anna Christie* in 1930, *The Emperor Jones* in 1933, *The Long Voyage Home* in 1940. Most experimental and daring of all was *Strange Interlude* in 1932. Characters relayed their inmost thoughts about incest ("my heart pounding at the thought of seeing her again"), hereditary insanity ("You don't mean Nina's going to have a . . ." sound of maniacal laughter . . . "That's my husband's sister—hasn't been out of her room for years."), nymphomania ("lips on my lips . . . strong arms around me, spooning, necking with the patients . . . I've been bad, Charlie.").

Clark Gable seemed somewhat ill at ease with Norma Shearer as his partner in a therapeutic mating experiment.

If the actors and actresses of the Thirties seem slightly more than life-size, it was because the starring system with its seven-year contracts made gods and goddesses of Gary Cooper, Tyrone Power, Clark Gable, Fredric March, Errol Flynn, Cary Grant, Bette Davis, Marlene Dietrich, Joan Crawford, Claudette Colbert, Rosalind Russell, Norma Shearer, and Katharine Hepburn. Sometimes a star transcended the limitations of human clay and became a legend. There were three ways that this could happen: the star could a) die young, b) refuse to give out interviews and retire from the screen, or c) have the more intimate details of her sex life described posthumously to an audience numbered in millions. Ingrid Bergman later on was to take a fourth route, by having a son out of wedlock. In the Thirties she made her first bow to a fiercely loyal public in *Intermezzo*. Jean Harlow, who qualified under categories *a* and *c*, has had the best publicized legend of them all. Harlow made her first big hit as the tough blonde of *Hell's Angels* in 1930. Subsequently a certain sameness about her screen roles seemed to set in: daughter of the underworld in *The Secret Six*, a gangster's moll in *Public Enemy*, the temperamental movie star of *Bombshell*, the tough chick of *Dinner at Eight*. She was Lew Ayres' albatross in *Iron Man*, Spencer Tracy's wife in *Riffraff* and China Doll in *China Seas*. One of her most entertaining films was *Red Dust* with Clark Gable. Her casting problems could be summed up in the anguished question: "What kind of a whore am I now?"

In *Suzy* and *Personal Property*, she took a crack at the let's-take-off-our-shoes-and-jump-into-the-fountain-cute-girl-in-boy's-pajamas type of comedy. Her only musical, *Reckless*, brought forth the comment that singing was best left to Jeanette MacDonald. Jean Harlow died in 1937 at the age of twenty-six. The details of Miss Harlow's boudoir life have already been raked over the coals by Irving Shulman, and in two movies, one starring Miss Carroll Baker. Suffice it to say that it was a hell of a life and a hell of a legend, and that the amiable and much maligned girl, who late in her career was found to have an engaging comic gift, was indeed a *Bombshell*. It is interesting to note that for all her emotional difficulties there was no Harlow picture whose filming took more than three months.

Greta Garbo's allure was more subtle. Richard Griffith and Arthur Mayer, the authors of *The Movies*, summarize it thus: "For the old, bold movie vamp, Miss Garbo substituted the more complicated and credible charmer—doomed neurotic, torn by inner conflicts. She was poison to men and to herself, yet held in her eyes the promise of Cleopatra. Her eyes had held a direct invitation throughout various silent films of the Twenties. When Maurice Stiller, her Svengali, went back to Sweden Miss Garbo refused to speak to interviewers and became to her detractors "a sphinx without a secret."

The silence was broken in 1930. "Garbo talks!" the ads proclaimed. Nearly everyone of the right age remembers the ad; few remember what she said to start off. Her first words in *Anna Christie:* "Gif me a viskey, ginger ale on the side—and don't be stingy, baby." She appeared in *Grand Hotel* and *Queen Christina* in 1933, *Anna Karenina* in 1935.

By 1936, as Griffith and Mayer say, "the legendary face had both hardened and softened into a mask of tragedy." Garbo, according to an MGM executive, was "the only one we could kill off." All those unhappy endings, however, were giving her stature. In *Camille,* in 1936, she was transformed by director George Cukor into what he describes as "a sorrowing statue" and gave a performance that swelled the membership of the Garbo cult. In 1939 it came as a delightful surprise in *Ninotchka* to discover that the Tragedy Queen could be a laugh riot.

Garbo the movie queen died with her retirement in the early Forties. Garbo the Legend still lives on. New Yorkers are sometimes lucky enough outside of Schrafft's or over a counter at Bloomingdale's to get a glimpse of the fabulous face.

Carole Lombard, like Harlow, died young. She was, quite simply, everybody's darling. She could play a dizzy society girl, as in *We're Not Dressing* with Bing Crosby in 1934. She played thankless roles, as for example in *Fools for Scandal* in 1938 opposite Fernand Gravet. (Gravet got his job because of a superficial resemblance to the Duke of Windsor.) She took a crack at tragedy as the female half of a Depression-ridden couple with Jimmie Stewart in *Made for Each Other* (1939). But it is as a comedienne that she will be remembered: in *Twentieth Century* with John Barrymore in 1934; in *Nothing Sacred* (1937), as a girl who, through a series of mishaps, attends her own funeral; above all, as bored and beautiful Irene Bullock in *My Man Godfrey* (1936).

Irene Bullock wins William Powell in a scavenger hunt. The ground rules for this favorite 1930s sport are laid down by Miss Lombard as follows: "A scavenger hunt is just like a treasure hunt, except in a treasure hunt you find something you want and in a scavenger hunt you find things you don't want, and the one who wins gets a prize, only there really isn't any prize, it's just the honor of winning because all the money goes to charity if there's any money left over but then there never is."

Among the other idle rich in the picture was Mischa Auer, a sad-faced Slav who could imitate a gorilla. Miss Lombard, Mr. Powell, and Mr. Auer point up once more the great Hollywood paradox of the Depression—that the pictures which have stood up best from the decade of Social Significance deal mainly with high jinks in the high surtax brackets.

The popularity of many an adult star, unlike that of Miss Lombard, waned before the end of a seven-year contract. There was one class of performer whose talents were even more ephemeral—the child actors and actresses who stormed the gates of Hollywood doing everything from soft shoe shuffles to bird imitations. It had all begun with that cosmic moment in the early Thirties when Shirley Temple was taken from a series called Baby Burlesks and sent for an audition in the Fox Studio. She won a part in *Stand Up and Cheer* (1934), and the rest is history. She was loaned to Paramount for *Little Miss Marker* and later featured in *Baby Take a Bow* and *Now and Forever. Bright Eyes* got her star billing and an Oscar as the outstanding personality of 1934. Between 1934 and 1939 some of the films she made were *The Little Colonel, Curly Top, The Littlest Rebel, Poor Little Rich Girl, Heidi,* and *Rebecca of Sunnybrook Farm.* She was No. 1 at the box office and at the age of ten was making more money than FDR.

She was an accomplished little dancer. Each picture contained some cute song and dance routines: "You Gotta Eat Your Spinach, Baby" and "But Definitely" in *The Poor Little Rich Girl* (it was particularly cute that she pronounced it "definally"). There was a Dutch dance in wooden shoes in *Heidi.* In *Captain January* she tap-danced down a forty-five-foot lighthouse stairway delivering a line at every turn.

She spread good wherever she went. In *Stand Up and Cheer* she was involved in a never-never land where a Secretary of Amusement was pitted against a bunch of crooks bent for some abstruse reason on prolonging the Depression. In *Little Miss Marker* she was left as payment on an IOU and had a mellowing effect on a bunch of Damon Runyon gangsters. In *Now and Forever* she was teamed with Carole Lombard and Gary Cooper and acted once more as a force for good upon a group of international swindlers. The sex of Kipling's *Wee Willie Winkie* was changed out of deference to Shirley. She brought peace between her crusty old uncle, Old Boots (played by C. Aubrey Smith), and Cesar Romero, a Latin character actor somewhat miscast as Tribal Chief Kohda Khan.

Every studio began auditioning child stars in the hope that lightning would strike twice.

Shirley's co-thespians were legion. Some, like Jackie Cooper, who had made his first big hit in *Skippy* in 1931, had guardians who wisely stashed their money away. Jackie Coogan, already a has-been in the Thirties, was worth five million dollars before he could balance a two-wheeler and had bought his own Rolls-Royce at the age of ten. His adult life was spent selling airplane parts, playing summer stock and night clubs, burlesquing his great role in *The Kid* (1920), playing monster parts on TV, and renting out the Rolls-Royce for period scenes.

Among others, Jane Preston, Scotty Beckett, Richard Ralston Arlen, Virginia Weidler, Carmencita Johnson, Ronnie Cosby, Buster Phelps, Edith Fellows, Billy Lee, Dickie Moore, Bobby Breen, Gloria Jean, Baby Le Roy, and Jimmy Fay are all candidates for the Where Are They Now Sweepstakes.

Jane Withers, like Shirley Temple once a hot Fox property, has dropped her screen career for the more profitable business of making TV commercials. Freddie Bartholomew, a talented little English actor, followed his triumph in *David Copperfield* by appearing with little Cora Sue Collins in Garbo's *Anna Karenina,* and in *Little Lord Fauntleroy* in 1936. In Kipling's *Captains Courageous* he played the brat who was fished out of the ocean by Spencer Tracy, who later made a man of him. For a time Freddie's fan mail exceeded that of Clark Gable. Freddie is a Vice-President of Benton and Bowles. Like Shirley Temple Black, he is one of the few to land on his feet.

It was nevertheless a bad time for grown-up players. "The nervous director," wrote June Hampton in a 1934 *Photoplay,* "once furious at the least delay, is now off in some corner with The Child (they speak of him with reverence) perched on his knee. Together they are going over the scene. If it takes an hour or days even, what of it? The Child must understand. Let the adult actors stand around and get corns if they want to. The child is the one who will draw in the shekels."

One could sympathize with W. C. Fields, who was alleged to have spiked Baby Le Roy's orange juice, when one read of the plight of Helen Mack in *You Belong to Me*. She approached the director to inquire how she had made out in the seventeenth take, only to be informed that he had been so busy watching *wunderkind* David Holt that he had forgotten that she was in the picture.

Dolly Dimple and Bobby Bounce often gave out gratuitous advice on acting. In *Imitation of Life* little Baby Jane Quigley looked up strangely at Claudette Colbert at the end of a scene. "It's wrong. It's wrong," she cried. "She said it wrong." Claudette admitted that she had changed a word and promised Baby Jane to be a better girl in the future.

One of the greatest hams of all time was Mickey Rooney. In *Orchids and Ermine* he played a cigar-smoking midget. He appeared in the Mickey McGuire series and somehow seemed to turn up in practically everything from *Riffraff* to *Ah! Wilderness*, from *Manhattan Melodrama* to *A Midsummer Night's Dream*. In 1937, in *A Family Affair*, he played his first role as Andy Hardy with Lionel Barrymore as his father, the Judge. Judge Hardy's role was abdicated to Lewis Stone, who played it until 1946, when, with *Love Laughs at Andy Hardy*, the series was finally laid to rest. In 1939, 1940, and 1941 Mickey had replaced Shirley Temple as Peewee Box Office Champ.

As Andy Hardy's colleague, Judy Garland often gave him a dose of his own medicine when it came to upstaging. Singing "Alone" and "Nobody's Baby" in *Andy Hardy Meets Debutante*, she avenged Lewis Stone, Wallace Beery, and Lionel Barrymore, to mention only a few who had suffered from Mickey's determination to walk away with anything up to a death scene. Another footnote to the longest adolescence in history: Well after Mickey was embarked on one of many real-life marital disasters, he was still going to Lewis Stone for information about the birds and bees, introduced inevitably by a blushing request for a man-to-man talk.

The offshoots of the star system were legion. They ranged from Shirley Temple dolls to movie palaces, from Hedda Hopper to tours of the Homes of the Stars. There was Pickfair and San Simeon, and Norma Shearer's "Provincial French cottage." There was the Fifth Avenue Theatre in Seattle, where a monstrous golden dragon grasped for a white globe below, "symbolic of the Pearl of Perfection." Movie theater architecture came in a variety of exotic styles: Egyptian (Grauman's Egyptian), Hindu (Loew's State in Syracuse), Chinese (Grauman's Chinese in Los Angeles, the Oriental in Chicago), Hispano-Persian (the Missouri Theatre in St. Joseph), French baroque (the San Francisco Fox), Siamese-Byzantine (the Fox Theatre in Detroit).

But nothing could compare with the magnificence of New York's Roxy. Gazing at the Roxy rotunda with its huge green marble columns, its twenty-foot chandelier, its gilded catafalque, its 2½-ton rug (the largest oval rug in the world), a Hokinson child in a *New Yorker* cartoon was depicted as asking, "Does God live here?" Buckingham Palace had nothing on the Roxy when it came to ritual. The changing of the guard ceremony at the palace was matched at the Roxy by the daily Changing of the Ushers.

It was the fan sitting at the Roxy—thirsty for details of life in Screenland—who imparted such formidable power to two commonplace ladies on the coast: Louella O. Parsons and Hedda Hopper. Louella Parsons as a writer was dreariness incarnate. She could misquote the most common cliché ("Oh to be in England now that it's May"). She had gotten her start at the Essenay Studios when Gloria Swanson was chasing Wally Beery, when Mary Pickford's mother was trying to get her daughter's salary upped to fifty-five dollars a week, and when Ben Turpin was a cross-eyed office boy who was said to bring the company luck. William Randolph Hearst offered her a job on the New York *American*. At the height of her career Lolly was syndicated in twelve hundred papers. Her nose for news led her devoted followers to overlook her style.

A case in point involved her biggest scoop—the news of the Fairbanks-Pickford split-up in 1935. It was announced over lunch to Lolly by Miss Pickford, who later claimed she had no notion that she was speaking for the record. Louella's version had been a bit different. Mary had said, "Douglas and I are separating." She had insisted that Lolly write the story forthwith. Miss Parsons claimed to have been too shocked to speak but had finally acceded to "brave little Mary's orders."

In 1934 Louella O. Parsons became emcee of a radio program —*Hollywood Hotel*. The stars who appeared on it were recompensed by a free case of Campbell's Soup, and after their second stint they were allowed to specify the variety. Only Greta Garbo demanded additional financial remuneration. The program established Louella as a force, though it was dropped after four years when James Cagney and the Screen Actors Guild put down their collective foot and announced that man did not live by Campbell's Soup alone.

Such was the power of Miss Parsons that she almost managed to scuttle Orson Welles' *Citizen Kane*, which presented an extremely unflattering picture of Miss Parsons' employer.

Hedda Hopper became a pundit in 1938. Her hats also became a Hopper trademark; her accuracy was somewhat suspect. Indeed, at a Hollywood party, Miss Hopper once suggested that Hearst's San Simeon be turned into a national shrine. She waxed eloquent on what a bonanza the castle of Mad Ludwig of Bavaria had been to Austria.

Lesser literary lights were engaged in the business of reporting on the doings of the stars. Who were the Box Office Darlings of 1937? . . . Who was the greatest screen lover of 1933? . . . These were the cosmic questions that occupied the readers of *Photoplay* and *Modern Screen*, along with those ideal Hollywood marriages which had generally ended up in the divorce court by the time the magazine went to press. Sometimes the public might be titillated by the tale of what Shirley Temple ate for breakfast or by a confession of weakness—like the one indulged in by Hedy Lamarr in "Hedy Wine."

Miss Lamarr, like Luise Rainer, was one of Hollywood's exotic imports. She had come out in the Austrian import *Ecstasy* in 1937, and with much heaving of bosom she had looked with distaste upon her aging husband, and longingly upon symbolic matings which took place between flies on the window pane. A nude swimming scene was such a flagrant violation of the Production Code that one had to journey to a different city to see it. Managers of movie houses often advertised scenes from *Ecstasy* (with adhesive tape covering Miss Lamarr's shame), scenes which were excised from the cut version—a fact which the patron did not realize until safely ensconced in the theater. *Photoplay* in 1938 told how Hedy was just plain folks and hated being an "Ecstasy girl," attempting with little success ("She's just about as much an Ecstasy girl as I am.") to present the star as a product as American as corn pone and apple pie.

By 1938 fans had something really important on their minds: the search for Scarlett O'Hara. David O. Selznick had announced that the role would be played by an unknown from the South, and had even devoted two years to going through the motions of looking for her. Every actress in Hollywood saw herself as Scarlett. Might it be Tallulah Bankhead, smoldering Miriam Hopkins, red-headed Erin O'Brien Moore, flashing Paulette Goddard? Selznick was reported to have considered Margaret Tallichet, Arlene Whalen, Liz Whitney, and Katharine Hepburn. The role was offered to Norma Shearer, who did not consider herself worthy of it.

Rival studios thought they might beat Selznick to the punch. Bette Davis, who had built up quite a reputation as a mean girl since her performance as Mildred in *Of Human Bondage,* all but spit tacks in *Jezebel,* kicking aside the code of Southern chivalry, biting her lips to make them red, giving amiable aristocrat George Brent the air. It did not win her the role of Scarlett, though it was suggested that the only person who could play Scarlett after Bette Davis' performance was Paul Muni.

Warner Brothers, which had produced *Jezebel,* had another string to their bow. Rachel Field's *All This and Heaven Too* was scheduled for production in 1940, with Bette Davis as a love-crossed governess and Charles Boyer as the Duke de Preslin. *Gone With the Wind* was sometimes referred to as GWTW and Warners alluded to ATAHT—as it turned out, a trifle optimistically.

Photoplay interviewed some of the aspiring Scarletts, including Paulette Goddard, whose desire to play the part had her on the brink of hysteria. Of the group, *Photoplay* put its money on Miss Hepburn. Vivien Leigh, an Englishwoman, furnished a surprise ending to the search by unexpectedly walking off with the most coveted role in cinema history. Disappointed xenophobes saw her as a spurious daughter of Dixie.

If the search for Scarlett made the fur fly, the child stars made the treacle flow. In September 1938, Sara Hamilton visited a few of the kiddies in their native habitat and recounted their doings. Little Billy Lee informed *Photoplay*'s reporter that the red button on top of his skullcap was his "tail light." "Fred MacMurray," *Photoplay* said cryptically, "can't get over him."

Then over to "hazel-eyed, honest-souled, straight-from-the-shoulder" Virginia Weidler. "Make it ten," said Virginia when asked her age. "Studio reasons. Always chopping off a year." Besides her hazel eyes and honest soul, she boasted "two chicken pox marks above her right eyebrow, sixty-two freckles across her perfect little nose and six owls in her attic," and the fact that she thought Queen Victoria was a figure from American history.

George Ernest of the *Jones Family* was interviewed in the company of his best friend Marvin Stephens. *Photoplay* solemnly reported the following epic interchange:

> "Well, good night Marvin," he'll say at the end of day's work on the set.
> "See you tomorrow" and for a moment the two friends will stand in the center of a huge movie set, hands raised in salute, and then go.
> Two American lads off for home.

In *What Makes Sammy Run*, Sammy Glick gives a musical tribute to the "little people" who, he feels, abetted his greatness. In the long run they were the ones who had the last laugh. The character actors of Hollywood were grouped in a 1934 edition of *Photoplay* by studio.

Basil Rathbone, Roland Young, Elsa Lanchester, Una O'Connor, C. Aubrey Smith, and Cedric Hardwicke might be said to furnish the personnel for the English Division of Minor Players. There was also a Latin Division who peopled the gambling hells, ran the night clubs and peddled an occasional tomato. Prominent among them were Henry Armetta, Cesar Romero, Joseph Calleia and Eduardo Cianelli. The Latin Division had a way of turning ugly. In *Riffraff* Joseph Calleia portrayed a sinister purveyor of cheap labor. Eduardo Cianelli could be egghead ugly as the gangster in *Winterset* or just plain ugly roughing up the girls as the proprietor of a clip joint in *Marked Woman.*

The Negro Division furnished such hewers of wood and drawers of water as Hattie McDaniel, Rochester, Stepin Fetchit; such song-and-dance men as Paul Robeson and Bill Robinson.

There were the eccentric millionaires described above, without which no musical would have been complete. In addition there was Lionel Atwill, the corrupt captain of industry, Walter Connolly who took up the cudgels for free enterprise in Hecht and MacArthur's *Soak the Rich.* Eugene Pallette in *My Man Godfrey* was an amiable tycoon who wanted to go to jail so that he could get up and do an honest day's work without worrying about who was going to pay the bills.

The women—God bless 'em—came in all sizes and shapes: good old shoes, like May Robson and Alison Skipworth; Maria Ouspenskaya, who could travel at the drop of a hat to India when *The Rains Came,* or who could act broadminded for Dr. Ehrlich when he announced what he'd been up to with that magic bullet. Dame May Whitty was a good old shoe who always found herself mixed up in something sinister, as in *The Lady Vanishes* and *Night Must Fall.* Beginning with *Dead End,* Marjorie Main was a poor old shoe who never had sufficient upward mobility to make it out of the slums.

There were fluttery women like Billie Burke and Alice Brady, who portrayed Carole Lombard's flighty mother in *My Man Godfrey.* Mary Boland was one of the screen's leading birdbrains. Spring Byington fluttered but had moments of depth as Marmee in *Little Women.* It was Fay Bainter who first gave Jezebel a name.

The worldly women included Helen Vinson and Binnie Barnes (who was one of the wives of King Henry VIII, but who was more at home in modern dress). The archetypal worldly woman was society bitch Gail Patrick—in real life an amiable performer—who sneered obligingly while Shirley Temple broke up her love affairs, or as Irene Dunne popped up coyly at her husband's side on her honeymoon.

Paramount had its stable for the De Mille spectacles, *The Sign of the Cross, Cleopatra,* and *The Crusades.* These included Warren William, Henry Wilcoxon, and C. Aubrey Smith, Dean of the English Division—who also carried the banners of Empire in *Lives of a Bengal Lancer* and was generally to be found when the dawn came up like thunder out of China 'cross the bay.

United Artists' *Stagecoach* brought together Claire Trevor, whose disreputable trade was disclosed to John Wayne when he found a bunch of fancy women whooping it up on the site of the old homestead. Also among the passengers was John Carradine, prominent also in *The Grapes of Wrath* and as Rizzio in *Mary of Scotland*—in short, wherever the script called for someone sinister with the features of a razorback hog. Donald Meek was aboard the *Stagecoach,* as was Andy Devine. Devine was so devoid of period sense that it mattered little whether he was in a Stetson or in more contemporary dress in *Hold 'Em Yale.* He was always to be found when the script called for a comic who had lost his voice.

The same could be said for Thomas Mitchell, who won an Academy Award for his performance in *Stagecoach.* That time he happened to be a doctor. In *Lost Horizon* he had been a stock manipulator. In *Gone With the Wind* he was Scarlett O'Hara's father. He was called to the colors whenever the script demanded someone grizzled.

It was all but impossible for a character actor to break out of the mold. Frank Morgan for years played someone who giggled. He amazed critics with his excellent acting as a non-Aryan professor in Phyllis Bottome's *The Mortal Storm.*

If his was a rare departure from a rigid orbit, there were compensations. The character actor was spared the publicity build-up of an Anna Sten, a Rochelle Hudson, a Fernand Gravet, a Miliza Korjus, or a Sigrid Gurie. But any of the latter would have traded their eyeteeth for the steady income of a Charles Bickford, a Henry Daniell, a Jessie Ralph, an Allen Jenkins, a Raymond Walburn, a Cora Witherspoon, or a Helen Westley. More durable than many stars were Thelma Todd and Patsy Kelly, queens of the selected short subject. Minor players were mixed, matched, loaned, put into doublet and hose, and they became part of the landscape for many who were never sure whether they were watching Donald Meek, Donald Woods, or Donald Crisp. They were better off than many whose names rated larger letters. They outlasted children whose careers started out so promisingly—giving the interviewer a big yawn or kicking Clark Gable in the shins.

What of father who came in from the cold to forget his troubles? Did he really believe that Bette Davis had given up "everything" in *Dark Victory* to live in a cottage that cost $12,000 a year to run? Did he seriously think that Loretta Young and Clark Gable would be off in the frozen north in *The Call of the Wild* without anyone ending up in the wrong sleeping bag? Did he believe that Irene Dunne and Randolph Scott were off on that desert island with "nothing happening"? Did he believe in MacDonald and Eddy as they did the Wienerschnitzel Waltz through the kingdom of Graustark? Did he think that child stars were really unspoiled, or that Shirley Temple had come up with the cure for the Depression? Decency's double standard was shown up when Joseph Mankiewicz's *All About Eve* implied at last that two people were living together. No one was shocked that they were doing it. All were surprised that they were doing it in a *movie*.

Hollywood in the Thirties operated under an alien set of assumptions. The ninth beatitude in this Shangri-la was an unwritten one. "Blessed are the meek who serve the star—for they shall always work." Today the Roxy is only a nostalgic line in a bright revue ("There was a lobby!"). The marquees of old movie palaces advertise bargains in celery and lamb chops. With their passing so went those chaste Production Code heroes and heroines. Racier talent is recruited from foreign capitals. It is hard to remember the days when all moral problems were simplified—for ninety minutes— till one left the theater and went out into the world.

Movies in the Thirties were not long out of the days when moviemakers went West to find sunlight, wrote scripts as they went while slapsticking up and down the concrete runways that were to become Hollywood and Sunset Boulevards. D. W. Griffith and the first close-ups were not far behind us in the Thirties. And yet here we were, all of a sudden, with scripts and money and scenery and turntables and crowd scenes of extras, building to a technnical virtuosity as yet unsurpassed—and to an impact upon the public not always fully appreciated by the very people who were turning the pictures out.

One famous director—long since gone on to bigger and better

things—has been enshrined by film historians for movies whose endings he barely remembers today. Nostalgia for the Thirties? He dismisses it with a wave of the hand.

"The gangsters in fact were so sweet and everybody was so well behaved. Even the villains . . . there was something likable about them. It's a dear dead world. It doesn't touch any raw nerves."

Ça va.

But those of us who were part of the dear dead world did go to Saturday matinees and sit through two or three full showings, on occasion bringing a meal along with us. We did know practically every line of dialogue by heart. It was not unusual to find a teenager who could—God save us—go word for word through the book and lyrics of *Naughty Marietta*. Some of us changed the signs at the local movie theater to earn free passes to the Saturday night show. Teenagers of those dear dead days listened endlessly to apocalyptic rumblings from their parents. "You'll never amount to anything if you spend all your time reading *Silver Screen*." There was the breathless anticipation as we listened for "Louella's first exclusive" on the radio, or as we licked the neapolitan ice cream off the top of the Dixie cup to get to the picture of Greta Garbo.

Echoes from that dear dead world could be heard in unexpected corners of the earth. Ann Frank's room was embellished with pictures of Hollywood movie stars. A snapshot of Shirley Temple was found by a GI on the body of a Japanese sniper. Long after John Wayne made his first halting declarations to Claire Trevor in *Stagecoach*, Yves Montand is making a fortune singing about what goes on "dans les plaines du Far West."

Chapter 14

The Muse on the Picket Line

Playwrights, authors, and artists have always been divided into two classes: those who aim frankly at the market place and those who think at least that they are speaking to the ages. Other practitioners of the arts, dancers, actors, whose contributions are of a more ephemeral nature, make a distinction between performing for the lumpenproletariat and performing for the discriminating few.

In the 1930s the avant-garde, which thought it was speaking to the ages, was almost to a man dominated by the "social conscience." As Caroline Bird pointed out, the best seller lists of the Sixties would be denuded if everyone who once admired Soviet Communism and despaired of American capitalism had been struck by avenging lightning. We would never have had Mary McCarthy's *The Group,* Edmund Wilson's *The Cold War and the Income Tax,* Vincent Sheean's *Dorothy and Red.* Murray Kempton would be under interdict along with Max Lerner. *The New Yorker* would have to do without Richard Rovere, S. J. Perelman, Muriel Rukeyser, Dwight MacDonald, James Thurber, and Dorothy Parker. There would have been no Heywood Broun, no Lynds of Middletown, no Ruth McKenney, not even a Gypsy Rose Lee.

Among those who endorsed the 1932 Communist presidential candidates Foster and Ford were Lincoln Steffens, whose autobiography was a 1931 best seller, Erskine Caldwell of *Tobacco Road,* John Dos Passos, and critic Malcolm Cowley.

When Stalinist periodical *The New Masses* ran a symposium on *How I Came to Be a Communist,* some writers, not members of the Communist Party, stated that only socialism could save the country. Among them were world-famous novelists Waldo Frank and Sherwood Anderson. Others who opted for a watered-down form of Marxism included Max Lerner and city planner Lewis Mumford.

Mark Van Doren in the Thirties was leading the radical revolt against the apolitical pleasantries of the Algonquin. Philip Rahv had earned the mantle of the "Dr. Johnson of Radical Intellectuals." Even such a mild literatus as Clifton Fadiman was contributing to *The New Masses.* Edmund Wilson had written *Axel's Castle* and saw the USSR as "the top of the world where the light never really goes out." He got as annoyed as would Rachel Carson in a later decade at lethal pesticides. Mary McCarthy bored from within the movement, storing up for future reference every blemish on the faces of the faithful. Alfred Kazin has remarked on her ability to expose some Comrade's secret weakness and then turn around in genuine surprise that "her victim as he lay torn and bleeding, did not applaud her perspicacity."

In painting, Picasso's *Guernica* was the great political tract of the age—and there was a surprising amount of leftist ferment among milder souls. Emily Genauer recalls the proceedings of the First American Artists' Congress in 1936. The speeches called for action against economic depression and the impending disaster of war. The artists represented ranged from Stuart Davis to the dean of academic sculptors, Paul Manship. "It must be impossible," said Miss Genauer, "for a younger generation to imagine a day when men of disparate esthetic approach joined in a common cause."

The type of dance which depicts the fall of Barcelona is one of the lost art forms. Like other artistic statements of the Depression it was supposed to make a clean break with the past.

When Gertrude Stein departed from subject, predicate, and verb, when Thornton Wilder's *Our Town* was put on without scenery, when painters drew lines in imitation of Mondrian, Klee, or Kandinsky, threw spinach at canvas in seeming imitation of Picasso and Braque, when sculptors created mobiles like Miró's paintings or birds without feathers or beaks like Brancusi, or sought inspiration, like Epstein, in daring themes such as "Pregnant Woman" or a "modern" treatment of Christ, it was all part of the rebellion against the tyranny of form. The status quo got its licks too. Progress was the sister of Protest and both of them often carried Party Cards.

The outpourings of the social conscience were not always solemn. A description of the arts in the Thirties would have to include many of the quality magazines, particularly the humorous magazines. *Ballyhoo* in its day contained some extremely entertaining asides on big business and particularly the big business of advertising. In the limbo of magazines which have not had the will to survive, along with the old *Life*, the *American Mercury, Liberty, Collier's, The Woman's Home Companion*, there is one much lamented casualty—*Vanity Fair*. The March 1936 issue of *Vogue* bore the legend, "incorporating *Vanity Fair*." *Vanity Fair* appealed unashamedly to the snob market. Along with Robert Benchley and Frank Crowninshield it had Dorothy Parker, who wrote elsewhere in the Thirties, "There is no longer I. There is WE."

Whatever her intellectual commitments, Miss Parker could be both acid and apolitical. She dedicated in *Vanity Fair* a Valentine tribute to Alexander Woollcott which began: "When I was young and charming—at which time practically nobody was safe from buffalos . . ."

With so little to laugh at, it was extraordinary that so many were so funny. Who is the Dorothy Parker of the Sixties? Where are the Bronxites dear to the heart of Arthur Kober? The early offerings of Noel Coward seem a good deal wittier than anything that has hit Broadway since. Robert Benchley gave his faltering, euphemistic treasurer's report, and Ogden Nash wrote, "When called on the phone by a panther, don't anther." What other decade could have produced George Kaufman and Moss Hart, Howard Lindsay and Russell Crouse?

The New Yorker gave a lighthearted view of everything including the class struggles. Good as the current generation of *New Yorker* cartoonists may be, they don't seem to be in quite the same league with Helen Hokinson or James Thurber. We are grateful that George Price, Whitney Darrow, and Charles Addams are still practicing, that Mary Petty still obliges with a cover or two each year.

Whatever happened to those Gluyas Williams Literary Renegades, the girl going off with the villain in the big car, the Kathleen Norris heroine who didn't wait for Mr. Right?

"Why must you fight society?" the judge asks sternly of the small delinquent in the Whitney Darrow cartoon. The Mary Petty maids —note that there are two of them *and* a butler—say as they bring in the drinks, "This is the round that starts them weeping for the Spanish Loyalists." Two Alan Dunn cocktail party guests assure each other, "Oh it's very simple. Our little group simply seizes the powerhouses." Carl Rose does his marvelous May Day Parade of the Capitalists. A Gluyas Williams tycoon goes with great pomp and fanfare to the safe deposit vault and in the privacy of the inner sanctum blows the dust out of an empty box. Helen Hokinson's matrons are usually too set in their ways even to know of the existence of any classless society. Yet one of those indomitable club chairladies was to remark: "The vote is now fifteen to one that we deplore Mussolini's attitude. I think it would be nice if we could go on record as *unanimously* deploring Mussolini's attitude."

Most of the output of Broadway was as lighthearted as *The New Yorker*. In 1930 Evelyn Laye was playing in *Bittersweet*, a Ziegfeld production with Noel Coward songs. In 1934 Fannie Brice appeared in the last Ziegfeld Follies. Murder took place at the Vanities. Puritans went to bed to save firewood in the *Pursuit of Happiness*.

But an example of what could happen on Broadway in the Thirties is best shown in 1936–37. This was the year of George S. Kaufman and Moss Hart's *You Can't Take It With You;* Mr. Kaufman's *Stage Door* with Edna Ferber; Noel Coward's *Tonight at 8:30*. Theatergoers got a comic view of the Worker's Paradise in *Tovarich*. The Bronx came to Kamp Killcare in *Having Wonderful Time*. It was the year of *Yes, My Darling Daughter*. Clare Boothe Luce's *The Women* was history's liveliest, most acid-mouthed hen party. While musical comedy has already been treated in another chapter it must be pointed out that Kaufman and Moss Hart were affiliated with Richard Rodgers and Lorenz Hart in 1937—a happy union of wit and witty tunesmiths in *I'd Rather Be Right*.

Remember Shirley Booth in *Three Men on a Horse*, Ed Wynn in *Hooray for What?*, Monty Woolley as the irrepressible *Man Who*

Came to Dinner. The list is endless. Those hardy perennials, the Lunts, wooed, slapped, kissed, tickled, and hugged throughout *Arms and the Man, At Mrs. Beam's, The Second Man, Caprice, Reunion in Vienna, Design for Living, The Taming of the Shrew,* and *Amphitrion 38,* the last named a satire (in classical Greek costume) on married love.

Let's Face It in 1941 was stamped with the imprint of the war years. The curtain came down on that great age of comedy which began so unpromisingly with darkened theaters, and which was marked by the chant of the eternal Greek chorus that the theater was dying.

Something a bit weightier? By all means. There were verse dramas: Maxwell Anderson's *Winterset* and *High Tor,* winners of the Drama Critics' Award in 1936 and 1937. There was John Steinbeck's *Of Mice and Men.*

The Provincetown Playhouse was the setting for the cosmic torments of Eugene O'Neill. Shakespeare? Take your pick between Leslie Howard's *Hamlet* and Gielgud's *Hamlet.* Though Walter Huston did lay something of an egg as *Othello,* you could have seen Maurice Evans as Richard II or Falstaff. There was no end to weight* and yet, strangely, no limit to lightness.

Then there were the lost art forms of the Thirties—the unpretentious little domestic comedy which couldn't make for a week today and still pay the stagehands: *Springtime for Henry, Big Hearted Herbert, George and Margaret* (a delightful evening, during the

---

* Lillian Hellman's study of Lesbianism in a girl's school, *The Children's Hour,* was not for kids. Moral dilemmas of doctors were presented in *Men in White.* In *Merrily We Roll Along* a man who had been the center of a vitriol-throwing incident involving a wife and a mistress, was taken through the years back to his days as a college valedictorian: portrait of man going downhill in reverse.

History? In 1932 there was *The Barretts of Wimpole Street.* There was Helen Hayes with her cheeks stuffed out like a squirrel's for *Victoria Regina* in 1936, Raymond Massey on the rear of a campaign train in Robert Sherwood's *Abe Lincoln in Illinois.* Maxwell Anderson's *Mary of Scotland* and *Elizabeth the Queen* were there for anyone who wanted a double cultural dose of petards and pentameter.

James Cagney, Spencer Tracy, Joan Blondell, Clark Gable, and Humphrey Bogart were among those who used Broadway as a point of departure for Hollywood. Bogie played a well-dressed juvenile in *Chrysalis* in 1932 until in 1935 in *The Petrified Forest* his features contorted into a snarl—so profitable that it never disappeared. Van Johnson and Gene Kelly were launched on Hollywood careers in 1940 by John O'Hara's *Pal Joey,* with Kelly as the immortal heel and Van Johnson as a chorus boy.

course of which George and Margaret never show their faces).
Dennis King, Joe Cook, Bert Lahr, Bobby Clark, and Edna May
Oliver paraded through a series of revues. Victor Moore rubber-
faced plaintively through *Of Thee I Sing* in 1931 and *Let 'Em Eat
Cake* in 1933. The revue form as embodied by *At Home Abroad,
Set to Music,* and *As Thousands Cheer* is as dead today—outside
of a few spare and intimate rooms in Greenwich Village—as a Ben
Jonson masque.

Always there was Erskine Caldwell's *Tobacco Road.* Year after
year audiences went to it in the hope of seeing something dirty.
The Parents' League sounded the warning year after year—in vain.
Keep your children away. "If Tobacco Road exists, what are we
going to do about it?"

But even in the front seat of a Broadway play one was never entirely aloof from the social struggle. Certainly the message was
pounded in by Sidney Kingsley's *Dead End* and Caldwell's *Tobacco
Road.* The lighthearted Lunts acted in an animated pacifist tract—
Idiot's Delight. In *Idiot's Delight* the forceful arguments were all
given to a Communist. The play was filled with throbbing sympathy for the "little people." The wicked munitions maker or "mer-
chant of death" was chided by the actors: "Who is it did this dirty
trick on a lot of decent people?" or "He can give you all the war
news because he *made* it." The social gospel cropped up in *I'd
Rather Be Right*—that joint enterprise of Kaufman, Rodgers, and
the Harts, Lorenz and Moss (not related).

I'd Rather Be Right was actually a spoof on FDR, but the authors launched a witty broadside against two liberal bogeys:

> *I'll never die of hunger*
> *I'll never die of thirst*
> *I've got one son with Du Pont*
> *And another one with Hearst.*

A munitions maker—more lightly regarded than the one in *Idiot's
Delight*—appears to demonstrate his new spring line of artillery. "I
trust you got our calendar last year?" says he to the President. "We
have a new one this year that I'm sure you'll like. It has a beautiful
motto: Peace on earth, good will to men."

The theater in the following decade never succeeded in throwing off the influence of Oklahoma. The years of fast, cheap, literate entertainment might well inspire nostalgia as one stood in line in the Forties to watch endless figures in pantalettes and high-button shoes, off to endless fish fries and nuttin' parties—to an endless succession of Agnes De Mille ballets in the wake of Ado Annie and pore Judd.

The fiction and *nonfiction* of the market place represented to a large extent an actual flight from grim Depression. In the market place one might find everything from the works of Edna Ferber, the phenomenally successful, phenomenally craftsmanlike Somerset Maugham, to the slick, magazine level of Faith Baldwin and Katherine Brush and the Cinderella stories of Kathleen Norris. Much of it took the reader away from sordid reality as did the white spiral staircases of Hollywood and the tapping of Rogers and Astaire.

The Good Earth, Pearl Buck's 1931 best seller, transported the reader to far-off China. In *The Fountain* by Charles Morgan in 1932, a man escaped from outward reality into a world of inward reflection. *Shadows on the Rock* by Willa Cather (1931), *Anthony Adverse* by Hervey Allen (1933), Stark Young's *So Red the Rose* (1934), Kenneth Roberts' *Northwest Passage* (1937) were literary costume dramas which were free from the social gospel.

In nonfiction the self-help book then—as always—furnished publishers with eatin' money. *Life Begins at Forty* (1932) by Walter B. Pitkin was first on the nonfiction list in 1933, second in 1934. *Live Alone and Like It* by Marjorie Hillis in 1936 was one of those books which depicted to lonely women the morale-building effects of a glass of good wine and a rose on the solitary dinner tray. Religious books were also important. Where would the publisher have been without Lloyd C. Douglas' *The Magnificent Obsession,* the story of a brain surgeon whose "personality investments" paid big spiritual dividends? The publisher, too, lived very happily on dividends from Douglas' *Green Light,* listed by *Publishers' Weekly* as the top fiction best seller of 1935. The fuller, more dynamic life was depicted in *Wake Up and Live!* by Dorothea Brande in 1936, in Dale Carnegie's fantastically successful *How to Win Friends* *and Influence People,* in *The Importance of Living* by Lin Yutang in 1937. The full, rich, dynamic life in which others are subtly bent to one's will varies little from decade to decade.*

The international situation was reflected by the popularity of Gunther's *Inside* books, by Sinclair Lewis' *It Can't Happen Here* (1935), by Vincent Sheean's *Personal History* (1935), and *Not Peace But a Sword* (1939), and Negley Farson's *Way of a Transgressor* (1936). By 1939 it was Antoine de St. Exupéry who was airborne in *Wind, Sand and Stars.* Anne Lindbergh had ventured into the forum with unhappy results during the America First period when she suggested that if Nazism were *The Wave of the Future* (1940), it was best to dive in boldly and ride along with it. For those who took a dim view of the Führer there was *The Revolution of Nihilism* (1939) by Hermann Rauschning. With *Mein Kampf* it was always possible to get the story straight from the horse's mouth.

Some nonfiction best sellers of the early Thirties debunked the economic system. *Oh Yeah* by Edward Angly in 1931 was a collection of glib prophecies made by bankers and statesmen at the outset of the Depression. *The Epic of America* by James Truslow Adams in 1931 questioned the truth of the American Dream. *100,000,000 Guinea Pigs* by Arthur Kallet and Frederick John Schlink in 1933 showed how consumers were duped by cosmetics that poison the face, by gelatine made of glue, by foods that do not nourish, the gas logs that asphyxiate, by fat reducers made of cascara, by pesticides that ruin the trees and kill the birds.

By the late Thirties and early Forties the tone of nonfiction had changed. In 1938 Margaret Halsey's *With Malice Toward Some* turned witty barbs against the British. There was a fondness for

* The fare was extremely varied. Many books sold because of some off-beat merit of their own like the collections of short stories by Saki or, in a different vein, Clarence Day's *Life With Father.* Others made it because the author was some sort of celebrity. Alexander Woollcott's *While Rome Burns* owed its popularity in part to the fact that its author was a "character," the guiding spirit of a radio program which was enormously potent in promoting the fortunes of books. Woollcott, it was said, could "make" a book singlehandedly. Anne Morrow Lindbergh, who later regaled women with the delights of solitude and contemplation in *Gift From the Sea,* was up to much the same thing in the Thirties except that she was then airborne and could tell of voyages at Lindy's side in matching aviator suits in *North to the Orient* (1935) and *Listen! the Wind* (1938).

such figures as Bellamy Partridge's *Country Lawyer*. *The Horse and Buggy Doctor* by Arthur E. Hertzler described that antediluvian figure who appeared with his black bag and re-created at length the day he brought the patient into the world. In 1938 he had yet to go the way of the one-horse shay.

There were a lot of good yarns in the Thirties: *My Son, My Son!* by Howard Spring, *The Rains Came* by Louis Bromfield, *Lost Horizon* and *Good-bye, Mr. Chips* by James Hilton, *The Yearling* by Marjorie Kinnan Rawlings, *All This, and Heaven Too* by Rachel Field, and *Rebecca* by Daphne du Maurier. But the best of all possible yarns was in a class by itself—*Gone With the Wind*.

Gone With the Wind, the book you couldn't put down in 1936, appeared as a film in 1939 and was to become Hollywood's biggest money-maker. (*The Sound of Music* has recently been named as a serious contender for this laurel, but a coming GWTW revival at reserved-seat prices makes it a good bet that no mere novice will get the better of Scarlett O'Hara.) If Margaret Mitchell could have looked ahead to the late Forties and early Fifties, she would have known that she had started something. Could she only have seen the conflict of loyalties, the families torn asunder by historical novelists, the brothers on opposite sides of the French Revolution, the Wars of the Roses . . . you name it; could she have observed those breasts pressing against the bodices of crinolines, undulating demurely and provocatively beneath a Puritan's gray and white frock, acting as promontories from which fell Empire sacks . . . would it have stopped her from burning Atlanta?

In Bohemia, however, in the haunts where the avant-garde actually congregated, it was fashionable to take the class struggle hard. The question one asked of a work of art was: Is this document socially significant?

Joe Gould was a Village character—Harvard 1911—"Magna Cum Difficultate." (He was a classmate of Richard Whitney. T. S. Eliot, Walter Lippmann, Alan Seeger, and Heywood Broun had graduated the year before.) For years he had been wandering about the Village getting handouts from Harry Panagakos, who wrapped up steaks and chops left over by diners at the Athens Restaurant and

distributed them among hungry Bohemians. Gould also haunted
the Sheridan Diner, creating tomato soup from ketchup and water,
jotting snatches of conversation in greasy notebooks alleged to contain a massive "Oral History of Our Time."

After his death, the "Oral History" proved to exist only in
Gould's mind. While he was alive, you knew it when he was in a
room. His strange wit was as pungent as his unwashed body. Often
he would imitate a sea gull. He claimed to have translated into sea
gull many of the works of Henry Wadsworth Longfellow. He called
Maxwell Bodenheim a "niminy piminy poet, an itsy bitsy poet,"
who had read nothing but Floyd Dell, Ethel M. Dell, and the
Rubáiyát. Along with the "Oral History" he carried copies of little
magazines like Ezra Pound's *Exile*. He considered his own poetry
more than equal to Bodenheim's and Longfellow's.

> *Who killed the* Dial?
> *Who killed the* Dial?
> *"I," said Joe Gould*
> *"With my inimitable style*
> *I killed the Dial."*

In the Thirties he wrote one entitled "The Barricades":

> *The prissy hedge in front of the Brevoort*
> *Is but a symbol of the coming revolution*
> *These are the barricades*
> *The barricades*
> *The barricades*
> *And behind these barricades*
> *Behind these barricades*
> *Behind these barricades*
> *The comrades die*
> *The comrades die*
> *And behind these barricades*
> *The comrades die*
> *of overeating*

Suddenly he was almost run out of the Village. The hands with
the half-eaten lamb chops were angrily withdrawn. Since Gould
killed the *Dial*, Bohemia had undergone a sea change. Whereas the
talk had once revolved around sexual emancipation, people behind

the prissy hedge were talking of dialectical materialism and the dictatorship of the proletariat.

Behind the hedge they might still be discussing Freud but they were also reading Thorstein Veblen's *Theory of the Leisure Class, The Autobiography of Lincoln Steffens,* and Maurice Hindus' *Humanity Uprooted.*

The Harvard dissenters, the single taxers, the Socialists, the early psychoanalysts, the Village rebels may have been united against Joe Gould. That was not to say that they were united among themselves. Max Eastman, Sidney Hook, and Eugene Lyons were not welcome at the offices of the *New Masses.* Eastman had expressed a contempt for dialectical materialism and the others had in some way or other lapsed into heresy against Stalinism.

Also persona non grata at the *New Masses* was V. F. Calverton —born George Goetz—founder of the *Modern Quarterly* and author of many articles on "the pulse of modernity." He thought he could go through Marxism, cafeteria-style. He would free marriage from Mrs. Grundy, society from the oppressors, and Karl Marx from Josef Stalin. His place on Morton Street was a haven for anarchists, revolutionaries who remembered Engels. He had served Alexanders, heaven forfend, to moderates, the hated Mensheviks!

Malcolm Cowley, book editor of the *New Republic,* was in the vanguard of smart literary Stalinism. He had driven an ambulance, drunk with Hemingway, and roamed the Village streets with Hart Crane. A seersuckered Hemingway in his own right, Cowley handed out books to review—and Kazin often cooled his heels in the *New Republic* offices. Only old Joe Gould, puffing on a grotesque inch of cigarette and munching a ketchup sandwich, was patient enough to await the fruits of Cowley's largesse. "I had an image of Cowley," Kazin recalls, "a passenger in the great polished coach that was forever taking young Harvard poets to war, to the Left Bank, to the Village, to Connecticut."

Kazin professed the deepest contempt for the Harvard or Yale graduate of the Twenties who now worried in the *New Masses* whether Proust should be read after the revolution and why there seemed to be no simple proletarians in the novels of André Malraux.

There were also those behind the prissy hedge who were there just because it was the thing to do, and who were ill fitted for the class struggle because they saw its comic side.

A vaudeville turn of the day ran somewhat as follows: "Comes the revolution you'll eat strawberries and cream." "But I don't like strawberries." "Comes the revolution, we'll *make* you like strawberries."

There were those who carried placards for the Scottsboro boys, who turned down a side street and went home because their feet hurt. There were those who were unpopular behind the hedge, who dared to poke fun at the whole thing. The *Daily Worker* in the late Thirties suddenly became very kitschy. A supplement called the *Progressive Sunday Weekly Worker* even had a cover devoted to that literary mercenary Louis Bromfield, whose novels appeared on the coffee tables of Suburbia. Inside were hints on taking stains out of slipcovers, articles on the meaning of May Day for the kiddies, and even a comic strip, *Little Lefty*. Some of the more lackluster revolutionaries dared to twit the Comrades, saying they were going to run up cookies from a recipe by that veteran agitator and grand old woman of the party Mother Bloor or make a brassiere from a *Worker* pattern out of two handkerchiefs.

These scoffers notwithstanding, in what would now be the Off-Broadway Theater, one had to have a message to survive. Actors in the WPA theater tangled with issues that were admirably visceral, and in the play *How Long Brethren* brought the class war down to a homely plane by protesting vigorously against wage cuts. Orson Welles' Mercury Theatre put on a production of *Julius Caesar* with Brutus as a liberal intellectual and Caesar as a fascist dictator. Welles as Brutus was dressed in a shabby overcoat and the stage was innocent of scenery—another relic of an outmoded past.

The Social Theatre, part of the Federal Theatre Project, featured lines of soldiers in dun-colored uniforms marching amid black platforms on stages bereft of scenery. The pacifist audience thrilled with horror as a spotlight glinted on sharp bayonet points.

Cheryl Crawford, Lee Strasberg, and Harold Clurman were members of the Group Theatre—an earnest organization which featured Morris Carnovsky and Stella and Luther Adler defining the issues of the time in "clear, cogent, inescapable relation to the public." Other brave experiments were *One Sixth of the Earth,* a Communist production which came to Madison Square Garden in 1939. Far more engaging was *Pins and Needles,* produced by labor Stage, Inc., in 1937. This company of garment workers went on until 1939 wittily pleading the cause of unionism with a catchy tune that might have been the leitmotif of the entire decade, "Sing Me a Song with Social Significance." There was no room for a little theater which simply offered entertainment. The University Players ran one of the first summer theaters and were responsible for a moribund repertory company in Baltimore. Despite a roster of future stars—Henry Fonda, Jimmy Stewart, and Margaret Sullavan—they folded in the early Thirties. They just didn't have a chance.

Having had all the advantages, they failed because they gave the public warmed-over Princeton Théâtre Intime, when the taste of the time ran to Clifford Odets. How could *The Torch Bearers* or *Mr. Pim Passes By* satisfy the public which hungered for Odets' *Awake and Sing,* for the "agit-prop" play, *Waiting for Lefty,* for *Golden Boy?* What had the University Players' production of *The Trial of Mary Dugan* to offer in the way of dialogue to compete with Odets' mighty lines from *Waiting for Lefty?*

> JOE: It's conditions.
> EDNA: We're at the bottom of the ocean. . . . We're stalled like a flivver in the snow. My God, Joe, the World is supposed to be for all of us.

Many of the outpourings of the avant-garde were little more than animated political tracts. In many works of the time the reporter moved in with varying degrees of success upon the creative arts. There are passages of tremendous power in James T. Farrell's *Studs Lonigan* and in John Dos Passos' *U.S.A.* and *1919*—all considered by most of the left to be suitably visceral.

Farrell explores the lower-middle-class Chicago Irish background as ruthlessly, as fully, and as literally as a photographer at a parochial school graduation. Dos Passos invades the scene in *1919* with actual headlines and newsreels of contemporary events: DEMPSEY KNOCKS OUT WILLARD IN THIRD ROUND: Newsreel XXI "Goodby Broadway Hello France"; HER WOUNDED HERO OF WAR A FRAUD, SAYS WIFE IN SUIT. It is never difficult to divine Mr. Dos Passos' political orientation. The *U.S.A.* trilogy ended with an unemployed man trying to thumb his way down an American highway. (Oh, the bitter irony of that American dream!) To read these two socially conscious authors today is to doubt that Truman Capote is really the father of the nonfiction novel.

One of the most effective tracts of the time was presented in photographic form. Erskine Caldwell salved his conscience for the money he made off *Tobacco Road* by writing text for eloquent pictures of real po' whites taken by his wife, Margaret Bourke-White. *You Have Seen Their Faces* as late as 1937 showed a mother and child sitting on the ravaged steps of a once magnificent Southern mansion where many families grubbed about in rooms at five dollars a month. Wheelless cars languished in overgrown back yards. The flesh-and-blood denizens of *Tobacco Road* gave wry commentary on their plight. A couple tend a Franklin stove in a lean-to open to the wind. "I spent ten months catching planks to build this house and then the flood washed the side off. Doggone if I don't like it better."

As director of the WPA Theatre, Hallie Flanagan evolved something called a "living newspaper." Many of her living newspapers earned the approval of the *Daily Worker*. The most famous were those on housing which added the phrase "one third of a nation"* to the language, and "Triple A. Plowed Under" which commemorated the demise of FDR's farm program. She joined the Federal Theatre in 1935 and stayed with it until it shut down in 1939. She returned to Vassar College where she inspired a whole generation of drama majors to find inspiration in the Gastonia strike and to write plays whose message could be summed up like a subject for debate. "The Question Before the House" for example "posed" or "addressed itself to the problem" of "How long can a liberal college remain liberal when its students are moved intellectually and emotionally to participate in a labor crisis outside its gates?"

The dancer was equally eager to man the barricades. Charles Weidman's group included in its reportoire many numbers that were intentionally amusing. Martha Graham preferred to stick with

---

* One third of a nation was ill-clad, ill-fed, ill-housed.

the spirit once satirized by Fannie Brice in a skit called "Re-Wolt."

At Bennington College in 1938 Miss Graham did a dance called *American Document,* which Lincoln Kirstein in the *Nation* saw as using for "a basic impulse a structure of philosophic or moral concepts." The group, clothed in clean transparent colors, came in like "a troop of erect peacocks driving a chariot." A spirit of deadly earnestness hovered over these Indians as they lamented the spirit of the land they had lost. Miss Graham, in severe white, did a Puritan duet with a partner "naked except for white shorts and a dark coat of tan," who spoke Jonathan Edwards' words on damnation against an antiphon from the Song of Songs. The slaves were emancipated and there was a finale of "contemporary self-accusation." The whole thing was framed in "the basic skeletal structure of a minstrel show" and opened and closed with a parade doing the cakewalk and the minstrel strut. (Better watch that, Miss Graham.)

Mr. Kirstein found that the work had the purity of a "useful Shaker wood-turning." He conceded that its purity was a little rough on the "shy-eyed" of all ages. It was so serious that it could only touch those who had the courage to look at it. There was a certain amount of wriggling among the shy-eyed in the audience—who may not have been motivated by any flinching from reality. When she polished off the program with a number that was meant to be funny there were many who were relieved that it was at last respectable to laugh.

The poets of the Thirties were a law unto themselves—and they presented the party faithful with many a dark night of the soul. One could laud the fact that the dactyl, the spondee, the period, and the comma were going the way of rice powder and the corset. Some of the poets who experimented most boldly with new verse forms had social philosophies that were nothing short of alarming.

T. S. Eliot was certainly busy throwing off the shackles of Robert Frost when he wrote *The Waste Land*—a work from the Twenties which remained the Bible of college English majors up through the early years of World War II.

It was equally certain that Eliot had black clerical leanings. If only he would stop messing about with the Fisher King and riffling the Tarot pack, and come to grips with social reality. W.

H. Auden took a very frivolous view of Marxism. William Butler Yeats, like Eliot, had done much of his work in the Twenties and seemed bored by social reality. He was more attracted by some mystical mumbo jumbo about gyres and spherical cones. One of the controversies which raged in the columns of the *New Masses* concerned Archibald MacLeish's *Frescoes for Mr. Rockefeller's City*. Was it as Mike Gold and Granville Hicks claimed, a work of "the Fascist unconscious"?

Ezra Pound was politically irresolute in the Thirties but later on left little doubt that his fascism was perfectly conscious. One could wish for a bit more of the class struggle in e. e. cummings, however much one might laud his referring to himself as "e. e." rather than E. E. Only old Stephen Spender was really politically reliable, having turned out, between 1936 and 1939, poems about the Spanish Civil War with fancy titles like "A Stop Watch and An Ordnance Map" and "Ultima Ratio Regum."

Others among the rare few who got the imprimatur were Kenneth Fearing, who used Guggenheim funds to damn the Guggenheim Fund, and Chicago's Carl Sandburg who raised the standard of revolt in the City of the Big Muscles.

As in Proust's *Remembrance of Things Past,* the avant-garde was torn. Edmund Wilson tried to rehabilitate the whole disreputable lot in the *New Republic* by finding a place for the techniques of Cummings, Joyce, and Eliot as weapons in *The Literary Class War*. On Morton Street they wondered whether lightning would strike as they attended the Federal Theatre production of Eliot's *Murder in the Cathedral*. All were agreed on one thing, however. Intelligibility and the sonnet form were for ladylike poets with triple names.

As the rebellion against traditional form was an artistic axiom of the Thirties there were certain characteristic genre paintings. They came from both sides of the prissy hedge. One was the portrait of charming, fey, and picturesque poverty. The Sycamore family of *You Can't Take It With You* made firecrackers in the basement and did ballet routines instead of going to the office. The play raised certain gnawing doubts as to whether Grandpa Vanderhof got the same amnesty from the butcher, the grocer, and the bank as he did from the United States Government. He didn't believe in the income tax and was happily emancipated from paying it by a fortuitous mistake in identity.

William Saroyan burst upon the literary scene in 1934 when *Story* magazine published "The Daring Young Man on the Flying Trapeze," a piece about a young man walking through the streets and dying of hunger. In successive works Saroyan transmuted hunger into gold. Everyone was poor in *My Name Is Aram*. Everyone was Armenian. Everyone was from Fresno. There was Cousin Dikran and Uncle Khosgrove; Mourad and his father Zorab, and John Byro "an Assyrian who, out of loneliness, learned to speak Armenian." All of them lived life to the fullest along with their author, who counseled his readers: "Forget everybody who ever wrote anything. Try as much as possible to be wholly alive, with all your might, and when you laugh, laugh like hell, and when you get angry, get good and angry. Try to be alive. You will be dead soon enough."

When Saroyan encountered Joe Gould, a spirit whose lust for living was every bit as unchanneled as his own, it must truly have been a moment for one of *Vanity Fair*'s Impossible Interviews.

John Steinbeck's great best seller *The Grapes of Wrath* showed refugees from the Dust Bowl in a poverty that was neither fey nor pitcuresque. He did turn out in such works as *Tortilla Flat* and later in *Cannery Row* a good many tramps who arrived at cheerful philosophical truths from their homes inside abandoned rusty boilers.

Frederick Lewis Allen has pointed out that *The Grapes of Wrath* would not have done as well in 1932 as it did in 1939. In the early Thirties, poverty, if depicted at all, had to be painted in flattering pastels.

The prolific Robert Nathan produced in 1933 a book called *One More Spring*. It is worth recapping the plot of this genre painting to end them all. It concerned an antique dealer named Jared Otkar, a violinist called Morris Rosenberg, and a young woman named Elizabeth Cheyney, who dreamed of a wealthy husband but could only boast of adventures with swains who offered her "soda pop and a ribbon or two."

After leaving his antique shop, Mr. Otkar takes up residence in

Central Park where he is joined by Mr. Rosenberg and Miss Cheyney—also destitute. A man named Sweeney, who dreams of scraping up thirty dollars to take violin lessons from Mr. Rosenberg, finds an abandoned tool shed for his three protégés to live in. Otkar moves in his last remaining antique—a bed embellished by cupids. These three gentle souls engage in various adventures: catching and cooking pigeons, stealing a pig from the zoo, braving the Mrs. Grundys who object to Miss Cheyney's presence in the tool shed, and, finally, saving the life of a suicidal banker who has just flung himself into a lake.

Romance blooms. Mr. Otkar moves south with Elizabeth to warm weather and probably ultimate starvation. Mr. Rosenberg is adopted by the wealthy banker, who becomes his patron and starts him on the road to hollow financial success. It is not Mr. Rosenberg's feat which enlists the author's sympathy. (Most violinists would trade their bows for hollow financial success in any age, let alone in 1933.) We are asked to admire Mr. Otkar, who has turned down a job at the bank "which would have drawn him back into a world in which he no longer believed."

It was a tribute to Nathan's gently humorous style that he could invest starvation with positive charm. Others were finding the real thing less romantic. *One More Spring* shed a rosy glow over life in Central Park until better times steeled America to read about Steinbeck's Dust Bowl.

The-hell-that-war-is school of thought also produced its share of genre paintings. Many were of the vein of the Lunts' *Idiot's Delight*. Walter Millis' savage picture of Woodrow Wilson was popular on campus about the same time as George Santayana's best seller, *The Last Puritan*. Erich Maria Remarque's *All Quiet on the Western Front* presented war as the real villain with the soldiers of both sides as the victims. Even such an apolitical movie as *Dinner at Eight* had Wallace Beery as the heavy in the role of a bellicose politician. *The President Vanishes,* one of Hollywood's rare think pieces, was about a President kidnaped by evil warmongers.

Cousin Dikran in *My Name Is Aram* gives a speech in school to thunderous applause explaining how the Great War made the world safe for democracy. One of those wise old men so common in Saroyan's Fresno rebukes him gently. Dikran is only eleven but from a grown man "the horror of that remark would be just a little too much for me to endure." (The old man then goes through a Saroyanesque progression, taking off his shoes and sighing audibly, "These crazy, wonderful children of this crazy, wonderful world.")

In Dos Passos' *1919,* Clemenceau, Wilson, and Lloyd George play poker with the Saar, the League of Nations, and Fiume "and oil was trumps." "Meestair Veelson" was the subject of a most unflattering portrait as was J. P. Morgan, who smoked a big black stogey, was famous for his few words—yes and no—and for the special gesture of the arm that meant "What do I get out of it?"

The section of *1919* about the body of an American, Dos Passos' tribute to the Unknown Soldier, struck the same note as the hair-raising advertisements of World Peaceways, where babies were held up by their mothers in pictures captioned "To be killed in action." The Dos Passos peace pamphlet was also the last word in syntax and thought.

WhereastheCongressoftheUnitedStatesbyaconcurrentresolution adoptedonthe4thdayofmarchlastauthorizedtheSecretaryofwartocause tobebroughttotheunitedstatesthebodyofanAmericanwhowasamember oftheAmericanexpeditionaryforcesinEuropewholostthislifeduringthe WorldWarandwhoseidentityhasnotbeenestablishedforburialintheme-morialamphitheatreofthenationalcemeteryatArlingtonVirginia.

A Greek chorus seeks assurance that the Unknown Soldier is a WASP. "Make sure he ain't a dinge, boys. . . . Make sure he ain't a guinea or a kike." A bouquet of poppies is placed on the tomb by—you guessed it—Meestair Veelson.

It is one of the forgotten ironies of history that when this particular mood passed and liberals once more endorsed Meestair Veelson's global views, reactivated by Franklin D. Roosevelt, these views were handsomely underwritten by Roosevelt's archrival—the Anglophile House of Morgan.

There was one more literary period piece which more properly belongs to the Twenties, The Provincial Comes to Town or, in its extended version, The American Goes to Europe. One of Ernest Hemingway's best books, *The Sun Also Rises,* dealt with doomed love among the Lost Generation in Europe. Hemingway also produced a hell-that-war-is work in 1929, *A Farewell to Arms,* and his socially significant picture of the Spanish Civil War, *For Whom the Bell Tolls.* Writing classes emulated his spare, telegraphic style. He added two clichés to the language. The lovers in *For Whom the Bell Tolls* were forever "making the world move" and his manly phraseology was often satirized by the euphemism "obscenity in the milk." (Pioneer that he was, Hemingway still belonged to an age which did not spell out four-letter words.)

The provincial to end all provincials who ever came to town was of course Thomas Wolfe. Wolfe's enormous size, as man and as novelist, made him a legend. It was said that he wrote his vast, sprawling novels standing up, resting his paper on the top of an icebox. Maxwell Geismar, who edited *The Portable Thomas Wolfe,* remarked that to call the work of Thomas Wolfe portable was a contradiction in terms. When Wolfe visited V. F. Calverton's, the place on Morton Street seemed too small to contain him. Asheville, North Carolina, had also been too small to contain him. Constitutionally sickly, he had damned the stinking bandages that the midwife applied to his infant navel and the spiritual poverty of the bigoted "drugstore faces" which surrounded him. Somehow his family had scraped together enough money to send him to college—first to Chapel Hill and later to Harvard. Eventually he reached New York, "the Enfabled Rock."

Look Homeward, Angel (1929), *Of Time and the River* (1935), *The Web and the Rock* (1939), *You Can't Go Home Again* (1940) tell the story of his Odyssey. The books are filled with what Geismar describes as "the weltschmerz of the hinterlands." In *Look Homeward, Angel* his hero, Eugene Gant, struggles to free himself from those belly bands and drugstore faces. *Of Time and the River* tells of Eugene's adventures in Europe. Gant comes back to the Rock and in disembarking has been mysteriously transformed into George Webber of *The Web and the Rock.* He has an affair with a woman named Esther Jack and at the end of the series affirms his faith in America, though it seems that he, at least, can't be happy anywhere.

Wolfe was a rarity among serious writers in the Thirties. He was badly hit by the Depression and was desperately poor in New

York; yet he never wrote a novel which by any stretch of the imagination could be called proletarian. Faulkner's Mississippians and John O'Hara's country club set seemed to be the only other creations by major American novelists who totally escaped the proletarian stamp.

The Enfabled Rock was no more congenial to Wolfe than Asheville. George Webber was forever berating Mrs. Jack for the shallowness of her friends. Their small talk covered adultery, cellophane, Calvin Coolidge, the talkies, the Shubert brothers, green toilet paper, Alice Foote McDougall, Lynn and Alfred and the Theatre Guild. (Wolfe suffered immeasurably when Lawrence Langner and Armina Marshall's Theatre Guild turned down his play.) Everything was "swell" or "grand" or "lousy" for these shallow New Yorkers, "released by the miracle of the age and science from all the plights of hatred, love and jealousy, of passion and believe, which had been rooted in the structure of man's life and soul for twenty thousand years."

Yet as he dramatized the long list of people and institutions that bugged him, Wolfe displayed something which wasn't so evident when we were very young—a gift for satire. In addition to giving a good idea of what people were talking about in the twilight of the speakeasy era, the conversation of Esther Jack's set, slightly updated, can still be heard at any cocktail party with the mildest pretensions to chic. The traveling Americans in *Of Time and the River* could be transplanted bodily to Europe of the 1960s. There is a dreadful familiarity about the ominous excursions to Biarritz, the Pyrenees, Rheims, led by a smartly camouflaged games mistress. When she says, "We're not going to be bound down by any program, any schedule. We shall stay where we like and go anywhere our sweet selves desire," just don't believe her—that's all.

We still meet people who go to Spain "to get a little writing done." Wolfe has captured that moment which turns hostile cab drivers into friends, which makes the brandy taste stronger and the cappuccino better. Something good has suddenly materialized in a strange city, banishing half-admitted unfashionable terrors, giving point once more to favorite witticisms—one of those hated "drugstore faces" from which emanates the blessed sound of *English*.

We have all met that 99 44/100 percent pure boulevardier Frank Starwick. Starwick is a cosmopolite of such formidable proportions that poor Eugene submits humbly to having his gaucheries ridiculed and being the butt of every joke in the Paris cafés because he has so completely missed the *point* by hauling out a Berlitz School book and trying to master a few key French phrases.

After various adventures have removed the scales from his eyes he realizes that half-formulated dreadful suspicions about Starwick are true. Imitating Starwick's accent, Eugene turns on him:

> "Dull! How can they be *dull*, Frank? Don't you see they're French. Now this boy here, for example," he pointed to a bus boy of eighteen years who was noisily busy pulling dishes from a table onto a tray, "Isn't he a *sweet* person Frank? . . . and there's something *very* grand and enormously moving about the way he piles those dishes on a tray . . . I *mean,* the whole thing's there —it really is, you know—it's like that painting by Cimabue in the Louvre that we both like so much—you know the one of the Madonna with the little Madonnas all around her. I mean the way he uses his hands—Look!" he crooned rapturously as the bus boy took a thick blunt finger and vigorously wiped his rheumy nose with it. "Now where, where, Frank," he said ecstatically, "could you find anything like that in America? I mean the grace, the dignity, the complete unself-consciousness with which that boy just wiped his nose across his finger—or his finger across his nose— Hah! Hah! Hah! I get all confused Frank—really! the movement is so beautiful—and fluid—it's hard to say just which is which. . . ."

The writers and artists of the Thirties have a quality in common— the excitement which came of a complete break with the past.

Most of the authors who produced major works during that decade never equaled them later on. Hemingway's *Across the River and Into the Trees* hardly inspired a freshman to imitate it. We have few contemporary idolators of James M. Cain. John O'Hara writes with the old vigor but his world is still the America of the Depression whether he roams through Gibbsville or Hollywood. Those who have tried to recapture the excitement of breaking with the past find that they are working with slightly shopworn materials. "Obscenity in the milk" has become a bit tame since Norman Mailer came out with a real obscenity repeated and (misspelled, albeit) in *The Naked and the Dead*. It would not take any contemporary reader as long as it took Eugene Gant to diagnose Starwick's problem. The connoisseur of Genet, Tennessee Williams, Edward Albee, or even William Inge will wearily peg Starwick from the moment he opens his mouth as a small-town queen.

In the arts of the Thirties can be found the clue to the Depression paradox, the failure of the working man to see himself as the protest novelist saw him—as a proletarian. John Dos Passos reached a far smaller audience than Hervey Allen, Somerset Maugham, James Hilton, Lloyd C. Douglas, or Louis Bromfield, because a really big best seller was often made into a movie. We remember Margo's departure from Shangri-La far better than such proletarian novels as Jack Conroy's *The Disinherited* (1933), Robert Cantwell's *The Land of Plenty* (1934), or Edward Newhouse's *You Can't Sleep Here* (1934).

The WPA workers, who flocked thirty strong to do a job which could have been performed by one reasonably adroit boy scout, were at heart ashamed of their dirty blue collars. After Pearl Harbor their atrophied talents were once again in demand. They flocked to defense plants to begin their triumphal ascent into the middle class. In a brilliant review of a recent collection of protest literature, Charles Poore gives a clue as to how the proletariat had been able to put the dirt on the collar out of their minds. He also gives a clue as to why the horrors of the Depression are sometimes recalled more vividly by the guilt-ridden rich than by the poor who experienced them first hand. A boy in a penthouse might read a novel about breadlines and bank holidays. A girl in one of those scabrous Erskine Caldwell Southern mansions might read a book from the local library and dream that she was Scarlett O'Hara.

Speaking of Scarlett—this ultimate creation of the market place stands up as well as any character created by those who wrote for the few. A rerun of *Gone With the Wind* seems less dated than all the brave manifestoes of the Thirties which went something like this:

thecastratitherottingcorpsestheschemingstatesmenlifeinallitsblank ghastlyfutility. . .Ontheotherhandthecrazymadwonderofit

Was it for this that the train whistle beckoned in the lonely night? Was it for this that I graduated high school and went out to follow my dream into the rosy-fingered promised land of the future? . . . Was it for the screaming headlines

EXTRY, EXTRY, READ ALL ABOUT IT

What does it mean when my boy friend kisses me while smoking a cigar, asks PUZZLED.

In the Wasteland-that-is-Broadway people from that other
    world where they catch trains after the theatre
fall over each others feet after hearing Noel say
    i love you so terribly
        Gertie
i told the printer to set this dampoem up just the way it was
and he put in capitals
    Trotskyite
and semicolons
you can go to obscenity hell, Lovestoneite
who killed vanity fair
we socially aware
with our long hair
    we killed vanity fair
letshaveit again class whichis the cruellest month
    last one in the water gets to spend eternity with max
        Eastman . . . .

Well, say what you will, with a library card and a fifty-five-cent balcony seat the 1930s was not a bad time to be young.

Chapter 15

The World of Tomorrow

In 1939, when the worst of the lean years were over, a little light became visible at the end of the tunnel. In Flushing Meadows outside New York City the Trylon and Perisphere, symbols of the New York World's Fair, rose as a soaring testament to the City of Man.

A carnival air pervaded the World of Tomorrow. Frederick Lewis Allen recalls bold modern architecture, fountains, gardens, waterfalls leaping off buildings, fireworks, a sense of festival. "General Motors and Remington Rand sat cheek by jowl with the WPA. Soviet Russia presented her delights to people who would presently compare them with Eastman Kodak's delights. There was Coca-Cola on every corner and the horns of the buses jauntily played 'The Sidewalks of New York.'"

"I still have my Heinz pickle," recalls another rapturous Thirty-niner. "Also a handkerchief featuring the Dionne Quintuplets—one on each corner and in the middle, Annette." Blowing one's nose was a challenge, he added, to avoid sacrilege.

In 1939 the foreign exhibits formed one of the Fair's most exciting areas. The vast, comforting presence of the British Empire was much in evidence—like those large pink areas on the map—symbolic of regions where the sun never set. Fairgoers could see the Magna Carta in the British Pavilion or have a pub crawl in Merrie England amid picturesque grog shops named the Jolly Mermaid, the Cheshire Cheese. Their Britannic Majesties took in the Fair en route to Hyde Park for that famous hot dog with the Roosevelts, creating great good will, even though the British Pavilion did try to establish that George Washington was really an Englishman and the stars and stripes a British coat of arms.

The three countries which were ruled by dictators had created problems. The $8,000,000 Soviet exhibit teemed with spies and pictures of happy proletarians. A replica of a Moscow subway station challenged comparison with the spur of the I.R.T. line specially constructed for the World of Tomorrow.

The Russian pavilion, an impressive structure of red porphyry and marble, was topped by a huge gold worker holding an illuminated star. He towered menacingly over Independence Hall, a less imposing colonial structure which resembled a bank in Westchester. According to a tale that is probably apocryphal, the height of the nearby parachute jump was slightly increased so that the worker lost a cubit or so of stature to this symbol of capitalism at play. In 1940 an irate Soviet government crated up the worker and sent him back to Vladivostok.

A group headed by Dr. Frank Kingdon wished to restrict the Germans to an exhibit of pre-Nazi culture, but the Führer refused to play. The World of Tomorrow had no reference to the cultural achievements of the Third Reich. Italy contributed an impressive bit of Mussolini modern, topped by the goddess Roma, and with a cascade of water foaming down a flight of steps to a pool. Italy's chimerical military adventures were chronicled on a map of black copper and marble. The Hall of Transportation was a tribute to those trains which the Duce had caused to run on time.

Ideological rumblings along the Avenue of Flags hardly concerned John and Jane Doe. What they might remember best was the food. There was wonderful smörgåsbord in the Norwegian and Swedish pavilions, dainty *bains-maries* full of scrambled eggs, little meatballs in broth, thin slices of native cheese, thick rich Tilsits, smoked salmon, artichoke hearts, pickled herring. There was Rumanian game, Belgian sorrel soup, Turkish coffee, Mexican chili, strawberries from Luxembourg in Moselle wine. There was French turbot, sole, lobster thermidor, *poulet farci en cocotte*. Two posh World's Fair restaurants, the French Pavilion and the Belgian Brussels, were so good that they moved downtown to become part of the permanent landscape of New York.

It was also possible to eat sukiyaki in a Shinto shrine. The Liberty Bell picked out in cultured pearls testified to the Japanese genius for imitation. Pearl Harbor—an innovation two whole years in the future—would put the kibosh on another of Mr. Moses' projects for the Forties. His plan to turn the Japanese pavilion into a teahouse for posterity was quietly given a "So solly."

In 1939 one could attend for a whole season—limitless admissions—for fifteen dollars. The regular fee was seventy-five cents for adults, a quarter for children. When Grover Whalen found himself in financial difficulties he responded by cutting the admission to fifty cents. This was not to mention the special concessions to students, teachers, and children or the souvenir books of tickets good for five admissions and six admissions to amusement concessions. In 1939 a five-and-dime restaurant served passable food. This price list would be remembered nostalgically by those who revisited Flushing Meadows in 1964–65.

The World of Tomorrow was a pleasant spot to kill an evening. Dotted about it were ample places to wet one's whistle—the Schaefer Center, Ballantine's Three King Restaurant, the Rheingold Inn in Sun Valley. People took dates on the roller coaster, the bobsled, or parachute jump, or to jitterbug in the Savoy hotspot—to the music of Harlem's great swing bands.

Those amusement concession tickets were good in Admiral Byrd's Penguin Island, the Auto Dodgem, Frank Buck's Jungleland, the Live Monsters Show. "Believe-It-Or-Not" Ripley was represented as he had been in Chicago in 1933. More sedentary souls could enjoy *The Hot Mikado* or Billy Rose's Aquacade, priced on the theory that all God's chillun got forty cents and most of them sit in the cheap seats.

At George Jessel's Little Old New York, Steve Brodie leaped nightly from a replica of Brooklyn Bridge. Amid horsecars, hansom cabs, cobbled streets, and old-time prize rings one might encounter Lillian Russell, Lily Langtry, the Florodora Sextette or Edna Wallace Hopper—placed for once in her proper historical setting.

In 1939 the spirit of Major Bowes had led the public to provide much of the entertainment themselves. They were content to sit around picturesque gardens taking color photographs, listening to broadcasts over WNYC, competing in the safe-driving contests or bakeoffs.

The World of Tomorrow left is legacy to the ages. The Westinghouse Time Capsule 1 offered Queens residents of 6939 microfilmed newspapers and magazines, a *World Almanac,* the Lord's Prayer in three hundred languages, *Gone With the Wind,* an address by FDR, an account of a Miami fashion show. There were pictures of Fred Astaire, Jesse Owens, Sonja Henie, Joe DiMaggio, Frank Lloyd Wright, Albert Einstein, Adolf Hitler, and a 1938 issue of *Life* with Errol Flynn as cover boy. There was also a can opener and a Bible which—out of respect for revelation—was not microfilmed.*

A gigantic cash register had ticked away in 1939, totting up the head count of visitors which even then was not quite sufficient to put the Fair in the black.

Almost all of them brought with them genuine wonder at the marvels of science. If a scientist could light bulbs in the Trylon and create sound in the Perisphere with cosmic rays there was probably nothing that he couldn't do. Some of the splendors of science were exhibited in 1939 for the first time. Kodak showed the Grand Canyon in color at various times of day on multiple screens. Doors opened, Kodak's first color films were on sale. The crowd repaired to a courtyard for a bit of do-it-yourself. G.E. showed the first complete television studio. Du Pont had the hit of the Fair—the stockings of tomorrow. That first pair of nylons was a tough act to follow.

The G.M. Futurama was the hit of the 1939 Fair. John and Jane Doe toured America in moving chairs, traversing smooth

---

* The later capsule, No. 2, buried in 1965, gave a misleading impression of a civilization dedicated to weightier pursuits. There were works by Albert Camus, John F. Kennedy, Adlai Stevenson, Jackson Pollock, Linus Pauling, Dag Hammarskjöld, Winston Churchill, Andrew Wyeth, and Vannevar Bush. Future archaeologists were left to make what they would of Eugene O'Neill's *A Long Day's Journey Into Night,* from bits of the Dead Sea Scrolls, and from the piece of the heat re-entry shield from the Mercury Aurora 7 Spacecraft. Rivaling Flynn and Astaire was a current record of the Beatles singing "A Hard Day's Night." It was assumed that the world five thousand years hence would be equipped with microfilm projecting machines and hi-fi equipment which would do justice to Ringo and Paul. There was also a credit card and a computer memory unit.

bands of concrete, navigating overpasses, underpasses, superhighways, clover leaves, and turnoffs. John and Jane were dazzled by the vision of the highway of the future when a car would go fifty miles an hour through the center of town.

The World of Tomorrow was also rich in the department of culture. It brought together a collection of masterpieces from the Louvre, the Uffizi Gallery, the National Gallery in London, the Rijksmuseum in Amsterdam. There were the exquisite Thorne Miniature Rooms—tiny period interiors scaled an inch to a foot.

Most expressive of the Thirties was the personality imposed on the Fair by industrial designers Raymond Loewy, Donald Deskey, Walter Dorwin Teague, and Norman Bel Geddes in conjunction with sculptor Paul Manship, painter Rockwell Kent, and countless unknowns who depicted men with a capital M engaged in progress with a capital P.

Paul Manship died in 1966 at the age of eighty, one of the few sculptors in history who ever made money. In the League of Nations monument at Geneva, in the Soldier's monument at Thiaucourt, France, in "Prometheus" in Rockefeller Plaza, he captured perfectly a fleeting popular mood. Flanking the long avenues of the World of Tomorrow were Manship statues. In the shadow of Trylon and Perisphere was a Manship sundial of the Fates. Near a statue of George Washington was Manship's "Moods of Time," a nude figure holding a sun. A horse prances across a slightly obscene composite of unidentified human organs. A figure of Day reaches out to meet the challenge of the Future. A Manship sculpture transports the viewer back to a prevailing mode of winged horse, symbolic figures whose diaphanous garments were lashed by the winds of "Speed" and whose loincloths were embellished with signs of the Zodiac.

Also working in an alien period style were the WPA artist and the contributor to the IBM exhibit (IBM, precomputerized in 1939, limited itself to encouraging the arts and to displaying a harmless-looking collection of office machinery). Some WPA art was concerned with literal renditions of grimness: "Sharecropper," "Not Wanted," "Bureau of Relief," "The Hungry," "Driven Away," "Seeking Work," "The Dust Bowl." But the affirmative mood of *The People, Yes* was also expressed in pictures with themes as American as apple pie: "A Maine Vacation," a Southern Pacific depot, Detroit smokestacks, an Illinois farm, a little boy looking at derricks in an Arizona copper camp. The undulating wheat stalks, the experiments in contour farming, the emergent America of the New Deal were heralded by pictures with such titles as "Reclamation of Eroded Farmland."

In the pavilions themselves the Wheel of Industry style came to its fullest flower. In the "activated mural" at the Ford exhibit pistons churned, gears meshed, engine parts whirred. In bas relief at the Food Focal Building straining farmers plowed rippling earth, bringing "Grain for the City's Bread." Another overalled figure wrestled with the udder of a cow, acquiring "Milk for the City's Children." The Petroleum Industries Building showed "Labor in the Plant, in the Laboratories, in the Field." Identical clean-limbed figures gaze at experiments in test tubes, or flexed their muscles amid chimneys and tanks. Workers—amid belching smokestacks and revolving paddle wheels—held bolts of lightning. Sportsmen met in peaceful, manly competition. The Metals Building paid tribute to the Power of Communication. One winged figure representing the future stood poised for flight while the past hung tentatively back as airplanes roared and the four winds lashed at a sheet around (his? her? who knew?) loins. In front of the Home Furnishings Building a naked figure with uncut hair and Neanderthal features held promise of future intellectual striving. He had acquired from some cave a round scroll embellished with an eagle and a book. He was titled "Aspiration" and symbolized Man's Upward Climb.

What would the fairgoer looking at these murals have thought if he could have seen what the World of Tomorrow had in store for him?

Many would disagree that their World of Tomorrow would be in any way altered by the outside events which had already altered the 1940 Fairgrounds. The grass was green and clipped. The walks were lined with tulips from Holland. People still queued up at the Kodak show and the House of Jewels, sat in pleasant beer gardens, rowed around the lake or went to Lew Lehr Day and Charlie McCarthy Day.

But in the World of Today, on June 14, 1940, the Germans

had entered Paris. The swastika flew from the Ministry of Marine, the Chamber of Deputies, and the Eiffel Tower. In July the British people were battening down the hatches—waiting for Marshal Goering to translate into action his boast that "There is no such thing as an unconquerable island."

The Royal Band no longer paraded from the British Pavilion to Merrie England. The King was too busy for a holding action in this particular outpost of Empire. The Czech pavilion had closed. The Brussels dispensed sorrel soup and the Norwegians still dished out smörgåsbord in the uneasy knowledge that the folks at home were ruled by Quislings. A brouhaha broke out over King Leopold of Belgium who had given only a token resistance to the Wehrmacht. His statue was removed from the Belgian exhibit in June. He was reinstated in October. When the Fair closed, the Polish employees had no country to go back to. Marshal Pétain broadcast greetings from Vichy in November 1940. Unperturbed by the rise and fall of cabinets, by a tomorrow that would involve collaborationists, Resistance figures, and Charles de Gaulle, the French pavilion in July staged a walking race for waiters.

Four typical fairgoers were probably less interested in these matters than the fact that A.T. & T. was offering, by lot, free long distance calls for Mother's Day. Lights would go on on a huge map showing how the call was routed. It was assumed that when you got hold of Mother, you would try to say something pleasant to her, fulfilling the characteristically hopeful message on the Communications Building. MODERN MEANS OF COMMUNICATION SPAN CONTINENTS, BRIDGE OCEANS, ANNIHILATE TIME AND SPACE. SERVANTS OF FREEDOM OF THOUGHT AND ACTION. THEY OFFER TO ALL MEN THE WISDOM OF THE AGES TO FREE THEM FROM TYRANNIES AND ESTABLISH CO-OPERATION AMONG THE PEOPLES OF THE EARTH. Take that boy over there, Princeton '37, looking at his Fair Guidebook in front of the League of Nations Building. He is playing hookey this afternoon from the job as a runner in a bank which he got through his father's pull on Wall Street. He is an ex-member of the Veterans of Future Wars at Princeton. The *March of Time* came to Princeton to interview them and described them in the newsreel as "likely pieces of cannon fodder." They were a witty bunch. They didn't take the thing too hard.

A gentleman didn't put himself in a class with the FERA students or the "black men" by joining, as he would if he joined the ASU.

He reads—from the Guidebook—and thinks on what he reads: "That circular turret on the League Building symbolizes *Unity,* the base of the five races of mankind." *That's a hot one. Why even the catalogue copy sounds apologetic.* "The Exhibit makes no false claims, issues no propaganda or false pleadings . . . If the League can make even a modest contribution toward international appeasement, toward substituting cooperation for conflict and thus laying the groundwork for lightening the burden of armaments, it will have fulfilled the hopes of the many nations which have united to build on American soil this contribution to the World of Tomorrow!" *If we stay out of this mess,* he thinks, *it won't be any thanks to the League.*

This young pacifist cannot know that the World's Fair information booth will soon be a recruiting center, that in two years he will be in the army. After the war, because he is one who will survive, he will successfully guide the destinies of a large corporation and will be instrumental in landing several government contracts. He will anxiously comb the financial page for talk of a "peace scare."

How about that raggedy Italian kid in front of the General Electric mural by Rockwell Kent? His dad came over here because he expected America to look something like that. He's not quite sure what those figures are doing, whooping it up in primitive masks, or the role of that printing press in Man's Upward Climb. But those people walking so hopefully over that broken machinery have something to say to him. Their hands are outstretched toward the stars in a sky where two symbolic figures float above the landscape. The meaning of those cloud-shrouded skyscrapers in the distance is crystal clear. The streets of tomorrow will indeed be paved with gold.

But they're not quite paved that way right now. *The Literary Digest poll in 1937 said that Landon would win. They were wrong. They only spoke to people who had telephones.*

They should have come to Dad. If they'd been able to reach him, he could have told them. . . .

Well, on the Consolidated Edison diorama they say you can see

*the subways going and everything, and maybe the old man won't
be too tired to take in RAILROADS AT WORK. . . .*

One day in the 1960s the son of this ragged boy will have something that none of the rest of the family dreamed possible. One day they will call from Democratic headquarters and urge the ragged boy of yesterday to vote for Lyndon Johnson. Of course he will vote Democratic. He always has. But he will close the conversation with a proud footnote. "We argue a lot," he says, reproducing the air of lively debate which pervades the home. "My son—the bright one—the college man"—here his voice trembles with pride—"is for Barry Goldwater."

How about that frightened little girl, clinging to her father's hand? It was Children's Day and she got in for a dime. She loved the Eskimos in their air-conditioned igloo. She listened to herself on the Voice Mirror. Who ever would have thought she sounded as bad as that over the phone? Now she is looking at a panel in front of the Food Focal Exhibit. What does it mean? (On a wild surrealist landscape an avocado, with five jewels glowing from its skin, surmounts a scabrous mountain peak. A flight of lobsters wings its way into the mountains. A transatlantic aqueduct spills roses into the desert. An eye blinks mysteriously from a cave. A clock inside a can races backward.) It is lousy with symbolism but the little girl is thinking about something else. She does not realize that the avocado's five jewels are the five nutritional elements, that the airborne lobsters represent modern transportation, which makes it possible to have fresh fish in landlocked mountains. The clock running backward shows the victory of canning over the harvest. The aqueduct is irrigation. The blinking eye symbolizes the triumph of Vitamin A over night blindness.

The little girl ponders more concrete problems. At school she is teased because she comes from a crummy part of town and wears funny-looking clothes cut down from her mother's. Last night she overheard them saying that they might even be kicked out of their ramshackle home. The fact that Daddy is taking her to the Fair today is ominous. He's had a job for a couple of years now. Whenever he has had time to play on a work day in the past it has meant trouble.

One day the little girl will marry a man who will buy her a fine house, and, after saddling her with two children, will leave her.

The drawers of the big house will be filled with piles of telltale rubbish. She has never overcome those childhood squirrellike habits—collecting cardboard, putting weights in it and selling it by the pound. She haunts the corner of the supermarket where the cheapest grade of meat is sold. She buys day-old bread. Amazing, the neighbors say, that with the children in private school and that big, expensive white elephant on her hands the children have anything to eat at all. But meat once a week isn't bad at a good address; day-old bread tastes better with the kids in Country Day.

And how about that fellow over there looking at the mural in the Belgian pavilion showing the benefits of colonial rule in the Congo. Why should he complain? It didn't bother him when Amos 'n' Andy broadcast from the Fair. What could be more natural than the fact that all the Belgian scientists, teachers, and missionaries are white, while everyone of *his* color is dressed in loincloth, sharpening a primitive instrument, or pushing a wheelbarrow? What else had he a right to expect? In Chicago and St. Louis they made his relatives strike-breakers. When they got into the union and asked for equal wages, nobody would hire them. There was an outcry when the Communists wanted to give relief on the same basis as the white man. Everyone knew that colored people have always lived like animals. At the 1965 World's Fair he would be one of many who threaten a stall-in on opening day.

All four of these fairgoers bore the mark of the Depression. Their World of Tomorrow was hardly the land promised by Rockwell Kent.

Yet all of them once believed wholeheartedly in a future that would have nothing in common with the evil old past.

They were really doing Europe a favor by staying out of the mess and improving the flavor of Coca-Cola, the "drink everybody knows" which would come as close as anything to unifying mankind into One World. There was enough trouble at home. What energies the four fairgoers had left from the daily struggle were spent in the rush toward the glittering future. Everyone was headed in the same direction: those scientists making Fords out of soy beans, those furniture designers in the International Style, those creative workers in spun aluminum, those neo-Proletarians in the Marxist study group, the debutante Fair Guide brushing elbows with real proletarians between trips to Armando's. The smoke-stacks belched. The paddle wheels turned. The winged figures un-leashed their bolts of lightning. The literati worked in eccentric type faces and obscure verse forms. Henry Agard Wallace and H. G. Wells would lead us to the promised land, just over the hori-zon in the mural. We would be happy there for the dream was geared to a figure as good, as honest, as strong, and as vacant as those overalled workers, with emotional needs that were 50 percent nylon and 50 percent rayon acetate.

The World's Fair Supplements in the daily papers hit a uni-formly optimistic note. Everyone saw a better day in store for the assembly line, in the pulpit, on the farm—for tomorrow's worker, tomorrow's woman and tomorrow's child. "Machines are ministers to man," wrote Henry Ford in the New York *Times*. David Sarnoff of RCA spoke of "the might of the speeding word." Dorothy Can-field Fisher wrote of recapturing the "moral vitamins of the cer-tainty of being useful." Six months before the invasion of Poland, Arthur Krock saw the future through a somewhat clouded crystal ball: "The fabric of federalism will be used as a translucent canopy, not as the material of fascist tunics black, silver or brown." H. G. Wells, who had demolished the world in *Things to Come,* could not resist the impulse to build it up again more gloriously than ever. He saw "nothing in sight that will stanch the flow of inven-tion." He foresaw that the "progress made in indexing and docu-menting knowledge should produce a far clearer-headed common man in this diversified town countryside about the world to which the World's Fair points us." In a final transport, he inquired, "Will there be universal good cooking or is my utopian steak running away with me?" Not only was John Doe to rival Einstein, Jane was transformed into Escoffier.

Already the World of Tomorrow was coming into being. The air-conditioned rooms which had mesmerized visitors to the Cen-tury of Progress were in 1939 a reality. The words "air cooled" appeared in the mid-Thirties in ads for department stores. The Pharmacy of the Future in The World of Tomorrow gave a pre-

view of the self-service drugstore. One of the marvels predicted by
H. G. Wells involved four men in different cities all talking over the
same telephone connection, the "conference call" so dear to the
heart of today's ad men.

The gears churned, the pistons went, automobiles and roads were
springing up. The Futurama was coming to life—underpasses, overpasses, crosswalks, turnoffs, car pileups on what are sometimes
laughingly known as "distressways."

The "flow of invention" would scatter families, churn up super-
markets and shopping centers, and "suburban" developments fifty
miles from town. The car was putting Americans in touch with
rural free delivery routes in Texas. It was making walking at night
an obsolete activity in the average suburb—and a crime in Beverly
Hills.

The flow of invention would go on long after the World of Tomorrow was torn down, after Russia had picked up its marbles,
crated up its exhibit and taken it home . . . after the parachute
jump had been carried off to an amusement park still visible from
one of those Futurama superhighways. What of that vast building
that seems so strangely familiar today? It is a bit of the World of
Tomorrow currently housing a transvestite revue in Sheepshead
Bay. The omnipresent rats were there waiting for the demolition
squads to get through. Some race memory takes them back to those
days before a city dump was transformed into the Avenue of Pa-
triots, the Court of Power—when garbage made glorious grimy
mountains against the New York skyline, and Flushing Meadows
was a decent address.

And today's civic planners wring their hands over the prospect
of an unbroken line of hotdog stands stretching from coast to coast.
We may well ask ourselves: Where are those moral vitamins and
Lucullan cooking? "Oh diversified town-countryside, what happened?" Paul Manship, you led us down the garden path.

Epilogue

Déjà Vu?

The day we realize we're getting old—so the saying goes—is the day that the cops begin to look young. Another sure sign is the sudden realization that the tigers of our youth are either toothless or dead. It isn't just Joe Louis. The liberal who spent his youth picketing Hearst newsreels finds himself in a town where the Hearst paper has gone out of business and feels a little like Sherlock Holmes minus Professor Moriarty. Did we ever think we'd see the day when Owney Madden would contribute to combatting juvenile delinquency? Did we ever think we'd feel sorry for Louis B. Mayer as he spent his last years in a futile proxy battle to get back into a studio that no longer wanted him, as the taste of America had long since transcended Andy Hardy? We lost track of Father Coughlin around 1940 after his brand of social justice was suddenly no longer in demand. How curious to learn that he was hanging around the Shrine of the Little Flower in Royal Oak all the time, before his superiors retired him at last to become a pastor emeritus. The final straw is the realization that Lolly Parsons' column is written by someone else. We think back to the days of her awesome power and it comes to us, "My God, she's just a little old lady." We know ourselves to be as anachronistic as the parchment-skinned aristocrat clipping coupons in some safe deposit vault, fighting a rear-guard battle against a dead president, who is as remote to today's schoolchildren as Washington or Lincoln.

And yet . . . all of a sudden the landscape begins to look slightly familiar. Is it because another New York World's Fair has made us conscious of a discrepancy between the world in which we live and the world as seen by General Motors, Bell Telephone, and IBM? The millennium was as close as prosperity when the Fair opened in 1939 with its glittering preview of television, color photography, and synthetic materials, the hopeful feet marching across maps with their promise of better things to come in the form of intercontinental rockets. Now we have the prosperity and the rockets, but the millennium eludes us. Nobody expects it tomorrow or even the next day.

Throughout the industrial section in 1964–65 we were assailed at every turn by a secret *caveat emptor*. We rode past the undersea community in the updated GM Futurama and we thought to ourselves: "They can take their Aquascooter and their hotel at the bottom of the ocean. I'm just too *old* to start living under water." At the Bell System exhibit we saw the telephone of tomorrow—where we could watch on a television screen and see our party writhing at the other end of the line, trying to think of an excuse to get out of coming to dinner. Doubt assailed us immediately. "Surely the bastards don't seriously expect me to walk around the house with my clothes on."

We remember reading that the CIA has discovered a way of bugging an entire building. We remember all that was expected of communications in 1939 as we search our martinis for listening devices concealed in the olive.

We visited picturesque Belgian Village in 1965. Somehow we were unimpressed. We have just seen the switchboard girl off to Paris by jet. Also at the airport were two Italian grandparents who read the *American Weekly* and were on relief during the Depression. Their granddaughter, like many of her generation, realized *their* dream of a trip back to the Old Country. She is as unimpressed as we are by its ersatz counterpart on Flushing Meadows. She prefers the real thing to a hoked up and bankrupt burgomeisters' hall— complete with Belgian waffles, cobblestones, and Muzak.

And speaking of Belgium . . . there has been an agonizing reappraisal of those enlightened colonials in the Congo.

In 1964 the face of the ghetto was everywhere in the background of the Fair. Chanting by civil rights groups drowned out bits of President Johnson's opening address. Many people stayed home because of the threatened stall-in. In 1939 the average Negro would have been lucky to have a car to stall.

During the 1964–65 World's Fair a red-faced Chrysler Corporation withdrew the words "dem" and "de" from the dialogue of the Chrysler puppet show. The NAACP had protested. Blue puppets were transformed to yellow puppets lest the image of the black-faced minstrel be revived. The Fair closed before anyone could assess what this might do to the sensibilities of the Japanese.

There are everywhere alarming evidences of Things to Come.

We visited the Underground Home, one of the less popular exhibits (Admission, $1.00 adults; children 50¢), a three-bedroom house protected from fire and radiation fallout. The pill was not sweetened by the fact that in the evenings the patio becomes a "discothèque." Most people push to the back of their minds the picture of themselves munching the emergency canned goods and drinking from their covered water supply, as the Beatles play (thanks to an electrical system miraculously spared by the mushroom cloud) that late twentieth-century artifact, an LP of *A Hard Day's Night*.

Moving over to the IBM pavilion where it was the so-called benefits of science which were being depicted, a "People Wall" hauled spectators up to a theater where a little man popped up through the floor showing how computers aided us all—from the train dispatcher to the captain of industry—operating much like a hostess seating a table and toying with potentially explosive combinations of dinner guests. Sitting in the dark we recalled uneasily that a computer had recently handed a girl a traffic ticket with a complete record of speeding and parking violations. More doubts assailed us. That computer which makes the switchman's job so simple will end by abolishing it entirely. Another of those half-buried memories stirs . . . of a breadline. We come away with the feeling that we have seen the face of our mortal enemy—that glib little man and those cute machines which he labors so hard to introduce to us, as if it were the folks next door.

On the way home from the Fair we got lost on the 1939 GM Futurama come to life. Though we have driven the route for twenty-five years, the roads had all been "improved." A whole nexus of confusing traffic signs had been put up in special honor of Peace Through Understanding. Underpasses, overpasses, crosswalks, confronted us in bewildering profusion—Northern Boulevard, Shea Stadium, Whitestone Bridge, Van Wyck Expressway. All the signs pointed in different directions. Three of them went to the same place. (The question of *which* three caused a bewildered traffic commissioner to scratch his head and to plead to newspaper reporters, "Show me the way to go home.")

We remembered the free-flowing traffic in the 1939 Futurama. We gritted our teeth, jammed on the brakes, settled in for the bumper-to-bumper traffic and reflected grimly, "Fifty miles an hour through the center of town *indeed!*"

The World's Fair becomes a memory. The demolition squad takes the ball and crane once again to our follies and aspirations. Something else seems familiar.

Today clamorous groups picket the Dow Chemical Company, protesting the manufacture of napalm. In the Thirties the evils of munitions manufacture were once demonstrated to a group of booing peace paraders by the felicitous appearance of a Du Pont truck.

Today cowled figures walk in sheets and death masks behind a coffin bearing the legend "American Dead 4,000—Vietnamese Dead 1,300,000." In 1940, pacifist students paraded about in gas masks and carried cardboard coffins marked "Student of 1940—Dead in 1941."

The older generation rails at draft card burners who say, "I don't care to fight in this particular war." They forget the years between 1933 and Pearl Harbor—a sizable number of young men, often with the approval of college faculties, took the Oxford Oath which read, "We will refuse to support the government of the United States in any war it may undertake."

Among those who have chided youth for its attitude is Kingman Brewster, Jr., President of Yale, who considers that student draft deferments foster "a cynical disregard for national service and corrupt the aims of education."

Youth, in Brewster's generation, one would assume, was spoiling to get into the fray, particularly since the fray in 1940 was considerably closer to home.

The Luftwaffe began daylight raids on Britain. Adolf Hitler promised that "no matter what happens, England will be broken . . ." Churchill was to say, "We are fighting by ourselves alone; but we are not fighting for ourselves alone."

(As Winston Churchill said when he discovered himself later in uneasy alliance with Josef Stalin, "I have only one purpose, the destruction of Hitler. . . . If Hitler invaded Hell, I would make at least a favorable reference to the Devil in the House of Commons.")

Stirring words. Did America concur?

On September 16, 1940, Franklin D. Roosevelt signed the Wadsworth Selective Training and Service Act, providing for the registration and conscription of all able-bodied men between twenty-one and thirty-five. Conscientious objectors, would-be bed wetters, cases of punctured eardrums and flat feet caused a wave of angry editorials in the interventionist press. "Where Do You Stand?" the *Atlantic Monthly* angrily demanded. Youth gave it back to the editors with both barrels—considering all they had heard about the horrors of war, not without some justification.

"WE Stand Here," one such rebuttal ran.

"WE acknowledge the challenge to defend America in the Americas as the test of our patriotism and courage. But we can by no standard accept the defense of England as the *automatic* measure of our loyalty to American ideals. . . .

"And what of the things we should be fighting for? Democracy and freedom would obviously have to be scuttled. That would not matter so much if there were some hope of their restoration after the war. But even if we had the promise of the man in power, conditions would make the return of democracy impossible.

"We have not yet recovered from the scars of our last effort abroad, little as it was in comparison with the demands of victory under present circumstances. . . .

"And most of all, intervention seems to us a fantastic *moral* proposition. The lesson of the last war writes too plainly the fact that out of the devastation and hatred of wholesale war does not come any promise of a fair peace or a lasting order. . . .

"We take our stand here on this side of the Atlantic . . . because at least it offers a chance for the maintenance of all the things we care about in America, while war would mean their certain extinction."

Speaking of *déjà vu,* the author—Kingman Brewster, Jr.

Mr. Brewster, President of Yale, meet Kingman Brewster, isolationist undergraduate.

Anyone who rioted on Randall's Island to the music of Benny Goodman or who fondly recalls Glenn Miller and the lively, danceable music which emanated from Frank Daily's Meadowbrook, will find no meeting of minds with young people on the subject of the "big band sound." Benny Goodman, having turned to playing clarinet concertos by Mozart, seems to be unjustly relegated to the same limbo as "Jeannie With the Light Brown Hair."

The musical bridge comes from quite another source. A mother who has steeled her nerves to a torrent of "folk-rock" suddenly hears a long lost chord. She says to a teenage son, "That's a re-recording of an old song isn't it?" An album with a picture of five pimpled youths in shoulder-length bobs is brought forth. The explanatory notes are read. Mother did indeed know best. Why? "They said, 'Hello, Central,' and nobody says that anymore," Mother explains. She has just read the alarming news that it is now possible to dial Europe directly. (A few bugs still remain and numbers like 200-2-33-10-11, which put the Vice President of A.T. & T. in touch with the UN in Geneva will soon become a commonplace. No problems with the Cyrillic alphabet.)

"Furthermore," continues Mother, "boxcars don't go to Memphis or Nashville or St. Louis. That was in *my* day."

Buried down there in the unconscious is the memory of a world divided into the rich folks and the po' folks who traveled by boxcar. Of course . . . *Leadbelly.* "Where do the boxcars go nowadays?" Mother asks. The teenager having miraculously discovered a common idiom replies, "To L.A."

The ground broken, the teenager son introduces another enthusiasm, an irritating nasal whine, accompanied by discordant noises on guitar and harmonica. The artist is singing a paean to "Rainy Day Women." "Rainy Day Women," Mother is a bit shattered to learn, is slang for what we used to call "reefers."

Once the ear became accustomed to the dissonances, Mother came to enjoy this sinister hill-billy *manqué* and the clash with composer-guitarist Bob Dylan's original, destructive, and formidable mind.

To one brought up in the Thirties, Dylan is the most fascinating of the current crop of young guitar players. Born in an age of affluence he found it necessary to create his own depression. Spiritually he was fortunate to come from a small pocket of poverty. While not exactly the Dust Bowl, Hibbing, Minnesota, was a town whose major industry, the iron mines, had gone sour. "I was raised in a town that was dying," he says. "There weren't no need for that town to die. It was a perfectly valid town."

(Young Dylan is perfectly at home with the poetry of García Lorca, the plays of Bertolt Brecht, the philosophy of Martin Buber, the verse of Yevtushenko, and the po' white twang, like the long hair and Huck Finn cap, all seem to be part of the image.)

In another installment of the autobiography he tells us: "I ran away when I was 10, 12, 13, 15½, 17 an' 18." The thread of racial turbulence which went through his youth provided him with the stimulus of a cause. In 1954, during the course of his third bolt for freedom, the Supreme Court handed down its decision on segregation in the public schools. In 1955 he returned home briefly and wrote love songs to Brigitte Bardot. At this point Martin Luther King was rising to national eminence through a bus boycott in Alabama. When Dylan was a high school junior in 1957 the National Guard was called out to escort Negro children into a high school in Little Rock. In 1960 Negro college students staged their first sit-in at Greensboro, North Carolina.

In 1960 Dylan gave up Minnesota and headed for New York. He had taught himself to play the guitar and tried for a while unsuccessfully to invade the rock 'n' roll field, dominated by the bland figures of Fabian and Frankie Avalon. Doors were shut in his face and he took refuge in Greenwich Village. During his peregrinations he went to the bedside of his idol, Woody Guthrie. He composed songs and eventually landed a job at Gerde's Folk City. His first LP *Bob Dylan* sold 4200 copies. He became the hit of the Newport Festival. A more recent one, *Highway 61 Revisited,* sold 360,000.

His total sales of 10,000,000 records throughout the world would indicate that there are a number of young people around with an inexplicable nostalgia for hard times.

Rock 'n' roll before Dylan had dealt with laments of unhappy high school lovers with overtones of pregnancy at recess. With such Dylan compositions as "Masters of War" and "Blowin' in the Wind" popular music became imbued with the social gospel which the Hit Parade seemed to have escaped in the years when everyone actually *was* starving. He became the darling of folk singer Joan Baez, and the poet laureate of the civil rights movement. His earlier records were on themes as political as one of Hallie Flanagan's Living Newspapers. "A Hard Rain's Gonna Fall" was inspired by the Cuban Missile Crisis. "I Will Not Go Down Under Ground" was triggered by a controversy about people who were buying up shotguns to keep less provident neighbors out of the fallout shelter. When James Meredith entered the University of Mississippi, Dylan wrote "Oxford Town." "With God on Our Side" is his astute and mocking tribute to those who have marched with legions of angels supporting them into battle behind such battlers for *Lebensraum* as Teddy Roosevelt and Adolf Hitler.

Dylan remained, however, always *sui generis*. His album *Bringing It All Back Home* caused his more socially conscious followers to boo him at the Newport Folk Festival and to accuse him of selling out to Mammon. Not only had he sung a folk song to a rock 'n' roll accompaniment (construed as a shameless knuckling under to teenage purchasing power), but he had turned from external social protest with such offerings as "Maggie's Farm," "It's All Right, Ma," and "On the Road Again" to exploration of some private inferno. "Mr. Tambourine Man," and the "Gates of Eden" are a private travelogue through a strange landscape undertaken under the influence of heaven knows what exotic stimulant. His followers bewailed that somehow he had lost "the proletarian touch."

In *Highway 61 Revisited* we follow him deeper into the world of dwarfs and hunchbacks and geeks, our guide a foul-mouthed T. S. Eliot, who hates chambers of commerce, colleges, insurance companies, and "road maps for the soul."

His abandonment of the soapbox preach may have stemmed from a truth lost on the thinkers of the Depression—that effective polemics do not always add up to Art. As the apolitical Bob Dylan put it, "Burning draft cards isn't going to end any war or save any lives. If someone can feel more honest with himself by burning his card, that's great; but if he's just going to feel important, that's a drag . . ." or "The word 'message' has a hernia-like sound. And message songs as everybody knows, are a drag. Only college newspaper editors and single girls under 14 could possibly have time for them." "I'm a liberal," he says, "but not to the extent that I'll let Barry Goldwater move in next door and marry my daughter."

In the bland years of Eisenhower equilibrium, the rumble of protest was more or less confined to the pelvic undulations of Elvis Presley, those early sit-ins that took place when Bob Dylan was still in Hibbing High School, or to the novels of Jack Kerouac.

Pearl Harbor had changed the peace parader into a creature at once more selfless and more sheeplike. One instructor who had taught school in the Thirties was appalled at the returning GI who came back to college. Instead of faces aflame with wholesome hatred of their parents, he would look out on roomfuls of docile notetakers gazing toward the platform, waiting to be told what to think. When the Korean War came on, the postwar student distressed his elders by accepting his draft notice like an inevitable if unwelcome bill in the mail. It is difficult for the young to win. During the McCarthy era one could sympathize with their desire to play it safe and keep their mouths shut. The protest singers of the Sixties have made up for lost time. What are things coming to when the Beatles announce that their group is more popular than Christ or when a controversial ensemble makes a record called "Group Grope"? The young are playing a cat-and-mouse game with their elders, sneaking God knows what-all into lyrics sung with discreetly incomprehensible diction. *Time* magazine recently ran an article on the game of Let's Talk Dirty. Does Frank Sinatra's "Strangers in the Night" involve a homosexual pickup? Is the Beatles' "Day Tripper" really the lament of a man who has discovered his girl is a prostitute? Is Lou Christie's "Rhapsody in the Rain" really a saga of intercourse to the rhythm of windshield wipers? Ten years ago who could imagine anyone daring to record one of the recent hits by the

Rolling Stones with the lyrics—let alone the title—"I Can't Get No Satisfaction"!

A new type of pop scholarship has been born which also gives the feeling of *déjà vu*. It harks back to the era when the arch square of all tme was Robert Frost, when a poet one could understand was ranked with Edgar Guest. Mick Jagger and Bob Dylan are past masters at obfuscating the issue and there were no such rewards to the prurient in *The Waste Land*.

But the *déjà vu* in the case of Bob Dylan goes deeper. The world he is against is the world of the Thirties. Proletarian or not, he sings of unjust wars and the follies of religion, corrupt bankers, people dying on Kansas farms, fathers in back alleys scrounging for food, a Negro maid killed by a white master, satiric retellings of the discovery of America ("Oh that hollow, hollow American dream").

His music harks back to those country square dances that fascinated Pete Seeger and Alan Lomax, to Negro blues which emanated from Southern jails—where broad lashes were laid on the backs of convicts, where bad niggers spat or did worse into goods they were forced to can on the prison farm. His song "Masters of War" recalled, to a New York *Times* writer, Maxwell Anderson and Clifford Odets. He even writes of a wicked munitions maker straight out of *Idiot's Delight*, bless his sweet old-fashioned heart.

In writing one of his hit songs, "Like a Rolling Stone," he says, "it wasn't called anything, just a rhythm thing on paper about my steady hatred directed at some point that was honest." To anyone over forty, it is obvious what the object was—us. He has replaced the boy-meets-girl ballad with the new hymn of hate where the product of a fashionable finishing school is forced by some unnamed financial reverse to hustle on the street. He has cut through the costly dinners, the fawning headwaiters, the delivery boys with hands extended for Christmas tips to ask: "Take away your status symbols and what's left?" It's like a cartoon in the *New Masses* set to music.

It has often been pointed out that his tunes are familiar. Though he is hailed as a poet his lyrics sound somewhat laughable without accompaniment. It is perhaps fitting. Among other things he feels that the action is to be found in the big beat rather than in books.

The words call for the guitar (the harmonica's strapped to his neck), the throbbing, orgiastic protest against the status quo.

But he, like us, has an Achilles heel. He doesn't like it to be known that he was born Robert Zimmerman, that his parents were able to scrape together enough money to send him to college, which he left after flunking science for "refusin' to watch a rabbit die," that his father sent him to the wrong side of town to observe the poor and hopefully to learn the virtue of thrift. He once wore clean shoes and joined a fraternity. He prefers to dwell on his own depression, when he "rode freight trains for kicks, got beat up for laughs, cut grass for quarters, met a waitress who picked me up and dropped me off in Washington."

The strident, insistent music catches us naked without our credit cards. He has us pegged. In one of his musical tirades he says, "You've read all of F. Scott Fitzgerald's books." We rush to hide the copy of *The Great Gatsby*. Touché. But we have our revenge. All right for you, kid, but I haven't heard talk like that since the day the *Literary Digest* folded. You may not remember me but I've met you. You were the one who showed up just once, before realizing your mistake, with clean fingernails at the party for the Spanish Loyalists.

If movies and popular music are to be the artifacts, archeologists will unhesitatingly conclude that the Depression took place in the 1960s and that the Thirties were banner years for business.

The trips to Mexican bordellos, the boys on the bum in boxcars, the young bodies ravaged by VD (however camouflaged by those Ezra Pound lyrics) which are the stock in trade of the rock-'n'-roller were a fairly accurate transcription of what the mass audience of the Thirties couldn't face—a typical day in the life of a Scottsboro boy.

Such subject matter has ironically plummeted their young creators into surtax brackets where it barely pays them (or it becomes too expensive) to work.

The scatological lyrics of popular music probably should have us worried. Mother would have washed *our* mouths out with soap. Yet one feels at home in the presence of a familiar emotion. It seems better than the simpering vulgarity of "How Much Is That

Doggie in the Window?" Better rage at the powers that be than Patti Page, the Singing Rage. But as the coastline comes into view we recognize the outlines. Political extremism is once more fashionable. For the first time since World War II much of it is extremism of the left, but the *new* left? . . . Today college students make headlines by sending medical supplies to the Viet Cong, the patriotic hand-wringers forget the students who in 1940 ran swastikas up to the tops of flagpoles.

Youth Congresses and swastikas notwithstanding, when Pearl Harbor served notice of a clear and present danger a whole generation followed Skeezix's example and postponed their most cherished ambitions. All doubts were eclipsed by a common purpose and somehow the Republic survived.

We may look at a youthful rebel and think, "Maybe the army will make him cut his hair and take a bath." Yet we think back to cocktail parties where twenty-year-old Nixonites in sack suits talked of fringe benefits in large corporations. At least today it's the forty-year-olds who seem middle-aged.

God is dead? Respectable churchgoers we know protested as undergraduates in the Thirties against the "outmoded" institution of compulsory chapel. In the battle between faith and science before the bomb was dropped the undergraduate had a rough time of it in a college bull session trying to defend the Holy Trinity against H. G. Wells. Visiting ministers on campus preached to audiences who were ostentatiously doing crossword puzzles or playing pen and pencil games. The literary god of a whole generation, Mr. Hemingway, parodied the basic Prayer as follows:

Our nada who art in nada, nada be thy name. . . .

Rebellion is everywhere. One is as surprised by casual fornication at the Bijou as by the spectacle of the New York Yankees in the cellar. Who could have foreseen that "taking a trip" would involve anything more sinister than a train ride to Schenectady?

Picket lines are back in fashion. The Communist Party has come out in the open again for the first time since 1939. Can we be in for fresh calls to free thought from *The Daily Worker, The Workers' Rational Living Library,* or *Sane Sex Life and Sane Sex Living?*

As time has not stood still for Louella Parsons and Charles

Coughlin, yesterday's campus radical is today's investor in mutual funds. We know that shoulder-length hair will thin. Sensitive angry faces will acquire jowls. Waistlines will broaden and motorcycling jackets will look as out of date as Gene Sarazen's plus fours. Bob Dylan, it is reported, has quietly acquired a few more bourgeois trappings—a wife, a baby, a town house. He has, it seems, lost the first and most important round.

To turn to lighter things, beach pajamas are back. Magazine writers have discovered the fact that Bogey was "cool" and Joe Gould was a Bohemian. Our children may have found the parody of a Rogers-Astaire dance in a revived *You Can't Take It With You* a bit dated, but we notice they were roaring with laughter at the final curtain. *The Man Who Came to Dinner* was back in our midst, if not improved by his stay in the time capsule. The much-revived George S. Kaufman is one of the hottest playwrights on Broadway. On a subway poster beneath a girl of formidable mammarian development someone has written, "This is typical of a Fascist sub-culture." Another bit of graffiti urges Judge Crater to please call his office.

Recently an article in the New York *Times* asked its readers the question, "Can pretty little curly-haired Belle (Bubbles) Silverman, precocious singing star of radio, grow up to be a real live opera star? Can Belle, Bubbles, or ultimately Beverly, once featured on radio's *Our Gal Sunday* make the jump, not only from Sea Gate to Back Bay, but from soap opera to grand opera?"

Belle (Bubbles) happens to be Beverly Sills, ex-player on *Our Gal Sunday* and Major Bowes winner, currently featured at the New York City Opera. Doesn't every one of us beam with pride and say, "We always knew she could do it"?

The remaining years of the century may arouse delight, disgust, and more than a little apprehension. But there is the excitement in the thought that after a long, long absence, we may be coming home to a land where the natives speak a tongue we understand.

Bibliography and Acknowledgments

INTRODUCTION

The Depression landscape was re-created with the help of *The Invisible Scar* by Caroline Bird, David McKay Co., New York 1966; *The Desperate Years* by James D. Horan, Bonanza Books, New York 1962; *Since Yesterday,* by Frederick Lewis Allen, Harper & Bros. New York 1940; *Middletown-Muncie,* Margaret Bourke-White, *Life,* May 10, 1937.

For the liberal dilemma reminiscenses of disenchanted left-wingers were invaluable: *Part of the Truth* by Granville Hicks, Harcourt, Brace & World, New York 1965; *Starting Out in the Thirties* by Alfred Kazin, Little, Brown & Co., Boston 1962. *The Daily Worker* back file and *I Led Three Lives* by Herbert Philbrick trace the fluctuations in the Party Line as a result of Stalin's dealings with Hitler.

Capone and Co. were lined up by *Esquire* in *When Crime Paid.* *Newsweek* gives examples of instant nostalgia in *It's What's Happening,* April 25, 1966. The New Deal is contained in a nutshell in *A Concise Dictionary of American History,* ed. by Thomas Cochran and Wayne Andrews, Charles Scribner's Sons, New York 1962. The fact that a swastika was hauled up a flagpole on an American campus was documented by the New York *Times,* April 20, 1940. *Time,* October 13, 1941, describes the *Switch About War* which took place a year later. Samples of the Depression diet are from *The Group,* by Mary McCarthy, Harcourt, Brace & World, New York 1963.

CHAPTER 1—THE LEAN YEARS IN FUNNYLAND

The background of Funnyland is from *The Desperate Years* by

James D. Horan, Bonanza Books, New York 1962, and from *The Big Change* by Frederick Lewis Allen, Harper & Bros., New York 1952. Funnyland characters go through their paces in the New York *Daily News,* the New York *American,* and later the New York *Journal-American,* the New York *Herald Tribune* and the New York *Sun.* The *March of Time* documentary on *America's Youth,* April 1940, deals with the true-life contemporaries of Skeezix and Harold Teen.

CHAPTER 2—SUNDAY AT HOME

For a vivid picture of life at the grass roots, I am much indebted to Barbara Blakemore. The Sunday school curriculum was culled from the *Christian Herald* back file and from the *Christian Endeavor Guide,* Christian Board of Publication, St. Louis, Mo., 1935. The information on fads is from Allen's *Since Yesterday* and Horan's *The Desperate Years.* The Old Gold contest was described in detail in *Life,* September 6, 1937. The origins of Monopoly were relayed by Marc Haefele. Conditions on the ski slopes were from *Esquire,* February 1939, "You Have to Have Snow." For a liberal scientific, geographical, and sexual education, I consulted the incomparable *American Weekly.* The Uncle Don story, considered by many to be apocryphal was actually recorded on *Pardon My Blooper,* LP 2, Side 1, Jubilee Records.

CHAPTER 3—PORTRAIT OF THE STONE AGE
OR HOW WE LIVED BEFORE TV

Sam Slate and Joe Cook supplied much of the information in this chapter in their lively history of radio *It Sounds Impossible,* The Macmillan Co., New York 1965. Also indispensable: *A Pictorial History of Radio* by Irving Settel, Citadel Press, New York 1960; *Not So Long Ago* by Lloyd Morris, Random House, New York 1949; the *Variety Radio Directory* and the *Radio Annual.*

For early stunts on radio, I referred to "Pole to Pole," *Newsweek,* July 7, 1934; for early radio performers, "Some Radio Entertainers" by Gilbert Seldes, *New Republic,* May 20, 1931. Fred Allen ruefully retraced his career in *Treadmill to Oblivion,* Little, Brown & Co., Boston 1954.

Periodicals of the time were a gold mine of information. *Fortune,* January 1938, was my authority on Toscanini. Philip Hamburger covered the "All American Breakfast" in *The New Yorker,* August 10, 1946. *Newsweek,* September 28, 1942, gave a view of "Breakfast at Sardi's." Henry Morton Robinson revealed radio's weightier side in

"Information Please," *Reader's Digest*, January 1939. *Life* visited "The Quiz Kids," August 5, 1940, and "America's Town Meeting of the Air," October 16, 1939. Leonard Allen made some sense of the ASCAP-BMI feud in "The Battle of Tin Pan Alley," *Harper's*, October 1940—a subject also touched on in *A History of Popular Music in America* by Sigmund Spaeth, Random House, New York 1948.

I am indebted to Russell Sanjek of BMI for a starry-eyed view of country music, and to Theodore Strongin for looking over this whole section.

CHAPTER 4—THE SERIALS, THE SOAPS, AND THE PULPS

Here, as elsewhere I depended on the total recall of Marilyn Schafer. More soap opera background was provided by *Not So Long Ago, It Sounds Impossible;* by Merrill Denison's view of "Soap Opera," *Harper's*, April 1940; "The Hummerts' Super Soaps," *Newsweek*, January 10, 1944. James Thurber's articles on "Soapland," *The New Yorker*, May 15, May 29, June 12, July 3, and July 24, 1948, are the all-time classics in the field.

Sidelights on the queens of Soapland came from "Helen Trent and Ma Perkins," *Life*, September 9, 1957; "Life With Molly," *Time*, September 26, 1949; *Molly Goes Marching On* by William A. H. Birnie, *American*, November 1941; and from the personal reminiscences of Julie Stevens, who as Helen Trent found romance for many years "at thirty-five and even beyond."

Other Soapland denizens are described in "Pepper Young's Family," *Christian Science Monitor*, June 7, 1941; "Life in One Man's Family," *Newsweek*, February 6, 1939; "Family Affair," *Newsweek*, May 8, 1950. For information on the indomitable people who plot the soaps, I am indebted to Robert Carrington and Irna Phillips.

The saga of the Fresh Air Taxicab is related in a series of magazine articles: "Time Remembered," *Time*, March 31, 1958; "Blackout," *Time*, January 25, 1943; "Amos 'n' Andy Again," *Newsweek*, October 18, 1943; Amos 'n' Andy's "10,000th Performance," *Time*, December 1, 1952.

Famous comedy teams are "Vic and Sade," *Time*, December 27, 1943; Fibber and Molly come "Up From Peoria," *American*, March 1942; "An Introduction to Goodman Ace," a thesis submitted to the University of Wisconsin by David Magidson introduces Goodman and Jane. "Henry the 3rd," that durable teenager, was profiled in *Newsweek*, September 6, 1943.

The Lone Ranger makes his debut when "WXYZ Wins Showmanship Award," *Life,* December 27, 1937; rides triumphantly in "Hi Yo Silver Lining" by C. B. Boutell, *Nation,* January 11, 1941, and proves in *Newsweek,* February 2, 1953, that "Purity Pays." For the doings of *The Lone Ranger, The Green Hornet,* and *The Shadow* I am further indebted to the nostalgic rebroadcasts on Station WJRZ.

Barney White opened the doors to Pulpland by providing an entree to the Argosy Publishing Co. Street and Smith's rival pulp empire was described in *The Fiction Factory* by Quentin Reynolds, Random House, New York 1955. Doc Savage's doings are chronicled in the Bantam reissues of *Meteor Menace, The Man of Bronze, The Thousand Headed Man*—all by Kenneth Robeson, all published in 1964. Thanks are due to Charles Michelson for the loan of a pearl of rare price—a bound copy of *The Shadow Magazine* for 1936.

CHAPTER 5—HAPPY DAYS ARE HERE AGAIN

For the Big Picture, I relied on *The Wonderful Era of the Great Dance Bands* by Leo Walker, Howell-North Books, Berkeley, Calif., 1964, and Leonard Feather's *The Encyclopedia of Jazz,* Horizon Press, New York 1955. Also helpful were those old stand-bys, Slate and Cook's *It Sounds Impossible* and Spaeth's *A History of Popular Music in America.* Martin Williams recalls in *Hi Fi Magazine,* April 1962, the days when "The Big Bands Played Swing."

Much biographical material comes off the covers of record albums, to wit: *Libby Holman Sings,* MB Album 101; *Songs That Brought Sunshine Into the Depression,* Stereo Fidelity Records Album SF 6300; *The Sound of Harlem,* Columbia Jazz Odyssey Album, Volume III; *The Street* by Charles Edward Smith, Epic Records SN 6042; *Bing: A Musical Autobiography,* Decca Records; *Benny Goodman,* 1937–38 Jazz Concert, Columbia Records; *Glenn Miller the Stylist,* RCA Album; *Cole Porter Revisited,* RIC Album, all supplied by Stuart Harris.

Martha Gellhorn gives one view of Rudy Vallee in the *New Republic,* August 7, 1929. He gives a self-portrait in "I Stand By," *Pictorial Review,* August 1936. The view of an unabashed and adoring fan is given in the *Literary Digest,* May 22, 1931.

The second seal on the rock is described in Bing Crosby's *Current Biography* 1941 profile; in "The Kid from Spokane," *Collier's,* April 27, 1935; "The Groaner," *Time,* April 7, 1941, and in a review of *Waikiki Wedding* in the *Literary Digest,* April 3, 1937. The last challenger—Frank Sinatra—is described in *Current Biography,* 1943; "The

Voice That Makes Women Swoon," *Life,* May 3, 1943. For an account of the Libby Holman case, the New York *Daily News* refreshed my dim tabloid-fed memory. The material on Leadbelly is from *Life,* April 19, 1937; from *Take This Hammer,* Verve Folkways Album FV 9001; from John A. Lomax's *Adventures of a Ballad Hunter,* The Macmillan Co., New York 1947; and from the new edition of the *Encyclopedia of Jazz* by Leonard Feather, Bonanza Books, New York, 1960. I am also indebted to La Verne Owen for describing the build-up to the Lucky Strike Hit Parade top tune; to John Benson Brooks for answering endless telephone questions on such matters as "drooling into a kazoo." Harold D. Vursell supplied firsthand reminiscences of Harlem rent parties and recipes for Prohibition gin and juice. Ted Strongin was good enough to read it with a professional eye.

CHAPTER 6—IT'S FUN TO BE FOOLED

The samples of 1930s advertising come from the back files of the New York *Journal-American,* the New York *World-Telegram, Modern Screen, Christian Herald, Literary Digest,* New York *Daily News, Time, Life, Saturday Evening Post, American, Photoplay, Silver Screen, The Shadow Magazine, Dime Detective,* and *Dime Sports.* The material on whispering campaigns is from "Whispers for Sale," *Reader's Digest,* December 1934.

CHAPTER 7—THEY DON'T MAKE 'EM THAT WAY ANY MORE

A Pictorial History of the Automobile by Philip Van Doren Stern, The Viking Press, New York 1953, gives the chief automotive developments of the Thirties. Specific models are covered in Horan's *The Desperate Years* and in *Automobile Quarterly,* Spring 1962, Fall 1962, and Spring 1963.

The key silhouette change of the Thirties is described in *Streamline Vogue,* February 14, 1934. "Dream for a Driver" by Count Alexis de Sakhnoffsky in *Esquire,* December 1934, gives a picture of the archetypal streamlined car. Other examples of streamlining appear in his illustrated columns throughout the decade. The automobile industry's mid-Thirties offerings are handsomely illustrated in "Esquire's Preview Automobile Parade," *Esquire,* February 1935. The October 16, 1939, issue of *Newsweek,* and *Arts and Decoration,* October 1940, give a roundup of end-of-the-era changes.

The carriage trade is covered in "Cadillac Presents," *Vogue,* February 15, 1932, and March 1, 1934. "La Salle by Cadillac"—another

General Motors prestige product—is described in *Vogue,* March 1, 1934. "Airflow Chrysler" is shown in the same issue. The Cord appears in the November 1936 issue of *Esquire.* In *Esquire* February 1935 Count Alexis de Sakhnoffsky does a luxe safari in "Caravans for Jungles."

For views of the automobile industry in an unfavorable business climate, I turned to *Business Week,* September 9, 1931, "Auburn Makes Good in a Bad Year"; "Cord Out of Cord," *Time,* August 6, 1937; "Packard," *Fortune,* January 1937; "Studebaker's Light Car," *Fortune,* April 1939; "Hupp Up," *Time,* August 9, 1937; "Willys Overland," *Fortune,* July 1938; "Reo Revitalized," *Time,* April 26, 1937. The skeleton at the feast is ably described in *Fortune*'s June 1938 article "Used Car."

"Model T. Tycoon," *Time,* March 1941, describes the peculiar genius of Henry Ford. Lee Strout White paints a charming picture of Ford's most famous creation in "Farewell My Lovely," *Reader's Digest,* July 1936. Caroline Bird tells of some upheavals in the Ford shop in *The Invisible Scar.* Change rocks the Ford empire in "New Ford, New Fight," *Business Week,* February 1, 1933; "Purge and Pistol," *Time,* October 11, 1937; "The Radio Pastor of Dearborn," by Harvey Pinney, *Nation,* October 9, 1937; "The Ford Reich," *Nation,* May 4, 1940; "23 Men vs. Henry Ford," *Time,* February 17, 1941; "River Rouge Revolt," *Nation,* April 12, 1941.

In another part of the firing line: "Strike Earnings GM," *Time,* August 9, 1937; "Government Declares Peace at GM," *Business Week,* June 22, 1940, "Of Arms and Automobiles," *Fortune,* December 1940.

To bring it all up to date: "Happy Mass Fop" by Tom Wolfe, New York *Herald Tribune Magazine,* December 5, 1965; "New Duesenberg Automobile is Unveiled," New York *Times,* March 29, 1966.

CHAPTER 8—JOSEPH INVICTUS

The sports chapter is based on *The Tumult and the Shouting* by Grantland Rice, A. S. Barnes & Co., New York 1934; *The Greatest Sports Stories from the New York Times,* ed. by Allison Danzig and Peter Brandewein, A. S. Barnes & Co., New York 1951; *The Golden People* by Paul Gallico, Doubleday & Co., Garden City, N.Y., 1965; *The American Sporting Scene* by John Kieran, The Macmillan Co., New York 1941; *Information Please Almanac,* Simon & Schuster, New York 1965, and Horan's *The Desperate Years.*

Vignettes of Dizzy Dean are from "White Elephant," *Time,* January 17, 1940. Bob Feller was the subject of a *Time* cover story, April 19, 1937. *Time* covered Gene Sarazen's envoi to golf on June 17, 1940.

The Louis-Walcott fight was a poignant episode in *Out of the Red* by Red Smith, Alfred A. Knopf, New York 1950. Louis' tax problems were described in the New York *Times*. Clem McCarthy and Bill Stern were both subjects in *Current Biography*. For the fun-loving ways of the sportswriting fraternity, see the profile of "Toots Shor" by John Bainbridge, *The New Yorker,* November 11, November 18, and November 25, 1950.

CHAPTER 9—INSTANT CURRENT EVENTS

The Lindbergh trial was covered in "Since Yesterday" in the *Literary Digest,* December 29, 1934, and *Newsweek,* February 23, 1935. The sampling of genre cartoons and humor from the *Literary Digest* appeared on April 8, 1933, and November 13, 1937. The evolution of the *Reader's Digest* was traced in "Little Magazine" by John Bainbridge, *The New Yorker,* November 17, December 1, and December 15, 1945. Samples of *Reader's Digest* punditry came out in October 1930, December 1930, March 1933, and October 1939 issues of the magazine.

Sam Slate and Joe Cook, authors of *It Sounds Impossible,* describe the battle between the networks and publishers for the right to broadcast the news. The abdication of Edward VIII, the burning of the *Hindenburg,* Neville Chamberlain's views on Munich, Elmer Davis' announcement of the outbreak of World War II and Fiorello La Guardia running on the laundry ticket were all on Edward R. Murrow and Fred W. Friendly's Columbia LP *I Can Hear It Now.*

Father Coughlin was one of Raymond Gram Swing's *Forerunners of American Fascism,* Julian Messner, New York 1935. Gabriel Heatter was profiled by Philip Hamburger as "The Crier," *The New Yorker,* January 20, 1945.

Pictorial Review, August 1936, gave vignettes of Boake Carter, Lowell Thomas, and Gabriel Heatter in "It's a Small World." Vincent Sheean described a turbulent marriage in *Dorothy and Red,* Crest Books, New York 1963. Samples of FPA are from "The Conning Tower," New York *Herald Tribune,* July 2, 1931; HI Phillips from "The Sun Dial," New York *Sun,* June 26, 1937; Westbrook Pegler from "Fair Enough," New York *World-Telegram,* July 29, 1940, and from *Pegler, Angry Man of the Press* by Oliver Pilat, Beacon Press,

Boston 1963. Eleanor Roosevelt's sampling of "My Day," is from the New York *World-Telegram*, July 20, 1940.

"The Newsreels" by Thomas Sugrue, *Scribner's,* April 1937, was an invaluable source of information on Pathé, Fox Movietone, et al. Arthur Schlesinger, Jr., describes the role of the newsreel in Upton Sinclair's California gubernatorial campaign in *The Politics of Upheaval.* Secondary sources on the *March of Time* included "Time Steals a March," *New Republic,* February 9, 1938; a review of *The Ramparts We Watch, Time,* July 29, 1940; a letter on *The Ramparts We Watch, Time,* October 21, 1940; "The March of Time," *Newsweek,* February 9, 1935, and "Time Muddles On," *New Republic,* August 19, 1936.

I am much indebted to William Kyriakis and Michael Prush for admitting me to the Fox Movietone Film Library. Thanks also to Ted Kalem and Carolyn Owen for leading me to the remote subcellar of the Time and Life Building, which houses the dusty scripts of the *March of Time,* and with them the zeitgeist of a period.

CHAPTER 10—FREEDOM OF THE BEACH

The back file of *Vogue* is the great authority on freedom of the beach. Lesser sources include "The Long and The Short of It," by Betty Thornley, *Collier's,* November 9, 1929; "Must Women Go Back to Tripping Over Their Trains?" *Literary Digest,* November 16, 1929; "Swaddling Clothes," *Collier's,* February 22, 1930; "If I Were That Girl's Mother," *Parents',* August 1932; "Pajama Parties," by Ina Claire, *Collier's,* January 18, 1930; "Boy Dates Girl," *Scholastic,* February 26, 1938, and October 8, 1938; "Anything Goes in a Hat," *Life,* November 22, 1937, and "Red Revolution in Men's Clothing," *Literary Digest,* July 3, 1937.

For Empress Eugénie's economic overtones I turned to the New York *Times,* to "Knocking Out the Depression with a Cocked Hat," *Literary Digest,* September 12, 1931; "Prosperity Talks Through Its Hat," *Literary Digest,* October 10, 1931; "The Menace of the Ashcan Hat," *Literary Digest,* January 9, 1932.

College fashions were explored in *Vogue,* August 15, 1935, and *Life,* September 30, 1940; sports clothes in "The Sporting Thing," *Collier's,* January 30, 1932, and "Short Shrift," *Literary Digest,* June 12, 1937. *Vogue's* article on "World's Fair Fashions," February 1, 1939, previewed styles which have yet to materialize. The New York

Times Magazine, May 16, 1965, turns the clock back twenty-five years to that first run on nylons.

For a *Vogue*'s eye view of changing mores: "Thank You, Mrs. Conway" and "Tut Tut, Mrs. Conway," *Vogue,* January 1, 1939; also "Thank You, Miss Conway," *Vogue,* December 15, 1941.

The international situation encroaches on the fashion designer's ivory tower—"New All American Fashions," *Life,* November 18, 1940; "The Stylists Declare for Peace," New York *Times,* May 7, 1939, X, 5:1; "American Originals," *Vogue,* October 1, 1941; "Vivien Kellems Gives Veronica Lake Credit for Promoting Safety by Putting Up Her Hair," New York *Times,* March 26, 1943.

Chapter 11—Late Tubular and White On White

The decorating magazines were my chief authorities on late tubular and white on white: *American Home, House and Garden,* and *House Beautiful.* The shattering discovery that the Thirties are now a period came from "Design at the Crossroads," New York *Times Magazine,* October 31, 1965. This was also hinted at in a New York *Herald Tribune* feature on sofas upholstered à la Jean Harlow (January 16, 1966). The Hollywood touch was imparted to the home by Cedric Gibbons—"Every Home a Stage," *Ladies Home Journal,* July 1933.

The section on architecture style is based on *What Is Modern Design?* by Edgar Kaufman, Museum of Modern Art, New York 1953.

Descriptions of contemporary interiors were provided by Dorothy Draper's profile in *Current Biography;* by Alfred Kazin in *Starting Out in the Thirties* and by Mary McCarthy in *The Group.* Here too Marilyn Schafer was invaluable—being as much of an authority on decorating as she is on soap opera.

Chapter 12—The Expanding 400

The good old days were described in *The Age of the Moguls* by Stewart Holbrook, Doubleday & Co., Garden City, N.Y., 1953, and in "From Cotillions to Supper Dances, New York *Times Magazine,* May 6, 1964.

The passing of the ancien régime was portrayed in "The Poor Vanderbilts" by Amy Vanderbilt, *American Mercury,* February 1941; in the obituary of Mrs. Oliver Hazard Perry Belmont, New York *Times,* January 27, 1933; *Who Killed Society?* by Cleveland Amory, Harper & Bros., New York, 1960; and in "The Servant Problem," *Fortune,* March 1938.

The dispirited pleasures of the rich were covered in "Dinner on Fifth Avenue" by Helen Newport, *Reader's Digest,* September 1936; "The Younger Social Set," *Scribner's,* January 1936; "At the White House, at the Ritz," *Time,* January 9, 1938, "Debut in Texas," *Scribner's,* December 1938; "U.S. Deb," *Fortune,* December 1938; "Little Women of the World" by Margaret Fishback, *Atlantic Monthly,* March 1940; "Dazzling Parties Introduce Debs," *Literary Digest,* January 16, 1937; "The Great Debutante Parties of the Century Town and Country," June 1965, and "The Debbies in Brief" by Cholly Knickerbocker, New York *Journal-American,* November 20, 1938.

For the birth of café society Cholly Knickerbocker was Hearst's leading authority on the "glitterbugs" and the "dance list laddies." The nouvelle vague debutante was previewed by Esmé "O'Brien at 17," *Life,* December 27, 1937, and by "Girl Guide at the World's Fair," *Life,* May 22, 1939.

Elsa Maxwell deplored the doings of "Society, What's Left of It," in the *Ladies Home Journal,* March 1939.

Café society in full cry could be seen in the "Yankee Doodle Salon," *Fortune,* December 1937. Brenda Frazier took a hayride in a profile done by E. J. Kahn, *The New Yorker,* June 10, 1939, and played fast and loose with her suitors: New York *World-Telegram,* February 3, 1939, and February 9, 1939. A retrospective view—"What's Happened to Brenda," *Town and Country,* June 1965.

Vogue visited some of society's well-bred haunts in "Night Clubs," March 1, 1934. Cholly Knickerbocker recalled a tale of star-crossed bluebloods—"New York Society's Great Tragedies, Do You Remember Them?" New York *Journal-American,* December 20, 1937.

Discreet renderings of the Richard Whitney case is to be found in the New York *Times.* Back issues of the *Social Register* give an interesting view of socialites caught in the twentieth century's treacherously shifting sands of status.

CHAPTER 13—THE CELLULOID SAFETY VALVE

Much of the information on the movies is from *The Movies* by Richard Griffith and Arthur Mayer, Bonanza Books, New York 1957, and from *A Pictorial History of the Talkies* by Daniel Blum, Spring Books, London 1958. I also consulted *Not So Long Ago* by Lloyd Morris and *Since Yesterday* by Frederick Lewis Allen.

Child stars were discussed in "The Awkward Age, Curse or Blessing?" *Modern Screen,* March 1949. *Time* reviewed the candidates for the role of Scarlett O'Hara in *The Search for Scarlett O'Hara*, March 28, 1938. Reviews of individual movies appeared in *Outlook, Literary Digest, Newsweek,* and *Time.*

The lives of individual celebrities are covered in *Harlow* by Irving Shulman, Dell, New York 1964; "The Little Queen Hollywood Deserved" by Paul O'Neill, *Life,* June 4, 1965; "Hedy Wine" by Sara Hamilton, *Photoplay,* October 1938, and "She Can Do It Again," *Modern Screen,* February 1949.

Ben Hall gives a peerless portrait of the great movie palaces in *The Best Remaining Seats.*

CHAPTER 14—THE MUSE AND THE PICKET LINE

The interplay of the muse and the picket line in the Thirties is described in Caroline Bird's *The Invisible Scar. The New Yorker Album, 1925–1950,* Harper & Bros., New York 1950, gives a lively slick magazine view of the class struggle, as does *Vanity Fair,* edited by Cleveland Amory and Frederic Bradlee, The Viking Press, New York 1960.

Theatrical highlights of a banner year are described in the New York *Times,* January 9, 1966, II, "The Rialto—Oh, Those Thirties." *Joe Gould's Secret* by Joseph Mitchell, The Viking Press, New York 1965, gives a good picture of the crown prince of Bohemia. Alfred Kazin and Granville Hicks (in works previously referred to) give, along with the *Daily Worker,* insight into the struggles between Stalinists and Mensheviks.

The wicked munitions maker is recalled in *A Generation on Trial* by Alistair Cooke, Alfred A. Knopf, New York 1950. He does his hellish work in *The Road to War* by Walter Millis, Riverside Press, Cambridge, Mass., 1935.

Lincoln Kirstein reviewed Martha Graham's *American Document* in *The Nation,* September 3, 1938. *Newsweek* reviewed *The President Vanishes,* December 15, 1934. *Remains to Be Seen, I'd Rather Be Right, Julius Caesar* (in modern dress), *Richard II,* and *One Sixth of the Earth* were all reviewed by *Life.* On November 22, 1937, *Life* published highlights from *You Have Seen Their Faces,* Erskine Caldwell and Margaret Bourke-White's eloquent pictorial commentary on the decline of cotton country.

Evelyn Seeley probed the social conscience of the campus in "Geography, Youth and Idealism in the Colleges," *Literary Digest,* April 13, 1935. The University Players proved that talent without a social conscience was not enough. Their vicissitudes are described in *But*

Not Forgotten by Norris Houghton, William Sloane Associates, New York 1951. For what America was reading in the Thirties Alice Hackett gave an excellent roundup of *Forty Years of Best Sellers* in the *Saturday Review,* August 29, 1964.

In revisiting some literary shrines I reread *1919* by John Dos Passos, Harcourt, Brace & Co., New York 1932; *Poems 1909-1935* by T. S. Eliot, Harcourt, Brace & Co., New York 1936; *Collected Poems* by Stephen Spender Modern Library, New York 1954; *My Name Is Aram* by William Saroyan, Harcourt, Brace & Co., New York 1940; *One More Spring* by Robert Nathan, Alfred A. Knopf, New York 1933; *The Portable Thomas Wolfe,* ed. by Maxwell Geismar, The Viking Press, New York 1946.

CHAPTER 15—THE WORLD OF TOMORROW

The carnival air of the World of Tomorrow has been captured by James Horan in *The Desperate Years* and by Frederick Lewis Allen in *Since Yesterday.* Pundits explored its philosophical overtones in the New York *Times Magazine* section (VII), January 2, 1939. The New York *Times Magazine* section, March 5, 1939, was invaluable for its display of World's Fair Art. I am indebted to Mr. John Brunini for his on-the-spot reminiscences of the Fair and for his loan of an official guide to the *World of Tomorrow.* By unearthing a 1940 *Art News Annual* supplement of art on Flushing Meadows, my mother, Mrs. Henry A. Stickney, has explated for a lifetime of hanging onto 1911 calendars.

CHAPTER 16—DÉJÀ VU?

The return trip to Flushing Meadows along with the pacifist *déjà vus* is covered by various items in the New York *Times.* Kingman Brewster, Jr., the hawk, is quoted in *Time* June 23, 1966. Kingman Brewster, Jr., the dove, in the *Atlantic Monthly,* September 1940, with Spencer Klaw in an article entitled "We Stand Here."

The chronology of the Battle of Britain is taken from *What Happened When* by Stanford M. Mirkin, Ives Washburn, New York 1966.

For the life story of Bob Dylan I am indebted to *Folk Rock: The Bob Dylan Story* by Sy and Barbara Ribokove, Dell Publishing Co., New York 1966.

Profiles of Bob Dylan have appeared in *Look,* March 8, 1966—"The Angry Young Folk Singer"; *The Saturday Evening Post,* July 30, 1966 —"Bob Dylan, Rebel King of Rock 'n' Roll." *Bob Dylan—a Candid Con-*

versation with the Iconoclastic Idol of the Folk Rock Set appeared recently in *Playboy*.

Time, July 1, 1966, was my authority for the scatalogical ditties of contemporary youth.

To Harriet and Stefan Bjelavucic—an unclassifiable but indispensable acknowledgment—my thanks for the loan of *Life* (bound), January through December 1937, which spared me untold weary hours in the Public Library.

And to Lee E. Morris, my eternal gratitude for the informal clipping service which at times threatened to engulf me and to send me off to my reward in a sea of newsprint.

In the department of Without-whom-none-of-it-would-have-been-possible are the staff of The New York Public Library and The New York Society Library—and Sam Vaughan, whose patience and perspicacity brought order out of chaos.

Index

J